The Language of Public Administration

The Language of Public Administration

Bureaucracy, Modernity, and Postmodernity

David John Farmer

The University of Alabama Press

Tuscaloosa and London

∞

The paper on which this book is printed meets the minimum
requirements of American National Standard for Information
Science-Permanence of Paper for Printed Library Materials,
ANSI Z39.48-1984.

Library of Congress Cataloging-in-Publication Data

Farmer, David John, 1935–
    The language of public administration : bureaucracy, modernity,
and postmodernity / David John Farmer.
    p. cm.
    Includes bibliographical references and index.
    ISBN 0-8173-0784-2
    1. Public administration. 2. Bureaucracy. 3. Postmodernism.
I. Title
JF1351.F37   1995
350—dc20   94-32613

British Library Cataloguing-in-Publication Data available

TO: The U.S. Government
     The City of New York

AND TO: R. L. F. and E., G., M., and D.

Contents

Preface

COPING WITH THE practical problems of bureaucracy is hampered by the limited self-conception and the constricted mind-set of mainstream public administration thinking. Modernist public administration theory, although valuable and capable of producing even more remarkable results, is limiting as an explanatory and catalytic force in resolving fundamental problems about the nature, size, scope, and functioning of public bureaucracy and in transforming public bureaucracy into a more positive force.

This study specifies a reflexive language paradigm for public administration thinking. The paradigm is used to provide insights on public administration from the modern and postmodern perspectives. A major finding is that modernist public administration theory (as science, as technology, as enterprise, and as interpretation) encounters crippling dead-ends. The situation is aggravated by the limited scope of the discipline. The study shows how the postmodern perspective permits a revolution in the character of thinking about public bureaucracy, and this is explored by considering imagination, deconstruction, deterritorialization, and alterity. The language of public administration, as distinct from its modernist manifestation, does not face dead-ends.

The study implies the need for an expansion in the character and scope of public administration's disciplinary concerns. It implies that public administration research and discourse can have more long-term and fundamental benefits by strengthening the link between practical concerns and philosophical perspectives. It illustrates, for instance, how consciousness of the impact of our conceptual frameworks can permit theorists and practitioners to struggle away from a unidimensional and distorted understanding of public bureaucracy. It shows how the study and practice of public administration can be reinvigorated.

Acknowledgments

In writing any serious book on public administration, it is worth repeating that primary acknowledgment must be given to the practitioners and thinkers from whom one has learned. Despite barbs and criticisms hurled against public employees, public service is, in my view, an eminently worthwhile calling. I am proud to have been a public administrator, and the dedication of this book to two former employers is heartfelt. It is hard to have worked for employers such as the city of New York and the United States government without gaining some insights, a few scars, and many good memories. I learned most about public administration theory from such practitioner contexts.

Thanks also to those who reviewed the text of this book. Thanks for the feedback from my colleagues in the Department of Political Science and Public Administration at Virginia Commonwealth University, especially the contributions of Leigh E. Grosenick and Amin Alimard. Thanks to Laurin L. Henry, my former dean, who for several years also joined me in teaching a doctoral seminar on administrative theory, and to Hans S. Falck, professor emeritus of Social Work. Thanks to the two anonymous reviewers selected by the publisher. Thanks to Malcolm M. MacDonald, Kathleen Swain, and the excellent editorial staff at The University of Alabama Press. Thanks also to Rosemary L. Farmer, my companion in all things. Responsibility for any misperceptions and misunderstandings in the text remains, of course, with the writer.

Public administration theory has a rich literature, and there are also rich related literatures. A book such as this seeks to engage relevant parts of those literatures. This brings to mind the lines from *The Metalogicon* of John of Salisbury: "Bernard of Chartres used to compare us to puny dwarfs perched on the shoulders of giants. He pointed out that we see more and farther than our predecessors, not because we have keener vision or greater height, but because we are lifted up and borne aloft on their gigantic stature." Thanks to the following publishers for their permissions to quote from their publications:

From *Report of the Ad Hoc Committee on the Future of Public Service Education and Accreditation* by NASPAA Ad Hoc Committee, copyright © 1992 by National Association of Schools of Public Affairs and Administration. Used by permission.

From *American Public Administration: Past, Present, and Future* edited by Frederick C. Mosher, copyright © 1983 by The University of Alabama Press. Used by permission.

Reprinted with the permission of The Free Press, a division of Macmillan, Inc. from *Administrative Behavior: A Study of Administrative Making Processes in Administrative Organization,* Third Edition, by Herbert A. Simon. Copyright © 1945, 1947, 1957, 1976 by Herbert A. Simon.

From *The Post-Modern and the Post-Industrial: A Critical Analysis* by Margaret A. Rose, copyright © 1991. Reprinted with the permission of Cambridge University Press.

From *Naturalistic Inquiry* by Egon Guba and Yvonna S. Lincoln, copyright © 1985 by Sage Publications. Used by permission of Sage Publications, Inc.

1

Introduction

A LANGUAGE IS more than a tool for thinking, for conceiving and communicating thoughts. It is also a factory of ideas, approaches, intuitions, assumptions, and urges that make up our world view; it shapes us. Consider national language differences. When the French speak of a window, they assume a different shape than the American's window. They do not think of two rectangles, one on top of the other; rather, they think of the shape of French windows. They assume a different shape when they speak of bread; they assume a long, thin object rather than a rectangular shape. When the French speak of a legal rule, they have in mind something different from what the English mean by the same term; they do not think in terms of a particular case. Examples abound.[1] Stamped into the code mechanism of language is substantive character, reflecting and shaping our view of the world.

Wittgenstein is among those who have made the nature of language clearer. Language, for him, is not a private affair; it is essentially public and social. It is created and maintained interpersonally by a language community, and we participate in a variety of language games. Wittgenstein gives the example of a builder and an assistant to illustrate a primitive language.[2] The language consists of the words *block, pillar, slab,* and *beam.* The builder calls out the words, and the assistant brings the respective stone. The words and the action constitute the language game. Wittgenstein's use of the term "language game" emphasizes that the speaking of language is part of an activity or part of a form of life.[3]

Public administration theory is, in an important sense, a language. Public administration theory certainly is a collection of substantive information. As the name implies, this collection should include at least one theory. It could also include—or it may not include—laws, hypotheses, interpretations, or other propositions. Nevertheless, public administration theory is more than a mere collection. This substantive information, which reflects what some have thought and said about public administration practice, is arranged. The arrangement does not need to be either complete or completely consistent; nevertheless, it is recognizable, and the arrangement has consequences. The idea of information being "arranged" can be recognized more easily by making a parallel with computer-stored information; information processed and retained electronically is structured by the computer program. The structuring effected by the computer program has consequences in such terms, for example, as delimiting—or bounding—the form and content of information acceptable for processing.

The way in which public administration information is arranged is the language of public administration. Part of this arrangement is expressed in what we consider to be our ordinary language; for example, our understandings are shaped and constrained by the existence, denotations, and connotations of words such as *public servant, bureaucracy,* and *private enterprise.* Another important part of the ordering is the thought patterning that has been created by the way in which public administration theory has developed, for example, in views of the scope of the subject, of acceptable methodology for pursuing the study of public administration, and of the kinds of statements about public administration that are considered to be significant information. These patterns are, to a greater or lesser degree, shared by public administrationists. They constitute the subculture of such thinkers, the language game or games of public administration theorizing. This arranging or ordering governs the way that thinking about public administration can be conducted. By influencing the way ideas can be added, this arranging tends to shape new knowledge. Governing the way in which we speak about public administration, this arranging constrains the examination of old knowledge. This arranging serves as the vocabulary, syntax, and grammar of thoughts on the subject. Viewed as a language, public administration theory reflects the welter of assumptions, intuitions, ideas, approaches, fears, and wishes that shape understandings of public administration and that guide the doing of public administration.

Exploring the possibilities and potentialities for "rearranging" constitutes an important hermeneutic activity that should be a guiding component of a reinvigorated public administration theory. Such rearrangements may be expected both at the surface and at a deeper level in the language that is public administration theory. Understanding and interpreting arrangements and underlying factors should provide insights about the forms of life of the speakers of that language. Exploring the recesses and inner logics of the language of public administration might be compared by some with interpreting dreams; it can reveal some hidden forces that shape the activities of the dreamers.

What can, and should, be done about the nature, size, scope, and functioning of public bureaucracy? How should claims about the "dead weight" of bureaucracy be understood?[4] Can public bureaucracy be transformed into a more positive force for realizing our common dreams, improving the impact of governmental administration on both citizens and public servants? Should we aim further to invigorate public bureaucracy—to obtain the lusty benefits of enterprise in public organizations? What can be accomplished to ensure that a country's bureaucracy is an optimal contributor to, and not a drain on, the rest of society? How can governmental management be developed so that it shows greater initiative, spirit, and competence—

married with ethical and effective results? These and similar questions are legitimate and pressing concerns for those wanting an improved quality of life for human
beings. Such questions are also of concern to those professional public administrators who are as frustrated (no less than governmental leaders and clients) by the
negative aspects of the "system." Even if all agreed on an "ism" (capitalism, social-
ism, or any other "ism"), a fundamental impediment to realization of the social
dream would be our relative ignorance of how best to transform bureaucracy.

Public administration theory, the language of public bureaucracy,[5] should be
the dynamo that provides light on such public administration questions. A claim of
this book is that modernist public administration theory, although valuable and capable of producing even more remarkable results, is limiting as an explanatory and
catalytic force in resolving such pressing questions about the problems of bureaucracy. Part of the book is devoted to explaining that the logic of public administration theory, as it is, encounters limits as a matter of logical necessity. In each of five
major underlying lines of development, contraries are encountered for modernist
public administration theory. These five lines will be described and defined later
under the headings of particularism, scientism, technologism, enterprise, and hermeneutics.

Thinking about public administration and about bureaucracy, it is argued, can
work to transcend these limits. It can do so by adopting a reflexive approach toward
the language of public bureaucracy, giving a keener appreciation of the nature of its
own output and functioning. A reflexive language approach points to the entrap-
ment of public administration theory in modernist assumptions. It also points up
the possibilities available in postmodernity. Part of this book discusses aspects of
postmodernity that have a special relevance, and it goes into detail in terms of imagination, deconstruction, deterritorialization, and alterity. By seeking to reach beyond the modernist mind-set, public administration theory can be reinvigorated.

The aim of this book is to lay the groundwork for developing more satisfactory
answers to concerns (such as those raised in the questions three paragraphs ago)
about the nature, size, scope, and functioning of public bureaucracy—to explore the
use of a reflexive language paradigm for public administration. The word *paradigm*
is used reluctantly, partly because it may convey the notion of a theoretical magic
bullet. There is no theoretical magic bullet, no panacea, no quick fix for the problems of bureaucracy. There is no new miracle prescription, capable of being learned
in one minute or not, that explains all and fits all sizes. Nevertheless, paradigm is a
familiar notion in the public administration discipline, and its use, despite disadvantages, suggests the general direction in which we are heading.

The reflexive language paradigm, the reflexive interpretation this book explores for public administration, is a way of thinking consistent not only with modernity but also with postmodernity. In grammar, reflexive refers to a verb that has
an identical subject and direct object. For example, he *dressed* himself. In philosophy, reflexivity is a feature of what has been called perspectivism. A beginning can

be made by describing the reflexive language paradigm as one of individual and group engagement in a process of playful and attuned dialog with the underlying content of the language of public bureaucracy. The word *playful* is not intended to propose lack of seriousness;[6] it is used to suggest the creative realization of the opportunities suggested by the essentially hermeneutic character of public administration facts. The word *attuned* is used to suggest the creative opportunities available within the constraints of the reflexive character of thinking and of the relationship of language to thinking. The reflexive language paradigm is applied in this book by the interpretation of public administration theory in terms of modernity and postmodernity. The rationale for the paradigm is explained in the first section of chapter 2; the character of the application in the present book is discussed in the second section of that chapter. The nature of the paradigm is explained by the account, in chapters 3 through 14, of the application of reflexive interpretation. Reflexive interpretation is not another cookbook or ready-to-hand solution; we have passed that point.

The exploration does suggest that a radical change is needed in the way that we conceptualize the role and nature of public administration theory. A companion adjustment, given only limited attention in this book, is also required in the character of the other social sciences and action programs; in the latter sense, the account given in this book for public administration can be understood as a case study of the situation facing all the social science and the action programs such as social work, education, and health administration. A sea change is necessary in our traditional modernist attitude toward understanding the role and activities of thinking about governing. Without such a root-and-branch shift in the foundations of an understanding of public administration, treatment of the sort of questions we want answered will remain unsatisfactory. The visible hand of bureaucracy will remain heavy and inept.

It is helpful to address such fundamental and practical issues of bureaucracy within the context of our changed, and changing, times. Many students of American public administration are interested in prospects and trends. For example, forecasts of the future, such as those by Toffler and Naisbitt, have been popular.[7] Nevertheless, these sets of predictions, although they forecast amazing developments and point to a greatly changed world, do not clarify the move away from the fundamental mind-set of modernity. Other writers have described how we are passing from modernity to a new and fundamentally different era, which they have christened postmodern; others have different claims for postmodernity. For them, we have reached the end of the modern era, parallel to the end of the ancient world. As a first cut, let us choose from among the variety of descriptions of what might be meant by modernity and postmodernity; chapters 3 and 9 will add qualifications and note other views.

Modernity refers to the distinctive core of assumptions and beliefs about the power and nature of the human subject and human reason (and to related issues) that have constituted the dominant mind-set of the West for the last five hundred or so years, a period of so many technological, social, political, and economic "miracles." The project of modernity, in one view, holds up the prospect of an unlimited advance as if in response to Descartes's call to "master nature" and "enjoy the fruits of the earth without toil."[8] It equates the new subjectivity and reason with emancipation and continuing economic, social, political, and moral progress. This equation forms and informs our day-to-day cultural milieu.

Consider Max Weber's understanding of modernity; Weber is usually accorded a prime place in histories of American public administration. Modernity, for Weber, occurs through greater rationalization. Modernist rationalization, unlike the premodern view of rationality, provides for no natural pattern to which human beings should conform; the self is unconstrained. The nature of this rationalization provides for an abandonment of substantive reason that accepts some values as givens—the sort of rationality that St. Anselm would have accepted when he commented that he was not writing for Gaunilo "the fool." The individual self is now able to choose values, objectives, and meanings freely. This rationality is also explained as meaning the following of a rule, as contrasted with impulse or chance actions. As Shils explains it, "Weber meant by rationalization the coherent ordering of beliefs and actions in accordance with a unifying central criterion. . . . The systemization of belief is the elimination of logical inconsistencies, the disarming of demons, the denial of magical technology, the increased comprehensiveness or generality of a theory, and the reduction of all individual instances, whatever their diversity, to the status of general classes."[9]

As Brubaker explains, the "specific and peculiar rationalism" that distinguishes modern Western civilization includes, for Max Weber, a depersonalization of social relationships, a refinement of the techniques of calculation, an enhancement of the social importance of specialized knowledge, and an extension of technical rational control over natural and social processes.[10] Brubaker also points out that Weber has sixteen apparent meanings of "rational": deliberate, systematic, calculable, impersonal, instrumental, exact, quantitative, rule-governed, predictable, methodical, purposeful, sober, scrupulous, efficacious, intelligible, and consistent. Benefits can be obtained from this formal rationality, but they are secured at the cost of abandoning substantive rationality. For Weber, conflicts over ends—matters of substantive rationality—have no technically rational solutions.

Postmodernity transforms established ways of thinking, although no single set of postmodernist views exists; rather, postmodernists have different views, and many of them would deny the label. No positive program, no neat system of concepts, and no promise of future benefits are proposed. The title itself is not sacrosanct; next year, postmodernity might be called something else. The variety, the negative character, and even the reservation about the name are reflected in the description of postmodernism as "the name of the congeries of negativities that end the modern epoch. It [postmodernism] is the improper name of the transition from the age of irony to the age of parody. Post-modernism names no positive program nor system of concepts; it narrates no minatory tales, evokes no originary allegories of wholeness, and builds no foundations for future utopias."[11]

Postmodernists such as Baudrillard claim that a fundamental break with the modern era has occurred recently. Baudrillard describes those persons in postmodernity as living in hyperreality, which blurs distinctions between real and unreal. Models, in his view, replace the real.[12] Mass media, information systems, and technology are new forms of control that change the nature of politics and life. For him, boundaries are imploding between information and entertainment, between images and politics; society itself is imploding. Postmodernity, for him, is the process of the destruction of meaning. Like other postmodernists, he criticizes the ideals of truth, rationality, foundation, certainty, and coherence. For Baudrillard, history has ended. Postmodernity is characteristic, in his words, "of a universe where there are no more definitions possible. . . . It has all been done. The extreme limit of these possibilities has been reached. . . . All that remains is to play with the pieces. Playing with the pieces—that is postmodernism."[13]

Clearly, ideas so challenging cannot be summarized or presented fairly in two or three paragraphs. Postmodernists, it is suggested, are setting out to say some things that cannot really be said; yet the ideas may be true. For example, a common postmodern idea is that there can no longer be any overarching explanations of society or of the world. This idea leads immediately to a reflexive difficulty; the claim that no overarching explanation exists is itself an overarching explanation. The postmodernist is attempting to say the unsayable, and that attempt has led to a torrent of words and word plays and to not a few sloppy ideas. Nevertheless, postmodernism should not be dismissed for such reasons.

Others who criticize postmodernism, such as the critical theorists of the Frankfurt school, say that modernity has not yet played out its hand. Jürgen Habermas and other critical theorists view modernity as an unfinished project. They urge a reconstructive, rather than a deconstructive, approach. They reject the postmodernist break between modernity and postmodernity, and they accept some distinctions in critical theory that postmodernists reject. For instance, postmodernists would reject the very idea of social systems. Nevertheless, critical theory and postmodernism both criticize modernity.

Critical theorists point out what they consider oppressive features of modernity. For example, Horkheimer and Adorno, in their *Dialectic of Enlightenment,* discuss the development of new forms of social domination in modernity. They write about the system ensuring obedience through the synthesis of instrumental rationality and capitalism—with the use of mass communication and culture, science and technology, and bureaucratized and rationalized state apparatus. They state, "The fallen nature of modern man cannot be separated from social progress. On the one hand the growth of economic productivity furnishes the conditions for a world of greater justice; on the other hand it allows the technical apparatus and the social groups which administer it a disproportionate superiority to the rest of the population."[14]

It will become clearer in chapter 3 that a leading implication for thinking about public administration is that modernity strives for thinking and for theory that are understood to give epistemological assurance. Chapter 9 will explain that, by contrast, postmodernity promises no such assurance, no certainty. Thinking about public administration within the mind-set of modernity will be understood as including the search for grounded knowledge, reaping the benefits of reasoning considered to be well founded. Thinking within the mind-set of postmodernity will be seen to include a working out of the radical consequences of abandoning what are considered the false epistemological and other illusions of modernity.

Adequately addressing the issues of bureaucracy requires attunement to the insights suggested by such literatures as those on modernity and postmodernity.[15] It is hard to envision the future. In the conformity of the 1950s, it was difficult to see the flower children and the rioting of the 1960s. In the 1960s, it was hard to anticipate either the oil crisis or the order of the 1970s.[16] In the 1970s, it was hard to anticipate that in the 1980s big cars would again become fashionable; it was hard to foresee the fundamental changes in what today is the former Soviet Union. Nevertheless, a common element exists in each situation: the changes are always surprising. The world and the possibilities have shifted in the last fifty years; they may shift more, and in even more radical ways, in coming years. Then again, this shift would be a non-issue if those postmodernists who speak of the end of history are right. Nevertheless, to use the modern-postmodern framework, the reader is not required to make a commitment to any capability for future (or fortune)-telling. At a minimal position, she can regard this situation as an "as if" exercise, a heuristic device. In considering the central issues of bureaucracy, it is dangerous not to guard against the seductive falsehoods of the apparently obvious; the most seductive are the misperceptions that "common sense is always sense" and that "no radical paradigm shifts are possible."

The importance of questions about bureaucracy is likely to be seen as more pressing as the problems continue to deepen. It will become more important, in the words used earlier, to find ways of transforming public bureaucracy into a more positive force for realizing our common dreams. The problems faced by government are becoming more acute, and examples can be given of such "new" problems in the now "old" areas of environment, energy, hunger, rising populations, rising expectations, and nuclear proliferation. The record shows how governmental bureaucracies have been expanded and developed in order to cope.[17] Nevertheless, the ineffectiveness gap appears to grow in a somewhat Malthusian way; as improvements in the capability to cope increase at an arithmetical rate, the level and complexities of problems grow, as it were, at a geometrical rate. The limitations and corruptions of government are experienced by more and more people. This ineffectiveness was reflected in recent years in the headline of one popular magazine that asked, in the wake of a scandal at the U.S. Department of Housing and Urban Development, "Is Government Dead?" It is reflected in the United States by the fact that more than one successful presidential candidate has "run against the bureaucracy, against Washington."[18] Are established patterns of thinking adequate to effect more than temporary or marginal reversals of such a negative slide?

This book is intended for five main groups of readers. The first group includes politicians and influential people who, now or in the future, can make a difference in administration. The second group contains the public administration theorists and other students of public administration. The third group consists of public administration practitioners. The fourth includes social action and social science professionals, whose achievement of programmatic purposes requires a difference in administration. The fifth consists of those (to use Almond's term) in the "attentive public" who recognize that a difference in administration is essential if we are to maintain our quality of life.

The book will also be of interest to a sixth group, those with an interest in modernism, postmodernism, and contemporary society. The contemplative literature, if we may characterize it in this way, on postmodernism is now more than a cottage industry. That literature describes bureaucracy negatively, but its analysis stops short. Thinkers about modernism and postmodernism should have analyzed bureaucracy more deeply. They should have entered into dialog with public administration thinkers, those who specialize in the language of public organizations. This dialog requires not only an "action" literature but also respect for the real achievements made in public administration theory.

This book is about public administration concerns, however. Philosophical ideas are discussed where they are relevant to these concerns, but the intention is not to "do metaphysics." A distinction can be drawn between the implications of philosophy for social thinking on the one hand and, on the other, both philosophy for philosophy's sake and any implications of social thinking for metaphysics. Therefore, this book spends no time, for example, in explaining why neither the recognition of the hermeneutic character of social phenomena nor the talk of reflexivity in social thinking entails—although neither does so entail—any ontological commitment to multiple worlds. The focus is on the language of public administration.

Undeniably, members of any discipline tend to have difficulty reading a book that does not limit itself to the canon and habits of mind of that single discipline. The primary difficulty often is not that of understanding; it is the use of unfamiliar images, names, and examples. Differences exist even in writing styles. Philosophers would have difficulty in reading public administration books; the publications do not have the same set of common assumptions and expectations or the same set of familiar writers. Public administrationists, despite the "big-tent" attitude noted in chapter 2, can find the habits of mind accepted in philosophy to be equally annoying. The first part of chapter 2, for instance, mixes both public administration and non–public administration examples in the discussion of the hermeneutic character of public administration theory and "facts." Some may find even the repeated use of any unfamiliar word, such as hermeneutics (if it is unfamiliar), to be upsetting. Such irritation is a small part of the price we pay for the overspecialization of knowledge. Theatergoers are invited to enjoy the play by suspending their disbelief. Readers are asked to steel themselves to the variety.

This book is written with empathy for the habits of mind of those who work in bureaucracies and of those who think about bureaucracies. The writer's background in a variety of governmental functions makes this attitude unsurprising. It is warming to hear good stories about the good work of public agencies and public employees—how needed help was provided, how the child was saved from a certain fire by a brave employee, how the system worked. The important achievements of the public service deserve respect. Nevertheless, we should not deny what seem to be fundamental difficulties: the Kafkaesque aspects of bureaucracy and of the emerging environment of bureaucracy.[19]

The book is divided into three main parts, and it may be helpful here to have a general overview of these parts. The first part is introductory, consisting of chapters 1 and 2. Chapter 2 discusses the characteristics of the reflexive language paradigm, the rationale for the paradigm, and the general method of this study. The rationale includes establishing that public administration theory could have a different character than it now has. For this reason, the chapter explains how and why public administration theory and facts are socially constituted, and it describes what it means to claim that a public administration observer is an active image cocreator. Such background material is important because one intention of this book is to show the value of using reflexive interpretation. It is useful, first, to gain insight into why we understand as we do and, second, to explore possibilities for alternative sets of assumptions to yield different understandings.

Chapters 3 through 8 constitute the second main part. These chapters provide an analysis of the language of public administration in a modernist context. Chapter 3 describes the distinctive set of assumptions that underlie the modernist view of the world, and it discusses different ways of understanding the claim that these assumptions make up a modernist perspective. It describes this mind-set of modernity as shaping the underlying lines of development followed by public administration theory. Subsequent chapters (4 through 8) analyze modernist public administration theory in terms of these lines of development, lines named particularism, scientism, technologism, enterprise, and hermeneuticism. Chapter 4 focuses on the nature and limitations imposed on the study of public administration by the particular scope of the discipline, a scope shaped in part by the modernist trend toward increasing discipline autonomy and specialization. Chapter 5 analyzes the nature, contraries, and blind spots that result from the development of public administration as science. This analysis includes a consideration of some complexities facing administrative ethics. Chapter 6 examines the limitations that result from conceptualizing the development of public administration in terms of technology. Chapter 7 discusses the contraries and blind spots that limit the line of development that attempts to apply private enterprise solutions and public choice analyses. Chapter 8 turns to consider public administration developed as a hermeneutic activity. It explains how the search for rational meaning is limited by another set of blind spots and contraries. By the conclusion of chapter 8, the reader will see that modernist public administration theory has yielded useful results and can produce even more beneficial results. Nevertheless, the reader also will see that modernist public administration is logically limited in its capability to understand and upgrade bureaucracy. Each of the chapters shows that a particular line of development inevitably ends in paradoxes and blind spots.

Chapters 9 through 13, the third main part, discuss the language of public administration in a postmodernist context. They show how it is possible to go beyond the understandings available within the modernist frame of reference. Chapter 9 presents an account of postmodern perspectives and examines how such perspectives can be understood. A picture is drawn of a postmodernity that negates the basic mind-set of modernity. Subsequent chapters (10 through 13) analyze four interests on which postmodern discourse would focus. These interests are imagination, deconstruction, deterritorialization, and alterity; each is indicated to have significance for the study of public administration. Chapter 10 discusses the catalytic effect of imagination on public administration in postmodernity, an effect paralleling the role described for rationalization in modernity. Chapter 11 gives an explanation of deconstruction and describes the deconstruction of texts and narratives as a valuable public administration activity. Chapter 12 outlines the radical changes in the character and organization of public administration and other thinking in postmodernity, and it does so in terms of the concept of deterritorialization. It describes public administration theory as it is known in modernity as terminating. Chapter 13 explores ethical attitudes of postmodernity, examining their implications for public administration in terms of a tendency toward what is explained as antiadministration.

By the conclusion of chapter 13, the utility of looking at bureaucracy and public administration through the contrasting lenses, the opposed mind-sets of modernity and postmodernity, will have been illustrated. The reader will see the value of using reflexive interpretation to go beyond a unidimensional understanding of the language of public administration. The next chapter turns, then, to analyze the reflexive language paradigm, the basis for the paradigm, and the methodology of this study.

2

Method
Reflexive Interpretation

Being that can be understood is language.

—Gadamar[1]

We cease to think when we refuse to do so under the constraint of language. . . .
Rational thought is interpretation according to a scheme that we cannot throw off.

—Nietzsche[2]

EARLY VISITORS TO the moon did not expect to encounter entities such as a government, a budget, a paycheck, or a supervisor. Such public administration entities are not natural kinds; they are not givens. Public administration entities and facts are socially engineered and socially constituted. The ideas, entities, and facts represented by words such as *crime, budget, government, employee, and public sector,* as discussed below, are examples of social constructions.

Public administration theory is no less socially constituted than any other public administration "fact" or understanding. This theory, which conditions the way we see bureaucracies, could have a different shape and character than it now has. Using the language of public bureaucracy may be seen as a choice similar to (and with similarly profound consequences) the "choice" that the French made to speak French and the "choice" the Spanish made to speak Spanish. This social constitution and this choice do not imply that any theory is as good, or as bad, as any other. Nor do they mean that choices do not have consequences for the way we live. For example, it might be expected that a theory that recognizes its social constitution has advantages over one that does not.

Envelopes, or interacting layers, of meaning are involved in the generation of public administration "facts." We can simplify and speak of twin envelopes. One is the layer of meaning that surrounds and constitutes the object being studied. The other, interrelated with the first (which is why the adjective *twin* is used), is the envelope that surrounds and permeates the subject who is doing the studying.[3] The latter is the layer of meaning that is contributed by the observer—the scientist, the scientific community, and society. Such hermeneutic enveloping is a feature of any social or behavioral science, such as economics, sociology, or psychology, and the same is true of the understanding of public administration facts.

The first two sections of this chapter discuss the reflexive language paradigm and the rationale for it, and the third section provides methodological information on the present study. Discussion of the rationale in the second section begins by pointing to the twin envelopes that surround any study of public administration practice. The explanation of the hermeneutic context is simplified in the sense that we are using as a framework a modernist model of "subject understanding object" and that we speak only of two hermeneutic envelopes. Comment is then offered on the perspectival and other issues raised by the reflexive paradigm. The third section begins by explaining why public administration theory is chosen as the language of public administration and as the subject of analysis in this study, the present case. It goes on to discuss more specifics of the nature of this interpretive analysis, including the initial vantage point of the present study.

THE PARADIGM

The reflexive language paradigm was described in chapter 1 as a process of playful and attuned dialog with the underlying content of the language of public bureaucracy; the reader is referred to that description. The reflexive language paradigm indeed is not another ready-to-hand or cookbook explanation. A playful[4] and attuned dialog with the underlying content of the language of public bureaucracy and a single step-by-step methodology are incompatible; reflexive interpretation is a matter of art.

Reflexive interpretation is an art that seeks to draw out and use the consequences of the hermeneutic, reflexive, and linguistic character of the way in which we should understand and create public administration phenomena. It is an art that examines the set of assumptions and social constructions that constitute the theoretical lens through which we see, and it speculates about an alternative set or sets of socially constructed assumptions (that form another lens) through which we could see. The interpretation is reflexive because, for one reason, the focus is on the lens and on alternative lenses, rather than on the objects that are "seen" through the lenses; the attention is paid to the act of seeing and options for seeing.

A first aim of this art, then, is to analyze the set of assumptions—the form of the language—that shapes our constitution of public administration facts. This analysis would include exploring and evaluating the connection between the set of assumptions and the "facts" and possible alternative "facts," and it might include assessing the characteristics of that set of assumptions for producing such facts. For this purpose, choices are required. Modernity is chosen for this first interpretation, and thus our first attention is directed to the dialect of modernity. The most basic ideas are identified within the core of the modernist mind-set, including the fundamental philosophical thinking and other reflections about the human condition, about knowing, about society, and about what is. Also identified are the lines of development that this core would imply for the social constitution of an action discipline such as public administration. The choice is made to pursue this analysis (and why this analysis is considered to be critically important will become clearer as postmodernity is discussed) in "dialog" with the texts and the literature that relate to the subject. The choice is made to identify the logical characteristics of these lines of development; in this case, the modernist lines seem to lead toward contraries or paradoxes. This last sentence is written in the form "The choice is made" because another person may well opt for an alternative approach to reflexive interpretation. A second aim would be to explore a similar interpretation for another set of core assumptions. This attempt would require some modification in view of the nature and condition of the second set of assumptions (e.g., if the second set has not yet yielded any "facts"). Postmodernity was selected for this second cut at interpretation, and thus the second attention was directed to the dialect of postmodernity. Writing of lines of development is inappropriate to the basic attitudes of postmodernity, but it is possible to interpret attitudes of significance for thinking about our topic. Postmodernity, unlike modernity, would not lead someone to the project of public administration, and any interpretation should respect that difference. Additional steps, with yet other sets of assumptions taken, could have been added indefinitely. Any listing of methodological steps is oversimplistic and faulty, however; for one thing, it is inconsistent with an assumption that no Archimedean point really exists. This consideration restresses the need to avoid formulas, even the one in this very sentence.

Reflexive interpretation is concerned with why we see (understand) what we are seeing (understanding) and with the possibilities for seeing (understanding) something different by changing the lens. To continue this lens example, I can say that the primary interest is not the astronomical bodies that I can see through my telescope (eyes); the interest is the telescope (eye) itself. It is suggested that a way of thinking and theorizing about public administration phenomena, being what they are, is to assume that the nature of the public administration telescope (eye) will determine what I see. Another person might go further and take the position that, the state of the human condition being what it is, the telescope does determine what we see. The term *lens* here refers to the mass of assumptions, the underlying theoretical framework, through which we look. We cannot escape having a framework, but we need to be conscious of the way that it shapes (creates) what we see. A leading concern is why we are seeing what we are seeing and whether we could see it differently; it is reflexive interpretation.

The reflexive language paradigm is best introduced by explaining its rationale and the character of its application in the present case, and that explanation is the purpose of this chapter. My understanding of the paradigm is shown in chapters 3 through 14 in the account of its present application. An entry point into the rationale and the paradigm is through recognition of the ineluctably hermeneutic context of the generation of public administration facts and other understandings. No un-constituted way of looking at any item exists. A second step in the entry is apprecia-tion of the difficult idea that it is helpful to assume that our context is to be trapped in perspectival views and that no Archimedean point is available from which we can view the panorama absent a perspective; our view of social facts is assumed to come from the inside. A third step in the entry is recognition that the act of constitution is inescapably conducted within the context of language because thinking is embed-ded in language. Gadamer's and Nietzsche's comments quoted at the beginning of this chapter are consistent with this view.

RATIONALE FOR THE PARADIGM

Consider the social construction of entities, the hermeneutic envelope that sur-rounds and constitutes public administration objects. Karl Popper describes three worlds.[5] World 1 is the world of material things. World 2 entities are thoughts in peo-ple's minds, mental phenomena. World 3 consists of objective structures that are the products of minds, the cultural heritage. The objects of public administration and social science study, like the meanings of flowers in the language of flowers (see de-scription of flower language dictionaries later), are in World 3. Public administra-tion and social science objects are, as has been said, social artifacts.

Consider the concepts of *crime, budget, government,* and *employee* in the United States. Understood as they are, these concepts fulfill particular purposes and achieve certain results. Would it have been possible for these social artifacts to have been constructed differently? Yes, it would have.

Whether and how much crime goes up or down are functions, in part at least, of the particular concept of crime. The Uniform Crime Report in the United States emphasizes part 1 crimes, generally street and property crimes; it downplays par-ticular crimes (such as economic crime) and ignores the more fundamental co-authors and breeding conditions of crime. Thus, we add up the numbers of bank robberies and rapes and murders and auto thefts (adding apples and pears, as if one robbery equals one rape equals one murder equals one auto theft), and we exclude embezzlement, kidnapping, and drug offenses from the calculation of the part 1 crime level. We ignore the policy of a corporate organization (such as a bank) to maintain existing security levels where the organization decides that its costs do not justify expenditures on extra security arrangements. Alternatives chosen in bank security policies (as in parallel organizations) surely have effects on behavior that will enter the crime statistics. If a bank management forecasts that its decision on the level of security expenditures will be associated with twenty-five robberies and one employee death per year (compared with fifteen robberies and no deaths at a higher security expenditure level) and if five robberies occur, how many crimes does that total? If the same management has the same expectations and if no robberies occur, was there no crime? (In another possible world, there might well have been a name for such more fundamental authors—or co-authors—of crime. One possibility is a "Warwick," which refers to a corporate or organizational policy that generates crime. The analogy is to the Earl of Warwick, recognized in Shakespeare's *King Henry VI* and elsewhere as a "maker of kings"—in the sense that an organization can be a maker of criminals and criminality. In act 3, scene 3 of Part III, Shakespeare writes, "Warwick, peace; Proud setter up and puller down of kings.") The point is that the social construction of *crime* is critical.

The concept of a *budget* has changed radically in American government. At one point, a budget was seen as a recording device that we associate with line items and green eyeshades. At a later time (with a lot happening in between), it is seen as a process of planning-budgeting-evaluating. Nineteenth-century legislative budgeting is a different concept from executive budgeting, and it has different results. A budget viewed as an instrument of fiscal policy, as an economic tool, is a different object from what it could have been before Keynes's 1936 *General Theory of Employment, Interest and Money*. The rational-comprehensive budget is not the same object as the budget that is the embodiment of Lindblom's incrementalism.

Government is no less a socially constituted entity. Consider a particular government, for example, the U.S. government. If asked to point to the U.S. government, should the respondent point to the White House? Congress? Old Glory? A regional office of the Internal Revenue Service? The Pentagon's north parking lot? Consider government in general. It is not clear where government ends and nongovernment begins. It is not clear why the dictator who supervises our work in the private enterprise office is not governing us; he or she certainly gives us orders, rewards, and punishment. In earlier decades supervisors both in public and private enterprise would take more of an interest in the kind of activities that the employees did after work; for instance, the New York City Police Department in the 1960s is reported to have expressed interest in the marital fidelity of middle-management personnel. In earlier decades, supervisors would take an interest in the employee's choice of work clothes; for a man, a tie was required at all costs. The existence of quasi-governmental entities such as public corporations and nonprofit corporations also raises questions about the nature of government. So does the existence of community associations, which seem to be a form of private government. According to the Community Associations Institute, 130,000 such associations were in existence in the United States in 1989. Examples of large associations (virtual towns) are the 21,000-population Leisure World and the 27,000-population Woodbridge Village, both in California. Just as it is unclear what is a government, it is unclear who does government work. This point is more than an academic quibble because the conceptualization changes understanding of the problem and solutions. For example, we can look to the fire service as the primary source of fire prevention and extinction, and we can think that problems can be solved with simply more firefighters, better firefighters, and better techniques. On the other hand, we can see fire prevention and extinction as primarily a function of a set of quasi-anarchistic structures, of which the fire service is but one input.

Meaning and social constitution are provided by our language—by the language of the reader and his or her group. Consider F. H. Bradley's example of the language of flowers.[6] In the language of flowers, some flowers have meanings and others do not. How did some flowers become meaningful? Clearly, it was because the flower-reading public gave the meaning to particular flowers. The very idea of a flower language is a social artifact.

Jean Marsh reports that flower language dictionaries and books were fashionable in England from the days of George IV until the early years of Victoria's reign; the fashion came somewhat later in the United States. Marsh quotes one flower language book as explaining, "A party walking in a garden, through the means of flowers presented to each other, may carry on a conversation of compliment, wit and repartee."[7] She tells us that, for example, a person handed an ivy geranium sees that she is being asked, "May I have your hand for the next quadrille?" An American cowslip conveys the proposition, "Divine beauty; you are my divinity"; a wild daisy means, "I will think of it"; a dried white rose means, "Death is preferable to loss of innocence"; and a Japan rose (a sort of backhanded compliment, apparently) means, "Beauty is your only attraction." Jean Marsh lists the meanings of seven hundred flowers and plants. Clearly, not all plants in the world have meanings. Equally clearly, the meaning is provided by human beings through the public language shared and applied by the reader. When the flower language user sees the Japan rose, she sees the meaning in the flowers, but she is mistaken. The meaning, unlike the petals, is not in the flowers.[8]

Employee (or *labor*) is no less a socially constituted entity than a flower word. The socially determined nature of the *employee* was recognized by, among others, Herbert Simon. Simon writes in his *Administrative Behavior* that one "of the socially determined roles in many societies is that of 'employee.' The particular content of the role—the degree of obedience expected—will vary with the social situation. The American workingman today, for example, probably has a narrower zone of acceptance, so far as the employer's instructions are concerned, than his father had."[9] Examples can also be found in Lester Thurow's *Head to Head.*[10] Thurow contrasts the way that employees are viewed and treated in what he calls communitarian societies (such as Germany and Japan) and in individualistic societies (such as the United States and Great Britain).

Acceptance of the claim that knowledge is socially constituted, it should be interjected, need not imply that no other constituent factors exist. The extent of social constitution may be limited, in some views, by physical or other factors. The facts that a person can neither fly like a bird nor live underwater like a fish can be understood as physical realities that limit and help to shape the social construction of reality, for example; the fact that a person has a perishable body and life provides parameters within which social reality can be created. The Marxist view, as another example, is that social constitution is determined mainly by economic factors. The substructure, where the means of production shape the class and other relations in a society, act on the superstructure. The superstructure, of which the prevailing philosophy and social theory are components, react on the substructure; the substructure and the superstructure continually interact. The Marxian view is that, in this way, the means of production act as limits to (and determinants of) social constitution.

The claim about the social construction of "facts" such as those studied in public administration should be relatively uncontroversial among those interested in the philosophy of social science. The claim has been long discussed in such fields as sociology, education, and psychology.[11] Of course, such claims have been made by those public administrationists interested in interpretive and critical theory, but it is not clear that the claim is as widely recognized as it could be among those concerned with public administration.

Consider the hermeneutics of the human observer, the other twin of the hermeneutic layers. The hermeneutic character of the subject is no more avoidable by the public administration observer than by any other observer. Gulick, embracing his idea that the functions of the manager can be summarized in the acronym POSDCORB, could be expected to notice whether an agency head made no provision for, or took no account of, planning or organization. (As we know, POSDCORB stands for planning, organizing, staffing, directing, coordinating, reporting, and budgeting.) He pioneered the construction of a social reality of the manager as a POSDCORBian. Insofar as her view was the POSDCORB lens intended by Gulick in 1937,[12] a manager would not see an administrative world where a major task of the administrator was to maintain external relationships. Surely, we have all encountered administrators who complain that they have been so busy in external meetings that they have not had time to do their "proper" job, where their proper job is seen as dealing with their subordinates and superiors. That view is seeing the world through POSDCORBian eyes. Leonard White, author of the celebrated administrative histories, is also described as having "seen" and written the accounts in his first two volumes from a POSDCORBian perspective.[13]

Imagine New Public Administration devotees conducting an analysis of the operations of an agency. New Public Administration was the movement that held that an important part of the administrative function is to emphasize relevance, equity, fairness, and representation. Imagine now that the same agency is being analyzed by disciples of Frederick Taylor. The latter would see the activities of the agency through the lens of administrative efficiency, a different socially constructed reality.

The devotees and the disciples would see different administrative facts; each would construct a different world picture from what they saw.

The view that social science is a matter of the cumulative accretion of knowledge through the work of the human subject neutrally observing the actions and interactions of objects—letting the facts speak for themselves—is untenable. It is difficult to cling to the view that the mind is some kind of passive receptor of outside entities such as impressions or ideas—that the mind can work on these ideas (combine, compare, and so on) but that it receives the impressions as they are, naked. The views of Locke and others in this tradition reached a culmination in Hume, who characterized the mind as a bundle of such impressions and ideas.[14] For Hume, the mind is really nothing but a bundle of perceptions; he holds that the permanent self cannot be justified by introspection.

Facts cannot speak for themselves. For one thing, facts can neither speak nor write; speaking requires a speaker, and both speaking and writing require a subject who has a language. Known facts can only be constituted through propositions; if propositions were derived from observation alone, it would still be necessary to express those propositions in language. For the realist to say that water consists of two parts of hydrogen and one part of oxygen requires, for example, not only a certain state of the world but also the language to express the state of that world. Facts cannot speak for themselves because, for another thing, the subject cannot "see" objects without mediation. Subjects necessarily see objects through some conceptual system that is manifested in the language they use. It is more than saying that subjects see objects through the mist of their language, through the veil of their conceptual apparatus. This description implies that the knowing subject is separate from her language and conceptual framework. In fact, the relationship of subject and language used is more intimate. Some might want to say that the subject's mind is structured by the language in which she operates.

It seems more realistic (at least) to view the subject as an active shaper of the image received, as the active shaper of the object generated in the consciousness of the mind. Kant, a thinker who changed the face of Western philosophy, emphasizes the subject's active role. In the *Critique of Pure Reason,* the subject (e.g., the scientist) sees only the world of appearance.[15] For Kant, what is seen (or heard, touched, and so on) is the resultant of what is provided by the interaction of the subject and the thing-in-itself. Physical reality, as it is in itself, is beyond our seeing. For example, consider what seems such a clear feature of the world as it is—space. Kant holds that space is subjective in that its existence depends on the subject.[16] That we may not see the world (or space) simply "as it is" has been illustrated by recounting reports of the experiences of some patients with cataracts. The patients are adults who have been "blind" since birth as result of their cataracts and whose cataracts are then removed. After their operations, such people are said not to see tables and chairs in their "appointed" three-dimensional space points; rather, they see blurs of light.

Minton and Shipka, for instance, claim that "the patient is immediately confronted with a wall of brightness containing color patches that blend indistinguishably into one another. The flood of sensations is absolutely meaningless. . . . There is no awareness of shape or size, nor any idea of distance. . . . Only after long and painful experience do the patients come to have an idea of objective space."[17] The authors quote Marcus von Senden: "The newly-operated patients do not localize their visual impressions; they do not relate them to any point, either to the eye or to any surface, even a spherical one; they see colors much as we smell an odor of peat or varnish, which enfolds and entrudes upon us, but without occupying any specific form of extension in more exactly definable way."[18] The moral is that the subject is, at least, an active image cocreator.[19]

Recall the old story that asks us to imagine that we need spectacles in order to see. When I wear eyeglasses that have red lenses, I see the world as red. I get so used to seeing the red world that I come to believe that the world really is red. When I change to eyeglasses that are blue, the world becomes blue. I am entitled to doubt that the world is either red or blue. Am I entitled to say that it is neither red nor blue? No, it might or might not be. Am I entitled to say that the world is colorless? No, it might or might not be. Am I entitled to say, at least, that the world is not colored in the way that I see it colored? Without glasses, I have never seen—I can never see—the world. In the same way, we are condemned to see the world through the eyeglasses of a language. We cannot escape from the lens of language. We can see the world only in terms of some conceptual system, some perspective.

Public administration is no different in this respect than any other social science. Consider the case of the mainstream economic theorist. Such an economist proves useful in analysis precisely because he or she tends to see the world in terms of economic theory.[20] The negative side is that an adherent tends to have difficulty in seeing entities in any other fashion. The mainstream theorist will see a different economic world than, say, a Marxian economist. The nature of price is another example. As Richard Ebeling points out, "If, however, instead of defining 'price' only as a generalized constraint from the individual's point of view, 'price' is also looked upon as a social means for mutual orientation of individual plans in a system of division of labour, the one technique does not fit all problems."[21]

The forms of thought that constitute the observer—the sets of concepts and the cognitive and other baggage that make up a person's language in use—shapes that person's vision. These forms of thought are social and intersubjective. Certainly, idiosyncratic elements exist in my language and in yours; nevertheless, having said this, my language is in all important respects public if only because communication requires publicness. To be observers who communicate, observers must enter into a set of public language games.

The examples given earlier do suffer from the limitation that they do not provide a strong enough picture of the permeative character of language-in-use. Our language is our collection of sets of concepts. Beyond this, language can be regarded like cancer cells that invade, and that are invaded by, all of our being and all of interrelationships with the world. This point is consistent with Hegel's reference to logic being implicit in everyday language, the essence of mind.[22]

Whether public administration "reality" is socially constituted can be separated from the issue of the appropriate nature of the study of that reality; that is, hermeneutic constitution does not entail only hermeneutic analysis. Max Weber was one who held that social objects are socially constituted, but he also endorsed the positivist study of such entities. Berger and Luckman put it well when they write: "The sociology of knowledge understands human reality as socially constructed reality. . . . In sum, our conception of the sociology of knowledge implies a specific conception of sociology in general. It does not imply that sociology is not a science, that its methods should be other than empirical, or that it cannot be 'value-free.' "[23]

Positivist research on public administration issues should not be excluded merely because the subject of the research is socially constituted; its potentiality should not be belittled. Choice of method should depend, in part, on objective, and it seems straightforward to identify useful empirical-analytical objectives.[24] People can search for regularities of relationships in public administration and in the social sciences. Whatever the socially constituted entity and however it is constituted, that entity has qualities that can be explored; it has identifiable relationships with other socially constituted entities. Renata Tesch describes the discovery of regularities as being one of four major types of qualitative research. As she writes, "Some scholars carve out entities from the data that they regard as 'properties,' 'concepts,' or even 'variables.' In most cases they assume that there might be connections or relationships among them that are to be discovered. The regularities are viewed as a system of conceptual order. Other researchers are oriented more toward insightful description, where the structure is manifested in commonalities in the data, i.e. as certain patterns that repeat across the data."[25]

It is true that criticisms can be leveled at the status of, and the social science results of, positivism. On the issue of status, chapter 5 points to the contemporary inability to provide a consensus account of the privileged status of scientific statements. On the issue of results, it is arguable that public administration theory and the social sciences have failed not only to approach the superlative achievements of the physical sciences but also to achieve optimal understanding of public administration and social science issues. Public administration remains a prescience. It has never produced a lawlike explanation of the causal relationship between two events, for example; it has produced nothing at the level of "Every body continues in a state of rest or of uniform motion in a straight line unless acted upon by a force." Nevertheless, these problems are not the more significant difficulties. As chapter 5 explains, the positivist purpose is explanation rather than understanding. What positivism cannot do is to tell us enough about the spheres of values, purposes, and meanings—about the framework within which positivism, or any other approach, can be used.

The other fork in the road is to invest more attention and effort into seeking understanding through interpretation. The claim here is that, at the present state of development in our understanding, public administration theory can give direction and vigor to the study of public administration phenomena only by means of the latter fork. In a world or a sphere considered to be peppered with meanings, it seems natural to turn to a study of meanings. The antecedent phrase should be emphasized. The meanings, values, and purposes are not merely additional categories in the data set, grist for the positivist mill. Rather, they cogenerate the world and the research tools and assumptions that are being used.

Hermeneutics concerns texts; it is concerned with interpreting, with specifying significance, with achieving intelligibility. Texts, in this case, can be written texts or texts in the form of societal practices, institutions, or other arrangements or activities; as an instance of such arrangements or activities, recall that we often speak of "reading situations." Hermes transmitted and interpreted the messages of the gods; hermeneutics has a long history and an enormous literature, flourishing particularly in the last two centuries in Germany and elsewhere in Europe.[26]

Consider toys and eyeglasses. I do not wish to deny the value of positivist studies of toys, socially constituted entities. For example, it might be interesting for an entrepreneur to have the results of an empirical study indicating whether a particular design of toy will appeal to a certain age group; this person might also find it useful to have the results of an empirical study that indicate whether a certain size and shape of toy can be swallowed by children. Nevertheless, a study of the language of toys cannot be excluded. For example, it might be worthwhile for an entrepreneur to know how thinking about toys shapes what we and children think is a toy and what the purpose of a toy is; she also might find it useful to see how the structure of our thinking about toys reflects our socially constituted experience with the socially constituted objects that we call toys. There is value in "playing" with the language.

Substitute "public administration theory" for "eyeglasses," and substitute "modernism" and then "postmodernism" for "eyeglasses through which I see eyeglasses," in the following. In writing of a reflexive paradigm, the kinds of studies being suggested are studies of the eyeglasses through which (with which) I constitute the world. What does the nature of my eyeglasses tell me about the nature of the world I have constituted through them? What does it tell me about the nature of the world I "must" constitute through them? What seems to happen if I change the lens (e.g., from green to red)? What do my eyeglasses look like? What do my eyeglasses look like if (no, the following does not contain a typographical error) I change " 'the eyeglasses I use' to look at 'the eyeglasses I use' to look at the world?" Translating the foregoing questions, we have the following: What does the nature of public administration theory tell us about the nature of the public administration facts we have constituted? What seems to happen if we change from one set of public administration theory to another set? What does public administration theory look like (e.g., from a modernist perspective)? What does public administration theory look like from a different perspective (e.g., from a postmodernist perspective)? The preceding set of questions is an example of "playing" with the language.

Let us extend the example in one direction. The study of public administration can be expected to reveal a world of bureaucratic practice that will tend to match the fundamental mind-set of the discipline, the mind-set of the mainstream study of public administration. Public administrationists might see a public administrationist world—just as the economist might see a world governed by economic considerations and forces, the therapist might see a world of patients requiring therapy, the physicist (chemist) might see a world of physics (chemical) phenomena, and the trained witch-hunter might find a world of witches. The phrase "fundamental mind-set" here means the set of basic assumptions about aims and processes that govern accepted practice and thinking. It means the most basic objectives, motivations, metaphors, and energy sources that underlie the discipline. A radically different mind-set might reveal an alternative picture of the world. Subject to variations resulting from their own individuality (and with the exception of the odd deviant thinker), theorists educated to see the public administration world in one way will see the features and dynamics that their subculture is accustomed to describing and discussing. The nonspecialist will also be shaped by the character of a discipline that has been socially accepted. Fundamental mind-sets are not expected to remain static, however; they may adjust, perhaps in response to internalist and/or externalist forces. Nevertheless, archaeology of the subject will reveal the lasting impact of the original fundamental mind-set. The study of public administration is expected to be no different in this respect than any other discipline. It will have strengths and may have blind spots that can be traced to its fundamental mind-set. It is suggested that the way to this information is through study of the language of public administration.

The statement "All Cretans are liars," reported to St. Paul by a Cretan, is a classic example of reflexivity. (If the Cretan's report is true, the statement is false.[27]) Earlier, it was suggested that a useful heuristic device for public administration theorizing is to take the view that our context is to be trapped in a perspectival cobweb and that our view is always from the inside of the bundle of perspectives. In the same way, it was suggested that (because all our conceptualization and thinking are conducted in terms of language) it is useful to think that we are always trapped within the context of language and that we cannot look at the panorama from the outside. To say that all perspectives are socially constituted, on this assumption, is also a view that is socially constituted; it could not be said to be true *simpliciter.*

Two positions among those available on reflexivity are discussed here. One is to adopt the reflexive position as a heuristic device for the purpose of conducting public administration theory. The other position is to embrace reflexivity as an actual characteristic of the human condition. The former is all that is necessary to use the reflexive language paradigm in public administration thinking, but some may choose the latter. The discussion should begin by explaining how the former is possible.

Various views of the relationships of the special sciences and metaphysics are consistent with the general claim that the reflexive position can be adopted as a heuristic device for theorizing. One view will be suggested.[28] A special science, such as physics or sociology (or a discipline such as public administration), can be understood as standing by itself, and the theoretician can develop a number of alternative models or descriptions that work for the purposes of that special science, that is, for explanation or for understanding.

As illustration, let us redraw Synge's description between the R-world and the M-world.[29] The R-world, as Synge describes it, refers to the "real world, the world of immense complexity in which we live and move and have our being."[30] He contrasts this world with the various M-worlds that we have, with M standing for model. Examples of M-worlds are the Newtonian, which he calls M1, and the Einsteinian, which he calls M2. The accounts they provide cannot be considered in all respects true of reality. He continues, "Neither of them [i.e., M1 or M2] is right in the sense that it is an exact image of the R-world. No M-world can be that. But both of them are good images of certain features of the R-world, leaving many phenomena that they are both unable to deal with."[31] Clearly, M-worlds and the R-world are interrelated. Nevertheless, his general point (not peculiar to Synge, of course) is that it is muddled to equate "what is" with the models. Synge calls confusion of the M-world with the R-world the "Pygmalion Syndrome." As he writes, "I name [the confusion] the 'Pygmalion Syndrome,' after Pygmalion who carved a statue of such surpassing realism that it came to life—M-world becoming R-world in the mind of the enthusiastic physicist."[32]

The fact that our language (our theoretical framework) constitutes the world leaves open the question whether a uniquely correct way of describing the world exists. Kant's view, for instance, is that only one correct set of rules for constituting the world exists and that this set is applicable to all human beings. Hegel's view includes the idea that the way of viewing the world is created by our place in history, our language, and our society. An advantage of the heuristic avenue is that it sidesteps such issues, leaving the larger philosophical questions for another day. Arguably, it is not necessary to resolve deeper philosophical problems before conducting public administration.

Reflexivity has a large literature because its discussion is necessary for an understanding of thinkers such as Nietzsche, Wittgenstein, Heidegger, and Derrida; they all describe us as trapped within the conceptual cobweb of language. As Heidegger writes, "Human beings remain committed to and within the being of language, and can never step out of it and look at it from somewhere else."[33] In the *Tractatus,* Wittgenstein writes, "The limits of my language are the limits of my world."[34] Again, the perspectival difficulty may be one reason Nietzsche wrote in such an enigmatic manner; a perspectivalist does not wish to blurt out the "truth" because his or her statement cannot have a status greater than any other perspective.[35] Nietzsche chose to hint, to resuggest from another perspective, to say again from yet another perspective, and he chose to use various literary devices.

Nevertheless, as Hilary Lawson reports, Nietzsche, Heidegger, and Derrida—unlike Wittgenstein—do not avoid making general claims about the nature of language. A defensive and offensive line exist. With regard to the defensive, note Lawson's claim that much of the writing of Nietzsche, Heidegger, and Derrida is in response to the reflexive predicament, the predicament that their positions include "reflexive self-awareness which is paradoxical." Lawson states: "A simple reply to this whole predicament and one which will appeal to many analytic philosophers is to argue that to have arrived at this point is an indication of fundamental error. So long as we regard the enterprise of knowledge, the dream of the Age of Enlightenment, as intact, this argument will be a compelling one and the writings of Nietzsche, Heidegger and Derrida will remain of peripheral interest."[36] For the offensive, see Lawson's claim that Nietzsche, Heidegger, and Derrida are also concerned to push "the destructive aspects of reflexivity to their limit." He explains:

> In consequence, they can be seen to open up the post-modern world—a world without certainties, a world without absolutes. This new impact of reflexivity is in part due to a critical shift of focus, from the individual subject to the text. Thus from Nietzsche to Derrida we see the subject—traditionally the focus of philosophical thought as the place of experience, morality, choice and will—gradually abandoned.... The alternative modes of thought which these philosophers propose both rely on, and incorporate, a reflexivity which is all-encompassing.... For Nietzsche, Heidegger and Derrida, do not merely seek to change our views, but propose a new mode of thought.[37]

THE PRESENT CASE

Why is public administration theory being taken, in the present case, as the language of public organization? The languages of bureaucracy take various forms. In one classification system, four forms or types of language can be distinguished; other systems and additional forms can be identified. The first of the four forms is bureaucratic output itself. For example, a sanitation department might do a good (or bad) job of keeping a city clean, have no (or some) scandals, be staffed with no (or some) political hacks, and keep clean (or dirty) trucks. This form is language in the sense we say a boxer speaks with his gloves or a painter speaks with his brush. The second form is what bureaucrats say. For example, the unemployment clerk might say, in a pleasant manner, "How can I help you?" or, in an unpleasant manner, "Get behind the white line"; a manager might say, "Do this right away" or "Would you be interested in doing this?" The third form is what bureaucrats write (e.g., internal memoranda, public letters, and regulations). The fourth form includes the sets of theories that are believed to guide what bureaucrats do—public administration and any program specialty theory, such as engineering for public works engineers and such as medicine for public health doctors. Each of these language forms or types can be examined at the surface or at deeper levels. For example, at the surface level, it is useful to notice patterns of customer-friendly speech. At a deeper level, some may seek to analyze what they consider to be the underlying characteristics of the speech patterns.

Public administration theory is the language chosen for analysis in the present study. The other languages also present opportunities for analysis, and some work has been conducted on them.[38] The value of such approaches is significant. Certainly, the present choice is a matter of preference. Beyond this point, however, the choice of public administration theory as the language does have an advantage in that it is a more fundamental, more foundational language than the others. In important senses, it tends to lie underneath the other language types. As such, it probably offers more potential for deepening understanding and for effecting more large-scale change.

Consider any document exhibiting bureaucratese. Chapter 10 quotes part of a U.S. government purchase specification; it concerns the purchase of frankfurters, an item almost as American as apple pie. The specification is a typical example of bureaucratese. It is expected that readers can think of many similar examples; like me, they may have participated in writing them. Analysis of such bureaucratic output (the third form mentioned above) surely can be deepened by consideration of the underlying and more general language. Assume that analysis of the surface characteristics of such documents leads to the deeper view that what seems rational and desirable (necessary, in fact) when seen from within the bureaucracy can seem, when viewed from outside the bureaucracy, to be irrational and undesirable (absurd, in fact). Is this incongruence just a matter of perspective, a matter of the citizenry misunderstanding the practical problems of the bureaucracy? Is it the influence of, say, legal and political attitudes and pressures, or is it a matter of ineffective public management—something that could be corrected, say, by more effective systems analysis, more informed and better public employee judgment, and more training and better selected public personnel (maybe even using people with strong private enterprise backgrounds)? Is the problem with those particular bureaucrats or that particular bureaucracy or that set of bureaucrats and bureaucracies? Do even deeper reasons exist, perhaps connected with the nature of the bureaucratic and human condition, the nature of public management and organization theory, understandings about the nature of bureaucratic rationality embedded in the assumptions of public administration theory, other theories and pretheories, or some combination? Is yet another or companion reason connected with a lack of influence of public administration theory and with the underlying forces that account for whatever impact or lack of impact is involved? Do we not have to go to some depths to have hope of understanding this bureaucratic situation? Surely, we need to consider the more fundamental issues, and this consideration leads us (at a minimum) to the deeper level of public administration theory.

Faced with such situations, we should seek the more fundamental factors. We need to see what underlies such oddities (as odd as those in any dream) that the outside bureaucracy and the inside bureaucracy views do not match. Some will say the reason is obvious. A more meaningful approach is to examine what underlies in public administration theory—and what does not, and why. The starting point in the present case is to take public administration theory as the language of public organizations.

The procedure in the present study has been to borrow aspects of the hermeneutic approach developed in the wake of Gadamer, Habermas, Apel, and Ricoeur.[39] Nevertheless, it should be stressed that no attempt is made to follow any of these thinkers. The goal of the interpretation, of this methodological hermeneutics, is to produce a consistent and coherent account of the language of public administration. One way to begin, which is borrowed, is to start with a very general hypothesis about the interpretation of modernist public administration theory. This hypothesis directs attention to particular features of public administration theory, and then the resulting understandings are fitted into a coherent interpretation. The idea is that this process raises further issues because some features fit only awkwardly, then another interpretation is developed, and so on. The notion is that this forward-and-back series of iterations constitutes a hermeneutic circle. The inspiration and the debt are acknowledged, but (to repeat) no claims are made that I am doing what these writers do or that I am understanding the results in the same way that they would understand their results.

The task of the hermeneutic circle is to develop understandings by getting below the surface. Several analogies may help in understanding the process of interpretation used in this book. They are described here only from a modernist perspective; the situation is more complex in the postmodern context. One analogy would be to see the method of interpreting as ordinary rational analysis, one performed by examining public administration theory in the light of modernist and postmodernist claims. In this respect, the process could be understood as similar to what many philosophers do (i.e., developing and explaining claims, exploring claims from various perspectives, examining supporting arguments and counterarguments, modifying the claims, and reexamining). In this respect, the process could be regarded as similar to what many theoretical social scientists do (e.g., economists developing explanatory models, thinking the models through, examining the models in the light of what is known, and reformulating the models). In this respect, the process would be regarded as similar to what literary critics could do (e.g., probing the poem and interpreting and reinterpreting).

If this analogy were pursued, some might want the rational analysis—in a form of philosophical analysis—to follow a pattern such as that suggested by Anthony Weston. Weston writes, for instance, about "exploring the issue." He discusses the need to explore the argument on all sides of the issue, to question and defend each argument's premises, and to revise and rethink arguments as they emerge. Weston writes about "composing an argumentative essay," with "argumentative" here, of course, not having the negative connotation of everyday life. He discusses explaining the question, considering objections, making definite claims or proposals, considering alternatives, and developing arguments fully. Weston also talks about the "writing of the argumentative essay." He discusses the need to keep the introduction brief (one of his rules I think I have broken); to "clarify, clarify, clarify"; to support objections with arguments; and not to claim more than the analysis has shown.[40]

Another analogy that might help here is to view theory (recalling that we are speaking from a perspective that is not postmodern) as a dream and to understand the interpretive task to be a kind of dream analysis. Because public administration theory is socially constructed, the contents of the dream could have been different if the forces that underlie it had been different. In this analogy, we would attempt to analyze the content and the underlying forces by examining public administration theory (seen as a dream) in terms of elements of the modernist and postmodernist tendencies of the human condition.

If this analogy were pursued, some might wish to suppose that an analysis of the dream could be influenced by the principles Freud describes in *The Interpretation of Dreams* and elsewhere. For example, the object of our attention would not be the dream as a whole but rather the separate portions of its content. We are pursuing, under the headings of modernism and postmodernism, the parts of public administration theory. As another example, we would be conscious of the distinction between the manifest and the latent contents of the dream. As yet another example, we would be alert to the defenses, and (shades of the postmodern) we would remember Freud's caution that a core of mystery always remains at "the dream's navel, the spot where it reaches down into the unknown."[41]

When Freud wrote *The Interpretation of Dreams*, he seems to have been careful to reveal his thoughts gradually to spare the reader. For example, his chapter 2 tells us that a dream is a fulfillment of a wish; we wait until chapter 4 to be told that it is a disguised fulfillment of a repressed wish, and then we wait until chapter 7 to learn that the repressed wish is an infantile one. At first blush, the account of the process of interpreting public administration data might seem to face similar dangers. It is talking in a manner that might seem relatively foreign to a technological emphasis in the public administration discipline. It has spoken of hermeneutics; it has mentioned modernism and postmodernism; and now this account is topped off by the suggestion of a possible analogy with the interpretation of dreams. Nevertheless, there is no need for caution here; such strains of thought are established enough in public administration. For example, see the discussion of interpretationism in public administration in chapter 8, and see Denhardt on the Freudian contribution to public administration.[42] In addition, public administration has porous boundaries, a "big tent" attitude to ideas from other disciplines.

A hermeneutic circle requires an initial vantage point. On the basis of foreknowledge, the initial hypothesis for this study was that many critical features of the modernist public administration theory—constituted as it is—will lead to paradoxes. Such paradoxes might make more useful and comprehensible the insights to be gained from examining public administration in the postmodern context. An initial hypothesis in a hermeneutic analysis of this kind is usually very general, and this one fits that description. One reason is that the term *paradox* is itself general. Quine, more qualified than most regarding paradoxes, endorses the view that "a paradox is just any conclusion that at first sounds absurd but that has an argument to sustain it."[43] Nevertheless, he adds that the account leaves much unsaid: "The argument that sustains a paradox may expose the absurdity of a buried premise or of some preconceptions previously reckoned as central to physical theory, to mathematics, or to the thinking process. Catastrophe may lurk, therefore, in the most innocent-seeming paradox. More than once in history the discovery of paradox has been the occasion for major reconstruction at the foundations of thought."[44] Quine distinguishes three classes of paradox: the veridical, the falsidical, and antimonies. The veridical paradox occurs where the absurdity (the contradiction or contrary) is resolved, and the falsidical is where it is not. Quine distinguishes these kinds of paradoxes from antinomies, which he describes as paradoxes that produce a self-contradiction by accepted ways of reasoning. The antinomy is especially important because, as he notes, it points to an error in the pattern of reasoning and to a need to avoid that pattern.[45] A paradox's absurdity revolves around opposing or conflicting propositions, both or all of which are (or seem as though they must be) the case. Statements are opposed as contradictories, as the Kneales explain Aristotle's definitions, when they cannot both be true and cannot both be false; statements are contraries when they cannot both be true but may both be false.[46]

This study started with the general hypothesis that public administration theory would show paradoxes in the sense of contraries. The initial notion was that these contraries would come in terms of major results and procedures. Each in a set of major underlying lines of development was expected to yield significant results until a point was reached when it was clear that a contrary line of development should be pursued. It is necessary to be cautious because all paradoxes depend on assumptions (often implicit) and because paradoxes can sometimes be avoided by paying a high price in terms of sacrificing an implicit assumption. For example, the law of noncontradiction might be avoided by using a dialectical procedure, but that would be a desperate price.[47]

When the initial draft of this chapter was written, I did not know whether this general hypothesis would prove to be correct. In view of the fact that the hypothesis happened to work out, it is hoped that this account of the starting attitude does not sound like a tall claim; it is not. Any use of the reflexive language paradigm should be like a playful voyage into the relatively unknown, like a sailing at night over the wine-dark sea; and there must be play, an idea that may be associated with adventuring and with the notion that the voyage can be more valuable than the arrival. The first part of the hermeneutic circle consisted of working out an account of contraries for each of what were considered critical features of the underlying logic of the development of public administration theory, and it is contended that the subsequent six chapters (chapters 3 through 8) show how this initial hypothesis holds true for all the characteristics that are considered. Nevertheless, the conclusion is not negative; for one thing, the insights in the modernist context have utility, and, for another thing, we can seek to take the insights beyond modernity. The subsequent five chapters (chapters 9 through 13)—the second part of the circle—examine public administration theory in terms of postmodernism. Fundamental advance can be hoped for in a process that goes beyond, but does not neglect, modernism.

The focus of the study, public administration theory, is the canon or set of literature accepted by the public administration discipline. For readers less familiar with public administration, the outline of that literature can be made clearer by considering the view that public administration is a discipline. As McCurdy points out when he makes the claim,

> The evidence of disciplinary survival can be found in three features: first, a core set of values, knowledge and theory, usually associated with founders who enjoy an academically charismatic reputation: second, a dissectable or essential phenomenon which it can study, i.e. organizations; and third, certain trappings which include schools or university departments bearing its name, a society and an annual convention, devoted professionals, at least one journal, and hopefully, a government bureau or, better than that, a special agency in the Executive Office of the President.[48]

McCurdy adds that "neither its fragmentation nor its lack of a general theory disqualify [public administration] from the ranks of disciplines."[49]

Aspects of McCurdy's argument are unclear. For instance, we might wish to become clearer about the claim that public administration has a core set of theories and a core set of values (e.g., one may like to know how the core set of values is justified and what the place of dissidents is). Some of the claims should be refined because, as is, they are dubious. For instance, the second feature may be rejected by those who believe that the unit of analysis in public administration should be the individual (e.g., Ostrom), and the third feature seems arbitrary indeed. The precision of the entire set of features is also open to questioning. For instance, could astrology slip in under these terms? Astrology seems to satisfy the first two criteria but probably not the third. It seems wrong that psychoanalysis could be in the same boat as astrology in this respect because the former is reported to be taught in freestanding institutes rather than in universities. Nevertheless, it is true that, as McCurdy defines the term, public administration is a discipline.

It is also true that, despite questions, what lies behind McCurdy's criteria is persuasive. Although less defined than in some other disciplines, a canon of literature exists in public administration. A philosopher who had never heard of Aristotle or Kant, for example, would be lacking as a philosopher; an economist ignorant of marginality or national income analysis could be criticized as an economist. In the same way, a canon has been identified—and could be argued about—for public administration. The public administrationist who had never heard (limiting this comment to classical examples) of Follett, Barnard, or Simon would be lacking as a public administrationist; a public administrationist ignorant of human resources development or financial management could be criticized as a public administrationist.

McCurdy's second criterion indicates correctly that a field of study for public administration does exist, even though more disagreement exists about its nature than in some other disciplines. This disagreement should be seen in perspective. For example, philosophy thrives, but should we be surprised if philosophers disagree about the nature of philosophy? Disagreement is not uncommon, especially in social action disciplines, but it can be unnerving for those academics with a commitment to defending their turfs. There is legitimate disagreement about the "geographical" extent and shape of the subject. The view presented in chapter 7 regarding the scope of the public administration field differs from the views of those who speak in terms of what governments do, whether the unit of analysis is the organization or the individual. Chapter 7 states that the scope should encompass issues of the supply and demand of "publicness," whether or not the good or service is produced by a public agency, and explains what it means to say that a public good is one that can be consumed only collectively. The oddity of the present boundary line is suggested by the concentration on civil functions. Excluding the military from the scope of public administration seems more a matter of convenience than of principle.[50] Nevertheless, despite the difficulties, the view that a general field for public administration study exists is correct. One way of seeing that such a field exists is to apply a "no interest" test. The "no interest" test consists of asking whether no public administrationist (note that this sentence does not say every public administrationist) should have a specialist interest in a particular item of subject matter. For example, should no public administrationist have a specialist interest in governmental budgeting, governmental personnel, or governmental management?

McCurdy's third criterion reflects an externalist view of scientific development.[51] The externalist view is that knowledge is developed not merely by the internal dynamics of the subject matter. The view implies that knowledge is a social matter and that scientific knowledge is privileged because it was developed in a manner deemed acceptable by society. Society tends to delegate responsibility for epistemological acceptability to whatever group it considers expert. Oceanographers (or biologists, psychologists, or physicians) are major players in deciding what is scientific oceanographic (or biological, psychological, or medical) information; additional players include others designated as belonging to the scientific community, administrators belonging to the university community, and grants managers in relevant funding agencies. McCurdy is saying that players accepted as arbiters of the scientific and the academic would accept public administration. The fact that society accords a lesser such title to social action specialists than to physicists, for example, is interesting, but it is beside the general point. A public administration discipline and a mainstream set of public administrationists do exist.

The fundamental mind-set of the mainstream public administration discipline cannot be described as rigid, it is true. On the contrary, mainstream public administration theory lacks the conforming power it would have if the theory were more developed. The 1992 Report of the Ad Hoc Committee on the Future of Public Service Education and Accreditation, reporting to the National Association of Schools of Public Affairs and Administration (NASPAA), expresses it in terms of "creative pluralism." The opening two conclusions of the ad hoc committee's report read, "A creative pluralism is a prime characteristic of our field, one that reflects successive visions of the needs of American government and society that have shaped and reshaped advanced education for public service during this century. This pluralism was affirmed by NASPAA's constitution, which explicitly uses the key words that have characterized each of these successive visions—public administration, public affairs, public policy, and public management."[52] This pluralism, not unique to public administration, is reflected in the condition of the core set of theory—soft integration, multiple paradigms, and alternative purposes.

Using this term *creative pluralism* is, of course, more than giving the situation a positive spin. Seeing from different directions is valuable. A quantum increase in value can be expected, however, if the manner of seeing is adequate. The seeing should recognize the social constitution of public administration "facts" and it should be reflexive in the manner suggested earlier. It should relate the manner of seeing to what is seen, for example. In addition, probably the further apart the perspectives are, the better. It should become clear from chapters 3 through 8 that the perspectives given by the public administration, public affairs, public policy, and public management visions, if in the modernist tradition, are much closer together than the modernity-postmodernity perspectives. The same closeness will also be seen for the paradigms (such as organizational humanism, public choice, and classical) within modernist public administration theory. Nevertheless, in a sense the present application carries forward a value inherent in the notion of creative pluralism.

The "core set of values, knowledge and theory" to which McCurdy refers is more of a mixture than a compound. McCurdy himself refers to fragmentation and the absence of a general theory. Public administration does not have a core that is integrated to the same extent that economic theory, the core for economics, is unified. Waldo's distinction between "Big P. A." and "little p.a." reflects the character of the core of public administration theory. Waldo's distinction is one that no metaeconomist would have to make. As Waldo writes,

> In this essay I follow a practice I have recently adopted to help cope with the fact that "public administration" is a slippery term. I use Public Administration when the reference is to the self-conscious activity—teaching, research, etc. I use public administration when the reference is (a) to the activity "out there," that is, the object of the teaching, research, etc., or (b) to the total complex of phenomena and activities, public administration institutions, activities, teaching, research, etc.[53]

Waldo goes on to add, "But sometimes one shades into the other; and what if one wants to refer to them both? I have found no good solution to this problem." He is correct in stating that difficulties with his distinctions exist. (For example, it is unclear why Waldo should want to lump together under "little p.a." both his alternatives a and b. Another example, discussed in chapter 4, is the problematic notion of a "self-conscious study.") It is hard to imagine an economist wanting to say that "Big E" is the self-conscious activity (teaching and research, for example) and that "little e" is the activity our there or the total complex of phenomena and activities. Rather, would not the economist describe the substantive content of "Big E"?

The account given in the ad hoc committee's report of the development of public service education is worth quoting in part and summarizing:

> Anyone who understands the roots of public service education will know why a creative pluralism is a deep characteristic of the field. It could be said that four waves of innovation have swept over the higher education sector concerned with training for public service during the past hundred years. Each was set in motion by a distinctive vision of the needs of government and the society it serves. Each left the field with a distinctive set of curricular elements. The overlay of these elements has given the field as a whole a creative pluralism.[54]

Four waves are described. The report states that the first of the waves, "which created the early public administration programs, grew out of the intense desire of the progressive era to sever administration from politics and make it a field of specialized professional competence." The second wave was the public affairs movement, based on the rejection of the separation of policy and administration. According to the report, "A generation of economists and public administration specialists, many of whom had seen wartime service, joined hands to create new programs in public affairs and to give a public-affairs cast to the programs in public administration." The third wave was the public policy movement of the 1960s and 1970s, prompted by a perception of a need for policy analysts. The fourth wave was the public management movement. The report states, "The disappointment with the result of many of the public policy initiatives of the Johnson years gave rise to the view that the government might need a set of skilled policy analysts less than it needed a set of skilled managers who could build and administer programs and get things done." The report describes this wave as appearing in three developments: the public management programs in business schools, generic schools of management, and an emphasis on management in public policy schools. It also notes, "This pluralism was reflected in NASPAA's title when the National Association of Schools of Public Affairs and Administration was created and named in 1970, and the 'Scope of the Field' as defined by section 4 of Article 1 of our constitution includes all four of the key words—public administration, public affairs, public policy, and public management—associated with the successive waves of innovation that have passed over public service education." The report goes on to conclude this account by asserting, "We have from the beginning sought to give institutional support to the creative pluralism that has marked our field."[55]

SUMMARY

Public administration theory could have a different character than it now has, partly because public administration theory and facts are socially constituted.

The observer is an active image cocreator. The form of thought (or language) that constitutes the observer conditions her vision, and we cannot observe except through a language. More understanding and effort in public administration should be devoted to developing understanding through interpretation rather than through positivist research. The reflexive language paradigm is a useful heuristic device for this effort.

The reflexive language paradigm analyzes the language, the set of assumptions, that shapes our constitution of public administration facts. It is an art that examines the hermeneutic, reflexive, and linguistic character of the way that we understand public administration phenomena. It is concerned both with why we understand as we do and with possibilities for another set of assumptions (another lens) to yield different understandings.

The present hermeneutic study applies this reflexive language paradigm with the object of developing understandings below the surface level. As a preliminary view, the last section of this chapter considers some surface characterizations of the public administration discipline. The current study begins with an initial general hypothesis. The hypothesis is that public administration theory shows contraries in each of a set of major underlying lines of development. By the end of chapter 8, we will find that this hypothesis is substantiated.

We now begin the process of examining the modernism that shapes the present language of public bureaucracy. We will continue to see contemporary public administration theory as a limiting dialect of modernity.

3

Modernity
The Dialect

No country and no age has ever experienced, in the same sense as the modern Occident, the absolute and complete dependence of its whole existence, of the political, technical, and economic conditions of its life, on a specially trained *organization* of officials.
—Weber[1]

There is, for example, rationalization of mystical contemplation . . . just as much as there are rationalizations of economic life, of technique, of scientific research, of military training, of law and administration.
—Weber[2]

MODERNIST PUBLIC ADMINISTRATION theory is valuable, yet limiting. The public administration literature grows larger and stronger, but it is limited as an explanatory and catalytic force in resolving the problems of bureaucracy. These limits, as will be explained, are not merely accidental (a matter of expectations, of contingent historical developments) but also logical (a matter of the nature of the subject, of necessity). As a matter of history, public administrationists have gone from an early optimism about reform and about establishing a science to (or perhaps through) a period of concern about an identity crisis, a crisis about the nature of public administration. As a matter of expectations, it goes against the grain of modernism to suppose even now that the correct application of reason will not provide—in the public administration field no less than elsewhere—fundamental sets of solutions to the problems of bureaucracy. Nevertheless, it is not a matter of historical accident that relief from the burdens of bureaucracy can be promised neither to client nor to citizen from exclusive pursuit of the modernist set of public administration paradigms. The goal of explaining (or understanding) bureaucratic phenomena in the modernist intellectual context is out of reach as a matter of logic. The modernist dialect of public administration theory is limiting because its construction is such that contraries are presented in each of a number of critical features important for its development.

Public administration theory faces paradoxes along each important line of development examined in chapters 4 through 8. Particularism, scientism, technologism, the enterprise model, and modernist hermeneutics, pushed far enough, are such lines. The composite result is a view of modernist public administration theory with limits or walls in directions critical for increasing public administration's capability for explanation or understanding. Consider a side paradox for some in the hermeneutic line, for example—not the more fundamental contrary discussed in chapter 8 on the hermeneutic line of development. A hermeneutic cardinal mistake (sin) for those in this subcategory is to reify, but the essence of governmental administration in the modernist tradition is reification. It is a mistake that a modernist cannot avoid, and the punishment for this mistake is misunderstanding. On the one hand, the public bureaucrat and the student of bureaucracy must not reify; on the other hand, such reification cannot be avoided.

Consider this side paradox more fully. The first contrary for some (e.g., action theorists) in the hermeneutic tradition is that the bureaucrat (and the student of bureaucracy) must not reify. Reification is to treat social constructions as if they were unalterable natural kinds, as if they were givens. Thus, the bureaucrat reifies departmental policy with the statement, "Department policy requires me to . . . " She reifies when she says, "The function of management is . . . " She reifies when she exclaims, "The Constitution provides . . . " The second and opposing contrary is that the genius of modernist civilization impels reification. Consider the rule of law; it is a reification, and it is the centerpiece of our liberties (more reifications). Heroes such as St. Thomas More died for such a central reification. "Equal treatment under the law" and "equal bureaucratic treatment for equals"—these are reifications that can only be sacrificed at the price of abandoning what some consider the essence of the achievement of Western civilization (another reification). In administering the law, how can the bureaucrat avoid reifying the law? Certainly, the law can be tempered with mercy and even common sense or favoritism, but not to reify it is to ignore it. In administering a program for millions of clients, how can programs be administered impartially if program provisions are not reified? Bureaucracy itself, insofar as it is a tool of the legislature, is treated as a reification. Reification seems to lie at the heart of democracy no less than of bureaucracy.

What is modernity? What is the modernity that structures "modern" or "modernist" public administration theory? What is this general mind-set that shapes the way that we understand public administration facts and perspectives and that leads to the paradoxes that characterize modernist public administration theory? This shaping, it will be shown, has taken the form of manifestations of reasoning and rationalization that are associated with modernity's unique attitude toward the human subject. Discussion of the nature of modernity is necessary for the understanding of this shaping, this formatting, of public administration theory in terms of particularism, the positivist notions of science and technology, the primacy of enterprise, and modernist hermeneutics.

The matter of terminology bothers some, although it probably should not. We speak of modern, modernist, and modernity; other words sometimes used are modernization and modernism. Scott Lash writes that we should follow Weber and Habermas by using the word *modernization* for the process of cultural differentiation and social autonomization.[3] *Modernity* was what began in the sixteenth and seventeenth centuries and culminated in the Enlightenment project. *Modernism*, extending to the societal but starting with the "paradigm change in the arts which began at the end of the nineteenth century," is a reaction to the difficulties of modernity.[4] Generally, we can follow this convention.

CONTENT OF MODERNITY AND THE FESTIVAL OF REASON

In his 1980 account, Habermas defines modernity in terms of the intentions of the project of Enlightenment.[5] He also speaks about modernization; his account begins by recalling Max Weber's characterization of cultural modernity as the "separation of the substantive reason expressed in religion and metaphysics into three autonomous spheres . . . science, morality and art." They could then be treated as matters "of knowledge, of justice and morality, or of taste"; each would then be in the province of cultural professions of specialist experts. The project of modernity is the Enlightenment project. As Habermas writes:

> The project of modernity formulated in the 18th century by the philosophers of the Enlightenment consisted in their efforts to develop objective science, universal morality and law, and autonomous art according to their inner logic. At the same time, this project intended to release the cognitive potentials of each of these domains from their esoteric forms. The Enlightenment philosophers wanted to utilize this accumulation of specialized culture for the enrichment of everyday life—that is to say, for the rational organization of everyday social life.[6]

Public administration theory, we could interject, could be described as one form of this "rational organization of everyday social life." Enlightenment thinkers such as Condorcet expected, Habermas explains, that the arts and the sciences would result in the control of nature, understanding of the world and the self, moral progress, institutional justice, and human happiness.

On November 10, 1793, the Festival of Reason was held in Notre Dame Cathedral, and similar worship festivals took place throughout France. The festival can be taken as symbolizing the project of modernity. Thomas Carlyle describes, and disapproves of, the festival: "This . . . is our New Divinity; Goddess of Reason, worthy, and one worth revering. Her henceforth we adore . . . Reason again in her litter, sitting in the van of them, borne as one judges, by men in the Roman costume; escorted by wind-music, red nightcaps, and the madness of the world. And so, straightway, Reason taking seat on the high-altar of Notre Dame, the requisite worship is, say the Newspapers, executed."[7] Carlyle, missing the point, goes on to ask, "But there is one thing we should like almost better to understand than any other: what Reason herself thought of it, all the while. What articulate words poor Mrs. Momoro [stand-in for the goddess Reason], for example, uttered; when she became ungoddessed again, and the Bibliopolist and she sat quiet at home, at supper."[8]

A more perceptive appreciation exists regarding the meaning of the myriad of festivals held in revolutionary France, the culmination of the eighteenth century. This appreciation would not dismiss these festivals as mere political ploys or revolutionary aberrations. Henderson does the latter, adding, "It is an everlasting blot on the National Convention that it submitted to be a participator in all this anti-Christian mummery, that it allowed itself to be swayed by such evanescent passions."[9] Ozouf's interpretation is more sensitive.[10] Lynn Hunt, in the foreword to Ozouf's book, explains that most historians have been content to treat the Revolution's festivals (of the goddesses of Liberty, the celebrations of Reason, and the cult of the Supreme Being) as ineffectual or as "repugnant examples of a sterile official culture." Ozouf shows that "the festivals were more than bizarre marginalia to the Revolutionary process. The festivals offer critical insights into the meaning of the French Revolution; they show a society in the process of creating itself anew."[11]

This Festival of Reason can also be seen as illustrating the main themes of modernity. It exemplifies the Enlightenment project, intentions that constitute the project of modernity. The Enlightenment is a description of the prevailing attitudes toward the subject and toward reason that characterize Western European thinking especially in the eighteenth century. The term *Enlightenment* is usually taken as synonymous with the Age of Reason, a period that includes the seventeenth and eighteenth centuries.[12]

Modernity involves a rejection of traditional powers and conditions considered natural and unavoidable in premodern society, with the implicit consequence of more freedom and opportunities for the modern individual subject. Adorno and Horkheimer define the Enlightenment as the project of freeing the individual consciousness from the limitations and determination of the natural forces associated with the mythological phase of human history.[13] Such rejection and such reference to subjectivity is symbolized in the Festival of Reason. The old gods and the old religion that were considered part of the natural order were rejected; the subject was now unconstrained before the Goddess of Reason and was free to choose. Each worshipper at the Festival of Reason was defining herself without reference to God and to other such givens in the natural order. The self was the center of reference.

The Festival of Reason symbolizes the rejection of all values that previously were considered natural constraints within which one should (or better, must) live. Each worshipper was free to make rational choices about her own values and lifestyle and was no longer to be governed by traditional values and social roles. As Weber writes of modernity, it is in the individual's obligation to reason that values are now to be found. Modernity rejects a fixed conception of the good, and traditions are abolished, except to the secularity, scientism, and hedonism that flow from reason. As Weber explains, "We live as did the ancients when their world was not yet disenchanted of its gods and demons, only we live in a different sense. As Hellenic man at times sacrificed to the gods of his city, so do we still nowadays, only the bearing of man has been disenchanted and denuded of its mystical but inwardly genuine plasticity."[14]

The autonomous subject is the center of power at the Festival of Reason; as Carlyle knew, Mrs. Momoro did not have the traditional power to keep the worshippers in their places. Modernity located power in the subject, and the subject could now master her physical, social, and political environment. The self would achieve technological mastery of nature; as Lyotard puts it, human possibilities would be freed by mastering the conditions of life.[15] In political terms, this freedom would be reflected in liberal republican ideology, economic individualism, democracy, and the supremacy of the nation-state. This view is reflected in the individualism of Hobbes, Locke, and the other social contract theorists. It is also reflected in the context for, and in the character of, modernist theorizing about public administration. Such theorizing, for example, would occur in the context and in the shadow of the primacy of economic enterprise and the ascendancy of the nation-state.

The Festival of Reason shows the worshipping selves accepting reason. The claim "Reason is to the *philosophe* what grace is to the Christian" is a strong one.[16] Reason, in this description, is the means to salvation. The great scientific advances— those, for instance, of Newton—revolutionized the world. Newton's universe was essentially mechanical: it operated automatically according to certain recognizable laws. By the eighteenth century, the implications of these advances were more fully recognized. The supernatural was considered redundant. Reason, based on common sense and science, would produce progress and happiness. It was seen as practical. Public administration theory, like other modernist projects, would be constituted by this view of science. It would reflect a view of reason not hindered by the old gods and by value assumptions. Scientism would be a feature of public administration theory.

The very existence of the seventeen volumes of Diderot's *Encyclopedia* symbolizes this emphasis on the practical use of reason. Reason was seen as useful in a world that placed heavy emphasis on utility. This period was the age of Adam Smith and Jeremy Bentham. The notion of progress was an Enlightenment creation, and it was to be realized through the use of reason. Reason, properly applied, would produce human happiness. This view of reason and rationality would come to shape modernist activities such as public administration theory. An emphasis would be placed on the technological, on technologism.

The Festival of Reason symbolizes the new equation; the divine force is now the force of reason. Reason was seen in the project of modernity as a creative and useful force that liberates the self from the crippling limitations of superstition, inflated claims, vice, and ignorance. These limitations are scathingly attacked, for example, in Voltaire's *Bornes de L'Esprit Humaine* (Limits of the Human Mind). Voltaire explains that reason had been "regarded as debilitated in many people by such cultural factors as the Church and priests, vice, superstition and poverty; people needed enlightenment."[17] As Kant puts it, "Enlightenment is man's emergence from his self-imposed minority. This minority is the inability to use one's own understanding without the guidance of another. . . . Thus the motto of the Enlightenment is 'Sapere aude! Have the courage to use your own understanding!' "[18]

Enlightenment reason, symbolized in the Festival of Reason, was seen as liberating for the self and for society. The key to the development of modernity, as the less optimistic Weber sees it and as noted in chapter 2, was rationalization. It also would become so for modernist public administration theory. There would be a progressive rationalization of society, and a separation of the spheres would occur. The theoretical, practical, and aesthetic spheres would develop within the terms of their own logic; discourse would divide. The division of discourse would eventually confirm subject matter boundaries for disciplines such as public administration— the separation of the public from the private and the political from the nonpolitical. Rationalization endorses particularism in modernist studies, the atomization of the scholarly and thinking realm.

Subjectively grounded reason was worshipped in the place of what had been considered an omnipotent God. Notice the inscription on the bottom of one of Bartolozzi's contemporary drawings. Henderson reproduces the "charming drawing of Love and Reason embracing," and he comments, "One is astonished to find so well known an artist as Bartolozzi lending his aid to the propaganda, though he was doubtless well rewarded for it."[19] Bartolozzi's inscription reads in part, "Peoples, can you look with indifference on Love, long blind but today without a bandage; on Reason, sublime, borrowing the torch in order to change through its beams the destinies of France? Do thou, Love of Country, and thou, sage Reason, set aflame the horizons of this vast universe! . . . And thou, God of the humans, Supreme Intelligence, make the French the avengers of debased mortals. And everywhere the shield with the three colors shall be the happy emblem of omnipotence."[20] Reason has a jingoist aspect, supporting a particular nation state, but it can function to help the nation-state achieve the benefits of rationality for all mortals.

The Festival of Reason can also be interpreted as symbolizing the subject-object relationship of modernity. The subject is the worshipper, and reason is the means for picturing the world, the object. The mainstream concerns of modern philosophy, from Descartes to the present century, have been epistemological and foundationist. As Madison puts it, "[What] characterizes that form of logocentric metaphysics of presence known as modern philosophy is that it seems to realize philosophy's traditional goal of achieving a basic, fundamental knowledge of what is by turning inward, into the knowing subject himself (conceived of either psychologistically or transcendentally), where it seeks to discover grounds which will allow for certainty in our 'knowledge' of what, henceforth, is called 'the external world.' "[21] Subjectivity is fundamental in modern philosophy. This subjectivity includes an identification of mind with personal consciousness, and the subject and nonsubject distinction is the most basic. The individual is the foundation of philosophizing, and a goal of the philosophy is to ascertain what and how I can know and to ground what I know in the individual. Consider Descartes's search for a foundation of knowledge; it is modernist self-assertion. As Blumenberg states, "[M]odernist self-assertion is an existentialist program, according to which man posits his existence in a historical situation and indicates to himself how he is going to deal with the reality surrounding him and what use he will make of the possibilities that are open to him."[22] In this view, the end of modernity is the end of this epistemologically centered philosophy and the end of subject encountering the objective world.

Modernity, then, is the age of the centered subject. That statement is a way of summarizing the epistemological and foundationist character of modern philosophy. "What is" is explored in terms of what appears to the individual subject and how this knowledge can be grounded in that same individual subject. As seen later, postmodernity is described as an age of the decentered subject.

This description of modernity can be made clearer by considering Heidegger's view of the emergence of the subject leading to world picturing. One sense in which the self is centered is that the world consists in what the subject pictures, and Heidegger claims that this picturing is uniquely modern. Heidegger writes:

> When we reflect on the modern age, we are questioning concerning the modern world picture. We characterize the latter by throwing it into relief over against the medieval and the ancient world pictures. But why do we ask concerning a world picture in our interpreting of an historical age? Does every period of history have its world picture, and indeed in such a way as to concern itself from time to time about that world picture? Or is this, after all, only a modern kind of representing, this asking concerning a world picture?"[23]

Heidegger also writes, "To be new is peculiar to the world that has become picture."[24] This act of picturing accounts for the fundamental ways in which the modern individual understands; for example, the conception of reason as mathematically grounded, in Heidegger's view, connects with the power of representation. The subject is at the center because the subject is the representor, the picturer. Reason is instrumental for the subject. We can expect to find this view reflected in public administration theory and in other modernist enterprises—in scientific, technological, and interpretive work.

POST-ENLIGHTENMENT PESSIMISM

Habermas poses a question. The twentieth century, for him, halted the Enlightenment expectations. The separation of the theoretical, practical, and aesthetic spheres has led to autonomy, to divorce from what he calls the "hermeneutics of everyday communication," and to "efforts to 'negate' the culture of expertise."[25] The undermining of the Cartesian paradigm also occurs in the nineteenth century by such thinkers as Hegel, Marx, and Freud, a topic discussed in chapter 8. (Marx speaks of the determining role of economic factors, for instance, and Freud writes of psychological forces.) Remembering the disillusionment of the twentieth century, should we give up the project of modernity or should we hang on to "the intentions of the enlightenment, feeble as they may be"?[26] Habermas's own reply is that we should not give up modernity as a lost cause. Instead, we should learn from the mistakes that have acted to negate modernity; we should understand modernity, as noted earlier, to be "an incomplete project."

For others, modernity is a dead end; there is no way to complete it. Some critics have written of the collapse, either inevitable or achieved, of modernity. Adorno and Horkheimer, for example, hold that modernity contains the elements of its own destruction, that greater rationalization leads to greater irrationality.[27] For yet others, the question is off the mark; for them, we have left modernity and have entered the era of postmodernity. Baudrillard, described earlier as having been a postmodernist, is an example. For him, the problem in the United States is "the crisis of an achieved utopia, confronted with the problem of duration and permanence."[28] He sees the problem for Europe as the crisis of unachieved utopia, a failure to achieve its ideals (e.g., the Enlightenment ideals).

The nineteenth- and twentieth-century pessimism about modernity is reflected in Weber and others. Weber describes the "whole cosmos of the modern economic order" as "an iron cage," with its "specialists without spirit, sensualists without heart" and with its "delusion" that it has attained a higher level of civilization than any other age.[29] Weber believes that bureaucracy would encourage uniformity. "Bureaucracy develops the more perfectly, the more it is 'dehumanized,' the more completely it succeeds in eliminating from official business love, hatred, and all purely personal, irrational, and emotional elements which escape calculation."[30] The only possible defense is "will," whatever will people can muster not to be treated like a herd. Nevertheless, as Kolb explains, Weber had little hope: "The most likely course would be a stifling bureaucracy disturbed from time to time by charismatic politicians who could put their personal passions into new values and awaken the will of the people. Then the charisma would pass, be routinized, and end by giving the bureaucrats more legitimacy. The system could be disturbed only from the outside by such irruptions of passion, but they would not prevent the iron cage from closing again."[31]

The euphoria and optimism represented in the Festival of Reason held on November 10, 1793, has been succeeded during the last two hundred years with some reservations and some disillusionment about modernity. Problems of performance have occurred. Why has increased rationalization given us results such as wholesale slaughter and the desecration of cities and the environment that rational people would oppose? Negative aspects of modern living have been recognized. For example, alienation, anomie, and the depersonalizing aspects of developments such as mass communications have been experienced. These problems are clear despite the work on rationalization conducted in areas such as public administration. The optimism of the Festival of Reason—the rational quest for knowledge in science and philosophy—now seems unfounded. Freud, among others, speaks out against the notion of social progress.[32] He tells of the modern marvel of the telephone that allows the father to speak with his son, and then he remembers the modern marvel of the train that made it possible for the son to move away in the first place.

The dilemmas of modernity appear no closer to resolution. The dilemmas of how to coalesce a community of free individuals, of how freedom and authority relate in a liberal society, and of the effect of commitment to equality on tolerance of differences are examples. Some critics of modernity have been conservative. Frank Knight of the Chicago School of Economics, for example, has doubted whether democracy is sufficient to preserve social order; he thinks religion is necessary.[33] Alasdair MacIntyre has argued for a reformulation of Aristotelian virtue ethics.[34] Some public administrationists reflect MacIntyre's view. For example, Cooper and Wright have edited a book that discusses "public administrators, some famous, some known only to a few, who have exemplified virtue understood as specific character traits and as the quest for a life of integrity in the practice of public administration."[35]

SPECIFIC AND PECULIAR RATIONALISM

The specific and peculiar rationalism[36] that characterizes Western modernity—that was celebrated in the Enlightenment and in the Festival of Reason—was thus reevaluated by post-Enlightenment thinkers. As noted earlier, Weber is one of the post-Enlightenment pessimists. Chapter 1 explained that he sees the calculative and means-ends type of rationality as progressively dominating society. One source of his pessimism is that he sees a formal rationality imperializing society; substantive rationality is excluded. For him, no rational way exists (as has been mentioned) of resolving value conflicts—and it is the latter that are important.

Max Weber advocates a fact-value distinction, and he uses the same supporting argument that we find later in Simon's *Administrative Behavior*. Weber argues that if values (or principles of value) are to be justified deductively, the difficulty always exists in justifying the ultimate value; that is, value A may be deduced from a higher (or more general) value B, and the higher value B may be deduced from an even higher value C. Nevertheless, there is bound to be a highest or ultimate value, and that ultimate value cannot be justified deductively because there is no value even higher. For Weber, the spheres of values and politics are ultimately nonrational and are characterized by antinomies. In the ethical sphere, Weber talks about what he sees as the clash between consequentialist ethics (considering an action's consequences) and deontological ethics (based on an actor's duties); the only way out he sees is to choose. In the political sphere, an example Weber gives is whether justice requires giving greater opportunities to those with greater talents or whether on the contrary "one should attempt to equalize the injustice of the unequal distribution of mental capacities."[37] Weber believes that questions such as these "cannot be definitely answered."[38] The kind of deductive rationality he considers necessary could not settle matters in the sphere of ethics and in what is for him the separate but interpenetrating sphere of politics. Therefore, the scientist, carrying out the norms of his specialty, should confine himself to the study of facts. Turner and Factor refer to Schmoller, who was on the opposite side to Weber in the *Methodenstreit* (Battle of Methods). As they put Weber's view, "Someone who presents values as facts is not merely undermining the objectivity of his hearers but is committing a kind of fraud upon them. Weber suggested that Schmoller was doing this."[39]

It is possible to see this Weberian dilemma (of formal and substantive rationality) working out in the development of administrative decision theory. Note March's comment on decision making: "If scientific progress is measured by simplification, this is a story of retrogression. From a simple perspective of anticipatory, consequential, rational choice, we have gone first to a recognition of the limitations on rationality, then to concern for internal conflict, then to history dependent conceptions of human action, and finally to an awareness of the profound ambiguities surrounding action in organizations. . . . Life has proven to be more complicated than our earlier mythologies of it."[40] The recognition of the limitations on rationality seems to be an adjustment to the dilemma that Weber describes.

It is correct that more complexity exists—what March calls "retrogression"—in the developments with which March and Simon are associated. Misunderstanding about the rationality used in public administration can exist if bounded rationality is not always recognized for what it is, that is, instrumental rationality. A decision is no less rational because the selected decision rule does not follow the model of comprehensive rationality that dominates microeconomic theory. Rational decisions can be made on grounds that involve less than comprehensive rationality. The comprehensive type of rationality requires thinking in terms of analyzing all possible alternatives and considering all possible consequences before choosing the best, the optimal, alternative. In other words, the model of comprehensive rationality seeks to optimize the chooser's stock of utility; the last unit of utility is eked from the set of possible options. Simon himself writes of administrative man's bounded rationality, where a choice is selected not because it is the optimal but because it "satisfices."[41] Cyert and March apply the idea of bounded rationality to private enterprise.[42] Bounded rationality involves considering a series of randomly ordered options, where the decision rule is that the first option that is "good enough" will be selected. More examination might reveal one or several better options, but the suboptimal choice is accepted as good enough. The bounded is not a case of limiting rationality. Rather, the comprehensive and the bounded are alternative methods of rationally making the best choices, and they are examples of mean-ends rationality.

Lindblom's theory of disjointed incrementalism, the most prominent alternative to Simon's account, can be taken as reflecting Weber's understanding of substantive rationality.[43] Insofar as it is prescriptive, Lindblom's theory pays attention to the dilemma of substantive rationality, seeking the best political results, and Lindblom believes that the interaction of interest groups will yield (in the manner of Adam Smith) the best results. His method is to rely on the interaction of whatever forces exist around any political decision that has to be made. Lindblom's disjointed incrementalism—also called successive limited comparisons, the branch method, or incrementalism—is similar to Simon's bounded rationality in that it accepts that the human ability to process information is limited and that some alternatives are neglected. It also contemplates a means-ends analysis of what "satisfices;" but Lindblom makes the important point that ends should not be selected without considering the feasibility of the means. Lindblom's process is decentralized, and it relies on the interactions of interest groups and voices that clash in order to muddle through to correct limited decisions or even nondecisions. For Lindblom, administrative decisions are made at the margin, and they are serial and remedial.

Amitai Etzioni's "mixed scanning" theory, a bridge between Simon's and Lindblom's accounts, is another attempt to cope with both formal rationality and substantive rationality. Etzioni himself thinks of his approach as neither rationalistic nor incrementalist. As he writes, "[Rationalist] approaches were held to be Utopian because actors cannot command the resources and capabilities required by rationalist decision making. Incrementalism was shown to overlook opportunities for significant innovations and to ignore the empirical fact that incremental decisions are often, in effect, made within the context of fundamental decisions."[44] By "rationalist," Etzioni has a certain kind of rationality in mind; for example, he has written that rationalistic "models tend to posit a high degree of control over the decision-making situation on the part of the decision-maker."[45] Etzioni's mixed scanning method distinguishes between a higher level where basic policy directions are set and a lower order where incremental processes work out the details. Planned rationality is contemplated for the higher level and then the details shake out on an incremental basis at the lower level.

This contrast between the comprehensively rational and the incrementalist approaches has been carried forward by others, especially in budgeting.[46] The planning-programming-budgeting system (PPBS), introduced into the Department of Defense in 1961, is an example of the rational-comprehensive approach. Aaron Wildavsky's view is an example of incrementalism.[47] Wildavsky's account is not only descriptive (a description of what is) but also prescriptive (a prescription of what he thinks should be). He thinks that budgeting ought to be incremental; he believes that incrementalism leads to better results. Part of these better results is that incrementalism is better suited to the political system.

ASSUMPTIONS OF DISCUSSIONS REGARDING MODERNITY

Consider some assumptions about discussions of modernity. One assumption is that we have inherited a coherent and distinctive Western heritage of ideas and attitudes even though some of the components may conflict and even though we may disagree about the nature and etiology of that heritage.[48] Modernity is expressed in various aspects of culture—in philosophical discourse, social theories, art and architecture, and other cultural manifestations. The claim that Western heritage is coherent and distinctive means that these manifestations are underlain by a common Weltanschauung, ragged at its edges perhaps but patterned at its core. The claim permits disagreement about which aspect or aspects of culture constitute the independent variable, shaping the other aspects of modernity. Habermas holds that modernity is a function of its "philosophical discourse," whereas others suppose that the philosophical manifestation is a dependent variable of other factors (e.g., Marxians would stress the primary role of economic developments). Others would deny both Habermas's and the alternative claims. For example, Cascardi declares that modernity is more than merely philosophical and also more than merely historical.[49] Nevertheless, despite such differences regarding specifics, the assumption is that modernity represents a distinctive mind-set.

Modernity is not merely an epochal matter. It is true that the mind-set of modernity has evolved during the last five centuries and that mind-set became widely established during that period. Berman speaks of three historical phases of modernity, for example. One phase is the beginning of modern life, from the beginning of the sixteenth century to the end of the eighteenth. The second starts with the French Revolution, and the third is the global spread that has led to a "world culture of modernism."[50] Nevertheless, the mind-set of modernity cannot be identified completely and exclusively with the last five hundred years or with any particular time period. Horkheimer and Adorno write of Enlightenment beginnings in the *Odyssey*, although agreeing that the Enlightenment reached its full development in the eighteenth century.[51] Weber writes of the rationalized lives of medieval monks.[52] Further, contemporary society contains exceptions to modernity, such as the Amish.[53]

We must beware of chronocentricity, the delusion that our generation is a chosen people. A certain hubris does seem to exist in concluding that our own age is unique or in deciding that we are at the pivotal point between eras. Of course, the eras are different, and difficulty exists in comparing periods such as our own and, say, the Hellenistic. Eugen Weber notes that the Hellenistic period had forms of postmodern and modern attitudes similar to our own. As Weber reports, the intellectual atmosphere of the Hellenistic period, which covered the period from the death of Alexander to the death of Cleopatra, was characterized by antirationalist trends. The period experienced psychological and aesthetic fragmentation; an interest in the self; a sense of depersonalization in the face of the megalopolis; a retreat from political involvement; exotic cults; peculiar fads; and reliance on mystery religions, astrology, and magic. It also had modernist tendencies, such as preoccupation with bigness, a bureaucracy interested in making rules, and an obsessive pursuit of wealth. Absent was a willingness to create within the limits of timeless forms. As reflected in the art (such as the Victory at Samothrace in the Louvre), the Hellenistic period strove for movement, sensuality, and openness. These examples from Weber do remind us of our own times.[54]

Greater difficulties arise when it comes to dating postmodernity, that is, when it comes to dating the end of modernity. One difficulty is exemplified by the fact that some thinkers do not see the modern and the postmodern as successive eras. As Rose tells us, "[T]he word 'post-modern' is not always thought to be subsequent to or later than the 'modern', but may both be contemporary with it, or, as in the writings of Lyotard, 'prior' to the modern."[55] (Lyotard's statement on this point is, "A work can become modern only if it is first postmodern. Postmodernism thus understood is not modernism at its end but in the nascent state, and this state is constant."[56]) This time relationship would depend on how one understands the notions of modernity and postmodernity. We could be speaking of two distinct eras, or we could conceptualize modernity and postmodernity in such terms as competing views. For example, it has been noted that the modern-postmodern debate "has in many ways become an explicit debate over the nature of culture and social production in the emerging 'postindustrial' society."[57]

Along these lines, one possibility is to see the modernity-postmodernity contrast as opposing mind-sets or tendencies (or, if not opposed, with one being the limiting case of the other) that are present in varying proportions in all time periods. The contrast can be sketched that revolves around the claims for reason, and various analogies can be drawn. One analogy is between this contrast and the Apollonian-Dionysian distinction. For nine months every year, the Greeks at Delphi celebrated the god Apollo, who was associated with reason; Dionysus took over the Delphic oracle for the remaining three months of the year, and this period emphasized the orgiastic, the ecstatic, and the irrational. Waldo makes such an Apollonian-Dionysian contrast,[58] and Nietzsche and Jung drew the distinction earlier.[59] As Nietzsche's contrast is described:

> Apollo, [Nietzsche] maintained, stood for rational control, science, awareness of the lines which can be drawn between things—above all the line which separates the observer from the observed—and, in general, the knowledge needed in order to manipulate the world around us and avoid catastrophes of every sort. Dionysus, on the other hand, stood for the desire to forget who or where one was, to break down the line separating subject and object, to melt into the world—uniting either with another person, a group, nature, a god, or the universe.[60]

Another analogy for the modernity-postmodernity contrast might be drawn with regard to the coexistence of the left and the right sides of the brain. This analogy is drawn only for illustrative purposes, and no match is proposed between one "ism" and any brain hemisphere (assuming that the account of brain hemispheres is true).[61] Another analogy might be drawn with the female and male components that both Freud and Jung thought constitute the person; for instance, Freud writes, "Pure masculinity and femininity remain theoretical constructions of uncertain content."[62] In some persons and group situations, modernism might now dominate; in others, postmodernism might dominate. The less dominant coexists, however.

Postmodernity can be seen as a limit on the range of reason. Some regard the reign of reason as so unlimited and so transparent that it will allow them to ascertain everything. This understanding applies to public administration no less than to any other discipline, but it is more obvious in the case of some philosophers. The Taylorist manager would seek rationally to lay out all the tasks of her subordinates; that manager has no doubts of the range of rationality. A philosopher such as McTaggart, depending on the unlimited reign of reason and on an unlimited capacity to say what is the case, believes that he can show that the existence of time is impossible. It does not occur to him to doubt the limits of reason. It also does not occur to him to doubt the limits of what can be said.[63]

Modernism, in this view, would be a form of the sayable; postmodernism, as hinted in chapter 1, would be a form of the unsayable. Modernity would reflect a complete faith in the capacity of reasoned language to capture the world. It would reflect optimism, claiming the potential for complete understanding. Postmodernity would renounce this faith, this optimism, and this claim to power. It would embrace the nettle of reflexivity. Postmodernism denies overarching explanation; it embraces the fact that this denial is itself an overarching explanation, and it rejects the seeking of an escape route through a claim that its denial is in a metalanguage.

Even granting the difficulties about dating modernity and about its relationship with postmodernity, it remains clear that an identifiable world outlook of modernity prospered, developed, flourished, and dominated in the postmedieval West. The verb *dominated* should be underscored. It was a world that came to explode with scientific achievements, technological marvels, and discoveries; knowledge hyperinflated, and ignorance and superstition promised to recede. Power and dominion grew over circumstances, the environment, and other peoples; we are all familiar with how capable we now are in such terms as producing wealth, curing diseases, traveling, building, destroying, and communicating. Gains were made in the political, social, economic, and other areas. Modernity fueled the achievements of this modern age; it is the set of assumptions and attitudes that found full expression in the Enlightenment project.

Public administration theory is a paradigm case of modernity. Modernity's view of the centered subject, the unconstrained subject engaged in an epistemological project in which truth and values require grounding in the self, has led to distinctive features of rationalization and reasoning in public administration theory. Much of public administration theory embodies the rationalizing spirit that the Enlightenment celebrated: the calculating or instrumental rationality that Weber describes, the purposive-rational rationalization that Habermas depicts. This rationalizing is manifested in the attempts to develop the public administration discipline along scientific and technological lines. It is embodied in attempts to include the values of capitalism within the bureaucratic enterprise. Part of public administration—the hermeneutic—is another form of this rationalization. This rationalization also led to particularism, the erection of public administration's subject boundaries; in fact, it underlay the very creation of public administration theory, bound up with the modernist notion of the nation-state.

We now need to look at critical features of the underlying pattern of logic that constitutes modernist public administration theory: particularism, scientism, technologism, the enterprise preference, and hermeneutics. Each is described in turn in the next five chapters, although no claim is offered about the ordering of these items; none is needed because the action has been synergistic. No claim is offered about the exhaustiveness of the list; others may wish to supplement or to divide the exposition differently. The list of features is adequate to show the basic modernist pattern that shapes the picturing of public administration facts.

SUMMARY

Various descriptions have been offered regarding the nature of modernity. Weber, for example, writes in terms of specific and peculiar rationalism; Habermas speaks in terms of the intentions of the Enlightenment project; and Heidegger writes of the subject leading to world picturing. A way of appreciating the nature of modernity is to focus on the Enlightenment and, in particular, on ceremonies such as the Festival of Reason. The set of underlying assumptions that makes up modernity has not been equally dominant throughout the five hundred or so years of the modern era. For example, significant post-Enlightenment criticisms and feelings of pessimism have been expressed.

Modernity is the age of the centered subject, whereas postmodernity is the age of the decentered subject. In modernity, the application of reason is considered to yield unlimited human progress, and a principal motif is rationalization. Modernity involves the rejection of traditional powers and values considered to be natural constraints. Substantive rationality is abandoned. The self is autonomous as it is liberated from superstition. Modernity is the age of the subject encountering the world, and philosophy is centered on establishing foundations and epistemology.

An assumption of discussions of modernity is that we have inherited a distinctively Western heritage of ideas. Modernity may or may not be an epochal matter, however. Modernity could be viewed as the set of assumptions that understands the range of reason to be unlimited; postmodernity could be seen as assuming a limit. Modernity could then represent the assumption that all facts are sayable; postmodernity would deny this.

Public administration is a paradigm case of modernity. This chapter is laying a foundation for the view that public administration theory is limited as a force in understanding and changing bureaucracy. Along each important line of development, public administration will be seen to face contraries.

4

Modernity
Limits of Particularism

> Among the many occupational and professional fields with which it grew up in this
> country, public administration was . . . unique in many respects. . . . It also differed
> from many of them in that most of its character depended in only a minor way upon
> intellectual and vocational developments in other nations. Though it had distant
> roots in some of British constitutional history, in the largely abandoned German
> cameralism, in foreign military reforms (adapted to the American military estab-
> lishment around the turn of the century), it was for the most part an American
> invention, indigenous, and sui generis.
>
> —Mosher[1]

DISCIPLINE SPECIALIZATION AND autonomy—accelerating discipline fragmentation—
are characteristic of modernist scholarship. Reportedly, until the close of the sixteenth century, a home library could contain all of learning. After that date, learning mushroomed and fragmented beyond the powers of the most avid private
collector. D'Amico describes the growth of the size of libraries during the Renaissance. He writes that Petrarch collected 200 volumes, "a magnificent collection by
fourteenth century standards." Printing increased collections, and D'Amico reports
that Columbus's son Ferdinandus had 15,000 titles. As D'Amico describes, "For a
short period of history—roughly the boundaries of the sixteenth century—the dedicated collector could shelve all of learning in his home. The moment passed; although private libraries grew precipitously in the seventeenth and eighteenth centuries, learning multiplied and fragmented beyond the powers of a single man to
collect its fruits in his library."[2] The social and other sciences evolved and proliferated, and subspecialties developed. The modern tendency toward fragmentation has
been taken to an even higher pitch in the United States. Various action subjects
emerged, with public administration being one of them. American public administration developed, like the other specialties, with a claim to a particular segment
or segments of the knowledge turf. Specialization or fragmentation—let us call it
by the neutral term *particularism*—is a leading feature of all contemporary disciplines and specialties; premodern universalism is no longer possible.

The boundaries of American public administration—the actual shape of the particularism realized in the case of American public administration—can be analyzed by considering each of the terms in the discipline's title. Contraries are evident; the urge for the universal and the focus on the particular are contraries. Insofar as it has been positivistic on the lines of the physical sciences, for example, mainstream public administration theory has an interest in the universal. Insofar as it is limited to the concerns and experiences of one nation (to nationalism) and to a particular fragment of social knowledge (to its particular form of discipline specialization and autonomy), public administration theory concentrates on the particular. Consider the focus on one nation as an example, and consider public administration insofar as it wishes to be scientific. A physics or chemistry discipline that yielded only culture-bound propositions would hardly be a modern science. Robert Dahl is one who says that public administration's claim to be scientific depends on developing "a body of generalized principles independent of their particular national setting."[3]

Blind spots can also be noticed. American public administration theory, by virtue of its nature, has yielded significant results. Nevertheless, there is another side of the coin. The *American* character of American public administration, serving to discourage what can be learned about non-American situations, tends to create blind spots in the treatment of areas such as corruption and governmental size. To the extent that public administration theory is the servant of a particular vision of constitutional arrangements and of a particular range of political philosophies (however fine), such blind spots will tend to occur where practices fail to fit the vision or the range. The *public* aspect of American public administration discourages a recognition of important commonalities between the public and private sectors. The *administration* component of American public administration has been an acute concern among public administration theorists, especially in the form of the politics-administration dichotomy.

THE *AMERICAN* ELEMENT

A manifestation of the particularism of the modern age is not only discipline fragmentation but also nationalism, and sometimes the latter has helped frame the precise shape of the fragmentation. The modern age has seen the creation and development of the nation-state and the power of nationalism. Reportedly, Max Weber praised those Florentines mentioned by Machiavelli "to whom the greatness of their native city is more important than the salvation of their souls."[4] For the contemporary nationalist, typically this choice is not the one to make. Some people take this particularism further, reaching such a pitch of nationalism that they equate it with universalism and see nation and world as equal. Others see the rest of the world with marginal interest. Nationalism has helped to shape the subject boundaries of American public administration.

The American element of American Public Administration can be examined under four subsections. The first subsection discusses evidence for the existence of the localism. But there has always been some ambivalence about this element, and thus the second subsection notes work not limited in this respect. The third subsection recognizes some advantage in conceptualizing public administration as an American project. The fourth notes the disadvantages, that is, the contraries and blind spots.

The local character of our public administration should be established first. Contrast public administration theory and economic theory in terms of claims for territorial or geographical relevance. Economic theory claims universality. The theory of the firm, the theory that analyzes the output and pricing behavior of firms under various market conditions, is proposed as applying to any capitalist firm, whether that firm is in Miami, Maastricht, or Mongolia. More precisely, all economic theory, no less than this example of the economics of the firm, is intended to apply to all geographical contexts insofar as it applies to any such context. The focus of theorizing about economics is the universal, and contributions to economic theory can come from Harvard, the London School of Economics, Tokyo, Delhi, or Durban. By contrast, public administration theory, as it has been developed in the United States during the last century or so, has had a primary focus on one country. Public administration theory in the United States, despite the exceptions noted in the second subsection, has been quintessentially American public administration.

The following three items reflect the view that the local public administration literature is largely dominated by a one-nation focus. First, recall the April 1992 account, summarized in chapter 2, of the nature of the subject by the Ad Hoc Committee of NASPAA, the accrediting body for university public administration programs in this country.[5] The report explained the content of public administration as being dominated by history. More interestingly, it was dominated by the history of one particular country, the United States.

Second, note a 1992 editorial in *Public Administration Review*. The editorial begins by attempting to explain why recent attempts to rebuild public administration theory and practice have not succeeded. It continues, "This is not surprising. Historically major reorientations in American public administration have been associated with the rise of a dominant political faction, party, or movement embracing a relatively coherent ideology that viewed administrative reform as essential to the achievement of its political objectives. Familiar examples include: the Federalists, the Jacksonians, the civil service reformers and Progressives, the New Dealers, and the Civil Rights/Great Society movements of the 1960s."[6] These are intranational events.

Third, consider the anthology *American Public Administration: Past Present and Future*. A classic in the field, this history and account of the discipline was the result of a collaborative project of the Maxwell School of Citizenship and Public Affairs and NASPAA. Mosher's account in the anthology contains the quote given at the beginning of this chapter. The punch line claims that American public administration "was for the most part an American invention, indigenous, and sui generis." Mosher continues his account by pointing out that, with minor exceptions, such as comments by Hamilton and Tocqueville, public administration as a subject for study and as a profession was largely ignored until the end of the nineteenth century. The scholars such as Wilson and Goodnow who took up the subject at that time did make use of European literature and examples, but, he continues, the real origins of American public administration lay in the cities.[7] Mosher contrasts non-American with American public administration thought. He writes, "[V]irtually all European administrative thought, literature, and education began with the nation-state and worked downward. In the United States, the progression was reversed."[8] The non-American thought is depicted as essentially irrelevant.

Mosher's introduction points to the place of non-Americans in the anthology and to the difficulty of international technology transfers. Referring to the anthology, Mosher points out that "of the many students and writers identified in the succeeding pages, only a very few were not Americans, and indeed these are principally footnote references: Weber, Fayol, Keynes, Urwick, Crozier and a few others."[9] Referring to the heavy involvement of the United States in technical assistance in public administration after World War II, Mosher comments that many "of our transient 'experts'—and no doubt more of their foreign listeners—were dismayed and chagrined that many tried-and-true American ideas, techniques, and formulae were not particularly useful, or were completely irrelevant, away from home."[10] With the contributors having consigned Max Weber and John Maynard Keynes to footnotes, Mosher hopes that this volume "may be of some interest both to those interested in cross-cultural communication about public administration of whatever nationality, and to those students and practitioners of the field in the United States."[11]

The claim that the in-group's situation and clients are radically different from anyone else's has been a theme in the history of American public administration. Public administration theory, as it has developed in the United States, has been influenced by the American dream. The dream is sometimes taken as synonymous with success, especially individual economic opportunity and achievement. Nevertheless, whatever else this dream contains, one idea that is often stressed is that American political life in important respects tends to be different. The idea is that, more than any other system, the American Constitution, in the broad sense attributed to Woodrow Wilson ("the dynamic fundamental order of the State"[12]), makes that success possible. Others may try to emulate, but success is found only in America or, as the dollar bill puts it, "novus ordo seclorum."[13] The notion is that the fundamental political system is so structured and crafted with regard to such terms as liberties and democracy that United States citizenship offers possibilities for human development unparalleled elsewhere. This idea is reinforced by the relative military weakness of Europe, the economic decline of all European countries except Germany, and the backward-looking attitude (represented in places by the retention of premodern forms such as monarchy and marked social distinctions) that is both charming and difficult to accept in a forward-looking superpower. This attitude is clearly important to public administration theory to the extent that the business of public administration is not only (in Woodrow Wilson's phrase) "to run a Constitution" but to run a particular constitution.

Some ambivalence can be identified regarding the issue of the American element, and some attempts have been made to go beyond the exclusivism just suggested. These attempts are reflected in comparative public administration, in some recognition of antecedents to American public administration, and in the "universalist" tendency in work conducted by theorists such as Simon and Ostrom.

The claim about nationalism is undermined by the comparative public administration movement, a subfield of public administration and comparative politics and an exception to the particularist tendency.[14] The movement began after World War II. Its contribution to the public administration field seems recently to have declined, and the impact on public administration has been limited. As Heady puts it, "American students and practitioners of public administration have from the beginning shown an interest in the administrative experiences of other historical and contemporary political systems . . . , but this has never been the dominant focus of attention for a field of study that has concentrated for the most part on American problems and American solutions for those problems."[15] George Guess categorizes comparative public administration's history in terms of postwar relief (1943–1948), containment-frontiersmanship (1949–1960), the alliance for progress (1961–1972), new directions (1973–1980), and private sector initiative (1981–present).[16] The two main interests, he reports, have been public administration pattern comparisons and international public administration. Guess evaluates the results in these words: "Despite this practical grounding in reality, many CPA [comparative public administration] studies shed pseudolight on nonproblems for which the entire field was often criticized for producing near-meaningless information." He believes that comparative public administration has become more empirical and policy relevant, more eclectic and interdisciplinary: "[It] may not be concluded that public administration remains its leading edge."[17] Heady characterizes present activity as at "a lower but still impressive level."[18]

Recognition of prior and foreign writings also tends to mitigate the localistic description of American public administration. Dwight Waldo and Daniel Martin are among those who emphasize the role of antecedents. As Waldo writes, "American self-aware Public Administration needs to be viewed as a part of the very long history that has been sketched. So viewed, it is not something altogether new and different, but another chapter in a millennia-length story."[19] He goes on to add, "But viewing Public Administration in historical perspective also reveals some unusual, indeed unique, features. It is recognizably the product of a specific historical period and a specific New World environment."[20] He asserts that Americans could and did learn from Western Europe but that the reasons for the excellence of European public administration cannot be transplanted. He states, "Administrative technology was, first of all and above all, deeply imbedded in culture, and in social and political arrangements."[21] Waldo's account of American self-aware public administration, as noted earlier, does suffer from difficulties in the meaning and significance of the notion of "self-aware study." In terms of meaning, it would be nonsense to say that a topic is conscious of itself. Therefore, the notion should be taken to mean that a writer writing on Y is conscious as she is doing it that she is contributing to a discipline including Y. This notion is vague, however, and the meaning will remain unclear unless it is specified precisely *of what* and *how* one must be conscious when one does the writing (e.g., all the content of the subject, part of the content, or merely that such a subject exists). Certainly, Wilson and Goodnow were aware of less administrative theory than Waldo is, and so the character of self-awareness may vary. In terms of significance, how and why Y changes when it is done self-consciously needs to be specified. Would it have been more (or less) geometry if what the Pythagoreans did had been (or had not been) recognized as geometry by them? Was it any less physics because Newton's central work was conceptualized as, and titled, *Mathematical Principles of Natural Philosophy?* It is not clear that the notion of self-awareness can carry the weight Waldo attaches to it.

The claim, usually unsaid and taken for granted, that American public administration should be portrayed as having a corner on the discipline is undermined by Daniel Martin's description of nineteenth century French public administration.[22] Martin states that "virtually every significant concept that existed in American public administration literature by 1937 (half the history of the field since Wilson's essay) had already been published in France by 1859. Most had been published by 1812."[23] He cites a number of publications in that article and in the section titled "History of Pre-American Public Administration" in his guide.[24] Examples are Charles-Jean Bonnin's *Principes d'administration publique* (published in 1812) and Alexandre Françoise Auguste Vivien's *Études administratives* (published in two volumes in 1845 and printed in a third edition in 1859). Martin lists and discusses ten principles that can be identified in this French literature, principles that were independently reinvented in American public administration. These principles are as follows: "a dichotomy exists between politics and administration"; "the scientific study of public administration will lead to the discovery of principles"; "administration can be taught to practitioners in schools"; "administrators must plan"; "bureaucracy must be organized into a hierarchy, preferably with single executives"; "the placement, training, and conditions of employment must be conducive to the organization's purpose"; "executives must make decisions, issue orders, and provide leadership within the organization"; "the various parts of work must be interrelated"; "administrators must keep chief executives informed of the impacts of policies and other needs of society"; and "budgets must be planned and financial accountability of administrators maintained."[25]

The claim for the localism of American public administration is also undermined by the work of scholars such as Herbert Simon and Vincent Ostrom. Simon's *Administrative Behavior* and later work are directed at establishing a science of public administration that centers on the behavior of making decisions. His conclusions about the nature of rationality and the function of organizations in facilitating rationality, for example, are not at all parochial. Vincent Ostrom's *The Intellectual Crisis in American Public Administration* and later work have resulted in popularizing the application of the public choice approach to the public administration context. Ostrom's book has some emphasis on the experiences of one country (e.g., in his theory of democratic administration). Nevertheless, the public choice approach does seek to apply economics and related concepts, and economics does have a universalist orientation.

Intracultural particularism does have advantages and arguments to support it. Some may wish to say that no intellectually respectable alternative exists. At a minimum, it should be said that intercultural statements are extremely difficult because (as Mosher may be suggesting) it is hard to notice the embedded confounding variables.

Niskanen's model of bureaucracy constitutes an example.[26] What is presented as a universal model (beyond time and space, even) turns out to have at least one hidden assumption that disguises the model's limited application and its particularism; it contains a variable that is confounding when the model is applied in certain cultural contexts. Niskanen's model presents the bureaucrat who seeks to maximize her bureau's total budget and whose bureau will produce at more than the socially optimal level. The bureaucrat's motives are "salary, perquisites of office, public reputation, power, patronage, output of the bureau, ease of making changes, and ease of managing the bureau," and "[a]ll except the last two are a positive function of the total budget of the bureau during the bureaucrat's tenure."[27] A confounding variable is the implicit assumption that bureaucrats are interagency immobile; if they are mobile, the bureaucrat's motives may not be a positive monotonic function of that bureau's total budget. It is true that interagency movement, despite attempts such as the Senior Executive Service, is relatively difficult in the United States government. Nevertheless, the model cannot be applied as is to all cultural contexts because significant interagency mobility does exist in other cultural contexts. In England, where Dunleavy makes this criticism of Niskanen,[28] interagency mobility is much greater. It is hard to spot confounding variables.

The national particularism of American public administration does have profound disadvantages in terms of contraries and blind spots. A contrary was noted earlier between particularism and universalism. The urge for the less bounded and the focus on the more bounded are also contraries. Insofar as it is interpretationist, public administration has an interest in interpretations that are as little culture-bound as possible. This interest in the intercultural is in facilitating insight. Without the intercultural interest, for instance, insightful questions can be overlooked. We can fail to ask productive questions, such as why we have 17,500 police agencies in the United States compared with the small numbers in other advanced countries (such as 2 in France) plus a larger and unknown number of private police agencies. Without the intercultural interest, important comparisons with others are impossible. Lester Thurow recommends that we use benchmarking, for example, to improve such items as our educational and productivity performance. He explains that a country that "wants to win" begins by studying the competition: "The purpose is not emulation but what the business world calls 'bench marking.' Find those in the world that are the best at each aspect of economic performance. Measure your performance against theirs. Understand why they are better. Set yourself the target of first equaling, and then surpassing, their performance."[29]

A discipline focused primarily on one nation tends to miss good ideas from abroad and even to downplay its own antecedents. No study of public administration should be satisfied, for instance, to exclude such items as Michel Foucault's studies of "governmentality." Governmentality is discussed in chapter 10; it has been described as reflecting Foucault's interest "not only in the political aspects of government, but also in [government's] pedagogical, spiritual and religious dimensions."[30] No discipline should be content to have less than the fullest connection with its own antecedents. For example, Thomas Jefferson and Alexander Hamilton did have administrative views, and these theories have been discussed by Caldwell, Mosher, and others.[31] Nevertheless, the character of police science and its connection with public administration, for example, has not been pursued, with the result that even the meaning of that science is not widely recognized. The term *police* differs from the narrow contemporary meaning; pre-nineteenth-century definitions of *police* can be found in terms of the "government of a republic," "civil government," and "government."[32] Beccaria, professor of political economy and science of police at the University of Milan, explains it this way: "Thus, the sciences, education, good order, security and public tranquillity, objects all comprehended under the name of police, will constitute the fifth and last object of public economy."[33] The science of police that flourished in the Enlightenment has been described as the "culmination" of a literature that developed through the modern period.[34] It came to be taught in the New World. In 1799, Governor Thomas Jefferson rearranged the professorships at Virginia's College of William and Mary, a university established three centuries ago, to include a professorship in law and police. George Wythe was the first to hold that chair, followed by St. George Tucker.[35] The subject of police that was taught by Tucker is described as concerning "the internal organization or regulation of a political unit, the control and regulation of such a unit through exercise of governmental powers . . . : such control and regulation with respect to matters affecting the general comfort health, morals, safety, or prosperity of the public."[36] Tucker believed that all graduates in law should be familiar with "civil history and with municipal law and police."[37]

A public administration that is so centered on one country tends to limit its theoretical power by inclining to craft the description of issues in terms that are unique to the United States. Theoretical questions asked in terms of particular organizations (e.g., requiring a description of the current practices of the U.S. Department of Justice) are essentially local. This point is not raised to imply that applied questions should not be asked about the U.S. Department of Justice. Instead, I suggest that the form and character of a discipline can raise or lower "barriers to the entry" of interesting theoretical issues.

On the matter of the human condition, interpretations that are realistic—that dovetail with our understanding of the nature of human beings and of human history, that recognize the dangers of hubris—are likely to be helpful. Because the United States is both a military and an economic superpower, it is hard to be cosmopolitan about the country's historical claims to uniqueness. Thurow speaks of this in the economic context,

> Why should one worry about making a perfect system better? . . . The view that the American system is perfect and cannot be made better comes from America's peculiar history. America's Founding Fathers (Thomas Jefferson, George Washington, Benjamin Franklin) were gods, or if not gods, at least individuals more perfect than anyone now alive. They designed a unique system that could last forever without improvements. It was, and is, perfect. No other country has founding fathers in the sense that the United States has founding fathers.[38]

Nevertheless, we are speaking of a sector where the feeling of uniqueness might be even stronger: the public, the political.

Examples of two blind spots resulting from the one-nation focus of American public administration are the minimal work conducted on corruption and the determinants of governmental size.[39] These topics have been treated; writings on corruption[40] and on size[41] can be found. For example, Rohr has discussed the "low road,"[42] and a literature on responsibility exists. Nevertheless, these topics have not been studied as extensively as they should. No references to either of these topics are made in the bibliographies compiled by McCurdy or Payad, for example.[43] No such articles—at the time of writing—have appeared in the last five years' editions of *Public Administration Review.*

Corruption, unfortunately, has a tendency to besmirch the corruption fighter and the commentator as well as the perpetrator. It borders on being a politically incorrect subject. For example, it leaves a person open to the illogical progression that resembles the children's poem about the kingdom being lost all for the want of a horseshoe nail: If you say that it is not just a question of a few bad apples, you are saying that the system does not discourage corruption; so you are saying that the system encourages corruption; so you are saying that the system is corrupt; so you are saying that the system is no good; you are saying that somebody else's system is better, and so on, and all for the want of saying that it is not just a question of a few bad apples. As the Knapp Commission Report on New York's police corruption explains it, the rotten apple theory—"a basic obstacle to meaningful reform"—is that "any policeman found to be corrupt must promptly be denounced as a rotten apple in an otherwise clean barrel. It must never be admitted that his individual corruption may be symptomatic of underlying disease."[44] It is more acceptable and easier to see the corruption in another person's country than in one's own. Discussing the role of dash in Africa and bribes in Italy is more pleasant than addressing such problems in our own backyard; it is easier for us to see that a discussion of Italian administration should consider the role of the Mafia than it is to understand that organized crime can be a factor in American public administration. A connection exists between some corruption and organized crime, and the United States does contain some crime organizations; as the Knapp Commission Report described the New York situation, "Organized crime is the single biggest source of police corruption."[45] It is natural for the particularist approach to encourage a blind spot.

Let us continue with this police management illustration. Despite the fact that no major police agency can afford not to have an internal affairs unit (a police unit that is within the agency and that is dedicated to policing its own police members), the police management literature still gives relatively minimal attention to the problems of corruption.[46] The first three editions of the standard text on police management, O. W. Wilson's *Police Administration,* did not even contain the word *corruption.* This omission was corrected in the fourth edition.[47] Nevertheless, the point remains. Furthermore, as the Knapp Commission Report explains so well, it is a systemic problem not confined to individuals or the police. As the Knapp Commission documents for New York, the second largest cause of police payoffs "is legitimate business seeking to ease its way through the maze of City ordinances and regulations"; and "in every area where police corruption exists it is paralleled by corruption in other agencies of government, in industry and labor, and in the professions."[48] The problem is not confined to a particular sector, such as elements dealing with the construction industry. In a context where organized crime flourishes and where private interest is highly valued, corruption is a general administrative topic. It is not one that should be swept under the rug, under a heading covering a related but narrower topic, such as "responsibility."

American public administration, focusing on such central themes as "getting things done through others"[49] or decision making, has not centered on the issue of size. It has given scholarly attention to most aspects, as it were, of the elephant except its size. Nevertheless, the elephant clearly is large, as the general public seems well aware. Such attitudes and the nation's budgetary situation have been especially fruitful in yielding particularist literatures on such topics as "doing more with less" and cutback management. Nevertheless, a particularist literature must have difficulty in understanding our problem in context. For example, the fact that governmental expenditure in the United States accounted for 34.8 percent of gross national product in 1987, compared with 27 percent in 1960, raises one set of questions and perceptions. To know that an increase has occurred in the relative size of governmental expenditures in all advanced countries during the last two centuries, especially since World War II, puts the questions in a different perspective. It also suggests other questions (e.g., about the differences in the rates of growth).

Several broad factors are candidate explanations of governmental size changes, and Mueller provides a good summary and review of the massive theoretical and empirical literature—literature from outside the public administration discipline.[50] The governmental role of providing public goods and eliminating externalities, the government function of redistributing wealth, and the effects of interest groups are three explanations that Mueller describes as being drawn from the classical theory of the democratic state—the "citizen over state" view of most public choice work.[51] The role of bureaucracy as catalyst of government growth (under which heading would be included models such as Niskanen's, mentioned above) and fiscal illusion as promoter of government size are two other explanations that Mueller characterizes as placing the state over the citizen.[52] The American public administration discipline surely should be concerned with such issues; it needs to be concerned seriously in developing a theory about the appropriate size or sizes of bureaucratic entities.

Despite any merits, the view that confines knowledge to the intracultural is limiting. If the eye looks too closely and too directly at, say, the petals on the flower, the close perspective can limit understanding of the object observed. It can be helpful to move the head further back and to notice the context, the sets of interrelationships, within which the petal is a petal. It can help to see the relationship of the petal to the flower, then to the plant, then to the other plants, then to the entire garden of plants and associated insects, and so on. Several perspectives can help to expand the understanding. Parochialism, the close look that sees nothing but the object under analysis, has its own limits.

THE *PUBLIC* ELEMENT

The particularism of *public,* the second word in American public administration, leads no less to contraries and blind spots. Differences exist regarding the appropriateness of this carving out of a border for the discipline between the public and the private. Recall the turf claims of the disciplines that crowd around and into the public administration space. The reference here, of course, is to academic turf—the small-minded struggles and posturings concerned with issues such as who shall teach it and who should be regarded as authoritative about it. Nevertheless, the struggles have a wider significance; for one thing, they shape how public administration practice is seen. The turf question goes both ways as some widen public administration to the generic study of administration and as others narrow it further to subparts of public administration. On the one side are the generic orientations that see "administration" (or organization or some other part) as subjected to an artificial distinction when it is limited to "public" or "business." On the other are the programmatic orientations that see "administration" (or some other part claimed as public administration turf) as essentially linked to particular programs. Examples are programs such as health administration, social work administration, parks and recreation administration, criminal justice administration, educational administration, or what some see as subprograms, such as mental health administration or higher educational administration.

It is true that currently, in important senses, government is indeed different. The public and private sectors play different roles; government regulates aspects of the private sector; public production and agency operations are conducted in a markedly political milieu, and the bureaucracy is part of the political process; public agencies are subject to different legal contexts, limiting their scope for functions such as personnel management and employee relations; and public agencies have distinctive relationships with the press and interest groups.[53] Nevertheless, limiting the scope of administration to the public sector does create a set of contraries and blind spots. A generic view would see administration as a universalist phenomenon that includes public, private, and third-sector activity; it offers greater prospects for evaluating the practices of each in general terms so that each will benefit from the other. It would hold that, essentially, "administration is administration is administration." The contrary particularist view focuses on what is special in public sector management. Some of the blind spots would cluster around the divisions between the two sectors; others would consist in tardiness in using the advances made in the excluded sector. The consequent loss to a public administration theory limited to the public sector should be recognized as real, just as the benefits of separation are real. For example, some people continue to believe that public managers should be recruited from the business manager group; in addition, the study of business management is noted for its emphasis on quantitative procedures. Similar sets of contraries and blind spots could be developed for the programmatic subspecialties such as health administration.

Three blind spots will serve as examples. First, there is a tendency in public administration and in business administration (and in politics and in economics) to overlook the fact that the public and private sectors are socially constituted. Second, the interrelationships between the two sectors are, for all practical purposes, necessary and intimate. Third, the basic operating principles of each sector have much to teach the other.

The public and private spheres are artifacts. They are defined and can be redefined; they can be re-created or even abandoned. Consider as illustration the account of the concepts of *private* and *public* given by Jürgen Habermas in *The*

Structural Transformation of the Public Sphere.[54] Habermas describes the rise in the early years of modernity of the "bourgeois public sphere," mediating between the public and private spheres. This sphere included the political club, the newspaper, and the journal—the scene of rational debate. Habermas then describes the decline of this sphere, which was increasingly taken over by private corporations and by state. The state plays a management role in the economy, and it takes over functions such as education and social welfare. Private corporations take over the public sphere; witness the rise of public relations and advertising, and witness corporations taking over culture. The rational individuals become culture consumers. Habermas writes of a refeudalization of the public sphere: "For the kind of integration of mass entertainment with advertising, which in the form of public relations already assumes a 'political' character, subjects even the state itself to its code. Because private enterprises evoke in their customers the idea that in their consumption decisions they act in their capacity as citizens, the state has to 'address its citizens' like consumers. As a result, public authority too competes for publicity."[55] This description is a much different socially constituted conception of the public and private spheres than is portrayed in the socially constituted view of public and private sectors implied in, say, Samuelson and Nordhaus's *Economics.*[56]

As another illustration, consider H. George Frederickson's conception of the *public* in public administration. Frederickson argues for a conception that distinguishes *public* from *governmental.* As he writes, "The public lives independently of the government, and government is only one of its manifestations."[57] He regrets that the meaning of the term *public* has "come to have such a narrow meaning in our time" and that we "think of the public as pertaining to government and having to do with voting and the conduct of elected officials."[58] In an earlier article, Frederickson expresses regret that neither an extensive literature nor "agreed-on theories of the public in public administration" exist.[59] He reviews what he describes as five perspectives on the *public,* and he finds each of them incomplete. The five perspectives are the public as interest groups, as consumer, as represented, as client, and as citizen. His views are in the tradition of the public interest literature.[60] Frederickson's view is that an adequate theory of the public should be based on the Constitution,[61] on an enhanced notion of citizenship, on systems for responding to the interests of "both the collective public and the inchoate public,"[62] and on benevolence and love.

The notion that independent and virtually self-sustaining public and private spheres could exist is so difficult to maintain that it is hard to imagine who could assume it. Nevertheless, some do; we find Heilbroner criticizing the view where "the government treats with the economy, and to some extent the economy treats with government, much as do two foreign nations."[63] The notion of an undisturbed private sector, existing independently of government as if it were a virgin forest, is incomplete. For one thing, the private sector must operate within a context of a legal framework, including at least a criminal law that protects the contracting parties. Consider, for instance, the economic significance of legal provisions limiting the personal liability of corporate owners.

Beyond this consideration, agreement is widespread in mainstream economic thinking that, despite the wealth-creating power and distributive effectiveness of the activities of self-interested entrepreneurs and consumers operating in a free-market pricing system, significant interrelationships are necessary to avoid the effects of market failures. Free markets are fabulous wealth generators, but they present difficulties that demonstrate a demand for public sector involvement. Chapter 7 discusses these difficulties; here we will note them only briefly. For example, the private sector requires public sector action at three major points. One point of action is the prevention of the suboptimal behavior of imperfect competition; the second is the mitigation of the recessionary swings of the business cycle; and the third is the protection against the underproduction of public goods and the promotion of economic growth. Chapter 7 also points to the differences in viewpoints about the character and extent of governmental action that are appropriate under these headings. For example, differences exist regarding the role of government in assisting its corporate enterprises to think in a more long-term manner, to compete more effectively with other nationals, and to develop supracompany strategies for development. Differences exist regarding the redistributive role of government in limiting the wealth inequities that seem inevitable in the free market. Differences exist not only between socialist and other societies but also within societies wishing to pursue a basic free market approach. Nevertheless, it is hard to argue against the need for effective interrelationship between the public and private sectors. The debate regarding government "intervention" is to think in terms that are of limited use; as Samuels observes, "What is normally considered 'intervention' is not the intrusion of government in an area from which government hitherto has been absent, but the change of the interest to which government gives its support or which government is used to support."[64]

The reverse flow is also important for public administration practice. The public sector is traditionally seen as outside the sphere of private enterprise. There is a lack of realism in not recognizing that entrepreneurs wish to trade with whomsoever can pay, that government is a source of wealth, that a tax exemption is the same as a subsidy, and that a political payment and an economic payment are often alternative ways to make money. The rational entrepreneur will also wish to influence the slope of the private enterprise playing field, and that impact can be sought through the public sector. The notion of an independent public sector is as untenable as that of an independent private sector. The idea of an undisturbed public sector, existing independently of private businesses, is no less incomplete. The public sector—and public administration—are bound within the economic environment, and the impact works in both directions. The public sector and public administration are affected by the shape and performance of the surrounding economy—by such factors, for instance, as the varying output, employment and stock market levels, and by the extent and character of industrialization and postindustrialization. Public administration practice affects the economy through such means as the levels and objects of governmental expenditures, the shape of revenue measures, direct and indirect regulation of business, and the government's own business activities.

For a discipline that is so concerned about the politics-administration dichotomy, public administration theory has a blind spot in its lack of concern regarding the economics-administration dichotomy. Is the governmental administration that is operating on issues of central concern to private entrepreneurs operating in the public or the private sector? Are governmental administrators operating in the public or private spheres when they are managing programs to regulate the maximum apartment rentals that are chargeable, when they are directing programs to assist businesses to secure export orders, when they are directing enterprises to shoot space rockets to Mars, and when they are managing programs that will decide the taxes that private businesses will pay? The socially constructed shape of our public sector is an expression (perhaps cause, perhaps effect) of a limitation in public administration theory.

THE *ADMINISTRATION* ELEMENT

The particularism of *administration,* the third word in American public administration, leads also to contraries and blind spots. First, the functional character that is represented in the term *administration* is reflected in most of the purposes and the substructure of the public administration discipline. Second, the pursuit of the functional encounters the competing and contrary need to focus on the political and the programmatic. This encounter may be a basis for the multiple paradigms and fluidity that characterize the study of administration. However, a more likely explanation is the lack of power in the guiding theory. Third, this paradox of the pursuit of the functional and the competing pursuit of the political and programmatic has yielded what discipline members call the "identity crisis." This crisis is represented by the politics-administration dichotomy. Fourth, these difficulties are more critical at the level that will be described and explained as macroadministrative. Each of these points are discussed, respectively, in the following subsections.

First, consider the claims that the purpose and substructure of public administration theory are essentially functional, and this organizing principle encounters a limit. The functional character of the discipline's purposes is indicated in such classical descriptions of the study of public administration as getting things done through people, POSDCORB, and in Simon's decision making. This functionality is reflected not only in its title but also in the typical way in which the subject is subdivided in university public administration curricula and public administration textbooks. Consider the essentially functional character, for example, of the coding system used by McCurdy in his bibliography: management, organization theory and behavior, technology of administration, comparative administration, public policy, urban and intergovernmental policy, bureaucracy, general surveys of public administration, and financial and economic policy.[65] Consider the headings used in the second part of Daniel Martin's guide: scientific management, Woodrow Wilson and administrative science, Max Weber and bureaucracy, employee motivation, leadership, staffing, decision making and expertise, budgeting and fiscal administration, and policy analysis.[66] Consider the major headings in Rabin's handbook: public administration history and organization theory, public budgeting and financial management, decision making, public personnel administration and labor relations, federalism and intergovernmental relations, policy sciences, comparative and international administration, public law and regulation, public administration pedagogy, data administration and research methods, judicial administration, political economy, and the profession of public administration.[67]

The emphasis on the functional has been neither complete nor entirely satisfying in public administration, and additions have been made in programmatic terms. The functional leads naturally to a prizing of the practical. The functions and purposes of the program administrator or administration—as expert developer, as doer, as achiever in an administrative context, as a functionary who can make an administrative entity produce what it should produce—are highly valued. The most highly prized quality, it seems, is the achieving of results, getting things done. An underlying motivational source—objective, metaphor, or energy spring—for the study of public administration is that required action can be laid out in terms that can be readily used by the administrator or administration. The purpose of the subject is indeed action. Action requires more than functional analysis, however; it also needs understanding of program content. The functional reaches a limit.

Second, the encounter of the functional and the programmatic may be a basis for the discipline's multiple paradigms and fluidity. The multiplicity of paradigms in public administration has been shaped largely by the discipline's environment; that is, the multiplicity has resulted from intellectual, political, social, economic, and other factors outside the discipline. This multiplicity is also related, probably in lesser part, to the scope of the subject matter, the logical consequence of internal forces. Such an internal explanation would appeal to the logic of the discipline; in this case, it would be the paradoxes presented by encountering the subject borders. If a solution or significant impact on a discipline's set of problems requires subject-matter resources and techniques that are outside the discipline, pressure will exist to import such resources and techniques. This pressure can be expected to succeed unless there is some blocking force, such as possession within the discipline of a set of theory or other resources that is strong enough to counterbalance the inward pressure.

The centrality of this multiplicity of paradigms and this fluidity can be established in terms of the heterogeneity of the discipline's parentage, the character of the core, the NASPAA view, and a comparison with other social sciences. Each is discussed in turn as follows.

Multiple and changing paradigms in the study of public administration do exist. This fact was also mentioned in chapter 2. The heart of mainstream "Big P.A.," as it is, is administrative theory or organization theory. Nevertheless, even here, there are numerous "paradigms." For example, Harman distinguishes what he calls classical, neoclassical, systems, later human relations, market, interpretive and critical, and emergence theories.[68] Aspects of this classification system can be criticized. For instance, it is unclear whether "emergence theories" really should be a separate category. Nevertheless, the point being made here is to emphasize the heterogeneity of the core.

This heterogeneity is also reflected in the parentage of much of the core. Public administration draws on psychology, sociology, political science, behavioral science, systems theory, and a variety of other subjects. It draws on some subjects more than on others. For example, probably it relies on organization theory more than on economics or moral philosophy. Some parts draw on one set of social sciences and other disciplines; another will draw on a modified combination. It is tempting to suppose that, on the basis of the idea that the whole is greater than the sum of the parts, the mixing of these theoretical perspectives radically changes the natures of the different perspectives. But the record is not clear that the whole has in fact been greater.

The very conceptions of mainstream public administration theory differ. Some have seen public administration in generic terms, that is, as a field of business (e.g., Wilson and Goodnow). Some have seen it as administrative science and think in terms of efficiency (e.g., Gulick and Urwick). Others see the subject area differently, making politics central. For example, Sayre thinks in terms of politics first and administration afterward. Waldo conceptualizes public administration as a field of study where the boundaries and nature are problematic. He thinks that public administrationists should act as if their discipline is a profession. Mosher likes the analogy between public administration and medicine, but concerning the nature of public administration theory he is not sure.

The NASPAA Ad Hoc Committee report, as discussed in chapter 2, notes that the emphasis on pluralism has existed since NASPAA's foundation and that the "value of this pluralism was underscored at our 1977 meeting in Colorado Springs when NASPAA pledged that program review and peer evaluation would encourage excellence according to several visions of public service education rather than upholding a single vision."[69] This pluralism, this heterogeneity, has been characterized in various ways. McCurdy presents a map of the development of three relatively independent strands, and he describes these strands in terms of three periods of development: the orthodox (1887–1944), the politics (1945–1963), and the program (1963–present). Others have provided other maps.[70]

Multiplicity of paradigms is, of course, a characteristic of a number of social science and related disciplines, and similar comments can be offered for all such disciplines. Clinical social work is an example of such a discipline. Rachelle Dorfman lists nine clinical social work paradigms and five metaparadigms.[71] Similar to the case of public administration, social work is an example where narrow boundaries exist (i.e., boundaries for a discipline addressing problems that require intellectual resources from beyond the established subject-matter boundary). The inward pressure for external intellectual capital is strong, and no intrasubject theory or other resource is strong enough to provide a counterbalance.

A contrasting case is provided by economics, which has a strong theoretical content. Little competition exists within economics for the mainstream paradigm although it has lesser traditions such as institutional and Marxian economics. There are similar boundary or scope problems, which the discipline is able to overcome by virtue of its strong internal counterbalance. (Nevertheless, economics' boundaries have widened from certain kinds of behavior to certain aspects of behavior.[72]) Economics has paid a price for its successful insularity, however. The loss for economics is that it tends to explain economic phenomena entirely in economic terms. Economic decisions, on the contrary, are neither shaped merely by economic considerations nor best understood entirely in economic terms; for instance, as the public choice approach suggests, there is a marriage of the economic and the political.

Third, the pursuit of the administrative (the functional) and the competing need to focus on the political (programmatic) has given rise to the politics-administration dichotomy issue that has long troubled public administration theory.[73] The traditional view is that the politics-administration dichotomy should be traced to Woodrow Wilson, considered the founder of American public administration. Wilson would separate the study of administration from politics, denying that American administration must be unique as a result of its politics being unique.[74]

Administration, for Wilson, is a field of business;[75] it was "a part of political life only as the methods of the counting-house are a part of the life of society."[76] As he writes in his well-known 1887 essay, "If I see a murderous fellow sharpening a knife cleverly, I can borrow his way of sharpening the knife without borrowing his probable intention to commit murder with it; and so, if I see a monarchist dyed in the wool managing a public business well, I can learn his business methods without changing one of my republican spots."[77]

Here, then, are contraries. On the one hand, delineating the field of public administration in terms of the politics-administration dichotomy gives rise to some blind spots; on the other hand, doing so on the contrary basis breeds other blind spots. Consider the former and the marble cake character of governing and administering. The dichotomy disguises the pervasive impact of governing on government administering, the real effects of politics on administrative practice; the realities are that administrative practices are socially constituted and that an important constitutive factor is the set of influences that should be labeled political. As another example, consider the scope provided to police and to other criminal justice program administrators to protect citizens who report being in fear of death or assault. Political action has been required to widen the range of administrative options (e.g., passage of stalker laws). The dichotomy disguises the impact of government administering on governing, the political part that administrators play in program policy making and other areas. As examples, consider the political impact of intelligence information that is shaped by administrative agencies; consider the political impacts of the sizeable congressional relations staffs and activities maintained by subordinate administrative agencies.

Now consider denial of the dichotomy. This denial of the dichotomy disguises the distinctive character of the set of administrative issues that, independent of politics, seems to be encountered in government. The nature of the distinctive character is an issue for public administration theory. Much of the distinctive character involves, as was suggested earlier, the peculiar problems associated with producing public goods. These peculiar problems are encountered mainly in public and not-for-profit agencies—and also, to a limited extent, in private enterprise. The lack of a profit discipline creates special difficulties, such as relative slowness in introducing innovations and a necessary tendency toward oversizing. As an example of the latter, note some of the public choice literature suggesting that governmental agencies can be expected to produce at output levels that are not socially optimal (recall the earlier reference to Niskanen's model, which argues that bureaucracies will produce twice the optimal output levels) and to produce "X-inefficiency" (a term used by Leibenstein).[78] Others may prefer other descriptions of the "distinctive" character. Some candidates (perhaps in combination) might be size and power (i.e., power over the rest of society and over other societies). Other possibilities include the problems of administering in a politics-swept context.

The dichotomy issue is sometimes poorly understood. The fact that the administrative sector is in practice interwoven with the political (or social or economic, for that matter) sectors is significant, but it is not necessarily decisive if knowledge is understood as abstraction. Even if it is mightily intertwined (as it is), a subject of study can be set up as if it were separate. If that setup were not possible, no political science (and no economics) would be possible because, on a descriptive basis, surely no politics-economics dichotomy exists. No social science divisions would be workable. Nevertheless, the question is whether the "as if" game is effective in the case of public administration.

The subject boundaries may be too limiting in at least two senses. Possibly the breadth of public administration (defined in terms only of administration) is too narrow to permit achievement of the discipline's goals; that is, needed intellectual resources may be available only outside the boundaries. In addition, the phenomena may be so interconnected that the division of subject matter prevents successful study of only part of the phenomena. Such a situation would exist, for example, if administrative phenomena were so interwoven with political phenomena that hypotheses (or conclusions) could not be developed that were entirely within the subject boundaries of administration. We will return to this issue in chapter 7, where social engineering is discussed.

The paradoxical limit just described is not encountered for all problems in public administration. Nevertheless, it is reached for many issues and is reached more readily as the problems approach what can be described as the macroadministrative theory level. Public administration theory serves a variety of clientele. For example, we can identify levels of macroadministrative theory, microadministrative theory, and micro-microadministrative theory. The terms here have been adapted from economics, where a distinction is made between macroeconomics (the study of economywide phenomena) and microeconomics (the study of such items as the firm and the consumer).

At the macroadministrative level, public administration theory may be seen as a matter for (or about) presidents, prime ministers, and princes and, of no less importance, for others wishing to think about this multigovernmental level. At this level, a concern may involve humankind's attempt through government to harness the human and natural resources to achieve political ends; another concern may involve how to humanize large bureaucracies and bureaucratic programs. The existence of such a practitioner need at this level is suggested by the oft-heard complaint about the difficulties that government leaders experience—in the West and in the East—in inducing the bureaucracy to bend to their wills. At the microadministrative level, administrative theory is a matter for (or about), among others, the governor of a state or province or for the head of a highway department. At the micro-microadministrative level, administrative theory is a matter for or about (among others) the individual practitioner, such as the budgeteer, the personnel analyst, or the first-line supervisor. (At each level, we must be careful to recognize that concern for administrative theory is not—and should not be—limited to practitioners.) Clearly, sublevels can be distinguished; the macroadministrative level may be subdivided into the global, the international, and the national, for instance. (A point here is that, in considering public administration theory, a sort of ecological fallacy must not be committed. One level should not be evaluated in terms of the record at another level.)

Administrative theory serves all levels of interest, but perhaps more has been achieved at the more microadministrative level than at the more macroadministrative level. If so, this situation is ironic because arguably the main need at the present time is at the macroadministrative level. The limit of separating the administrative and the political is most likely to be encountered at this level. This macroadministrative level is the most likely point of paradox between the decision to isolate the study of the administrative and the imperative of studying the political.

SUMMARY

Discipline specialization and autonomy—particularism—in public administration leads to contraries and blind spots. This chapter considers these limits under three subheadings: American, public, and administration.

American public administration focuses primarily on the concerns of one nation. Some exceptions to this claim exist, and some advantages can be seen in limiting the scope. Nevertheless, the disadvantages are greater. One set of contraries in such a focus is between any wish of American public administration to be a science and the reality that American public administration is a culture-bound subject. Another set of contraries is between any wish of American public administration to offer the widest interpretations and the reality that such interpretations are bounded by the focus on one nation. Blind spots include limitation on theoretical power, diminished capacity for picking up good ideas from abroad, and minimal attention given to subjects like corruption and governmental size.

The public character leads to three blind spots. It encourages a tendency to overlook that fact that the public and private sectors are socially constituted, that intimate interrelationships are necessary between the two sectors, and that each sector has much to learn from the other.

The administrative character, being functional, leads to a contrary. This contrary occurs when the functional encounters the need to focus on a competing and contrary organizing principle, the political and the programmatic. This encounter of the functional and the programmatic may be the basis for public administration's multiple paradigms and fluidity, but a more likely explanation is lack of power in the guiding theory. Pursuit of both the functional and the programmatic have yielded the identity crisis so much discussed in public administration theory. Such difficulties are more critical at what is described as the macroadministrative level.

No claim is made here that particularism is unproductive. On the contrary, particularism has been productive, and it could be more so—up to a point. Nevertheless, public administration does encounter the limits discussed in this chapter.

5

Modernity
Limits of Scientism

To place the matter squarely, it may be ventured that with all its attempts to emulate natural science inquiry, the past century of sociobehavioral research and theory has failed to yield a principle as reliable as Archimedes' principle of hydrostatics or Galileo's law of uniformly accelerated motion.

—Gergen[1]

Knowledge is not a series of self-consistent theories that converge towards an ideal view: it is not a gradual approach to the truth. It is rather an ever increasing ocean of mutually incompatible alternatives, each single theory . . . forcing the others into greater articulation and all of them contributing, via this process of competition, to the development of our consciousness.

—Feyerabend[2]

HERBERT SIMON, in his *Administrative Behavior,* seeks to establish an administrative science.[3] His attitude toward public administration is an instance of scientism, the view that the methods of the natural sciences are applicable to all fields of inquiry. He and others, such as Gulick and Urwick in the *Papers on the Science of Administration,* can be seen as seeking universalism for public administration theory by establishing the study of public administration as a science.[4] A second group of those pursuing scientism has attempted applied science, that is, to apply the results of other sciences (to the extent that they are sciences), such as behavioral psychology, to public administration problems. A third group has made extensive eclectic use of social science research methodology. Attempts have been made to develop "scientific statements" for both the practitioner and academic fields within either no framework or a loose action framework—in the general spirit of the sentiment ascribed to the 1907 New York Bureau of Municipal Research, whose founders were said to be "confident that if the citizenry only knew the facts about government it would take the right steps."[5] Perry and Kraemer indicate that 52 percent of the articles published in *Public Administration Review* between 1975 and 1984 reported empirical research; of these articles, 52 percent were cross-sectional and correlation analyses, and 37 percent were case studies.[6] Stallings and Ferris extend this work by examining public administration research published in *Public Administration Review* from 1940 to 1984; they note, "The recent history of research in public administration, as demonstrated by articles published in PAR [*Public Administration Review*], differs little from the state of affairs nearly a half century ago."[7] As Whelan puts it when reporting on Perry's and Kraemer's study, "[T]here has been a great deal of progress, but the research path has been an uneven one, particularly in a field that is still undergoing a process of definition."[8] In describing the "classic methods" of public administration research, Yaeger discusses "case studies, interviews, unobtrusive methods-records, participant observation, and surveys."[9]

A distinguishing mark of scientific or positivist propositions, unlike other statements such as the poetic, is that they are privileged in the sense that, if derived in accordance with scientific procedures, they are considered to give greater assurance of truth. It is more useful if conclusions on, say, what works and what does not work in government are scientific because scientific propositions are understood to be more reliable. On the one hand, there are advantages in establishing public administration on a scientific basis. On the other hand, limits are reached. First, the basis of the privileged status of scientific statements is not clear.[10] Second, the need arises to know about issues excluded from science, especially those relating to ethics and understanding.

A set of contraries, then, is between confining the study of public administration to the scientific process that denies epistemological status to value judgments and extending the study to include value judgments. The blind spots of the former consist of giving inadequate recognition to considerations of morality; the disadvantage of understanding public administration as a moral science is the loss of privileged positivist information. Another set of contraries is the clash between limiting the study of public administration to knowledge achieved on an intersubjective basis and extending such study also to include first-person knowledge.

Public administration theory does contain a literature on administrative ethics. When taught and studied as ethics in the administrative situation, the content is valuable. When taught as administrative ethics, the content, with the primacy of the adjective suggesting some confusion, is less likely to be helpful. Organizations do promulgate and enforce ethics, and organizational practices and standard operating procedures can be evaluated in ethical terms; for example, the April 1992 ethics manual of the U.S. House of Representatives is 493 pages long.[11] Nevertheless, we will discuss the limitations of seeking a metaethical anchor, as some public administrationists do, in the administrative area.

THE POSITIVIST AGENDA

Consider the positivist agenda exemplified in Simon for public administration and as explained by Donald McCloskey for economics.[12] Simon seeks to establish an administrative science by separating facts and values and by defining factual propositions as testable. Concerning values, he writes that an "administrative science, like any science, is concerned purely with factual statements. There is no place for ethical assertions in the body of a science. Whenever ethical statements do occur, they can be separated into two parts, one factual and one ethical; and only the former has any relevance to science."[13] Simon in his *Administrative Behavior* seeks to erect his administrative science on decision making that is instrumental. Goals are taken as givens, and administrative decision making is seen as a question of determining within a context of values what the criterion of efficiency requires from a consideration of the facts. The essence of this criterion of efficiency is reflected in the fourth principle of the United States Code of Ethics for Government Service, passed in 1958 and still in effect in 1992: "[S]eek to find and employ more efficient and economical ways of getting tasks accomplished."[14] As Simon himself defines it, "The criterion of efficiency demands that, of two alternatives having the same cost, that one be chosen which will lead to the greater attainment of the organization objectives; and that, of two alternatives leading to the same degree of attainment, that one be chosen which entails the lesser cost."[15] For him, "the correctness of an administrative decision is a relative matter—it is correct if it selects appropriate means to reach designated ends."[16]

By factual propositions, Simon means statements that are testable, and by testable clearly he means intersubjectively testable. He is interested not in private information but only in items that are publicly observable. As he says, "In principle, factual propositions may be tested to determine whether they are true or false—whether what they say about the world actually occurs, or whether it does not."[17] As chapter 11 discusses, logical positivism was still fashionable when he wrote *Administrative Behavior,* and, in the seven citations in his footnote on pages 45 and 46, he was merely making the philosophically unwise move of relying on the latest authorities. What he really wants to do is to rule out private and uncheckable data, private revelations. As Simon writes in the preface to the first edition of his book, "An experiment in chemistry derives its validity—its scientific authority—from its reproducibility; and unless it is described in sufficient detail to be repeated it is useless. In administration we have as yet only a very imperfect ability to tell what has happened in our administrative 'experiments'—much less to insure their reproducibility."[18]

Consider further what Simon was trying to achieve; consider a view from a sister social science. McCloskey rechristens positivism "modernism," and he gives some of the common expressions that reflect its influence: "That is just your opinion"; "My biases are such and such"; "I came to this conclusion on the basis of the facts"; "You're not being objective"; "That's a very subjective view"; "You are not being scientific; why should I listen?"[19]

McCloskey offers what he calls the "Ten Commandments and Golden Rule of modernism in economic and other sciences."[20] They are as follows:

1. Prediction and control is the point of science.
2. Only the observable implications (or predictions) of a theory matter to its truth.
3. Observability entails objective, reproducible experiments; mere questionnaires interrogating human subjects are useless, because humans might lie.
4. If and only if an experimental implication of a theory proves false is the theory proved false.
5. Objectivity is to be treasured; subjective "observation" (introspection) is not scientific knowledge, because the objective and subjective cannot be linked.
6. Kelvin's Dictum: "When you cannot express it in numbers, your knowledge is of a meager and unsatisfactory kind."
7. Introspection, metaphysical belief, aesthetics, and the like may well figure in the discovery of an hypothesis but cannot figure in its justification; justifications are timeless, and the surrounding community of science irrelevant to their truth.
8. It is the business of methodology to demarcate scientific reasoning from nonscientific, positive from normative.
9. A scientific explanation of an event brings the event under a covering law.
10. Scientists—for instance, economic scientists—ought not to have anything to say as scientists about the oughts of value, whether of morality or art.[21]

Item 3 will seem odd to some social scientists and public administrationists because questionnaire surveys are widely used. Nevertheless, the two Simon themes are well represented. Items 7 and 10 relate to the fact-value distinction; that is, metaphysical belief cannot figure in the justification of an hypothesis, and scientists ought not to have anything to say as scientists about the oughts of value. Items 2, 5, and 7 (again) relate to the requirement for intersubjectivity. Only observable data matter in assessing the truth of a theory; subjective observation is not scientific knowledge; and introspection cannot figure in the justification of a hypothesis.

STATUS OF SCIENTIFIC PROPOSITIONS

The status or foundation of scientific propositions seems much less clear than it was when Simon wrote *Administrative Behavior.*[22] The following account explains why it can be said that the status is unclear.[23]

Some students of public administration and some social scientists seem to embrace one of the nineteenth-century views of the nature of the scientific method, the view expressed in John Stuart Mill's *System of Logic.*[24] This view states that science begins with the objective observation of facts, that it proceeds by induction from a number of particular observations to the identification of regularities and thus to general statements or laws, that it proceeds to theories that explain one or more laws, and that both laws and theories are then checked for truth by comparing them with observed facts. A parallel empirical-inductive picture of science was developed by the logical positivists. For example, Rudolph Carnap, in his *Logical Structure of the World,* develops a rational reconstruction of our knowledge of the world, purporting to build up logically from the simplest elements of sensation.[25] This effort has problems. For example, sense data are private and thus nonverifiable, and Carnap views the nonverifiable as meaningless. Later, his starting point is the protocol or observation statement.

One problem with such an account revolves around the difficulties of drawing a general conclusion from a series of particular facts. Mill is aware of Hume's problem of induction. Hume points out that we can never observe causation. We can see one billiard ball strike another, but we can never see one cause the other to move. Causation is a psychological phenomenon; we come to believe in a necessary connection by observing the "constant conjunction of events." Hume also sees that the uniformity of nature, on which scientific explanation must rely, also has its grounding in our minds. We believe that the sun (or the earth) will rise tomorrow because it always has; the grounds for acceptance of the uniformity of nature lie neither in the logic or the facts of the world but in my psychology: "The supposition, that the future resembles the past, is not founded on arguments of any kind, but is derived entirely from habit."[26] The problem of induction is similar. The occurrence of any number of particular observances does not permit deduction of a general statement such as that offered in chapter 2 about the motion of every body. Hume states, "There can be no demonstrative arguments to prove that those instances of which we have had no experience, resemble those, of which we have had experience."[27]

Consider the well-known example of the swans.[28] If all known swans are white, people cannot conclude that all swans are white. Seeing yet another white swan does not confirm that all swans are white. A black swan might appear later. Mill believes, falsely, that he can get around the problem of induction by thinking that the problem applies only to low-level inductive generalizations. Therefore, he believes that it is possible to corroborate general statements by an appeal to the multitude of relevant particular observations.

The hypothetico-deductive model of scientific explanation, presented formally by Hempel and Oppenheim in 1948 and developed earlier and less formally by Karl Popper in *The Logic of Scientific Discovery,* offers a radically different picture of scientific method.[29] A scientific explanation, in this view, involves a universal law and a statement of initial conditions; the rules of deductive logic are then used to deduce a statement about the event to be explained. As Popper explains, universal laws are not derived by induction; they are merely hypotheses, and induction is a myth. For him, scientific theories are conjectures put forward for trial. All such statements and theories are provisionally true until they are falsified; all hangs on falsifiability.

One problem is that it is difficult to falsify. The Duhem-Quine thesis is that no scientific hypothesis is falsifiable because any test involves testing not only the hypothesis but also auxiliary hypotheses (e.g., about the accuracy of the measuring instruments). When the 1881 Michelson-Morley experiment failed to show differences in the speed of light when a light beam was transmitted in different directions in relationship to the movement of the earth, the hypothesis about the ether (which was the main hypothesis) was not rejected. Rather, the experiment was repeated in 1887. With the result still unsatisfactory, an auxiliary hypothesis was rejected. The researchers concluded that the measuring device was wrong, and the Fitzgerald-Lorentz contraction calculated how one arm of the measuring apparatus had contracted to account for the "unfortunate" result. As Duhem puts it, "The physicist can never subject an isolated hypothesis to experimental test, but only a whole group of hypotheses; when the experiment is in disagreement with his predictions . . . the experiment does not designate which one should be changed."[30] The Duhem-Quine thesis has become associated with the idea of the "underdetermination" of theories; that is, as David Oldroyd puts it, there is in principle "always an indefinite number of theories capable of accounting for some observed facts, and that any of the theories can be maintained no matter how much contrary evidence there may be, if sufficiently radical adjustments are made somewhere in the auxiliary hypotheses, not in the hypothesis under test at any given moment."[31] Difficulties in the way of falsification—and in the way of confirmation—also exist. Examples are the "grue-bleen" and other paradoxes,[32] the breakdown of the distinction between analytical and synthetic, and the recognition that observations are theory laden. The theory-laden nature of observations, for instance, is incompatible with the notion of the presuppositionless observer.[33]

Popper claims that the mark of good science is the making of risky, highly falsifiable conjectures that can then be tested. "The sun will shine next year" is less falsifiable, for instance, than "The sun will shine tomorrow afternoon." The latter has more empirical content, and Popper regards this line as a sufficient reply to Duhem's thesis. Popper contrasts the precise predictions of the new physics with what he sees as the flabbiness of Marx's theory of history and Freud's psychoanalysis. For Popper, a theory is falsified by the conflicting experimental facts and critical discussion of an alternative theory. In this case, a corroborated theory is one where a failure to falsify has occurred.

Popper indicates that we need rules against immunizing stratagems if we are to distinguish between science and nonscience. Immunizing stratagems are arrangements (e.g., in the auxiliary hypotheses) that can protect the central hypothesis from disproof. Popper proposes some twenty such rules. For example, he states that "those theories should be given preference which can be most severely tested,"[34] that "in the case of a threat to our system we will not save it by any kind of conventionalist stratagem,"[35] and that "auxiliary hypotheses should be used as sparingly as possible."[36] Popper adds that his only reason for proposing his rules is their fruitfulness. The rules are conventions.

In recent years, there has been less agreement in the philosophy of science. Falsificationism is rejected, for instance, by Lakatos, Kuhn, and Feyerabend. Lakatos examines the movement of science not merely in terms of individual theories but of scientific research programs.[37] Such programs, he argues, consist of hard-core and protective belt theories. The example he gives of the former is Ptolemaic circular motion, a hard-core theory that was protected from observational falsification by a protective belt of theory about epicycles and deferents. He distinguishes between progressive and degenerating research programs, and his claim is that research programs move not by falsification but by a positive heuristic.

Thomas Kuhn seems to have captivated the imagination in the public administration field, and perhaps other social science disciplines, in the sense that he has popularized the notion of paradigms. Kuhn himself thought that the social sciences present preparadigms. This positive reception could be because the social sciences seem awash with a multiplicity of preparadigms (or paradigms).

Unlike Popper, who gives a normative prescription, Kuhn, in *The Structure of Scientific Revolutions,* is interested in giving a positive description of natural science practice.[38] For Kuhn, there is no definite scientific methodology; this point is the critical one. Details of his position seem to have changed between editions of his book. In the first edition, Kuhn describes the history of science as consisting of long periods of normal science (characterized by problem solving within the context of an orthodox framework) that are interrupted by revolutionary science. During the revolutionary period, a paradigm or gestalt shift occurs. Examples of such revolutions are the Copernican and the Einsteinian revolutions. According to Kuhn in the first edition, there is such a radical paradigm shift that the paradigms are incommensurable. In the second edition, he abandons the notion of a paradigm as a world view. For him, a lack of communication between paradigms no longer exists; paradigms, now referring to smaller groups, interpenetrate.

Feyerabend's 1975 *Against Method* presents a strong view that scientific knowledge is in no sense privileged and that no preferred scientific methodology exists.[39] For Feyerabend, pluralism is essential to scientific development, and many world views are needed. Feyerabend thinks that observations are unreliable because they are tainted with theories; falsified theories, like astrology, may have truth in them. As he writes, "Knowledge is not a series of self-consistent theories that converge towards an ideal view: it is not a gradual approach to the truth. It is rather an ever increasing ocean of mutually incompatible alternatives, each single theory . . . forcing the others into greater articulation and all of them contributing via this process of competition, to the development of our consciousness."[40]

THE ETHICAL ENTERPRISE

"The rediscovery of the ethical enterprise" is the heading Carol Lewis uses to describe what she sees as a renewal of interest in administrative ethics.[41] She describes the theoretical roots of public administration—scientific management and human relations—as treating ethics concerns only instrumentally. She describes "the amoral machine" as having won in the Brownlow Committee, in Gulick, and in those supporting "the dogma of public administration that dominates even today"; the "developing social sciences such as sociology, anthropology, psychology, economics, and political science also contributed to the temporary triumph of amoral public management."[42] She sees administrative ethics emerging as "a concern in its own right" after such events as the horrors of wars, the harmful effects of some bureaucratic actions, and a realization of the limits of decision making. Such revival of the ethics enterprise as has occurred in public administration is a natural reaction to political and public interest in the subject, an interest reflected in developments such as the growth of ethics machinery in the federal government. Cooper notes that interest in administrative ethics has "mushroomed" since 1980, as indicated by such items as the demand for training sessions, the increase in journal articles on the subject, and attendance at workshops on the topic at the annual conferences of the American Society for Public Administration.[43]

There is a paradox for the scientific study of public administration in any such revival of interest and rediscovery of the ethical enterprise. This paradox lies in how to reconcile the positivist study of public administration with the normative enterprise. Performing administrative ethics is more than merely switching the specification of agency ends from "efficiency" to "efficiency moralized up." Its study is not susceptible to the scientific method; an important ingredient is philosophical analysis.

The history of ethics promises significant limits on the extent of the agreement that can be expected on what we ought to do and why we ought to do it. Disagreement can be found regarding whether core values exist, and disagreement can be found regarding particular values (e.g., "right to life" or "right to choose"). Disagreement exists about the status of moral claims (e.g., subjective or objective). Consider only two of the recent views on the nature of justice; Rawls[44] and Nozick[45] offer two divergent views, and, although we may prefer one, we must recognize that the other is not to be dismissed. It is tempting to agree with Joyce Hendricks, who concludes from her chapter on ethics, "Perhaps the most important lessons to be gained from this chapter are that . . . we are ultimately on our own in deciding what to believe, and . . . making moral decisions is hard work with no guarantee of reaching certainty. For many of our moral decisions, decisive reasons can be given; and for others, thinking through the issue as best we can will at least help us gain the clarity and focus necessary to make a reasonable and responsible decision."[46]

Consider these apple stories. Weber summarizes his position (which we also discussed in chapters 1 and 2) in this way: "The fate of an epoch which has eaten of the tree of knowledge is that it must know that we cannot learn the meaning of the world from the results of its analysis, be it ever so perfect; it must be rather in a position to create this meaning itself. It must recognize that general views of life and the universe can never be the products of empirical knowledge, and that the highest ideals, which move us forcefully, are always formed only in the struggle with other ideals which are just as sacred to others as ours are to us."[47] Whether Weber was right to speak of antinomies in the study of ethics is open to dispute. Nevertheless, at a minimum, there is a certain lack of closure in philosophical ethics—a lack that adds to the difficulty of any attempt (if such an attempt is even feasible) to join value-free science with the study of values.

A marble relief from 460 B.C. or so in the Archaeological Museum at Olympia tells another apple (albeit nonethics) story, which can be understood as symbolizing the difficulty of closure on such matters. It shows Herakles (Hercules) supporting the heavens while Atlas returns with golden apples from the tree of life, whereby on completion of this final labor Herakles gains immortality. The story in Genesis, which I assume is unrelated, is startlingly similar, although it reports a different divine reaction. In Genesis, the reaction included snakes crawling on their bellies, childbirth pains, and banishment from Eden. In the case of Herakles, the goddess Athena even gave him a hand.

Administrative ethics, looking at the ethics of individuals in organizations and the ethics of organizations, rightly has become more fashionable. Nevertheless, it can only be conducted properly if it is approached in a philosophical and universalist manner. That philosophy should play some part is certainly recognized. For example, Kathryn Denhardt argues that the further development of philosophical traditions is "necessary in that by focusing only on the current state of public administration the field risks developing a narrowly interpreted, self-serving ethic that will neither serve the test of time nor serve the public interest."[48] The danger of administrative ethics as an autonomous subject lies, I suggest, not only in the matter of philosophical skills but also in the possibility of making too much of the adjective "administrative." This refers to the mistake of seeking a metaethical foundation in the administrative realm.

Let us explain this problem by examining the additional difficulty of reconciling the universalism of the scientific method with any particularism in administrative ethics (e.g., in the development of an American administrative ethics). If a subject is landlocked in one nation, then finding ways of just endorsing contemporary local societal values can result; one of these ways is, as suggested, to justify administrative responsibility in terms of local societal needs. As it has in American administrative ethics, this justification can take such forms as endorsing obeying the existing law and subscribing to existing core values. Such regrettable moves are encouraged by the significant difficulty in specifying a content that can exert a rational or nonrational grip on administrators.[49] It is even harder to specify a content that could have a grip on someone with an emotional disposition to think otherwise, on someone not open to rational persuasion, or on someone who thinks that ethics are her private concern.

Consider Carol Lewis's claim, in her American Society for Public Administration publication, that "public managers are obligated to implement and comply with the law."[50] One of the anchors contemplated is the local law, especially constitutional law. As she writes, "Not all legal formulations are of equal weight. The oaths (noted below) . . . reflect the primary position of the Constitution. Public service is both rooted in and bound by the Constitution's provisions. They are the ethical manager's framework for action and the citizen's basis for trust."[51] First, her main reason for claiming this is her view that democracy depends on public trust through voluntary compliance. Nevertheless, it seems a stretch to go from "George is breaking what he considers an unwise law" to "George is killing democracy"; no free riding is allowed. She supports her argument by saying that public officials take oaths, and promise keeping and truth telling (even George's) are essential to democracy— as if a promise could always be trumps and as if "truth telling is truth telling is truth telling." Second, her prescription does not seem to have the capability to be universalized. Addressing the question of whether a manager who believes a law to be unjust or immoral is ethically obliged to comply, she seems to be saying that it could not happen here. As she writes, "If a public manager believes a law is unjust or immoral, is he or she ethically obligated to comply? Or does another, higher law prevail? Managers today know there exists the possibility of an unconstitutional order, an evil empire. . . . This argument is a red herring. It changes the subject from legitimate government to illegitimate regime. It changes the question from 'what now?' to 'what if?' It is irrelevant to the contemporary constitutional system of American public service."[52] She then goes on to consider unjust human laws, judged unjust in terms of religion or philosophy. In this case, she says that the "ethical manager may not use public office to dissent as a citizen."[53] The contrary case is easily made. It seems clear that the law and morality are not synonymous; the law can be made not only for moral but also for public order or for other purposes. Most public administrators would also recognize that often enough it is true that, in the words Dickens wrote for Mr. Bumble, the law is an ass: "If the law supposes that," said Mr. Bumble, . . . "the law is a ass—a idiot."[54] Those particular provisions of the law—constitutional or other—that instituted slavery, that provided for restaurants and other facilities for whites only, and that confined Japanese-Americans to detention camps were surely as Mr. Bumble described.

It is not improper to hold that core values exist and that they are possibly contained in a constitution. (It is not improper to maintain that the Constitution does not say what it seems to say, even for the odd view that the Founding Fathers did not exclude blacks from the rights of man: "The concession to slavery here was not in somehow paring the slave down to three-fifths but in counting him for as much as three-fifths of a free person."[55]) Nevertheless, it is unconvincing to hold that this matter does not have to be demonstrated provision by provision.

Kathryn Denhardt provides her analysis of the public administration models or frameworks that were in existence at various points during the last fifty or so years. Six of the seven models mention the need for the administrator to respect "core values." Two are given as examples:

> 1950's—To be ethical requires that an administrator examine and question the standards, or assumptions, by which administrative decisions are made. The standards should reflect to some degree the core values of our society though not relying exclusively on custom and tradition.

> After Rohr—To be ethical requires that an administrator be able to independently engage in the process of reasonably examining and questioning the standards by which administrative decisions are made. The content of the standards may change over time as social values are better understood, or new social concerns are expressed. An administrator should be ready to adapt decision standards to these changes, always reflecting a commitment to the core values of our society. The administrator must recognize that he or she will be held personally and professionally accountable for the decisions made and for the ethical standards which inform these decisions.[56]

Again, respecting core values is mentioned as part of Kathryn Denhardt's own specification, except, as she indicates, "the term 'core values' might be misleading and that instead the 'morality' of society might be a better term."[57]

A measure of arbitrariness seems to be involved in selecting particular values as "core." William Morrow, for instance, writes about what he calls "the enduring traditions of public administration."[58] For him, these traditions are procedural democracy, substantive democracy, efficiency, and neutrality. Consider the last item: why would it be chosen? Reasons may include that Morrow believes that neutrality is a good thing, that the opposite is hard to imagine, that some laws encourage it, and that other people have spoken in favor of it. On the other hand, governmental service has had a parallel tradition, usually smaller, of nonneutrality. Others have suggested other values; examples include avoiding a permanent elite, stressing individual autonomy, and focusing on the future.[59] Consider the last item: why should it be or not be chosen? Reasons for choosing it may include that most of us like to do it and that it fits with the entrepreneurial society. On the other hand, some look back on enduring traditions, on the Constitution, and on the intentions of the Founders. We could go either way with our enduring traditions about power. We could follow Jefferson and Madison and speak of a power-diffusing value, or we could follow Hamilton and speak of a power-concentrating value.[60]

If selecting core values is so arbitrary, why does a substantial body of public administration thinking speak of core values? Various possibilities exist. For example, perhaps the alternative is unsettling; it is not nice to say, "The idea that my country has core values is sentimental talk to which I will give only lip service." The reality that we should face (and discuss) is the possibility, introduced earlier, that a cultural core is not quite the same as a core that is also a moral core and that the former is being mistaken for the latter.

Regarding the Constitution and the core as authorities on morality, the reader may be reminded of Socrates's question to Euthyphro: "Is it holy because the gods approve it, or do they approve it because it is holy?"[61] Similarly, is it ethical because the Constitution says it, or does the Constitution say it because it is ethical? Is it importantly moral because it is in the core set of values, or is it in the core set of values because it is importantly moral? This point is critical because the notion of core values has little significance if it is entirely cultural rather than also moral; that is, a core moral value is not merely a value that (as a descriptive matter) is central to a society. The French can be seen as having cultural core values that include love of liberty and love of the French language. This claim is not as interesting as one that states that these cultural values have moral claims on the behavior of all French citizens. A core moral value is one that has a moral grip on our behavior—a moral claim to affect our behavior. It is not enough that the grip be merely legal or historical or traditional; we must see it as a moral obligation.

Consider more closely a purely cultural set of core values. For example, Ruth Benedict describes a culture as a coherent system of values that grows up around some central core preferences.[62] Practices, habits, and attitudes that are congenial with the core are retained as normal, and the noncongruent are rejected as abnormal. She gives some dramatic examples of how, in her view, the categories of normal and abnormal are culturally defined. She describes one Melanesian society that is built on paranoia. She writes that they are so preoccupied with poisoning that women never leave their cooking pots unattended; they believe that everyone else's food is poisoned, and so they never share seed. The crazy person in that society is not someone our society might call a homicidal maniac; it is the "man of sunny, kindly disposition who liked work and liked to be helpful." Another of her examples is the person exhibiting trance and catalepsy. Regarded in our society as deviant, a person with these manifestations is highly valued in many societies—and Benedict recalls that the ecstatic experience was the mark of sainthood in medieval Europe. Benedict's view is subjectivist. Societies have core cultures, but morality for her is only habit, what is normal for that particular society. If we became administrators in that Melanesian society's government (if it has one), we must remember to act in a paranoid manner, and we must design our programs on a thoroughly paranoid basis. Not to do so might be fatal, but surely no moral grip is on us to do so.

Undeniably, such a core set of values, social customs, or mores can have a powerful grip, but it is not a moral grip. Do you recall watching the recent (or any other) presidential inaugural? On that day and during the previous transition period and election campaign, the watcher hardly could have been unconscious of the work of building a political core of values and attitudes. The television and other images of the president-elect were crafted to project the attitudes and values that he wishes to be accepted by the nation. The imaging was also designed to develop a grip for these same messages, including development of a grip of acceptance of the democratic process (by comments on what are seen as the strengths of this governmental system [e.g., its capability to transfer power peacefully]) and of the personal worth of the new president (showing him as a compassionate person, showing him in regal settings). The appeal was made in emotional and intellectual terms, and the core set of values projected was crafted within the context of values projected by other sources in society. It seems misleading to reify such values, treating them as if they had lives of their own under such a heading as "the enduring values." These other value sets come from institutions such as schools (and not only from civics classes and ceremonies such as each morning's pledge of allegiance), families, churches, television, peer groups, work and play organizations, and other sources. The way in which societies develop and accept the ruling set of values has been explained in various ways; for instance, it can be explained in terms of a dominant class, or a dominant group, or in some other way. Many people, both supporters of the new president and others, responded positively to the projected set of values and to the implicit and explicit appeals for support; they had been gripped, to a greater or less extent. Others, especially supporters of the previous president, had not been gripped. Nevertheless, no one should say that the latter are morally wrong; no one should criticize any person who later changes his or her mind. There is no moral obligation in the grip; there is no "ought."

It is not enough to argue that procedural arrangements can be made in a society for letting public employees know the binding provisions of that society's morality. This argument could be developed by discussing several types of formal rationality; Kolb explains them and gives his view that it can be disputed which of the lines would be supported by Max Weber.[63] Formal rationality, it will be recalled, is where rationality does not include as given a set of values; by contrast, substantive rationality would include such a value set. Kolb distinguishes three kinds of formal rationality that fall on a spectrum. A decisionist model, he explains, is where values are installed by an authority such as a dictator or an oligarchy. A pragmatic model is where the administrative system evaluates and changes its own goals in the light of experience, where the goals are not specified from the outside but just grow like Topsy. A technocratic model is where no specified values exist beyond those of operating the administrative and other societal machinery efficiently. Later, Kolb mentions a bureaucratic society that legitimates power in terms of efficiency and some procedural rules. Nevertheless, the argument does not go through. There is no moral grip (as opposed to legal or other grip) in any of these alternatives.

To repeat the claim: no moral grip for ethical precepts can be found in administrative or political structure or in the mere fact that societies develop a set of attitudes (or prejudices) that continue for periods. It was part of the ethos, core set of values that gave coherence to the people, before the Civil War, that some persons should be slaves. Understandably, nonacceptance of this core value could impede a career or even social relationships, but the claim here is that this grip carried no moral obligation.

This claim is not to suggest that the fact of differing core values is decisive regarding whether there is a moral core for humankind. Undeniably, cultures have distinct notions of approved behaviors, and what is acceptable behavior in our own society changes over time. Nevertheless, some people, such as James Rachels, argue that some rules are needed as core values in any society.[64] His view is that differing behaviors often reflect the same underlying value. He quotes Herodotus's story about how the Greeks were horrified that the Callatians would eat the dead bodies of their fathers, and how the Callatians were horrified that the Greeks would cremate the bodies of their dead fathers. Although the practices differed, a common value existed: respect for the body of one's dead father. Rachels does not deny that some of our values, which we might mistakenly describe as "natural," are really only cultural derivations. Nevertheless, beyond these peripheral values, he sees some values as core—common to all societies. This core is more than a mere cultural phenomenon.

A philosophical question that this issue poses concerns the nature of a "moral grip," the character and operation of such an "ought." It is an issue for moral philosophy, and such questions tend to interrelate with other positions, such as the metaphysical. The variety of views is large. It is a variety that includes the idea that no difference really exists between ethos and ethics; that is, there is no such thing as a moral grip. It includes holders of intuitionist and natural law views (subscribing to various value sets); it includes others, such as Kantians and utilitarians, who support competing positions. Hume explains ethics in terms of emotions; Kant appeals to reason; Aristotle speaks in terms of eudaimonia; and so on. The nature of such a foundation, or grip, is beyond the traditional scope of public administration. Another limit is encountered, the discipline's boundary.

VERSTEHEN

The objective sought in positivist science is explanation, permitting the prediction and control that McCloskey mentions in his first rule for positivism (or modernism). This objective is sought at a price that includes information lost in terms of *Verstehen,* understanding.[65] The price includes rejection of first-hand knowledge in the sense of knowledge from within. Simon, as indicated at the beginning of this chapter, rejects such first-hand knowing. B. F. Skinner followed a similar course in psychology, and operant conditioning is the governing law. Others have followed suit (e.g., the behavioralists in political science and the economists to the extent that they rely on the theory of revealed preference). As Habermas sees Verstehen, "The problem of Verstehen is of methodological importance in the humanities and social sciences primarily because the scientist cannot gain access to a symbolically pre-structured reality through observation alone, and because understanding meaning (Sinnverstehen) cannot be methodically brought under control in the same way as can observation in the course of experimentation. The social scientist basically has no other access to the lifeworld than the social-scientific layman does."[66]

To comprehend this distinction between understanding and explanation, we should recall the distinction, long recognized, between human action and mere human behavior—between knowing as identifying reasons and knowing as identifying causality. Human action is behavior that we will, that we control, that we intend; behavior is any movement of the body or body part. Rosenberg describes it as the difference between a wink and a blink, speaking and snoring, jumping and falling, suicide and dying.[67] Nevertheless, definition of the terms presents problems, and the distinction between the two can present borderline difficulties. For example, J. B. Watson included physiological processes as behaviors; B. F. Skinner excluded these processes, and he took as his unit of behavioral analysis "molar behavior," such as running and blinking (or a pigeon pressing a bar).

In recalling the distinction between identifying reasons and identifying causality, consider the example of the jogger as presented by Rosenberg.[68] Why does the jogger jog? Is it because she believes jogging is good for her, and she wants to do things that are good for her—a reasons explanation? Or, is it because her daily jogging has had a physiological effect on her body, and she now experiences a "runner's high" when she runs and some physiological punishment when she does not run—a causal explanation? The relationship is complex. For example, sometimes reasons can be causes; sometimes causes can be reasons. The literature on causes and reasons is substantial and complex; Rosenberg has a useful guide to the literature.[69]

It seems natural to suppose that a science of human or societal behavior, such as public administration, would seek to understand actions. This search would involve understanding the reasons for (and not necessarily the causes of) the actions. Reasons that we usually consider sufficient explanations are those made in terms of beliefs and desires. As Rosenberg explains, this attempt to understand uses the basic principles of folk psychology. He offers what he characterizes as an "oversimplified general statement" that lies behind our folk psychology predictions of how people will behave: "[G]iven any person x, if x wants d and x believes that a is a means to attain d, under the circumstances, then x does a."[70] Significant problems exist with this idea, as Rosenberg and others have explained. As examples, this proposition cannot be falsified. It is hard to obtain information on beliefs and desires independently of consideration of the actions themselves, and the number of relevant beliefs and actions is so great that explanations of actions are hard to pin down.

Max Weber considers action explanations (including consideration of beliefs and desires) to be critical in social science, and he calls for the identification of a law to connect beliefs and desires and action.[71] For him, causation is a matter of laws, and his view (noted in chapter 2) is that the social sciences in this respect should be no different than the natural sciences. We can take this view to imply that Weber would have held that a basic approach needed in public administration would be to improve on the folk psychology noted above. In the intervening years, such an approach has had both supporters and opponents.

SUMMARY

The development of modernist public administration on positivist lines also leads to contraries, no less than does the particularism discussed in the last chapter. This development on positivist lines has taken various forms in public administration: establishing an administrative science, conducting applied science, and pursuing the eclectic use of social science methodology.

Scientific statements are intended to be epistemologically privileged. Nevertheless, as shown by a review of developments in the philosophy of science, the basis of this privileged status for scientific statements is unclear.

One set of contraries occurs when the study of public administration is limited to a scientific basis, denying equivalent epistemological status to value statements. This limit conflicts with a need to include value judgments, as reflected in recent interest in administrative ethics. Administrative ethics suffers from the difficulty of identifying a moral (as opposed to a legal, historical, or traditional) grip for core values. No moral grip can be expected in administrative or political structure or in the mere fact that societies develop attitudes and prejudices that continue for long periods. Another set of contraries faces a public administration that, as science, confines itself to knowledge achieved on an intersubjective basis. This aim is the wish also to include first-hand knowledge and Verstehen.

6

Modernity
Limits of Technologism

To speak of administrative technologies strikes me as a good way to designate the interrelated arts, sciences and so forth.

—Waldo[1]

Members of the civilization which initiated modern technology now express a fear of the Americanization of Europe, and state that fear in their identification of the United States with the pure will to technique. This may be an expression of their deeper fear that their own society in becoming sheerly modern has at last and perhaps finally lost touch with its primal.

—Grant[2]

Only human pride argues that the apparent intricacies of our path stem from a quite different source than the intricacy of the ant's path.

—Simon[3]

ADVANCED TECHNOLOGY IS a characteristic of the modern age. As Lynn White writes, modern technology is distinctively occidental, and Western leadership in technology (and in science) long predates the seventeenth-century scientific revolution and the eighteenth-century industrial revolution: "By the end of the fifteenth century the technological superiority of Europe was such that its small, mutually hostile nations could spill out over all the rest of the world, conquering, looting, and colonizing."[4]

Much of the study of public administration can be seen in terms of technologism—a matter of building public administration tools and developing public administration techniques. The bulk of this effort has been "low tech" and a matter of technics. By contrast, some has been a matter of science-based technical knowledge—what Mumford calls simply "technology." A modernist impetus toward moving from technics to technology has occurred, and some may see public administration developing in this way as a technological study of the artificial.

Conceptualizing public administration as technology can yield useful results.

It will be shown later that this conceptualization might lead to a narrowing of the theory-practice gap, but the development of public administration as technology also leads to some paradoxes. Conceptualized in such terms as administrative science or social engineering, the needs of public administration as technology require resources that are beyond the scope of public administration as a subject area to provide. There is a need for scientific knowledge, as public administration as technology is induced to go beyond the limitations of prescience; this need leads to the paradoxes that were described in chapter 5 under the heading of scientism. It also leads to a resource difficulty parallel to that noted in the previous sentence for public administration conceptualized as administrative science or social engineering. There is another paradox—that between public administration as promoter of technological system and public administration as facilitator of individuality. Before explaining these claims, we should look further into public administration as a matter of technology.

PUBLIC ADMINISTRATION AS LOW TECH

The claim is made that a line of development for public administration has been, and can be, as technology. The idea is not new. Recall Waldo, for example. He writes, "I view administration as a number of more or less interrelated arts, sciences, attitudes, and procedures that develop in history and flow through history. To speak of administrative technologies strikes me as a good way to designate the interrelated arts, sciences and so forth."[5]

This claim about public administration as technology is made within the terms of a broad understanding of the nature of technology. For example, the mistake should not be made of equating technology with physical technology. As Agassi writes, "Once we realize that equating technology with physical technology means the oversight of social and political technology, then we should be not so surprised at the great tremors to society . . . that technology causes; old-fashioned technology is too short-sighted for words."[6] It is better to see technology as having physical, social, political, and other aspects.

As Mitcham explains, many varieties of understanding of the term *technology* exist, some less broad than others. His examples of broad definitions are "any tool or technique, any product or process, any physical equipment or method of doing or making, by which human capability is extended" (Schon), and "what things are done or made . . . and how things are done or made" (Singer). His examples of narrower definitions would confine the term to material construction, limit it to the making and doing that is influenced by modern science, and restrict it to making and using artifacts. Mitcham explains the "large variety of apparently incompatible definitions" that have been offered and notes:

Technology has been variously described as sensorimotor skills (Feibleman), applied science (Bunge), design (engineers themselves), efficiency (Bavink, Skolimowski), rational efficient action (Ellul), neutral means (Jaspers), means for economic purposes (Gottl-Ottlilienfeld and other economists), means for socially set purposes (Jarvie), control of the environment to meet human needs (Carpenter), pursuit of power (Mumford, Spengler), means for the realization of the Gestalt of the worker (Jünger) or any supernatural self-concept (Ortega), human liberation (Masthene, Macpherson), self-initiated salvation (Brinkmann), invention and the material realization of transcendent forms (Dessauer), a "provoking, setting up disclosure of nature" (Heidegger), etc.[7]

He also gives citations for these summaries.

Public administration as technology would seek "knowing how" rather than "knowing that." The output of such a study could be product technologies or, more usually, process technologies; they could be high tech or low tech. The goals of public administration as knowledge building and public administration as technology differ. As knowledge building, the science of public administration seeks to explain; as hermeneutics, it seeks to understand. Public administration as technology seeks (in Karl Popper's terms) to build or to do. Nonetheless, technology also involves knowledge, and the line between knowledge building and technology—no less than that between high and low tech—is difficult to draw. Consider science and technology. There are examples of science-based technologies (e.g., the electrical industry, nuclear engineering, and biotechnology) and examples of technology-based sciences (e.g., mining, metallurgy, and medicine). Nevertheless, despite such a difficulty, the differences between science and technology are important. Technology does not have the same goals of universality and explanation or the same emphasis on grounding the claims in acceptable scientific procedure, and it has a willingness to apply know-how even when we are not sure why the know-how works. This attitude can lead to different results, as can be illustrated by considering the case of imprecise technologies such as the "proverbs of Public Administration," those noted by Simon.[8] He criticized their status as principles or science, but he saw them as criteria for describing and diagnosing. As low-tech technology, they can have value.

High tech (or new technology or advanced technology) is a somewhat slippery term. One description is that it includes "companies that are engaged in the design, development and introduction of new products and/or innovative manufacturing processes through the systematic application of scientific and technical knowledge."[9] This description is useful in that it makes clear that the term applies to processes as well as to products. It is not useful if it implies that innovation is necessarily more important than imitation. For example, Levitt claims that the greatest flow of newness is imitation: "IBM got into computers as an imitator; Texas Instruments into transistors as an imitator."[10] High tech refers not only to changes in new fields such as microelectronics, biotechnology, and telecommunications but also to changes in traditional industries. As Johnson puts it, "The essence of advanced technology would seem to be the ability to integrate and apply scientific and engineering knowledge to complex problems."[11] Measures used reflect these descriptions. One measure defines high-tech industries as those in which the proportion of the engineers, engineering technicians, computer scientists, life scientists, and mathematicians exceeds the national average.[12] The Bureau of Labor Statistics has developed definitions, with one similar to Markusen's.

> These three specific definitions consider an industry as high-tech if (1) its technology-oriented workers account for a proportion of total employment that is at least one and a half times the average of all industries; (2) the ratio of R and D expenditures to net sales is at least twice the average for all industries; and (3) it satisfies two conditions: (a) its proportion of technology-oriented workers is equal to or greater than the average for all manufacturing industries, and (b) its ratio of R and D expenditures to sales is close or above the average of all manufacturing industries.[13]

Notably, no government could even be measured on the basis of these definitions; being high tech is treated as entirely a private enterprise manufacturing matter.

Government and high tech could be closer bedfellows, although bedfellows they already are. Consider government, especially the Department of Defense, as a promoter and user of high-tech research. There are untold additional possibilities for high tech and public administration high tech in government. Recall the achievements and the possibilities of the electronic office.[14] Office automation has been described by Goldfield as passing through stages, all of which in only a few years probably will seem old-fashioned. These stages range from the first level, where office systems provide one or two isolated applications, such as word processing, to the fourth level, which is the "company-wide general-purpose office system . . . to provide extra facilities for the large base of terminal users. These facilities [would] typically include a standard user interface to mainstream computer systems, store-and-forward electronic mail, and content-addressable electronic information retrieval facilities."[15] This fourth stage seems radically less fundamental than the financial assembly lines, as represented by the automated teller and electronic money processing systems, that are revolutionizing the increasingly high-tech banking industry.

Public administration technology is essentially low-tech process technology, consisting of established sets of socially constituted human practices and procedures. Consider the public administration technologies of budgeting and organization. Other examples could be added (e.g., personnel or human resources development). Alternatively, these technologies might be considered as constituent subtechnologies within the single technology, public administration itself. Chapter 2 considered such practices in terms of their social construction; this chapter asks the reader to view the sets of practices as technological.

Budgeting, discussed as a social construct in chapter 2, can be seen as a low-tech technological instrument or instruments, a set of technical practices. The study of budgeting can be viewed as a matter of technology intended to develop and improve the technological instrument. Recall the developments—the improvements in the craft (or technology) of budgeting—that have been achieved. In budgeting, a history can be traced that moves from budgets as mere statements of expenditures and revenues to budgets as planning and management tools, and the issues have included the executive budget, itemization, and audit and control. Many "inventors," some celebrated and many unknown, have made pragmatic contributions to the development of the technology. The landmark advances in the United States government form a framework for discussing this strand of what can be seen as technological development: the 1912 Taft Commission; the executive budget in the 1921 Budget and Accounting Act; the 1939 White House Reorganization Act, moving the budget to the executive; the 1946 Employment Act, institutionalizing (as it were) the Keynesian view of budgeting; the 1949 Hoover Commission, speaking of performance budgeting; the subsequent change in emphasis from transactions to systems; the 1961 introduction of the planning-programming-budgeting system in the Department of Defense; the 1965 extension of the planning-programming-budgeting system to the domestic agencies; the 1968 adoption of management by objectives; the 1970 Legislative Reorganization Act, standardizing budget codes; the 1974 Congressional Budget and Improvement Act; and zero-base budgeting, introduced in President Carter's administration. All these developments were part of the movement from "green eyeshade" budgets (to repeat the term used in chapter 2) to budgets as instruments of executive management. To a large extent, we now have budgets that are much more effective policy-making and program administration tools. It is appreciated that some would consider the present budgeting system in the United States to be flawed; it is a system where the presidential budget is of less significance than it should be, for example, and where agencies and interest groups are encouraged to make their own accommodations with appropriate congressional committees and members of Congress. Therefore, we can expect continuing "technical" improvements to the set of practices and procedures that make up the technology of modern budgeting.

The art of developing and strengthening organizations is another example of socially constituted low-tech technology. Organizations are machines for programmatic objectives and other purposes; the study of organizations can be seen partly as a matter of technology, even though technology may be only a minor reason for hierarchy and centralization. The principles for constructing hierarchies can reflect the view of organization as a technological activity. During the life of public administration theory, various technical innovations and steps have tended toward centralizing management and control under the chief executive. A tendency to centralize under the president has occurred, and a history of such a tendency can be laid out for the U.S. government. The same is true for state governors and other chief executives. For instance, one of the more important low-tech technical improvements at the local level was the city manager movement early in the twentieth century.

ADVANTAGES OF A TECHNOLOGICAL EMPHASIS

Substantial gains might be expected from developing the study of public administration in terms of technology (i.e., pursuing the overall goal for the discipline of making and doing). More could be achieved along these lines. As noted earlier, this focus may help to address the theory-practice gap. Such a change and such gains will be facilitated if the emphasis is sought with a clearer view of the nature of technology.[16]

There is such a theory-practice gap. Typically, public agencies are not highly receptive to new ideas about public administration in the sense that the functioning of public agencies is not markedly knowledge-based. In other words, agencies are deficient in terms of being the clients and beneficiaries of public administration—or any other—theory. This point can be clarified by considering what the situation would be if public agencies had been able to follow Alice Rivlin's advice on management through experimentation. Assessing what she considers to be the quiet revolution effected by the then-recent budgetary innovation, Rivlin writes of the progress that has been made in identifying and measuring problems and in analyzing the initial costs and benefits of programs.[17] Nevertheless, she points out, little progress has been achieved in comparing the benefits of programs (e.g., curing cancer versus teaching children to read), and little is known about how to produce more effective social services. One of her suggestions (among several that included decentralization, community control, and a marker voucher system) is to gather the needed information through natural, random, and systematic experimentation.

Consider an example of what Rivlin says. Police Chief X, instead of simply instituting "good program B" throughout the city, would design the implementation of the program in such a way that information can be obtained regarding what works and what does not work. Good program B might be a new idea for reducing homicides. Rather than merely implementing the program for all, the police agency taking Rivlin's advice might conduct an evaluation and institute the program in area X and keep area Y as a control group. The police agency in this case would be doing what is now routine in medical research. An outstanding feature of police policy making and administration is that the police community simply does not know which programs work.[18] If principles similar to those used in police practice had been followed in medicine, medical practice would be less sophisticated than it is now.

Viewing public administration as technology suggests recognizing that practitioners should assume more ownership for public administration theory.[19] The study of public administration as technology, it may be thought, should not be left so much to academics; bureaucrats, in this respect, should assume more responsibility for bureaucracy. Of course, practitioners are included in the "discipline" of public administration (e.g., both practitioners and academics are active members of organizations such as the American Society for Public Administration). Nevertheless, more ownership by practitioners would be helpful, especially because so much of public administration technology remains a matter of technics. The help, although real, would be limited to the extent that these practitioners are trapped within the very systems they hope to redesign.

A more thoroughgoing practice of public administration as technology would require further development. For example, organization and incentives affecting the technology of public administration would need redevelopment. More effective arrangements are needed to facilitate the work of those who seek improvements in the sets, and systems, of nuts and bolts. Some practitioners see academics as unfit to be public administration theorists. They argue that it is difficult to appreciate the problems of administration without having been an administrator; for example, one can learn more about the complexities of personnel management by performing all the work that is required to fire an incompetent subordinate rather than by reading about it. They also argue that some people are "natural" administrators. The real merit in this line of argument is that progress in public administration as technology requires a reshaping of the craft. As a first step, it would be helpful if governments would establish public administration research and development units for the encouragement of public administration process technology.

Such a readjustment in public administration would be facilitated by an understanding of the wide scope of technology. The advantages of a clearer view can be grasped more firmly by considering the useful typology that Mitcham presents. He uses a three-dimensional grid. The first dimension in his typology is subject or material distinctions, such as between chemical and electrical technologies. The second is functional distinctions, and the third is social or historical distinctions. The most interesting of these are the functional or structural distinctions. He distinguishes technology-as-knowledge, technology-as-process, technology-as-product, and technology-as-will. These four categories can be collapsed into the two main ones mentioned earlier—process and product technologies; the others, concerning knowledge and will, can be expressed as subelements of the main two categories. Nevertheless, it is helpful to follow Mitcham's four groupings, and the reader is asked to think how public administration examples could be plugged into the categories.

Technology-as-knowledge is described as including unconscious sensorimotor awareness of how to make or use some artifact, technical maxims or prescientific rules of thumb, descriptive laws or statements, and technological laws. The proverbs of administration mentioned earlier constitute a public administration example. Technology-as-process is said to include inventing, designing, making, operating, and managing and the functions of planning, teaching, consulting, and systems engineering. Public administration systems analysis is an illustration. Technology-as-product is described as including utensils, apparatus, utilities, tools, machines, and automatons or automated/cybernated machines. A civil service examination might be a public administration example, albeit a humble one. Mitcham writes that technology-as-will has been described as will to survive, will to power, will to freedom, will to help others, will to make money, will to be famous, and will to realize any self-concept.[20] Here, leadership theory and ethics might provide examples applicable to the field of public administration.

Drawbacks to this line exist. Any "new" promise for public administration as a technology is dulled by the realization that a main part of public administration during its history has been, despite the scientific work and rhetoric, essentially technological. For example, the overriding motive force of the first forty or so years (the early years) of American public administration was reform—a notion that is roughly equivalent to technology in the sense of technics. *Technics* in this case refers to a technological approach that is not science-based; like potting or other crafts activities, it is prescientific. American public administration is usually considered to have been born in the 1880s with the publication of Woodrow Wilson's "The Study of Administration" and perhaps with the passage of the Pendleton Act.[21] These developments began a period of reform that is considered to have lasted until the New Deal. By the turn of the century, the frontier was closing, the population had grown, factories were becoming large, and the corruption and inefficiencies of government and other aspects of life were being recognized. This period was the time of an earlier "Great Society," and the need for reforms was considered urgent. Uveges and Keller, cited earlier, give the following subheadings to their description of public management in American life: 1880s, Intimations and Foundations; 1890s, Prelude Continued; 1900s, Transformation in Practice; 1910s, Reform Continued and Intensified; 1920s, Maturation of the Public Interest Model.[22]

In this period it seemed clear what ought to be done. The task of American public administration (insofar as there really was a subject or discipline of public administration) was to implement what can be called the public administration project: improve the personnel system, the budgeting system, and the organizational structure and (above all) establish a generalist class of public administrators who can manage the bureaucracies; this agenda was the essence of "the" American public administration project. Two caveats should be added. First, others may wish to change particulars (or ways of expressing them) in this listing of the agenda (e.g., emphasizing municipal reform). Second, it would be misleading to suppose that important developments in understanding did not occur during this period. Nevertheless, the claim is that the primary need—the major motive force—was reform, a matter of technics.

The influence of public administration as technology has continued; the "subject matter givens" (noted in the previous paragraph) have tended to influence American public administration throughout its history. Indeed, the history of American public administration during the last one hundred or so years can be traced in terms of these elements. The notion of the generalist administrator, for example, is an assumption—spoken or not—of most public administration education programs. Rather than have a program specialist (such as a physician or a lawyer) run a governmental agency (such as a health or a justice department), American public administration has been committed to the notion of a generalist public administrator, that is, the notion of a public administrator who can manage any program. The idea is that "public administration is public administration is public administration." The program might be commerce or labor, but the preeminent management skill needed for the program administrator is public administration (or its equivalent). The phrase "or its equivalent" is added because supporters of a generic view of management would wish to reword this claim about the generalist administrator; they wish to claim instead that management is management is management. Nevertheless, the point is that the notion of the generalist, whether it is circumscribed by the adjective "public" or extended to the generic, is the client-centered technology that is contemplated.

The public administration pitch, the technological pitch, has been demeaned by faddism often enough. An emphasis on technology as technics does carry the danger of encouraging faddism, the quick fix that does not fix. Recent examples are the "total quality management" and the "reinventing government" fashions. The history of public administration practice is replete with such fads and fashions, both on the large scale and in day-to-day local management. When the fad fails, a demoralizing effect on bureaucrats is seen, and the failure must lower the chances for the next, "better" fad. One of the difficulties might be that reforms in administrative techniques are typically introduced as permanent cures, when they should be recognized as the present temporary change (e.g., "This is administrative reform X; it will operate for one year, during which time it is expected to yield good results; and then we will stop doing it."). Such a suggestion itself looks faddish, however. The difficulty is that the pitch is queered not only for the fads but also for genuine technological change, such as use of the generalist public administrator. As long as public administration technology remains at the level of technics, there is less opportunity to separate the genuine change from the fad.

FROM TECHNICS TO TECHNOLOGIES

According to Bunge,

The process of massive conversion of technics into technologies started in mid-nineteenth century, and it is far from completed. Even recent inventions such as the airplane and the light bulb were the work of highly skilled and imaginative artisans, not of scientific engineers. . . . The main difference between [the scientific inventor] and his prescientific predecessor is that he can tap an immense fund of scientific knowledge to get ideas and test them. . . . [Technology] is not just a collection of recipes handed down from master to apprentice, but a process of R and D [research and development].[23]

Technics is a term for prescientific technical knowledge, it will be recalled; the term *technology* refers to science-based technical knowledge. We will indicate below how Mumford questions the assumptions of our commitment to the present form of technical and scientific progress. Nevertheless, Mumford recognizes the radical transformation effected by the impact of mathematics and the physical sciences on technology: "This shift from an empirical, tradition-bound technics to an experimental scientific mode has opened up new realms as those of nuclear energy, supersonic transportation, computer intelligence, and instantaneous planetary communication."[24]

Sociotechnology is technology of close relevance to public administration as technology; Bunge considers other technologies to be engineering, biotechnology, information technology, and general technology.[25] Sociotechnology, as Bunge explains, is considered to consist of social engineering and management science. The distinction is that social engineering deals with management on a societywide basis, and management science concerns a subsystem. Both this choice of focusing on "managing" (rather than another action, such as "communicating") and this division into two categories (rather than some other number) are open to the objection of arbitrariness. Also, the separation from information technology and general technology may seem odd. Nevertheless, the two categories can be adopted for the present because they do permit useful points to be made. Social engineering can be understood as addressing large-scale problems, such as criminality, militarism, poverty, and overpopulation. Management science covers any societal subsystem, such as a government or a private company.

This sociotechnology may be described more clearly as consisting of social systems engineering and management systems engineering. Systems includes conceiving systems as wholes, thinking of parts as interrelated, considering parts as relating to overall functioning, and understanding systems as related to their environments. Churchman talks about systems in terms of total system's objectives (and particularly performance measures of the whole system), the system's environment, resources of the system, components of the system, and management of the system.[26] As he says, every system is embedded in a larger system. Systems theory has been discussed in terms of the contributions of Talcott Parsons, Ludwig von Bertalanffy, and Daniel Katz and Robert Kahn. Katz and Kahn's open systems theory, for example, treats in biological terms the inputs, functions, and outputs of organizations as systems.[27]

Bunge's criteria for seeing sociotechnology as technology are imprecise, perhaps necessarily so. Sociotechnology in both forms is seen as differing "from its traditional counterpart in that (a) it makes use of some of the findings of social science research, (b) it involves fresh scientific research . . . , (c) it uses basic social science (as well as ideological and moral principles) to design (or redesign) sociosystems as well as to plan for their operation, and (d) it attempts to evaluate objectively the performance of sociosystems."[28] The meaning of the phrase "makes use of some of the findings of social research" depends on what one makes of the words "some" and "use." The words can be interpreted generously or strictly, that is, to include or to exclude. Bunge himself says later, "Contemporary management science, though on the right track, still has a long way to go before it becomes fully scientific."[29] The fact is that both management science and social engineering can be seen as either technics or technology.

Bunge assumes the modernist characteristic of technological rationalization, an increasing tendency to move from technics to the technological. This rationalization—the preference for technology as opposed to technics—can be challenged on two preliminary grounds. First, technology may not yield more important results than technics. Management technics and management technology may be cases in point. It is true that management, making appropriate use of information technology and systems techniques, can be productive. Nevertheless, even more important can be the perspectives provided by low-tech change in conceptualizations, the low-tech component of the loose agglomeration that Bunge describes as "the discipline that studies [scientific management] in the light of (a) principles and data drawn from psychology, sociology, and economics; (b) the scientific method . . . and the technological method . . . ; (c) scientific or technological procedures, such as the gathering of statistics, automatic information processing, computer simulation and quality control; and (d) models of organizations and processes, such as block diagrams, decision trees, and mathematical models."[30] Useful progressivity has occurred in the low-tech component of the technology of the manager, for example, and this progressivity is part of management science. Wren describes the history of management as consisting of what he sees as three broad periods: the scientific management era, the social man era, and the modern era.[31] He sees management thought as "the mirror reflection of managerial activity. . . . Management is both a product of and a process in its environment."[32] Granting that environmental factors are significant, it still seems possible to consider the contributions of public administration theory and practice on this point as constituting a continuing set of important technics—as the perspective changing from the "manager as hero figure" to the "manager as competent and humane leader." Recall Taylor, Follett, Barnard, and Simon.[33]

Perhaps the major contribution to the development of this socially constituted "technic" of the manager in Frederick Taylor's scientific management is, to summarize it, that the manager must know and specify the operative's task. Taylor's prescription at the turn of the century is the adoption of scientific management—the development of what he thinks is a true science (although he could have used the term "technics"), the scientific selection of the worker, scientific education and development, and intimate friendly cooperation between management and operatives.[34] He speaks of a need for a mental revolution by both workers and management.

Follett, Barnard, and Simon each specify the functions of the manager in a way that develops the notion of the "manager as competent and humane leader." In Follett's law of the situation, the manager is not seen as issuing orders; instead, the manager and her subordinates together identify the imperative in the common situation. Yet another illustration is Chester Barnard's specification of effectiveness in addition to efficiency, where effectiveness concerns the relationship between the organization's purpose and the organization's environment (and where efficiency refers to the relationships between the chief executive and her subordinates within the organization). The technics (or technology) of management is thus shown to have an additional socially constituted dimension. Another illustration is the specification (e.g., by Follett, Barnard, and Simon) of the importance of anticipation as part of the role of the chief executive; it constitutes a real technical advance. It involves a claim about the "vision thing" of the leader.

Second, the assumption of technological rationalization itself rests on assumptions about the nature of human beings and of technology. Consider Mumford's view of human beings. Mumford opposes the commitment to technical and scientific progress as an end in itself, mainly on the basis of his view that it misconceives the nature of human beings. Mumford sees the human being as a mind maker rather than as a toolmaker: "At its point of origin, then, technics was related to the whole nature of man. Primitive technics are life-centered, not narrowly work-centered, still less production-centered or power-centered."[35] He goes on to write of monotechnics (the pursuit of wealth and power by organizing work activities in a mechanical pattern) and the megamachine (the human machine that could build, say, pyramids). Consider the tenability of the Aristotelian view of technology in the contemporary context. Aristotle (in part) saw technology as a means to some further end. Technology is purely instrumental; technical objects derive meaning and value from the uses to which people put them. Others have stated that it is not clear that contemporary society's technology can be considered to be purely instrumental. A person's house is instrumental in that it is used for shelter, but the technology of the housing industry uses people and materials. Arguably, it is hard to distinguish means from ends, and it is possible to think of human beings as enmeshed in a technological context. We shall return to this argument later. The point of these examples here, it will be recalled, is to suggest that an understanding of technological rationalization depends on one's conception of human beings and technology.

LIMITS OF SOCIOTECHNOLOGY

An optimistic view of the possibilities of technological systems is that public administration as technology should be pursued on a basis that integrates not only systems and management notions but also ethical considerations. The alternative is to develop an ethics-free technology that, dedicated to the principle of efficiency (as has been much of public administration theory throughout its history), encounters the paradoxes discussed in chapter 5 for public administration as science. Gawthrop is a public administrationist who argues for such a megasystem of management, systems, and ethics.[36]

The question is whether such a megasystem is feasible. Among the difficulties is that the values introduced tend to be those of the systems manager (or owner). For instance, a familiar argument against systems theory is that systems analysis inevitably serves the interests of those at the top. The further and more fundamental difficulty is how society, accepting substantial autonomy of the subject, could develop the values that will be utilized. As was suggested in chapter 5, it is hard to assume for any society either a set of binding core values or a means for reaching agreement on such a core set. It may be supposed that perhaps it is just a question of limiting autonomy a little, perhaps on the lines of limiting free speech to the extent of denying individuals the right to cry "fire" in a crowded theater. It is not. Kenneth Arrow's possibility theorem shows that it is impossible to guarantee that any system for aggregating individual wishes can be made in such a way that does not violate even the trivial set of assumptions Arrow discusses.[37] Arrow's five postulates are trivial in the sense that they are requirements such as "transitivity" (if A is preferred to B and if B is preferred to C, then A is preferred to C). As Arrow explains, the conditions amount to "citizen sovereignty and rationality in a very general form."[38] They specify nothing much more complex, such as "fair" or "just."

Public administration as sociotechnology encounters additional paradoxical limits; it yields benefits within limits. Try a thought experiment. Think of a manager (a governor, a department head) with an electronic command and control room on the lines of a Pentagon command and control room. This domestic command and control facility might give contemporary, historical, and projected information on aspects of the status of all programmatic and administrative activities for which the manager is responsible and of the relationships of those activities to relevant aspects in the environment. It might conduct analyses using (after Bunge) the principles and data drawn from such subjects as psychology, sociology, and political science; it might be programmed, perhaps with the use of artificial intelligence, to conduct all kinds of scientific and technological procedures, such as sampling, computer simulation, and quality control; and it might execute all kinds of mathematical and other models. It might have all kinds of automatic execute procedures (parallel to automatic stock market buy-sell routines). The conclusion of this thought experiment surely would be that sociotechnological practice, both as social engineering and as management science, can be beneficial.

The first contrary, a variant of the boundary paradox seen in chapter 4, would be encountered as the sociotechnology met the limits of the subject's boundaries. Public administration as social engineering would encounter the boundary limit because more information and techniques would be needed beyond the limits of the public administration discipline. Social engineering problems typically have aspects that are not confined within the traditional public administration discipline; they might be economic, political, sociological, or other types of input. Public administration as management science would encounter the barrier less readily because its scope is narrower. Nevertheless, the politics-administration, or identity, issue is evidence of some of the discomfort. The discomfort is not so well recognized in parts of the barrier; the economics-administration issue, as evidenced in the study of public choice economics, was an instance suggested in chapter 4. Notably, the part of the example given from Bunge and in the previous thought experiment also lie outside the scope of the discipline (e.g., the provision that management science conduct its studies in light of the principles and data drawn from psychology, sociology, and economics).

Social engineering and management science can be—and have been—conducted without any reference to public administration theory. Nevertheless, barriers are still encountered, and they are the barriers that are the by-products of the fragmentation of the social sciences. It is not a simple matter to move among the radically different outlooks of the economist, the sociologist, the political scientist, and other social science specialists; the barriers between perspectives are substantial. Interdisciplinary study presents difficulties.[39] There are significant limits to sociotechnology, with or without a public administration component.

A second paradox lies in the difficulty of incongruence of system and system environment. The pursuit of public administration as sociotechnological system inevitability can encounter any contrary wish to meet the needs of the nonsystematic. First, systems tend to develop what some may consider, with overstatement, "lives of their own." By the nature of the demands of tending to their maintenance and development, sociotechnological systems tend to be reified. The system that is socially constructed comes to acquire a life of its own; the system acquires properties. Consider typical attitudes toward the educational or the military system. The system is said to act or fail to act; it is said to be facilitated or hindered; it is said to be a good system or a bad system; it is said to be more important than its individual parts. The conceptual system that is being attended comes to be seen as an entity that has its own needs.

Second, the nonsystematic can be seen in terms that Herbert Simon called (for a different purpose) "the inabilities of the behavioral system to adapt perfectly to its environment—from the limits of rationality."[40] These limits of rationality can be understood in at least two ways. They can be seen as the limits of rationality that come from the boundedness of the rationality of the particular system builders (or tenders). Chapter 3 noted Simon's contrast between comprehensive rationality (i.e., optimizing, choosing the best) and bounded rationality (i.e., "satisficing," choosing the first option that is adequate). Some may wish to see the limits on rationality in pragmatic terms. In a systems world subject to the relative bigness of output (population coverage, system complexities, and unpredictable and multiple changes in circumstances) in relationship to the system builder's knowledge and input resources, errors in a system builder's choices can be expected. Frequently, choices are not close enough for systems work, and significant customer difficulties result. Nevertheless, this aspect of the limitation is of little interest here because it is reasonable to hope to remove the limit through additional and better technological work. The limits of bounded rationality are not merely pragmatic, however; some limit is "rational." Limits are rational in the sense that it would be irrational, in terms of time and other resources, for a public official to spend more resources on an additional search if she did not have a rational expectation of finding another system so much better than a system currently available that the extra resources cost would be recouped.

The limits on rationality, to understand it in an alternative way, may be seen as the limits of rational systems in an environment made not completely congruent with such rationality because of the subjectivity of the people in the system's environment. This argument is a variant of the one discussed earlier in terms of aggregating ethical preferences. Modern subjectivity recognizes some right of autonomy by the individual; the questions are how much and whether rationality is also required. As a first step, assume that subjects are irrational. Rational discussions of subjectivity—the individual on the receiving end of the system—tend to dismiss the subjective choice for irrationality. Some systems have to cope with the irrational (e.g., mental health systems), and it is not completely clear, especially if Foucault's account of the nature of madness seems reasonable, why the subject should have to sacrifice the right toward some irrationalities. As a second step, assume that subjects are rational. A. K. Sen's theorem on the impossibility of a Paretian liberal may be recalled. On a rational basis, he examines whether three weak conditions are compatible. One condition is liberalism, defined as "certain personal matters in which each person should be free to decide what should happen, and in choices over these things whatever he or she thinks is better must be taken to be better for society as a whole, no matter what others think."[41] Another condition is Pareto optimality, an outcome where no reallocation could occur that would increase the utility of one person without lowering the utility of another. The third condition is unrestricted domain, which relates to freedom of choice. Sen finds that no social aggregation function can simultaneously satisfy these three weak conditions; that is, his theorem purports to prove that some situations exist where it is impossible to make social decisions that satisfy all three criteria.

Seeing the technology of the system as an end for study and seeing systems work as the scientific adjustment of system to its environment is exemplified in Herbert Simon's view of administration as similar to playacting.[42] The effectiveness of the performance (administrative process), to paraphrase him, depends on the effectiveness of the play (organization) and the effectiveness with which the players (organization members) "play their parts."[43] He asks how he could construct an empirical theory of administration that would go beyond the rules of good acting. He answers that his writings have attempted to show that administrative dilemmas arise from the inability of the behavioral system to adapt to its environment; rationality, for him, has limits.[44] The science of design, the technologism, that Simon explains in *The Sciences of the Artificial* focuses on the system. Simon asks his reader to consider a man and an ant. He explains that a man is simple when seen as a behaving system. The apparent complexity of a man's behavior, he continues, is largely a function of the complexity of the environment.[45] On the next page, Simon adds the quote given at the head of this chapter: "Only human pride argues that the apparent intricacies of our path stem from a quite different source than the intricacy of the ant's path."[46]

Complete understanding of the issues surrounding public administration as technology requires consideration of the relationship between the human and the technical. A public administration technologist presumably does not, but may, manage her technology for its own sake; she probably is managing it on the understanding that what she does will increase human well-being. The technologist then encounters an additional difficulty if she is not sure of the relationship between the human and the technical. Let us flag this uncertainty by quoting two differing views.

The first view is optimistic. Pope Pius XII seemed to reflect an Aristotelian view when he wrote, "Very far, then, from any thought of disavowing the marvels of technology . . . He [the believer] will even find it natural to place beside the gold, frankincense and myrrh, offered by the Magi to the Infant God, also the modern conquests of technology; machines and numbers, laboratories and inventions, power and resources."[47]

The second view is less optimistic, one consistent with the notion of human beings as trapped within sets on sets of technology that they once controlled. Nicholas Berdyaev writes,

> It is not an exaggeration to say that the question of technique has now become that of the destiny of man and of his culture in general. In this age of spiritual turpitude, when not only the old religious beliefs but also the humanist creed of the nineteenth century have been shaken, civilized man's sole strong belief is in the might of technical science and its capacity for infinite development. Technique is man's last love, for the sake of which he is prepared to change his very image. Contemporary events only strengthen this faith. In order to believe, man craved for miracles, though doubting their possibility; now he witnesses technique actually work "miracles." This problem is an anxious one.[48]

SUMMARY

Public administration, developing as a technology, encounters contraries. Much of public administration can be seen as low-tech process technology. Advantages exist in conceptualizing public administration as technology, such as the narrowing of the theory-practice gap. Nevertheless, the benefits that can be realized for this line of development, in addition to the lines discussed in the two previous chapters, are limited.

Modernist technological rationalization tends to move the study of public administration from technics to science-based technology. As technics, public administration is more open to the faddism that often occurs. As science-based technology, public administration meets the paradoxes of scientism discussed in the last chapter.

Sociotechnology, consisting of social engineering and management science, encounters a paradox as it meets the limits of public administration's boundaries. Public administration as socioengineering meets the boundary as more information and techniques are needed beyond the limits of the public administration discipline. Economic, political, sociological, and other types of inputs are needed. Public administration as management science less readily encounters this barrier because its scope is narrower.

There is a paradox between public administration as promoter of technological system and public administration as facilitator of individuality. A paradox lies in the incongruence of system and system environment. There can be limits in rationality, and systems do tend to develop lives of their own. It is too optimistic to suppose that public administration as technology can integrate systems and management and ethical considerations.

7

Modernity
Limits of Enterprise

The production of public goods can also be achieved by an entrepreneur who sets up in the business of supplying them at a profit.
—Laver[1]

Uphold these principles, ever conscious that public office is a public trust.
—House Ethics Manual[2]

THE EMERGENCE OF capitalism was "the most fateful force in our modern life."[3] Max Weber goes on to distinguish the "impulse to acquisition" from capitalism, from free enterprise. He describes as naive the idea that capitalism is this acquisitive impulse. Rather, the pursuit of profit is rationalistic, and it may involve restraining or limiting the irrational impulse. Furthermore, capitalism is the continuing pursuit of profit within a rationalistic system for adjusting economic means to this pursuit. The system, no less than the motivation, is a sine qua non for capitalism; it is as necessary as water is to a fish's existence. As Weber writes, the "impulse to acquisition, pursuit of gain, of money, of the greatest possible amount of money, has in itself nothing to do with capitalism. . . . But capitalism is identical with the pursuit of profit, and forever renewed profit, by means of continuous, rational capitalistic enterprise."[4] The pursuit of economic interest in a noncapitalist system is, in Weber's view, undesirable. Professor Tawney, in his foreword, quotes Weber to this effect: "The unchaining of the economic interest, merely as such, has produced only irrational results: such men as Cortes and Pizarro, who were, perhaps, its strongest embodiment, were far from having an idea of a rationalistic economic life."[5] This chapter considers economic motive and operating system together. This view is in contrast to many who speak too blithely of the worthwhile goal of transplanting the private enterprise spirit to public enterprise, of techniques for making public officials responsive to their customers. System and system motive should be considered together.

Both mainstream public administration theory and other modernist social thinking make contrary assumptions about fundamental features of legitimate motivation and organization in the public and private sectors. "Legitimate motivation" is used here to mean behavioral motivation that is approved or considered justified. With significant exceptions, basic assumptions about public sector motivation and organization constitute A; with significant exceptions, basic assumptions about private sector motivation and structure tend to constitute not-A. Although the historical origins are easy enough to trace, it is odd that we should have come to embrace such a bifurcated view.

With exceptions, the assumption is that the motivation of the public official should not be self-interest; the motivational engine of the private sector is taken to be self-interest. With exceptions, the assumption is that a fundamental evil in the organization of public agencies is duplication; the fundamental principle of capitalist organization is competition (only possible with organizational duplication). These contraries will be explored in this chapter. In doing so, it will be recognized that frustration with the limits of each avenue has led to proposals to pursue the alternatives; unfortunately, the alternatives are not the panaceas they seem to be to their proponents. A significant swath of public administration theorists, supported by some pundits, hold that the A group should welcome opportunities to switch to a not-A basis. The public choice model provides examples of a wish to change public sector assumptions; for example, some writers urge the merits of competition.[6] The socialist model provides examples of a wish to alter private sector assumptions. Substantial experience seems to suggest that, although (for example) the public sector change can yield good results, neither switch can give benefits beyond a point. Because our interest is in the public sector, the focus here will be on the limitations for the public sector of the alternatives; it will be noticed that the limits are not merely accidental.

MOTIVATION

Consider first the mainstream attitude toward the issue of motivation. Public and private in this respect are opposite sides of the same coin, interest. It is generally assumed that the public sector administrator should be motivated by a wish to serve the public interest: "Uphold these principles, ever conscious that public office is a public trust."[7] This is a congressional endorsement of the public interest motivation. At least four provisions of the Code of Ethics for Government Service, promulgated by Congress for the public service, provide injunctions against acting for private interest: "Never discriminate unfairly by the dispensing of special favors or privileges to anyone, whether for remuneration or not; and never accept for himself or his family, favors or benefits under circumstances which might be construed by reasonable persons as influencing the performance of his governmental duties" (principle 5); "Make no private promises of any kind binding upon the duties of office, since a Government employee has no private word which can be binding on private duty" (principle 6); "Never use any information coming to him confidentially in the performance of governmental duties as a means for making private profit" (principle 8); and "Put loyalty to the highest moral principles and to country above loyalty to government persons, party or department" (principle 1).[8]

"It is not from the benevolence of the butcher or the baker that we get our dinner—it is from his self-interest," as Adam Smith writes in 1776.[9] The butcher and the baker and the candlestick maker give us what we want neither because they are generous nor because they consider that we deserve, need, or are entitled to their products; they do it for self-interest. Self-interest has always been, and remains, a central assumption of mainstream economic theory. As Nassau Senior, a later classical economist, puts it in his first postulate. "That every person is desirous to obtain, with as little sacrifice as possible, as much as is possible of the articles of wealth."[10] We could have easily quoted later economic theorists (e.g., Léon Walras, Alfred Marshall, or Joseph Schumpeter) or any standard modern textbook (e.g., *Economics* by Samuelson and Nordhaus).

The distinction between the normative and the descriptive should be recognized. The congressional standard for public administrators refers to what ought to be, and the standard would not have been issued if it were not for the obvious fact that some public administrators in fact do not meet the standard. (As a descriptive or positive matter, self-interest has been recognized throughout the Republic's history as an important character trait. "If men were angels, no government would be necessary," Madison writes in *The Federalist,* No. 51.) Similarly, Adam Smith's and similar views are that the private entrepreneur should pursue his or her own self-interest. Some entrepreneurs may in practice exhibit altruism, but as Smith notes, "I have never known much good done by those who affected to trade for the public good."[11] The bifurcated way that mainstream public administration theory looks at public and private sector motivation is normative.

The analysis can be made overly complex by considering the odd situation of the "manifest-orientation contrary-deeper-motivation" group, those who, as it were, are oriented to do the right thing for the wrong reason. Some entrepreneurs could believe they are motivated by the public interest to make an optimal profit for themselves (i.e., their beliefs are such that they think it is in the public interest for them to act in their own interest). For example, a business owner might want to make a private fortune because she believes that this affluence will make everyone better off. Government officials could believe it is in their private interest to pursue the public interest. Nigro and Richardson endorse the latter in their account of Alexis de Tocqueville's "doctrine of self-interest properly understood"; as they explain, this doctrine "relies on the citizen's belief 'that by serving his fellows man serves himself in that doing good is to his private advantage.' "[12] They think that "self-interest properly understood" can be developed as "an effective corrective to acquisitiveness and individualism,"[13] and they go on to quote more of Tocqueville: "The doctrine of self-interest properly understood does not inspire great sacrifices, but everyday it prompts some small ones; by itself it cannot make a man virtuous, but its discipline shapes a lot of orderly, temperate, careful and self-controlled citizens."[14] Various approaches may be used to accommodate "manifest-orientation contrary-deeper-motivation." Nevertheless, it seems satisfactory to equate the term "motivation" as it is used in this chapter with manifest motivation, leaving deeper motivations aside for the present.

The conditional model, developed to analyze police resources allocation decision making,[15] provided for three types of situations. The first type, the programmatic-goal (p-goal) situation, reflects the traditional public administration view of the public administrator as the altruistic public servant. Such a p-goal resource allocator is assumed to be uninterested in any effects of her program or other decisions on her own welfare in the bureaucracy. She does not seek any return to herself qua bureaucrat. The goal of the p-goal resource allocator is to achieve the altruistic "public interest"; that is, such a resource allocator's goal is to maximize social welfare by producing optimal program output.

This is contrasted with the "bureaucratic man," the b-goal decision maker. The goal of this decision maker is not altruistic; rather, it is assumed to be to seek optimal bureaucratic self-interest directed toward the self-serving objective of personal career survival and growth. The model, acknowledging its debt to the economic tradition and to public choice writers, attempted to analyze b-goal decision-making behavior in terms of accumulating bureaucratic welfare (or clout or leverage). The third type is the mixed (the p-b goal administrator). The mixed form treats the programmatic (the p-goal) and the bureaucratic (b-goal) as polar extremes; it conceptualizes the resource allocator's goal as resulting from a choice of one from a range of self-interest/public-interest points. A main point of the conditional model is to argue that the choice of this point is influenced by circumstances and that these "conditions" or circumstances may be adjusted to give different results. In descriptive terms, a public administrator may operate from a combination of self-interest and altruistic-interest, even though she may be judged in public interest terms.

The description of p-goal and b-goal decision making as optimizing welfare, social welfare in the former case and personal welfare in the latter, is open to some ambiguity. Differences in principle exist regarding the nature of social welfare.[16] Some might think in terms of Pareto optimality, for example, but others may wonder why one or two individuals should not be made worse off in order to make many individuals much better off. There are differences about the nature of the public interest. The public interest could be what X wants, what X should want, what Y thinks that X should have, and so on. The ambiguity does not vitiate the distinction between p-goal and b-goal motivation, however. The p-goal public servant, as the title implies, remains one who caters in some way to the needs or wishes of those or whatever she serves. The p-goal civil servant is one who serves the interests of another, perhaps a president or a prime minister, a set of politicians, or an abstraction such as the general will or the nation. The approved and expected motivation is not self-interest.

The application of the p-goal and b-goal motivations to the two sectors is not straightforward, however. Should all public sector employees be motivated only by the public interest? Let us assume that program advocacy is part of realizing the public interest, as it may well be. For example, the U.S. secretary of veterans affairs would be expected to advocate for veterans affairs; the U.S. secretary of agriculture would be expected to favor farming, and so on. A slippery, but not inevitably sliding, slope exists here because subprogram, sub-subprogram, and "my job" advocacy are not far behind program advocacy. The honey pot ant investigator should surely take time and energy to advocate in favor of honey pot ant investigation, even if such advocacy reduces the amount of her time spent on investigation this year. Should all private sector employees be motivated by self-interest? Economic theory, with the exception of micro-microeconomics, rarely dips below the level of the owner of the firm. Unless the profitability of the firm is equivalent to individual employee welfare, the private sector employee who is motivated solely by optimizing the profits of the firm is like a p-goal person; she is being motivated by something other than self-interest.

A canard should be rejected. This false idea is that "response to market demand" and "self-interest" are necessarily synonymous; they are not. The situation whereby the customer demands widgets and the producer responds to the demand by supplying widgets says little about the self-interest of the producer. The situation whereby the governmental agency listens to the consumer of that governmental service and gives that consumer whatever is demanded says little about the self-interest of the governmental official. Techniques and approaches for encouraging officials to focus on customer satisfaction (e.g., the total quality management approach) do not deal automatically with the self-interest of the officials. It can be said that satisfying customers may be in the self-interest of the producer because it may be pleasing to the producer—or it may increase the odds of job retention. Nevertheless, satisfying one's own whims or the dictates of a political superior may be just as self-satisfying—and just as likely to result in job retention.

Self-interest, greed, is a relatively powerful motivational force, and it is the motive that is taken to underlie the activities of the entrepreneur. The wish is to see public organizations operating with the brute energy—taken to be self-interest—of the private enterprise entrepreneur. Public sector altruism, p-goal motivation, does not seem to be as powerful. Quine gives his view, for example, of the shortcomings of the rational grip for altruism—for altruism he describes as ranging from "a passive respect for the interests of others to an active indulgence of their interests to the detriment of one's own."[17] He notes the "familiar" arguments that have been used "to heighten the persuasiveness of moral precepts by appealing to reason."[18] One is the "myth of divine decrees enforced by sanctions"; the other is the argument from self-interest—that "we are all better off if we all respect one another's interests."[19] He states, "The fallacy is familiar too: any one of us may be even better off by infringing on another's interests, if the rest of society behaves properly. . . . The enlightened moralist thus recognizes that self-interest, however enlightened, affords no general basis for altruism. Altruists are simply persons who prize the welfare of others outright and irreducibly, just as everyone prizes his own."[20] Quine goes on to point out that "man's altruism is not always as abundant as we would wish, nor are arguments from self-interest the way to increase it."[21] He adds that evolutionary theory can account only for innate altruism toward kin (e.g., in one form nepotism and in no form p-goal). His advice is that we "play on whatever faint rudiments of fellow feeling [people] may be capable of, fanning any little spark into a perceptible flame."[22]

Therefore, we are left to use whatever nonrational means are available to fan the flames of devotion to public service. Propaganda, especially in schools, is helpful, but other emotional devices and appeals are available: deadeners such as television, bread, and circuses; exciters such as flags, socially recognized holidays, and patriotic exhortations; various forms of social approval and disapproval; and religion. In the public service, political-emotional appeals can be made (e.g., in the United States to the responsibilities of citizenship and to the uniqueness of the Constitution, in a monarchy to the magic of history and to the appeal of pomp, in the former Soviet Union to the worth of serving the proletariat, and various other claims and glory stories). The appeal is greater if an intellectual component is added.

The assumption that the power of the motivation of self-interest let loose can be used to galvanize the public service is one thing; the assumption that it will result in optimal social welfare is another.[23] Perhaps the latter assumption is another version of Adam Smith's invisible hand theory, that is, the operation of competitive market forces will translate self-seeking actions into optimal social welfare. Those who accept the latter view often are those who would reject the mainstream view that the economy requires manipulation to correct market failures.[24] The view that self-interest let loose in the public sector is sufficient to yield optimal social results is belied by much work in the public choice literature. Downs's pioneering *Inside Bureaucracy* contains a description of intrabureaucracy operations that argues for oversupply.[25] Niskanen's model, noted in chapter 4, describes how the self-interested and rational bureaucrat, intent on maximizing her budget, will interact with the sponsoring agency.[26] It was explained that Niskanen shows how, because of the tendencies of the bureaucrat and because of the bureaucrat's greater information about unit costs, a significant oversupply of the bureau's output will occur. Migué and Bélanger offer a model that shows managers pursuing nonoutput goals other than mere budget maximization, and it thus provides an alternative account of the same general problem.[27] The theoretical and empirical literature on this topic is large.[28]

What those who contrast motivation in the public and private sectors really want is probably the entrepreneurship so valued in the free market system. Views about the precise nature of this entrepreneurship vary. Consider the views of Alfred Marshall, Joseph Schumpeter, and Frank Knight, for example. The economic man, the entrepreneur, of Alfred Marshall is perhaps exemplified in John Galsworthy's *Forsythe Saga,* the man of property. For Marshall, the entrepreneur was a capitalist with leadership and judgment, a person of action and imagination—qualities, in his view, hampered by bureaucracy and size. Nevertheless, the entrepreneur achieved slow and continuous growth. The entrepreneur of Joseph Schumpeter is the capitalist who is responsible for economic breakthroughs, for the creative destruction that is involved in breaking out of the circular flow of small changes that characterizes the economy. This work of the entrepreneur lifts the entire circle as it makes a fundamental contribution, such as introducing a new product, a new method, or a new market. The leadership of the entrepreneur, exemplified by people such as Ray Kroc (leading the way for fast foods) and Ken Olsen (leading the way in minicomputers), is followed by copycats. Frank Knight also held that the work of entrepreneurs are beyond the routine character of managers. For Knight, entrepreneurs are capitalists who cut out their own tasks as they deal with uncertainty. Despite the variety of these descriptions, underlying agreement seems to exist that the entrepreneur is a profit seeker who organizes, leads, and assumes the financial and other chances of a capitalist enterprise within the capitalist context; a capitalist entrepreneur is concerned with amassing wealth.

Some people want to be able to say that some public sector entrepreneurs do exist. The examples that come to mind readily are various politicians or political appointees. Seekers and holders of major political offices have been seen as entrepreneurs, but are they functioning as capitalists? Those who obtain and spend campaign funds and who exchange votes and influence for financial support, although we may despise them for it, are coming close. One feature of an entrepreneur is that she not only organizes and leads but also shoulders the uncertainties involved in providing the overall financial resources of the enterprise; she is the impresario, the one who sponsors and produces. She is concerned about accumulating wealth. If Robert Moses or Robert McNamara is described as an entrepreneur, he is being recognized as someone who shapes, leads, inspires, and impacts. Nevertheless, are they the impresarios of the enterprise? Consider someone even more powerful—Churchill, De Gaulle, or Gorbachev. They shaped, led, inspired, and impacted, and they shouldered enormous uncertainties; entrepreneurs risk little by comparison. Do even these giants fail the capitalist impresario test?

It is tempting to think that the term *entrepreneur* should be widened and liberated from the notion of financial support and market risk. Certainly, the market risk borne by some entrepreneurs is small. This contention might be supported by discussing the golden parachutes that some private enterprise chief executive officers arrange for themselves; a corporate executive who receives $x million if his company fails is not taking a large personal risk, for example. Would it then be enough to say that anyone who shows significant action, imagination, creativity, and courage in managing is an entrepreneur? Some write precisely about public sector entrepreneurship; for example, Michael Laver and other public choice theorists discuss public entrepreneurship as one model for explaining governmental activity. One of Laver's statements is quoted at the head of this chapter. Others write loosely about the need for entrepreneurship in government. They may begin by arguing that a good prison warden or a good regional administrator, although not subject to market forces, could show the desirable qualities listed above: significant action, imagination, creativity, and courage in managing. They might then ask whether that public official is not the same as an entrepreneur. It is a poor argument. Qualities such as action, imagination, risk acceptance, and an urge to meet customers' needs are useful. Nevertheless, an entrepreneur in the bowels of a public bureaucracy, when such a person is conceived in the private enterprise model, is an oxymoron. Missing is the profit seeking. Missing from such a person is the drive to amass capital, capital that is not an end in itself but a means to amassing even more capital; this drive is part of the nature of an entrepreneur. When he explains the motivation and dynamic of the drive to amass capital, Heilbroner uses Marx's M-C-M' formula: "a process of continuous transformation of capital-as-money into capital-as-commodities, followed by a retransformation of capital-as-commodities into capital-as-more-money."[29] Working on developing the entrepreneurial spirit in the traditional bureaucratic situation, aided by the Hawthorne effect, can yield short-term payoffs, but such an innovation, conceptualizing the entrepreneurial spirit in private enterprise terms, can be expected to be ultimately self-defeating. The capitalist rationalization, the motivation supplied by the market, is missing.

Can this objection be met through a radical resystematization of the public sector? Perhaps large segments of the government can be taken to the market; perhaps the market can be taken to the public sector. Could a government be restructured on a market model to bring, as it were, the benefits of the winds of competition to the sleepy monopoly of government? Could we thus obtain the bottom-line results that come from the dynamism of the competitive entrepreneur, the real wealth that comes from the cut-and-thrust and no-nonsense private sector executive? As we will notice, advantages, limits, and contraries exist.

DUPLICATION, COMPETITION, AND WASTE

In the public sector, *duplication* and *waste* are virtually synonymous terms. In the private sector, *nonduplication* and *waste* are virtually synonymous. The word *virtually* is added to reacknowledge the exceptions.

Martin Landau provides an early exception in the public sector case, writing in favor of some redundancy in the public service.[30] He describes how zero redundancy is used as the measure of optimal efficiency and how the antiduplication view is widespread in public administration thinking: "The removal of redundancy is rarely, if ever, challenged in the technology of public administration. It is an article of faith, a commanding precept; and if its injunctions cannot be followed today, one can always dream of tomorrow."[31] Landau's argument is that duplication is not necessarily a sign of waste. For him, redundancy serves many vital functions; it "provides safety factors, permits flexible responses to anomalous situations and provides a creative potential for those who are able to see it."[32] Perhaps the most striking part of Landau's article is his opening example. He describes how he once experienced an emergency landing and how the pilot had afterward told him that safety factors are built into all planes: "For a commercial airliner is a very redundant system, a fact which accounts for its reliability of performance; a fact which also accounts for its adaptability."[33] Others have also recognized the value of some redundancy and of some forms of redundancy. For example, Lerner attempts to carry Landau's work forward.[34] His discussion includes consideration of three basic and two hybrid approaches to redundancy.

Granting the exceptions, the prevailing assumption of public administration practice and thinking is that duplication is wasteful. This repetition is made to illustrate, as Landau did in his article, how redundancy can be used to "suppress error."[35] The error being suppressed in this illustration is that of not recognizing that the claim is being made that redundancy is frowned on in public administration. Landau explains that the lexical view of redundancy, rather than the view of redundancy as an error suppressor, prevails in public administration. He notes that "in ordinary language, redundancy is said to exist whenever there is an excess or superfluity of anything. . . . Excess, as defined lexically, is something which is more than normal, the required, the usual, the specified. It is useless, superfluous, needless—terms which are variously employed to define redundancy."[36] Landau notes that synonyms of *excessive* are *immoderate, intemperate, inordinate, extravagant, exorbitant,* and *extreme,* and he adds, "If we need a time scale here, we can note that excessive has been used to define redundancy for some 400 years."[37]

The notion of natural monopoly in mainstream economic theory provides one of the exceptions to the competitive (the duplicative) principle in the private sector case. A natural monopoly is a firm or an industry where the average cost per unit produced declines rapidly over the entire range of supply (i.e., where the economies of scale are so strong that only one firm should survive). In this case, "a single firm, a monopoly, can supply the industry output more efficiently than can multiple firms."[38] Samuelson gives local electricity distribution as an example.

Mainstream economic theory favors competition, but it does not consider any and all kinds of competition to be adequate. Mainstream theory specifies the conditions under which an economy will produce and distribute goods and services as efficiently as possible. Allen Buchanan describes five conditions necessary in an ideal market in order to achieve an equilibrium state where, at Pareto optimality, no one can be made better off without making one person worse off:

1. Full information is available about the performance and quality of goods and services and the costs of all alternative ways of producing them, and all the cost of this information is zero.
2. Costs of enforcing contracts and property rights are zero, and property rights, including rights to the means of production, are established and stable.
3. Individuals are rational in this sense: their preferences are organized in a

transitive ordering . . . and they are capable of selecting appropriate means towards their ends.

4. (a) Transaction costs are zero . . . or (b) there is perfect competition . . . and no externalities are present.

5. Products offered in the market are undifferentiated—buyers cannot distinguish between the products offered by various sellers, and vice versa.[39]

On efficiency grounds, the case for the market depends on the extent to which actual markets can approximate this ideal. Nevertheless, Buchanan is able to assert that actual markets do not meet these conditions. For example, he is right that real-world transaction costs are never zero and that perfect information is hardly ever realized. He is right that actual business structures reflect monopolistic and oligopolistic features and that the externality condition is not met. He is able to add objections to the market mechanism even if that market is perfectly competitive. For example, he mentions the problem that perfectly competitive markets do not guarantee full employment.

Competition's invisible hand is handy but only up to a point. This view should not be misunderstood. As Rhoads says, "[E]conomists believe that in most situations free markets come closer to achieving economically efficient outcomes than do alternative institutional arrangements. . . . [F]ree markets with flexible prices coordinate the activities of millions of people in different countries in a remarkable way."[40] The free market economy acts as a system, as Weiss and others have explained (and his account is followed in this paragraph), in the determination of the kinds and volumes of goods and services to be produced, in organizing their production, in distributing goods, and in providing for economic development.[41] The system is characterized by specialization and interdependence. The development of specialization has led to an interdependence that is governed, without coordinative action or understanding, by the automatic and decentralized operation of the market mechanism. Central as regulator is the price system, whereby prices are determined by the interaction of supply and demand. Individual entrepreneurs and owners of resources, without central direction, are induced by monetary and other rewards to satisfy the preferences expressed by consumers with the ability and willingness to pay; the profit motive, the desire for optimal gain, brings together the factors of production in the proportions needed to produce the goods demanded. Circular flows of incomes and money occur among businesses and individuals, facilitating the operation of the economic system. The capitalist system, compared with the command economy, seems spectacular.

It is widely held that the competitive system, left to itself, can be expected to fail in important respects. Corrective intervention is considered necessary to avoid hurtful results in terms of inefficiency, inequality, and instability. For example, Samuelson (as was first mentioned in the private-public discussion in chapter 4) lists the ways in which the unattended free market will fail, the corrective governmental intervention that is required, and examples from current U.S. practice.[42] An unattended free market, as he explains, will lead to inefficiencies in terms of monopolies, externalities, and public goods. Samuelson states that the monopoly and market structure situation requires government intervention in such forms as antitrust laws; the externality problem requires intervention in such terms as antipollution regulations; and the failure of the market to produce some needed public goods requires governmental subsidies for such purposes as national defense and lighthouses. Samuelson explains that an unattended free market can yield unacceptable inequalities of wealth and income, requiring some income redistribution through such means as progressive taxation and income-support programs. The unattended economy will also be unstable, leading to such unpleasant results as inflation, unemployment, and low growth. Samuelson notes that governmental stabilization policies can be corrective through monetary and fiscal policies.

It bears repeating that some economists and philosophers would not subscribe to what seem to be such middle-of-the-road views. On the one hand, for example, are economists such as Milton Friedman, who is a monetarist; his radical proposals, as contrasted with his short-run proposals, include abolition of the central bank, abolition of open market operations, 100 percent reserve requirement for banks, no opportunity for private money creation, the setting of limits on governmental expenditure, and reliance on the personal income tax. Varieties of New Classical Macroeconomics exist,[43] and, as Grandmont explains, "in recent times, some (but not all) NC [New Classical] macroeconomists even went as far as to claim that the systematic (i.e., deterministic) part of Government policies should have no real consequences if properly understood and anticipated by the private sector."[44] Some analysts agree with Robert Nozick, whose views include opposition to any transfer payments.[45] On the other hand are those who would argue for more fundamental governmental interventions. For example, some people believe that more radical intervention is required because the market process "distorts" preferences, yielding a mismatch between revealed preferences and well-being. For an unsophisticated example, think of the drug addict; for a sophisticated one, see Cohen's argument that consumption and output are favored at the expense of leisure.[46]

The United States has long opposed nonduplication in the provision of most private sector goods and services. The 1890 Sherman Antitrust Act, for example, states the following: "Every person who shall monopolize, or attempt to monopolize, or combine or conspire with any other person or persons, to monopolize any part of the trade or commerce among the several States, or with foreign nations, shall be deemed guilty of a felony." Nevertheless, it is not a question of wanting nonduplication of any kind.

Mainstream economic theory favors competition of a particular sort; it favors perfect competition. It has long been accepted wisdom in economic theory that monopolies, acting rationally, will restrict output in order to obtain excess profits; by their nature, rational monopolies, if left unchecked, will act against the public interest. As was suggested in Buchanan's set of conditions, oligopolies also pose efficiency problems; for instance, collusion can lead to results similar to those in the monopoly case. Optimal results can be expected only when perfect competition exists, where all firms are price takers (i.e., where no one firm can affect market prices). Unfortunately, perfect competition accounts for relatively small proportions in advanced economies such as that in the United States. Accordingly, the United States devotes considerable energy toward encouraging the "right" kind of competition and toward combating what are considered to be undesirable competitive structure and acts. For example, it prohibits some business conduct (such as price fixing), and it uses regulations to control structure and other business practices.

TWO WINDS OF CHANGE

Two broad strategies can be used to inject competition into the provision of governmental services: privatization and intragovernmental competitive reorganization. Significant use has been made of both these strategies. Gordon Tullock once described them as the two most important practical results of public choice.[47] It is true that much more could be achieved by moving in both directions, but it should be recognized that both courses eventually give rise to contraries.

Privatization, the intended or incidental turning over of a function to the marketplace, comes in forms that are efficient and those that are inefficient. (Intended transfer has been much discussed in recent years, and it is exciting to see services such as some correctional programs being administered privately. Incidental transfer denotes a turning over that is a byproduct of another purpose [e.g., getting work performed by better qualified private sector specialists]. An example of such incidental transfer is the work performed under grants and contracts for the federal government, such as research for the National Institutes of Health.)[48] Efficient privatization is the transferring of a function or an activity to a structure that operates in a context that would lead, according to economic theory, to an optimal outcome. In other words, it might be transferring a function to an owner operating in conditions where she is a price-taker—the perfectly competitive situation noted in the previous section. Alternatively, where the new private enterprise is a natural monopoly (or where it is an oligopoly), appropriate public sector regulation and oversight would be beneficial—just as it might be for a local television cable company. The mere unloading of governmental activities onto the private sector may even be counterproductive. Such inefficient transfers are those where the function is turned over to the private sector in a manner where the winds of competition do not operate, where the competition is not socially useful, or where the appropriate oversight is not provided. Governmental contracts and grants with single-source suppliers or with buyers where the barriers to entry are so large as to preclude significant competition are examples of the noncompetitive case. Reports have been made of the Department of Defense being offered a claw hammer at a purchase price of $435.00, an antenna hexagonal wrench at $9,609.00, a coffee maker at $7,622.00, a flat washer at $387.00, a tool box at $652.00, and a toilet seat at $640.09.[49] The fundament problem is not the pricing system (all costs being piled on) being utilized but the conditions that, like the limited competitive market situation, permit such a pricing system to operate. Even where competition does exist, however, the competition is not always socially useful. Price competition in the private sector can be limited by product differentiation that results from, say, advertising. The contractor and grantee group can also achieve product differentiation by contract and grant proposal packaging and presentation, a sophisticated form of advertising.

What is the optimal size (absolutely or as a percentage of national product) for a government? What is the optimal size for a bureau? Does not size by itself bring its own privations for citizens and for government, and should the Founding Fathers have provided a check and balance for it? Does a bureau of some 53,400 employees (the 1980 U.S. Justice Department) or some 98,000 employees (the 1993 U.S. Justice Department) have significant diseconomies of scale, and what are these diseconomies in human terms? Absent focus on such questions, it is perhaps understandable that observers should become emotional and sloganistic about governmental size. Slogans, it is understood, can have value, even if they are intrinsically hollow. "Government should steer but not row" might be an example.[50] Privatization does have a significant literature,[51] but the difficulty in clarifying the larger issues about optimal sizes opens the gate for the emotional and the sloganistic elements. The size of government is such a large problem that it may be best to err on the side of too much privatization (i.e., transferring functions even when it is unsure that the new market context will be adequate or even when it is unsure that the oversight is sufficient in the case of the natural monopoly [or oligopoly]). The very size of federal administrative buildings is perhaps enough to persuade us, on intuitive grounds, that the federal government really needs another department—a Department of Privatization. Just let the eye and the mind take in the physical sizes of the buildings for the U.S. Department of Energy, the U.S. Department of Agriculture, the U.S. Department of Health and Human Services; look, by the way, at the righteous slogans stamped in their marble and concrete pediments; perhaps a symptom of "living inside the Beltway" is that the governmental buildings no longer seem too large to the insider. Other examples can be found. Such an emotional and sloganistic approach can pay off up to a point, but surely a limit to their possibilities exists. For example, the complexities of the roots of the size problem are great, as was suggested in chapter 4. Also, typically there are the political disincentives to downsizing (e.g., from interest group pressure). To repeat the point made in chapter 4, it is odd that public administration theory has essentially avoided this issue.

Only if thoroughgoing anarchism leads to optimal results can complete privatization be the solution to the problem of bureaucracy. Nevertheless, good mainstream economic arguments can be made for public enterprise—on the "market failure" lines suggested above (e.g., the underproduction of public goods). Just as serious is the problem that functions transferred into private oligopolistic and monopolistic situations would require some public oversight. A completely privatized society of the latter type would really be one with a government of a different type—perhaps does not steer but merely sets the parameters for the steerers. The question of the limits of privatization is more complex than we have suggested. The question, What is the optimal size of government? cannot really be answered without also asking, What is the optimal size of the private sector? and What is the optimal size of society? This point leads us to societal purpose and other questions.

Intragovernmental competition is extensive, and it could surely be even more widely used. It is valuable. Individuals and groups in the public sector are at times pitted against one another (e.g., in individual personnel evaluations linked to pay raises, in unit rivalries [e.g., in the military where bravo company might compete with alpha company—rah, rah, rah], and interbureaucratic imperialistic competition). Bureaucratic imperialism, explains Matthew Holden, is part of the process of clarifying the confusion and uncertainty that characterize the administrative world: "Competition between agencies, engendered by competition between constituencies, is a vital part of the process of clarification."[52] As he explains it, agencies have different dispositions (toward expansion, maintenance, or retrenchment), but bureaucratic imperialism arises because the administrative politician needs enough agency power, and power "is organized around constituency and constituency around jurisdiction."[53] Competition of sorts can also exist between governmental and private agencies (e.g., between the public railroad and private railroad in Canada and between the U.S. Postal Service and Federal Express in the United States). Parts of the government are structured on a competitive principle, and the democratic political context of administration is typically competitive. Competition between the four military services is an example of the former, a competition that comes together in the collaboration (and competition and collusion) of the Joint Chiefs of Staff. Another example is the voucher system for schools currently being discussed in various forms. Political parties, as an example of the usually competitive world of the politician, have been described as firms engaged in raising funds and exchanging platforms and promises for votes, and legislators and others have been seen as entrepreneurs engaged in activities such as logrolling.

It is suggested that not enough experimentation in the public service with intragovernmental competitive structuring has been conducted. The intraorganizational competitive mechanism is, by contrast, utilized on a significant scale in the private sector. For example, an automobile company might establish within its organizational bosom three or so subordinate and competing car companies; it would accept the disadvantages of duplication in return for the competitive advantages that such duplication permits. With some imagination, opportunities could be developed in almost all areas of the public sector. The military example is a fine "moral tale." At first sight, it might have seemed absurd that intraorganizational competition could have been introduced in the military area. Why would a single country waste resources by duplicating military organizations? Yet, historical accident has given most countries such a competitive military system—in a system that by its nature is established to compete with foreign military systems. Historical habit now makes the military intraorganizational competitive structure seem natural, just as habit makes it seem unnatural in other areas.

Two characteristics of public administration theory might make such experimentation more difficult. First, functional focus could be a problem. The case for intraorganizational competitive structuring is clearer in the private enterprise situation because the relative successes of competing units can be measured by the yardstick of net profit. Bottom-line measures in the public sector are relatively flabby, and they are more easily explained away by nonperformers. For example, which is a better police agency: one, other things being equal, that uncovers more crimes or one that prevents more crimes? Which is the better social welfare agency: one, other things being equal, that helps more people or one that helps more people not to need help? Public agencies (like private agencies) have several purposes, but the unifying bottom lines seem unavailable to the public sector. Greater use of intraorganizational competitive structuring is not likely until the measuring problem can be addressed more effectively. The main focus of American public administration theory, as discussed earlier, has been on functions such as decision making, policy analysis, managing, leading, and organizing. The discipline's own success has not been measured by its own performance in developing program performance measures. This view is not to deny the volumes of work conducted on performance measurement; it is recognized that probably the main reason is the difficulty of the problem. Nevertheless, we can ask whether the relative lack of success can be explained in some part by the functional emphasis of public administration theory.

A second characteristic might be the nature of the personnel component in public administration theory and practice. The profit pressure has provided a motivation for private sector executives to put similar competitive pressure on their subordinates. It is not clear that an equivalent pressure occurs in the public sector, and strong political and other disincentives against rocking the boat exist. For example, does a public sector leader—absent a performance yardstick—have a greater vested interest in all her subordinate leaders succeeding? If any of them fails, does not the leader have to accept responsibility for that failure? If the subordinates are supportive, does that not strengthen the leader's position relative to her superior?

The public personnel movement has been successful in developing procedures for protecting against much politics and cronyism in hiring and firing. Consider the overall thrust toward the development of merit and related personnel systems. In personnel, it was suggested earlier, a history of technological improvement can be traced that runs from the spoils arrangements of Jacksonian democracy to a merit system that would be capped by the "subject-generalist cum public-administration-specialist" (perhaps the Senior Executive Service in the U.S. government can be seen as a step toward the latter). The Pendleton Act of 1883 gave us a limited form of civil service, and it is difficult for us now to appreciate the enthusiasm that surrounded that movement and act. The development of what can be seen as the technology of personnel management in the United States government can be sketched through the 1923 Classification and Pay Act, extending application of civil service within the government; the establishment in 1939 of departmental personnel offices; the passage of the Hatch Act, limiting the political activity of federal civil servants; the Second Hoover Commission, speaking of a Senior Executive Service; and the 1978 Civil Service Reform Act. If those early reformers could have seen the establishment of the senior executive corps on something not completely unlike the model of the British administrative class, they might (if the dead can cheer) at least utter two cheers for the achievements realized in the technology of personnel management. Would the public personnel component of public administration theory have been more successful if it had focused more on encouraging more risk-takers to enter the public sector? Would that have permitted three cheers?

Such intraorganizational competitive structuring, although it has possibilities for encouraging the programmatic benefits that can come from a harsh competitive wind, can only be effective to a point. The competition that can be obtained from restructuring encounters the fact that the best that can be achieved in most cases is to create an oligopoly situation that is open to all the difficulties of such an economic structure. Consider the nature of the competition that could be obtained by splitting up, say, the United States Postal Service, on the automobile holding company model, into three independent and competing suborganizations. Competition would be introduced by such a reform. Nevertheless, the result would still be a set of oligopolies, and that situation does not promise the benefits of perfect competition. Oligopolistic competition tends to yield unproductive forms of competition or collusion.

THE PUBLIC CHOICE ROUTE

In 1973, Vincent Ostrom published his important book, *Intellectual Crisis in American Public Administration.*[54] A principal theme of the book is that public administration has suffered since its inception from reliance on the Wilsonian paradigm that has taken the organization as the basic unit of analysis and has focused on applying the efficiency criterion in improving the organization. The Wilsonian paradigm has seen public administration in terms of bureaucracy and has striven for bureaucratic efficiency through the principles of hierarchical organization, the cost calculus, and the exclusion of politics. Simon's challenge, as Ostrom explains, was to the foundations of public administration theory and to the notion that perfection in hierarchical organization is the most efficient; nevertheless, it retained the organization as the primary focus. Ostrom's view is that a new paradigm is needed, and he favors the public choice tradition, relying on the individual as the unit of analysis and utilizing the methods that have (in his view) proven effective in economic analysis. It is suggested that Ostrom was right that a crisis in American public administration exists (although not only for the reasons he gives), and it is unfortunate that the response to his call to arms has been so feeble. Public administration theory, speaking metaphorically, has opened an additional chapter in the textbook and created a space for yet another paradigm, the public choice paradigm. For example, public choice and economics are assigned one of the thirteen sections in a book cited earlier—Rabin's *Handbook of Public Administration.*[55] A new public choice paradigm has been recognized, but it has not revolutionized the study of public administration, and the crisis (if there is a crisis) remains.

Some of the implications for public administration theory of the important change that Ostrom proposes remain to be developed. Recall his views on the central organizing concept of public administration theory. As Ostrom explains his view,

> The theory of public goods is the central organizing concept used by these political economists in conceptualizing the problem of collective action and of public administration. This contrasts with the theory of bureaucracy as the central concept in the traditional theory of public administration. When the central problem in public administration is viewed as the provision of public goods and services, alternative forms of organization may be available for the performance of these functions apart from an extension and perfection of bureaucratic structures. Bureaucratic structures are necessary but not sufficient structures for a productive and responsive public service economy.[56]

Ostrom favors the approach of those "political economists who (1) use the individual as the basic unit of analysis (2) use the theory of externalities, common properties, and public goods to define the structure of events relevant to public administration (3) analyze the consequences that different organizational and decision-making arrangements have upon the output of public goods and services and (4) evaluate those consequences by whether or not the outcome is consistent with the efficiency criterion."[57] The "bureaucratic" or "governmental" view of public administration has prevented appropriate attention, it is agreed, from being given to the importance of quasianarchistic arrangements. In the administration of justice, for example, it has directed attention too much to institutions and institutional responses; this point may be appreciated by reflecting on the significance of such facts that institutions are not needed in order to compel people to queue in an orderly manner for buses. The "governmental" view leaves us wondering about the status of the intermediate sector, the nonprofit areas. More importantly, it also ignores the public aspect of private decisions.

As hinted in chapter 2, the field of public administration can be defined as being concerned with the supply and demand of publicness; roughly, a public good or service is one that can be consumed only collectively, rather than solely privately. Samuelson and Nordhaus define a public good as "a commodity whose benefits may be provided to all people—in a nation or town—at no more cost than that required to provide it for one person. The benefits of the good are indivisible, and people cannot be excluded from using it."[58] In 1954, Samuelson defined public consumption goods as those "which all enjoy in common in the sense that each individual's consumption of such a good leads to no subtraction from any other individual's consumption of that good."[59] National defense is the usual example of a public consumption good or service; if A is defended by a rocket site in Minnesota, A's consumption of the protective service does not diminish B's consumption of the same service. A private good or service, on the other hand, does not have this characteristic; in the latter case, all the utility accrues to the primary consumer. When A consumes boiled beef and carrots, that eliminates B's consumption possibility for A's boiled beef and carrots. Samuelson's original classification of goods and services into two polar extremes has subsequently been modified. Rather than a dichotomous situation, a range of goods and services exists with varying degrees of publicness. Even an apparently very private good or service has some publicness. When A eats boiled beef and carrots, one aspect of the publicness of that good is that hunger is less liable to drive A to steal B's boiled beef and carrots. Even the Minnesota rocket site may have some privateness (e.g., in defending the inhabitant of Florida from death more than it defends the Minnesotan). The public goods concept is more complex than has been indicated here. The continuum between pure publicness and pure privateness has four components: jointness or divisibility of supply, excludability, optionality, and susceptibility to crowding. Buchanan presents a box diagram that describes public goods in terms of one axis showing their "degree of indivisibility" and the other axis indicating the "size of the interacting group."[60] The spraying of a backyard against mosquitos is said to be indivisible in the sense that a neighbor's backyard also receives some protection, and that refers to the degree of indivisibility; the number of backyards in the neighborhood receiving this benefit, a function of the size of sprayer and judgment, refers to the size of the interacting group.

Much can, and has, been said about public goods, but a critical point is the following: the publicness of a good or service is not a function of organizational arrangement. That is, governments produce goods and services with varying degrees of publicness, and so do private enterprise firms. The term *publicness* is intended to reflect the fact that the production of private goods and services typically entails the associated production of a degree of public good, a degree of publicness. For example, private automobile manufacturers make private products such as cars; they also make an associated set of public goods and services, including (again, in economics terminology) the car's externalities. The makers of big cars, when the oil crunch came, were not just producing private products; they were manufacturing forms of publicness. Accordingly, when we speak of the supply and demand of a public good or service, we should refer not to the supply and demand of what governments produce. We should refer to the supply and demand for publicness in the goods and services that are produced by both private and public agencies.

It does seem useful to conceptualize the public administration part of public choice economics into two elements: the supply of public goods and the demand for public goods. The resulting utility occurs despite the difficulty that some items could well be allocated in either category (e.g., logrolling). The supply case is discussed here, and the demand side will be addressed at the end of this subsection. Here, it may be helpful to repeat the important conclusion about the example of waste, waste that is an inherent tendency in the structure of governing. The supply of governmental output—which is not coextensive with the supply of publicness— has been the subject of some public choice studies of significance for public administration. Certainly, a characteristic of government is that it has monopoly powers, and these powers must inevitably lead to waste. Breton is among those who developed a model of representative government that would support this view; he analyzes how the governing party will use these monopoly powers.[61] Mentioned earlier were the contributions of Downs, Niskanen and Migué and Bélanger, as was the extensive work on "political business cycles." All these works contribute to the view of government as rationally inclined to waste.

This characterization of government as uneconomic can produce the emotional reactions of either strong disapproval or enthusiastic approval, and so a caveat should be added. Certainly, a characteristic of governmental supply is that government has monopoly powers, and these monopoly powers inherently tend toward waste. The waste is not merely the result of bad leadership and management; it is a rational tendency in the monopolistic (or oligopolistic) structure of the public sector. The waste can be avoided, of course, in the same way that a rower can row upstream, but the rational tendency is analogous to the current. The public choice studies underscore and "explain" this supply-side characteristic of government, but the caveat is as follows: to say that government is wasteful is not to say that private enterprise is not. The conclusion about the public sector does not speak to whether monopoly powers and market failures are unlikely and insignificant in the private sector. At some times and places, it has been fashionable to think that public enterprise is wasteful and that private enterprise is not; at other periods and places, the fashion has been to think the reverse. Tullock talks, for example, about a recent change in attitude on the question of public and private imperfection: "This recognition that government is also imperfect, and that the proof of imperfection in the market does not indicate that one must turn to government, is relatively recent."[62] Both fashions seem unlikely. A more reasonable view is that both private and public enterprise have proved to be wasteful and that at least a proportion of the waste is not accidental.

Public choice economics consists essentially of the application of economic and related theory and techniques to the study of political science. As the journal *Public Choice* puts it in every issue, "Public Choice deals with the intersection between economics and political science. It started when economists and political scientists became interested in the application of essentially economic methods to problems normally dealt with by political scientists. It has retained strong traces of economic methodology, but new and fruitful techniques have been developed which are not recognizable by economists." The scope of public choice is demonstrated by the seven headings that Abrams uses in his coverage of the subject: axiomatic choice theory, elections, legislatures, spatial models, game theory, coalition theory, and collective goods.[63] Nestled within this subject is the part of public choice economics that applies to public administration.

Clearly, public choice enriches modernist public administration theory. The strengths of economic theory are added, and they are powerful. For one thing, economic theory can supply a perspective missing from much public administration theory. Economic theory is essentially deductive. By contrast, public administration theory is essentially inductive; it proceeds from the particular to the general. It is not claimed here that theory must be deductive; it is claimed that it is an advantage to use both capabilities. Interestingly, in a different connection and for a different purpose, Francis Bacon takes the same line in Aphorism 95 of Book 1 of his *New Organon*. There, Bacon compares the best scientific approach with the work of the bee, contrasted with that of the spider and that of the ant: "Those who have handled sciences have been either men of experiment or men of dogmas. The men of experiment are like the ant; they only collect and use; the reasoners resemble spiders, who make cobwebs out of their own substance. But the bee takes a middle course; it gathers its material from the flowers of the garden and the field, but transforms and digests it by a power of its own."[64]

Public choice economics also enriches modernist public administration theory because economic theorizing typically operates at a higher level of generality or abstraction. Economic theory may be applied to make predictions about General Motors and Al's Corner Grocery, but the language of macroeconomic theory is typically in terms such as the labor supply, the money supply, employment levels, gross national product, and the balance of payments. In addition, economics has a well-developed body of theory that is available for use; Wisdom goes so far as to say, "Economics is well-known to have fully-fledged theories in the hypothetico-deductive sense."[65] Like buying clothes off the rack, we need to make only minor adjustments. As Alec Cairncross says, "[I]t is often the most elementary propositions in economics, on which we all agree, that matter for practical purposes."[66] Cairncross quotes Lionel Robbins with approval: "[T]he most useful economic principles, when stated in their most general form, seem often mere banalities, almost an anti-climax after the formidable controversies amid which they have emerged. Yet experience seems to show that, without systematic training in the application of such platitudes, the most acute minds are liable to go astray."[67]

The utility of the public choice literature is a concern for some. Such concern, although understandable, is misplaced. For one thing, public choice is a fledgling subject. As Tullock points out, a fifty-year gap occurred between the publication of the *Wealth of Nations* and the point at which Adam Smith's basic ideas had more than a minimal effect.[68] Clear signs of the public choice potential exist (e.g., in the account of governmental supply-side and demand-side conditions). Nevertheless, public choice does have a strong theoretical tendency, and its practitioner impact has been small. The first public choice book reported to have made a significant policy recommendation was *The Calculus of Consent*,[69] and Tullock claims, "[I]f . . . we look for specific actual changes in government policy which can be attributed to public choice activity, I think we would find that there is none."[70] (I do not know whether his view remains the same today.) In that 1979 article, Tullock also notes two changes that might have resulted from public choice work: the recognition that government is also imperfect (i.e., like private enterprise) and the appreciation of the place of self-interest among bureaucrats and politicians. Fiorina doubts the latter claim.[71] In the same publication where Fiorina expresses doubts, Russell edits a collection of studies, including such headings as "Super-Rationality and School Tax Voting," "National Environmental Lobbies and the Apparent Illogic of Collective Action," "Practical Aspects of the Construction of Decentralized Decision Making for Public Goods," and "Resource Allocation Reviewing Role of Reviewing Courts," that make a case for the practicality of public choice.[72]

A difficulty does lie with the nature of public choice economics as it is developing, however. The mathematical bent, displayed in the trade journal *Public Choice,* tends to wall off the subject from those with a qualitative contribution to add. The following sentence also appears each month in that journal: "In general, *Public Choice* can be viewed as a field of interest to both economists and political scientists who are interested in theoretical rigor, statistical testing, and applications to real world problems." This statement is again reminiscent of the old "losing" battle between Gustav von Schmoller, a historicist, and Carl Menger, a neoclassicist. Nevertheless, this battle is not one that has been joined yet in the public choice case, and it would help if public administrationists and others would take a more assertive, less defensive, stance toward public choice theory. Economics and public choice are not branches of mathematics; mathematical economics, properly, is a branch of economics.

The criticisms that Vincent Ostrom levels against the mainstream public administration paradigm are convincing as far as they go. Ostrom is right that focusing on the organization has encouraged a tendency to consider only the supply side of the equation. He is right that no economic meaning exists in the notion of producer efficiency in the absence of consumer utility; perfecting supply arrangements makes no sense unless one knows how to optimize supply and demand. Improving arrangements for selling more boiled beef and carrots makes no sense if the demand in a particular market structure is for more fish; similarly, focusing exclusively on perfecting organizational arrangements for supplying a particular governmental product is fruitless without knowing the total structure of public demand. For instance, constructing more and better highways is not worthwhile unless we understand the specifics of the demand for such output.

The limiting difficulty is that it is not at all obvious how demand for public services can be measured. Much of public choice economics has been concerned with the demand for public goods—with an examination of methods for revealing preferences for public goods. These examinations have underscored and clarified the difficulties. The effective demand for private goods is reflected in the amount of money that people are willing and able to surrender in return for whatever volume of products they can buy; the market is the method for measuring the demand. Because of the imperfections that are inevitable in any marketplace (if for no deeper reason), it is superficial to claim that there is no problem of demand revelation in the private sector. Be that as it may, the problem is far worse in the nonmarket sector. It is a stretch to suppose that, by voting periodically for a representative, we in our indirect democracies are revealing the nature and strength of our demand for a particular public good (say, a particular policy alternative). Candidates stand on a variety of issues, and voting is not by issue; issues change, and new ones arise in the interelection years; and usually the intensity of votes is not measured. Consider the last point. In the marketplace, we do not merely vote for or against the purchase of carrots; rather, the intensity of our choice is indicated by the volume of money we are prepared to offer. In the political arena, 49 percent of the voters (with twice the intensity of feeling that is felt by the remaining voters) will lose against 51 percent. Consider the irrationality of some votes. A person may want more governmental services (e.g., help the homeless or help the military-industrial complex), less taxation (e.g., Proposition 13 or a tax cut), and no governmental debt or deficits (e.g., a balanced budget amendment).

Even with rationality assumed, different rules for aggregating individual preferences can yield different results. A Condorcet winner (choosing the issue or candidate who defeats all others, using majority rule, in pairwise elections) is not necessarily a Borda winner (choosing the issue or candidate who has most points, when n candidates are arranged by each voter in order of preference, and the first candidate is given n points, the second n-1, the third n-3, and so on), is not necessarily a plurality winner (choosing the candidate receiving the largest number of votes), and so on. Then, too, there are other ways for revealing demand that present aggregation problems, including "voting with the feet" (e.g., fleeing to the suburbs), contributing money (i.e., in the form of campaign contributions), protesting on the streets (e.g., pro-life or pro-choice), and revolution (e.g., in nineteenth- and early twentieth-century Mexico). Novel demand revelation processes have also been examined. For example, Thompson has proposed a plan whereby individuals reveal their demands by buying insurance against the victory of the least-favored alternative.[73]

The fact is, no ideal system for revealing demand exists. The reader is again referred to the claim that Arrow's general possibility theorem establishes that no aggregation mechanism (for summing the individual preferences into a social decision) exists that can give assurance of satisfying even a few weak assumptions about that aggregation process.[74] As Samuelson and Nordhaus comment, "Put differently, no voting scheme has ever been devised—and Arrow proved it impossible to find one—that can guarantee majority voting will be consistent and will move the society to its most desirable point."[75]

Public choice and economics are surely, like public administration theory, socially constituted. As Nelson points out, "The definition of economics is not immutable. Some working economists may, of course, see themselves as working in an age-old process of creating ever-closer approximations to Truth. The idea that economics is socially constructed should not, however, be novel to anyone with an interest in the methodology or the philosophy of science or who ever heard of Thomas Kuhn."[76] How could this be otherwise? The same arguments that are persuasive that public administration theory is socially constituted apply no less to economics.

Public administration practice and economic practice seem to have significant similarities. Both have an overriding interest in payoff, in practical results. From public administration practice, a person may want better governmental results, a better government, or better governmental treatment for herself. From economic practice, she may want a wealthier world, a wealthier country, a wealthier factory, or a wealthier self. Nevertheless, mainstream economic theory looks so different from public administration theory. It does so in such terms as being deductive, being mathematicized, and using a higher level of abstraction. Wisdom suggests that one factor for the success (and thus for the character) of economic theory is that it operates with " 'natural units'—units of money—which move."[77] This point is correct. Nevertheless, could economic theory have been otherwise if it had not been developed in large part by the nineteenth-century English gentlemen who had not only a philosophical tendency but also a subcultural aversion to "working in trade" and a hands-off approach to the economy? Could public administration theory have been otherwise if the discipline had not been pioneered by thinkers who believed in a set of particular intrusive remedies such as civil service reform? Regardless of such historical accidents, could not institutional economics or some other form not now be mainstream economics? These questions are not to argue for a preference; they merely underscore the socially constituted nature of economics and public administration. In other circumstances, could not public administration theory be grandly deductive, and could not economic theory be empirically oriented and inductive, looking first at General Motors and at Al's Corner Grocery? Could the present situation be reversed, with economic analysis looking more like the approach of the German historical school of economics?

This view of economics as socially constituted can be expected to clash with that of many mainstream working economists despite the growing literature on the philosophy of economics. Nelson also tells us:

A favorite pastime of economists is dumping on, expressing bewilderment about, or ridiculing the lack of "rigor" in the other social sciences. Classifying a work as "sociology" is an especially quick and sure-fire way of silencing it by removing it from the territory of serious conversation of economists. The hierarchical relations between the social sciences is especially evident in the ranking of journals within academic culture: having an article accepted for publication in an economics journal seems to be considered a coup for the sociologist or political scientist, but a publication in a political science or sociology journal by an economist (or in a sociology journal by a political scientist) is no harbinger of professional advancement. It may even be seen as an embarrassment.[78]

Economics is usually considered to be a more successful science than most of the other social sciences, and this success strengthens its interest in becoming even more like the even more successful physical sciences. Where such an attitude exists, economics is seen as a positivist enterprise.

Exploring the problems and status of economics would require another book. Nevertheless, it is not clear why, as a modernist social science, economics should have different expectations than modernist public administration theory with regard to encountering sets of contraries. It is unclear why in this respect any other social science or social action discipline should not face the same difficulties. For example, the modernist would not include value statements as economic science; yet the problem of economics at some point begs for consideration of value. As Frank Knight, founder of the Chicago school, writes, "Economics and ethics naturally come into rather intimate relations with each other since both recognizedly deal with the problem of value."[79] One of Knight's objectives, as he explains in his next paper, had been to argue "against any view which sets out from the assumption that human wants are objective and measurable magnitudes and that the satisfaction of such wants is the essence and criterion of value, and which proceeds on this assumption to reduce ethics to a sort of glorified economics."[80]

These avenues of rationalization for public administration theory—the overlapping economics and the public choice routes—present opportunities for further advances. Nevertheless, each of the avenues seems also to lead to the contraries and the frustrations discussed in this chapter. Other contraries can also be expected, that is, those emanating from the nature of modernist economics. To the extent that public administration theory utilizes economic theory, it can expect to reencounter such general contraries as are presented by economic theory itself.

SUMMARY

Entrepreneurship or the free enterprise capitalist spirit, when transplanted to the public sector, leads to contraries. The limits result in part from the fact that capitalism, or market free enterprise, is different from mere acquisitiveness. The latter represents capitalist self-interest but without the capitalist system. The free enterprise pursuit of profit, on the other hand, is rationalistic. Entrepreneurship in the public service, without the system of capitalist rationalization, is doomed to fail eventually. The capitalist (or market) system is a necessary ingredient for the effective functioning of entrepreneurship. The power of self-interest has some capability to galvanize the public service, but the result will not be optimal social welfare.

Contrary assumptions about legitimate motivation and organization govern the public and private sectors. The motivation approved for the public official is to serve the public interest, and the motivation for the private sector entrepreneur is self-interest. Organizational duplication typically is considered to be a fundamental evil in the public sector; the fundamental principle of capitalist organization is competition (only possible with organizational duplication). Exceptions do exist, and some are discussed in the chapter.

Attempts to adjust the public sector system to approximate the capitalist (or market) system can be made through privatization and intragovernmental competitive organization. Privatization and intragovernmental competition can produce benefits, but both avenues encounter contraries. Privatization in this respect can be efficient or inefficient in that mainstream economic theory does not favor all kinds of competition. Furthermore, as complete anarchism does not lead to optimal results, complete privatization is not a viable solution to the problems of bureaucracy. Because the best that can be expected through most intragovernmental competitive restructuring is the creation of oligopolies, optimal results cannot be expected.

Public choice economics has produced useful results for public administration. Especially important is Ostrom's argument that perfecting supply arrangements does not make sense unless one knows how to optimize supply and demand. The conclusions about governmental waste are also useful, but more can be realized from public choice analysis. For example, there is an opportunity to redefine the study of public administration in terms of the supply and demand for publicness, where the publicness of a good is not the function of organizational arrangement. Public choice economics adds a deductive element and operates at a higher level of generality; these are qualities from which other strands of public administration theory can benefit. More can be learned about the public sector by comparative study of both public and private sectors. Several points are made in this chapter (e.g., relating to motivation and to basic organizing differences). Nevertheless, the public choice route for public administration theory also leads to contraries, emanating from the nature of modernist economics.

8

Modernity
Limits of Hermeneutics

Reaching understanding in the lifeworld requires a cultural tradition that ranges across the whole spectrum, not just the fruits of science and technology.
—Habermas[1]

The form of the world into which he is born is already inborn in him as a virtual image.
—Jung[2]

THE MODERNIST PUBLIC administration search for meaning has yielded important re-sults—up to a point. On the one hand, the rational pursuit of meaning (and the pur-suit, by any means, of rational meaning) is useful. The pursuit of modernist public administration is grounded in rationality. It is correct that the practice of public administration has the elements of an art—in the same way that physicians and ten-nis players are artists. Nevertheless, the body of knowledge on which the adminis-trator-artist may or may not choose to act (like the physician and the tennis player) cannot be irrational. On the other hand, this rational pursuit encounters a contrary if the basis of rationality is seen as eroding, and if, as modernists do, it is taken that knowing should have a firm epistemological foundation. A contrary is encountered between a reliance on rationality and the understandings that have undermined this very rationality. This chapter will focus on one tradition (the psychological) that relates to the decentering of the subject, the undermining of this rationality.

Furthermore, blind spots occur if particular interpretations are always open to the possibility of newer and better interpretations. Is there a "right" interpretation? Some writers do set out to find the correct meaning of texts. Are there many, or an infinite number of, interpretations? Some consider the finding of meaning to be in-exhaustible; for them, no final meaning is achievable. Does any meaning exist out-side of the text that is being interpreted? Others, postmodernists, consider that meaning is no more than the interplay of signs. The utility is reduced if privileged interpretation is not assured in the sense that the scientific method has been consid-ered to yield reliable information.

What is the character of hermeneutic study in modernist public administration? What should be said about the limitations of the rationality used in the modernist hermeneutic methods (and in the scientific method) in studying public administration? This chapter is organized around these questions, but four preliminary caveats should be noted.

First, the word *hermeneutics* is being used here in the broadest sense; it includes all manner of writings that have a hermeneutic element. Critical theory is included, for instance. As Habermas sees it, critical theory requires both interpretive understanding "from above" and study of empirical factors "from below"; it requires a combination of conceptual and empirical analysis, a combination—in McCarthy's words—of "hermeneutic and structuralist analysis with system-theoretic and functional analysis."[3] There is a variety of schools and views of the nature and purposes of hermeneutics, and there is a variety of usages (and denials) of labels. Second, the interest in this chapter is in modernist hermeneutics, although writers such as Derrida and Gadamer could be mentioned as examples. Third, some may assume that meaning is hidden in texts and in situations and that the meaning awaits uncovering. Gadamer and Derrida (writers whose purposes are philosophical) would be among those who do not think that texts have meaning present in them. Those who suppose that meaning is present would be in a position similar to analysts and analysands who are trying to ascertain what really is the case that lies beneath the apparent, the real latent "secret" behind the manifest content. Fourth, categorizing comments about complex writers and movements is fraught with pitfalls. The public administration writers are included on the modernist side of the house. Nevertheless, as may become clearer in the following chapters, the distinction between modern and postmodern writing is open to disagreement. Derrida rejects the description "postmodern," for example, and Gadamer also has been described as a postmodernist.[4]

MEANING IN PUBLIC ADMINISTRATION

What is the character of hermeneutic study in modernist public administration? Those who have contributed to the hermeneutic element in public administration theory can be considered in terms of three categories: hermeneutics 1 (H1), hermeneutics 2 (H2), and hermeneutics 3 (H3). Recall that the term *hermeneutics* is being used in its most catholic sense.

The H categories are offered only for descriptive purposes, and no great weight should be placed on the use of this particular categorization system. A different classification scheme might be preferred. As one example, there is a division between action theory and interpretation. As another example, those who think that there are various levels of meaning might wish to indicate the level sought. For example, the writer can aim for surface (or near-to-surface) meanings; Waldo's work in *The Administrative State* might be in this subcategory. (It will be noted in what follows that this work could be categorized as H2.) Alternatively, the writer might aim for deeper meanings. Denhardt's *In the Shadow of Organization* is an example.[5] Denhardt describes the organization as a cultural symbol of the denial of death. He writes, for instance, in such terms as making the unconscious choice to cope with our fear of death by accepting the domination of organizations, and we need (in Denhardt's view) the assistance of critical theory to allow us to escape such domination.

The first grouping, the H1 category, may seem peculiar to those outside the public administration tradition. H1 represents the contribution from thinkers who might not realize that they have been public administration theorists, including some writers who might resent a suggestion that they are part of the public administration discipline. Thus, thinkers such as Jürgen Habermas, Theodor Adorno, Max Horkheimer, Michel Foucault, and Georg Hegel[6] could be "adopted" as part of the public administration discipline. The discipline of public administration has a tradition—happily—of recognizing as public administrationists some people who would not recognize themselves as such. Frederick Winslow Taylor, Mary Parker Follett, and Chester Barnard are prominent management thinkers who have been adopted. This tendency is reflected in the distinction sometimes made between self-conscious public administration and the non-self-conscious kind. A thinker such as Waldo writes public administration and knows that he is writing public administration, for example; a thinker such as Foucault makes a statement about pastoral power (a statement about public administration) and may believe that he is writing about governmentality rather than making a claim of critical importance to public administration theory.

The second category—the H2 category—includes those self-conscious public administration thinkers who did, and do, political or interpretive or critical analyses without recognizing them as being in a hermeneutic tradition. Much political writing relating public administration and larger political concerns would be in this category. One of the many examples of such political analyses is Appleby's *Big Democracy*.[7] Appleby writes about the differences between the public and private sectors, and he discusses his optimism about government control of bureaucracy despite the size of departments. Perhaps most thinkers in the H2 category would be aware that they are not performing science even if they do not consider themselves to be in a particular hermeneutic tradition. An example might be the kind of interpretive work that Harlan Cleveland has in mind when he argues that public administration should be treated as neither science nor rationalism but as "merely wisdom."[8] Among the theses he supports are that public administration in the 1990s will be the "art of making creative interconnections," and he urges, "Above all, let's put behind us the idea that the politics and administration of human endeavors are some kind of science."[9]

Examples of public administrationists conducting interpretive or critical studies, as Jay White indicates, are those who write case studies, reports of action research projects, descriptive histories, descriptions of administrative experiences, philosophical analyses, political theories, or social critiques.[10] In this article White is responding to a claim by Robert Cleary and Howard McCurdy that public administration dissertation research work is inadequate in that it fails to "meet the criteria that conventionally define careful, systematic study in the social sciences."[11] These criteria include purpose, validity, testability, causality, topical importance, and cutting-edge significance: in other words, good causal research. White's response is that these criteria represent an unduly narrow view of adequate research. He supports a theory of knowledge that would recognize interpretation and criticism: "The result is a theory of knowledge and its use which is broader than that of the mainstream social sciences and better represents the types of research that have been a part of public administration for more than 80 years."[12] He gives Waldo's *The Administrative State* as an example of work that has contributed to our knowledge of public administration but that would be discounted by Cleary and McCurdy's criteria of causality, testability, and validity. Through interpretations and criticisms, White holds, "a significant amount of knowledge about public administration has developed."[13]

The importance of the H2 category should be stressed. It could be said that hermeneutic reconceptualizations have been the factors that have at times changed the direction of the subject. Consider New Public Administration as a hermeneutic, as an H2, activity. It offered an interpretation, a reading or misreading, of the nature of organizations and the role of individuals within public agencies. New Public Administration, largely an outgrowth of the 1960s American domestic upheavals, was a counterestablishment movement. Among the perceptions it stressed, for instance, was the role in bureaucracy of values, equity, change, and participation. The New Public Administration conceptualized preference for decentralization, participation for clients and employees, greater accountability, equity rather than efficiency, non-bureaucratic organizational forms, understanding of social values, and the production in the bureaucracy of change agents who would make public administration more responsive. The reconceptualization resulted in experimentation with such initiatives as citizen participation in the formal structure of governmental bureaucracies (e.g., in Model Cities structures) and in the administration of programs (e.g., giving welfare clients a role in welfare program activities). A similar intent lies behind the ideas advanced for the Blacksburg Manifesto, the set of ideas that Wamsley characterizes as "Minnowbrook 1 with institutional grounding."[14] These ideas include recognizing the participant's role in the governing process of both the public administration (or public bureaucracy) and the public administrator.[15]

A case could be made that the engine of the development of the study of public administration has been essentially hermeneutic, a rereading of meanings and a search for meanings; causal science, in this view, might be seen as a bit player. Arguably, the discipline of public administration has advanced because of the reinterpretations of basic concepts (i.e., because of the non-self-conscious hermeneutic element). This element would include reinterpretations that are parts of scientific development. Some who consider themselves as conducting science have given a re-reading of public administration practice.

Consider decision theory. In attempting to lay the groundwork for a science of administration, Simon made important "hermeneutic" decisions about the nature of a decision. First, he made decisions the center of analysis. Second, he defined decisions in a particular way. Lindblom gave a different reading. These rereadings of the role and nature of a decision significantly shaped the study of public administration. Consider systems theory. The developers of systems theory permitted organizations to be interpreted in a way that is distinct from, say, the interpretation in neoclassical organization theory. This reading, or interpretation, gave a new understanding and meaning to "organization"; it changed the spectacles through which we see.

The H3 category consists of those public administrationists whose work includes (at least in part) self-conscious hermeneuticism. This H3 category can be divided into two subcategories: the interpretive and the critical. Interpretative analysis is intended to elucidate meaning, and critical analysis is intended to go further by pointing out oppressive features (such as repressed meanings) of societal and public administration practice. Of course, the borderline between these subcategories is not always clear, and some writers (e.g., Denhardt, according to White[16]) have written on both sides of this fence. Nevertheless, this discussion is not an attempt to minimize the importance of the distinction. Interpretation aims to understand; critical theory wants to liberate people, and interpretation is part of this process.

Jay White gives examples of three types of "unique and powerful theories of organization" offered by some public administration theorists.[17] He means critical theories, interpretive theories, and action theories. As examples of critical theorists, he offers Denhardt[18] and Dunn and Fozouni.[19] As an example of an interpretive theorist, he notes Hummel.[20] As examples of action theorists, he offers Catron,[21] Harmon,[22] and (as he should) himself.[23] Earlier, White offers some additional and some of the same names.[24] Additional citations are provided for Denhardt,[25] Diamond,[26] Schon,[27] and Argyris.[28]

The journals *Administration and Society* and *Administrative Theory and Praxis* are significant sources of H3 articles. Examples of the former are articles by Arthur Felt, Anne-Marie Rizzo and Dolores Brosnan, and Jay White. Felt adapts Habermas's concept of communicative competence in analyzing organizational communication failures.[29] Rizzo and Brosnan see themselves as building on Habermas's critical theory perspective and Forester's typology of communication distortion "to analyze sexual harassment as symptomatic of communication dysfunction in macrocosm."[30] White writes about administration in terms of action theory and literary interpretation.[31]

The use of interpretive and critical research in public administration can be examined from the points of view of two public administration writers, Michael Harmon and Robert Denhardt. Michael Harmon, associated particularly with action theory, gives a perspective (with a colleague) in his *Organization Theory for Public Administration*.[32] This view can be supplemented by consideration of applied phenomenology in the 1990 issue of *Public Administration Quarterly,* introduced by Ralph Hummel.[33] Robert Denhardt gives a perspective in his *Theories of Public Organization*.[34]

Harmon describes two public administration contributors to interpretive theory: himself (for his *Action Theory for Public Administration*) and Ralph Hummel (for his *The Bureaucratic Experience*). Denhardt also describes Harmon, and he characterizes Harmon's *Action Theory for Public Administration* as "[by] far the most comprehensive application of phenomenology to the field of public administration."[35] As for critical theory, Harmon describes work by Robert Denhardt[36] and John Forester,[37] and he comments on the work of managerial humanists such as Argyris and McGregor. He also cites work by Kathryn Denhardt, William Dunn and Bahman Fozouni, and Ralph Hummel.[38] Robert Denhardt notes that "few explicit attempts have been made to apply critical analysis to the study of public organization,"[39] but he does refer to Dunn and Fozouni,[40] Hummel,[41] Argyris and Schon,[42] and his own work.[43]

Harmon summarizes his argument in *Action Theory for Public Administration* in terms of eighteen propositions. The following is a truncated list. The full list and descriptions can be found in the introduction to the book and throughout Harmon's text.[44]

3. The primary unit of analysis in social theory should be the face-to-face situation (or encounter). . . .
6. Descriptions and explanation in social science should be primarily concerned with action, a concept that directs attention to the everyday meanings people give to their actions. . . .
9. The primary value in the development of a normative theory for public administration is mutuality. . . .
11. . . . Decision rules and institutional processes associated with them are the primary ingredients of organization "structure." Five kinds of rules are or can be employed in public organizations: hierarchy (unilateral decision), bargaining or market rules, voting, contract and consensus. . . .
14. Criticisms of classical responsibility implied by the action approach suggest an alternative and normatively preferred meaning of responsible administrative action, namely, personal responsibility.
15. Irresponsible administrative action is rooted in the cognitive processes that lead people to deny or simply not comprehend personal responsibility for their actions. These processes constitute the problem of reification.[45]

Harmon believes that the action theory, constituted by his propositions, provides (as he puts it in his proposition 18) "a framework within which 'applied' theory and administrative practices may be developed and critically evaluated."

Ralph Hummel's *The Bureaucratic Experience* first appeared in 1976. As Hummel puts it, it "originated as a lone protest against life in modern organizations, one intended to do no more than lay bare the underlying realities producing the agonies of the bureaucratic age."[46] Hummel explains that the second edition reworked the core chapters, added work of other writers, and led to the establishment of a "network of mutually supportive researchers, which continues as the Institute for Applied Phenomenology."[47]

Hummel summarizes the framework of *The Bureaucratic Experience* in these words:

> First, bureaucracy—whether public or private—is an entirely new way of organizing social life. It succeeds society, just as society has succeeded community. Second, bureaucracy, a world into which we are recruited, differs from society, the world into which we are born, in five ways (1) socially, (2) culturally, (3) psychologically, (4) linguistically, and (5) power-politically. Bureaucracy is a new society and a new culture. . . . Third, bureaucracy, because it differs from society in these five ways, poses special difficulties for people depending on where they stand.[48]

This view does seem, as Hummel's preface suggests, to be more in the vein of critical theory than interpretive theory. Hummel claims, for example, that bureaucracies have a one-directional acausal language—one that is "usually so constructed as to prevent both bureaucrats and outsiders from ever formulating questions that might attack the underlying assumptions of the bureaucracy itself."[49] Later, he goes further and makes the claim that one-directional talk is neither communication nor language. For him, it is information, a method of "talking" that is concerned with power: "The 'language' through which bureaucracy speaks to us is not designed for problem solving. . . . [B]ureaucratic language consists of fragments of information. These fragments each describe actions that the client must carry out if he or she is to become part of the system of administration which the bureaucracy represents—that is, if he or she is to become functional."[50]

The phenomenological "variant of interpretive theory," as Harmon characterizes it and as he tells it,[51] was introduced into the public administration literature in the 1960s. Hummel gives an account of phenomenology in a symposium report on the progress of phenomenology applied to public administration.[52] As he puts it, "[To] manage phenomenologically is to so approach things (people, conditions, objects) that they can show themselves as they really are. Any approach is phenomenologically oriented that enables an employee to show a manager what he really has it in him to do. Any approach is phenomenological that enables, say, political conditions to 'speak' to the manager thus revealing the conditions and restraints under which the manager must manage."[53] Applied phenomenology is contrasted, as Hummel indicates, with scientific management and rational management, including mathematics. Phenomenology has resulted, in his account, from the philosophical developments initiated with Husserl and from an "accumulation of management practices that could not be justified on scientific or pure rational grounds but that merely worked."[54]

Hummel claims that phenomenology has come of age. As he says, "Phenomenology, once only a critical tool, is explicitly or implicitly widespread in almost every function of management, including public administration."[55] The symposium report consists of papers on applications of phenomenology in various management areas. For example, Michael Harmon discusses applied phenomenology and organization. Harmon's view of applied phenomenology squares with Hummel's account; he says that it means "the activity of ferreting out practical lessons from what is best characterized loosely as a phenomenological attitude rather than a rigorous and systematic technique of analysis."[56] How he uses this view in his discussion is suggested by his definition of organizing as "a process of collective sense-making about what people have been doing, what they might want to do in the future, including (but not limited to) how they might want to do it."[57] Other papers are titled "Social Design in Public Problem Solving," "Psychological Phenomenology and Organizational Analysis," "Managing and the Crisis of Work in the Public Sector," "No Planning or Administration Without Phenomenology," "Interpretive Research: A New Way of Viewing Organizational Communication," and "Phenomenology and Organizational Development."[58]

There is a diversity of views within the philosophical movement that is known as phenomenology. *Phenomenology* is a term derived etymologically from *appearance* and *reason*. An appearance is interpreted as anything of which a person is conscious. Because of the diversity, a summary of phenomenological positions is difficult, but these positions include a wish to be free of presuppositions and a denial of the subject-object dichotomy. Applied to the social sciences, phenomenology is usually reported to be concerned with the "lived world" and with human relationships. The application of quantitative methods is considered inadequate. The intersubjective is primary, and human living is interpreted in terms of goals and meaning. Phenomenology has been discussed as going beyond the modern tradition in philosophy, it will be recalled.

It is valuable to see how an interpretive writer working in public administration sees the development of interpretive theory. Harmon traces what he calls the "European influence on interpretive theory" from German idealism—from Kant through Husserl and Weber. He describes differences between the latter two; he writes, "To Weber the sociologist . . . the idea of subjectivity is inherent in the descriptions of the meanings that constitute people's actions, in contrast to Husserl's philosophical concern with the innate structures of human consciousness."[59] He describes Alfred Schutz as seeking to merge Husserl's transcendental phenomenology with Weber's sociology. The primary disagreement of Schutz's existential phenomenology with naturalistic social science, according to Harmon, lies in the view that "the social world must be understood in terms of the subjective meanings or interpretations that people in the everyday world give to their experience."[60] He quotes Schutz as saying that social science should systematically "account for the way in which this social reality is constituted and maintained, in what ways it is intersubjective, or how actors in their common-sense thinking interpret their own actions and the actions of others."[61]

Harmon describes Peter Berger and David Silverman, both of whom followed Schutz, as presenting several ideas that form the "foundation" of the interpretive approach. These ideas are the action-behavior distinction, the face-to-face encounter, intentionality and intersubjectivity, and the problem of reification. The act-behavior distinction was discussed in chapter 5. The face-to-face encounter, rather than the system or the individual, is described as the primary unit of analysis. Under the next heading, Harmon notes that the social world is a product of consciousness: "Although seeming real and concrete in the way we experience it, the social world is really nothing more than the residue of our 'sedimented' experience."[62] Nevertheless, this creation is intersubjective, and this social creation is made possible by language. As he puts it, "Language is more than simply the instrument of communication; it is the essence of social existence."[63] The problem of reification, resulting from a forgetting of our creation of social entities, occurs when we have the false impression that social entities have a concrete independent existence: that is, they have a dehumanized existence.

David Silverman's "action frame of reference," in Harmon's view, provides the most direct application of Schutzian sociology to the study of organization theory. Harmon reports seven propositions that summarize Silverman's approach to organization theory:

1. The social sciences and the natural sciences deal with entirely different orders of subject-matter. While the canons of rigor and scepticism [sic] apply to both, one should not expect their perspective to be the same.
2. Sociology is concerned with understanding action rather than with observing behavior. Action arises out of meanings which define social reality.
3. Meanings are given by men to their society. Shared orientations become institutionalised [sic] and are experienced by later generations as social facts.
4. While society defines man, man in turn defines society. Particular constellations of meaning are only sustained by continual reaffirmation in everyday actions.
5. Through their interaction men also modify, change and transform social meanings.
6. It follows that explanations of human actions must take account of the meanings which those concerned assign to their acts; the manner in which the everyday world is socially constructed yet perceived as real and routine becomes a crucial concern of sociological analysis.
7. Positivistic explanations, which assert that action is determined by external and constraining social or non-social forces, are inadmissible.[64]

Harmon's own work uses Gibson Winter's intentionalist social ethics. Harmon explains that, unlike the leading interpretive sociologists, Winter attempts to derive ethical theory from an interpretive perspective. The social and active nature of the intentional self provides the basis for the ethical, and Harmon believes that a significant feature of Winter's conception of social ethics is the "we-relation."[65] By focusing on the face-to-face encounter (as Harmon describes the we-relation), Winter thinks it possible to derive such normative values as love and mutuality. Harmon's choice (in his proposition 3, above) of the face-to-face situation as the unit of analysis will be recalled.

Denhardt's 1984 summary of work on a critical analysis of public organizations is titled "Toward a Critical Analysis of Public Organizations."[66] As this title suggests, the emphasis of the summary is on work that will be conducted rather than work that has been performed. Thus, he says, "Specifically, a critical theory of public organizations would examine the technical basis of bureaucratic domination and the ideological justification for this condition, and would ask in what ways members and clients of public bureaucracies might better understand the resultant limitations placed on their actions and in turn develop new modes of administrative praxis."[67] Such an approach would, to paraphrase his account, include constructing its understanding of public policy formulation and implementation on a value-critical basis; laying the foundations for greater autonomy both within the bureaucracy and in its interactions with others; highlighting aspects of bureaucratic theory that limit the individual's part in the governing process; emphasizing the conditions of power and dependence that characterize organizational life, including analysis of communication flows and alternative management styles; and understanding the relationships between bureaucrats and clients. He ends that section with the hope, "Under such conditions, the public bureaucracy might even become a primary vehicle for societal self-reflection and critique."[68]

Such public administration theorists who have undertaken critical theory acknowledge indebtedness to the Frankfurt school and Jürgen Habermas, as Denhardt indicates in his book and earlier in an article written with Kathryn Denhardt. In his 1984 book, Denhardt discusses three items from that school: the critique of instrumental reason, the reduction of the public sphere, and the restoration of undistorted communication. Habermas's ideas on the public sphere were noted in chapter 4. On the critique of reason, Denhardt reports that the Frankfurt school sees itself as going further than Weber's analysis of calculative or mean-ends reason, and he quotes Habermas as seeing a solution in terms of communicative interaction. On restoring communication, he reports on Habermas's concern with language and how we must identify the distortion that results from domination. Robert and Kathryn Denhardt's 1979 article argues for the use of critical theory in studying public administration and for a continuing critique of domination.[69] The article discusses the "European critical theorists" such as Habermas and Horkheimer; for instance, it ascribes to Habermas the distinction between the sphere of symbolic or communicative interaction and the sphere of the purposive rational, the latter being instrumental. Among the points the article makes are that we find it difficult to escape the version of reality imposed on us by a rationalized society and that we "can fully engage in broad choices only by moving outside a system of regulation."[70] The article, relying on Farganis,[71] identifies four distinctions between critical theory and positivist public administration. The former is holistic, views reason as negation, is consciously theoretical, and is based on dialectical rather than functional analysis. The Denhardts write that applying critical theory to public administration would involve discovering the meaning of human action, and they want to achieve through praxis a linking of reflection and action. The critique of domination, in their view, is intended to restore "to the field of administration a sense of service and integrity based on the theme of enlightened action."[72]

MORE COMMENT ON HABERMAS

The most celebrated resistance to the abandonment of modernity comes from Jürgen Habermas (e.g., through *The Theory of Communicative Action*[73]). As suggested in chapter 3, his view is that modernity is an incomplete project. He acknowledges the barrenness of the "cognitive-instrumental" rationality of the subject conceptualized as having the two basic relations of representation and action as she stands against a world of objects. He understands that the Cartesian solitary thinker on whom reason is founded has been undermined. As Thomas McCarthy explains in his introduction to *The Theory of Communicative Action* (and the next three paragraphs, but not the fourth or fifth, follow his interpretation), the Cartesian paradigm and associated subjectivist orientation were challenged in the last century by Hegel, Marx, Darwin, Nietzsche, and Freud. The result is what Habermas calls a "desublimation of spirit" and thus a "disempowering of philosophy." He points out that forms of the Cartesian model underlie Husserl and logical positivism but that now we live in a post-Heideggerian, post-Wittgensteinian, poststructuralist age. As McCarthy explains,

> The spirit has been shown to be "infiltrated with the world" in such a way that "otherness is carried to the very heart of selfhood." This "twilight of subjectivity" is not merely an intraphilosophic affair. . . . It is the theoretical center of the stream of antimodernist thought. . . . The critique of "rootless rationalism" goes hand in hand with an unmasking of the anthropocentric, egoistic, possessive, and domineering aspects of Western individualism. . . . We cannot ignore the question of whether in the absence of an archimedean point outside the world, anything can be salvaged from these emphatic concepts and the universalist claims connected with them.[74]

Habermas wants a methodology for critical theory that combines the philosophical and the empirical (or scientific). Thus, he seeks to escape from the dead end that Weber presents for modernity (the increasing influence of calculative rationality and the impossibility of resolving value conflicts rationally) with two moves. One move involves his concept of communicative action, reaching for "communicatively shared intersubjectivity." The other move is to combine his idea of the "lifeworld" (a "culturally transmitted and linguistically organized stock of interpretive patterns") with system theory. He analyzes social evolution in terms of the "decoupling of system and lifeworld" and increasing differentiation within lifeworld and system.

Weber stressed the general encroachment of rationalization; Habermas highlights, as McCarthy explains, the forms and the lack of balance in the development. Within the processes of differentiation, Habermas describes the appearance of encoded forms of purposive-rational activity; he calls these forms "delinguistified steering media." Money and power are examples; he describes how modern lives are monetarized and bureaucratized. The monetary system is institutionalized (e.g., in property and contract law), and it interacts with other systems such as the political, for example; it acquires a momentum and directive force of its own. The private sphere is "undermined and eroded by the economic system." A similar analysis is offered for the public sphere (discussed in chapter 4), a sphere undermined and eroded by the administrative system.

Habermas's defense of the project of modernity involves turning from the philosophy of consciousness to a philosophy of language. He disagrees with Weber's claim that rationality has no prospects for rejuvenating itself. Habermas holds that the communicative forms of language, not the cognitive-purposive or instrumental, are primary. Orientation to reaching understanding, rather than orientation to success, is the "original mode of language use, upon which indirect understanding, giving something to understand or letting something be understood, and the instrumental use of language in general, are parasitic."[75] For him, reason does not need to be regenerated; it will regenerate itself because communicative reason is part and parcel of language.

This view is not at all a matter of merely claiming that communicative action "should" be primary, and it could be that the description of the public administration application of such views may have created such a false impression. The claim is that communicative action in fact has priority. For Habermas, language as communicative discourse is emancipatory, and communicative discourse is primary over other forms of action and discourse. Habermas's claim about the regenerative role of communicative reason parallels, as it were, the Marxist claim (and the Christian claim) that the success of the revolution (or of the Church) is inevitable; the triumph is inevitable regardless of what we do. After the 893 pages of *The Theory of Communicative Action*, however, it might not be clear why such a triumph must be inevitable.

THE PSYCHOLOGICAL CRITIQUE OF REASON

Hammers that weaken the modernist view are the critiques of rationality, undermining and decentering what the modernist sees as the foundation of reason.[76] The subject of reason—the reasoner—has been undermined by a variety of critiques, including the psychological. The rest of this chapter will focus on explaining the psychological source of this decentering; the other critiques, such as Marx's, could have been added. Both the conclusions of modernist interpretation and the results of the scientific method depend on reason. When the difficulties of deciding among nonprivileged interpretations is resolved (if they can be), the rock is reasoning. Nevertheless, is the rock still holding? Is it really a rock?

As Foucault points out, the modern *cogito* ("I think") must be different from Descartes's cogito because human consciousness is bound up in an unthought that is unclear to the cogito's thought.[77] As he explains, the subject of thought does not completely understand the subject as an object of thought. Descartes wants to determine an indubitable foundation for knowing, something about which he could be certain. He rejects various candidates, such as his body, because of various "unthoughts"; he notes, variously, that his senses have often deceived him, he cannot be sure that he is not dreaming, and he cannot be sure that an evil genius is not out to deceive him. He concludes, however, that he can be sure about one thing: the "I." "I" think, therefore "I" am. The "I" is the rock, the reasoner, on which he can start building.

Could not a parallel critique be developed of the organization, understood in Simon's terms as the basis of good reasoning? Who is the subject of an organization's reasoning? In Simon's view, it is the organization through the person or persons who direct (or make up) the agency. Simon explains that the organization is capable of being more rational than the individual. It is impossible, he explains, for a single isolated individual to reach a high degree of rationality because the number of alternatives is so great and the amount of information is so vast: "A higher degree of integration and rationality can, however, be achieved, because the environment of choice itself can be chosen and deliberately modified."[78] Then he concludes the introductory section to his chapter 5 by saying, "In the course of this discussion it will begin to appear that organization permits the individual to approach reasonably near to objective rationality."[79]

As noted, other critiques of the subject exist (e.g., the linguistic critique of the subject as constitutive of meaning and the critique that speaks [such as Adorno and Horkheimer's] of instrumental reason).[80] These critiques complement the psychological critique discussed here; this can be illustrated by considering a bare outline of the linguistic critique. In philosophy of language, the idea that the subject, with her experiences and intentions, is the source of meaning has been attacked by various philosophers, such as the later Wittgenstein. Such philosophy of language undermines the autonomy of the subject (the foundation of knowing) if it succeeds in demonstrating that linguistic systems of meaning come from a preexisting world revealed through language. The subject does not determine the meaning of words (or signs) by assigning the signs to particular objects or things; that is, she does not assign a name to a given meaning. Meaning is set by the life-form, the language game, in which the speaker is speaking. Meaning refers to the intersubjective use of the language. We take the transparency of our language for granted, but it shapes the subject.

Freud both shows that the notion of an autonomous subject is a fiction and undermines the claim that the subject's reasoning is rational. It is appreciated that his objective, consistent with Enlightenment goals, was to show how people could gain more control of themselves, but we are speaking of the implications of his work. Descartes's "I" is dissolved into an ego that mediates between the id and the superego. The "I" is an entity swept here and there by psychic forces. It is an entity controlled in part by its unconscious, subject to forces long since forgotten by the conscious ego. The subject's reason is the expression of psychic and social forces.

The subject is master neither of his own psyche nor even of his own dreams. The author of *The Interpretation of Dreams* writes that even the subject's dream is a disguised fulfillment of a repressed wish and that the wish is an infantile one. Except by analysis, the subject has no idea about this repressed wish and has long forgotten (repressed, in fact) the infantile wish. To understand the dream, the subject should pay attention to the layer cake and the entrepreneur models of the psyche and should be alert to the suggested structure (id, ego, and superego) and dynamics of the psyche, the underlying force. He or she should be alert to parallels to the sources of the dream's facade; Freud gives four such sources: universal human experiences, infantile material, the day's residue, and contemporary sensations. The subject should remember the problems of primary and secondary elaboration, including the problems of condensation, displacement, and symbolization. Again, the subject has been decentered.

Consider Freud in *Beyond the Pleasure Principle* and the implications for the autonomy and rationality of the subject.[81] Here, Freud advances his view that the judgments of each subject are shaped by the death instinct, the name given, as Laplanche and Pontalis explain, to a basic category of Trieb (sometimes translated as "instinct" or "drive"[82]) in the framework of the final Freudian theory of the instincts. Laplanche and Pontalis summarize Freud's doctrine of the death instinct in this way: It is opposed to the life instinct; it strives to reduce tensions to the zero point; its goal is to bring the living back to the organic state; to begin with, the death instinct is directed inward; it tends toward self-destruction; and it is "subsequently turned towards the outside world in the form of the aggressive and destructive instinct."[83] These points allow Laplanche to give a central position to the death instinct. For instance, Laplanche describes the death drive as "the very soul, the constitutive principle of libidinal circulation."[84] Even sexuality is the dance toward death, and so Laplanche can reverse the popular association of sexuality with life—for instance, seeing sucking the breast as hostile to life. Paul Ricoeur provides a complementary interpretation: "The extreme is this: living things are not put to death by external forces which suppress them, as in Spinoza; they die, they go to death by an internal movement. . . . Better—or worse?—life itself is not the will to change, to develop, but the will to conserve itself: if death is the aim of life, all of life's organic developments are but detours toward death, and the so-called conservative instincts are but the organism's attempts to defend its own fashion of dying, its particular path to death."[85] He quotes Freud, "[E]verything living dies for internal reasons. . . . the aim of all life is death," and he could have added, "The death instincts are by their nature mute. . . . [T]he clamor of life proceeds for the most part from Eros." In this account, deep uncontrollable forces shape what we want and how we think.

Carl Jung's account shows the subject even more dramatically in the unthought control of forces beyond the self. Consider Jung's notion of the collective or transpersonal unconscious, as Hall and Lindzey interpret and explain it.[86] It is a universal, inherited and shared by all people as the foundation of each of our personalities; it is a foundation that makes us more than metaphorically "one" not only with all the other billions of living people but also with all who have ever lived. This unconscious is a repository of latent memory traces not only from our racial history but also from our evolutionary and prehuman past. Part of the structural components of this unconscious are the numerous archetypes, permanent deposits in the mind from generations of experiences. Archetypes are entities, as Hall and Lindzey explain, such as energy, the hero, God, the earth mother, the demon, rebirth. Some entities are so developed that they are entire systems within the personality, such as the animus, the anima, and the shadow. Archetypes from our collective unconscious do more than merely shape our behaviors; they do more than feature in our dreams, rituals, and maladies. Jung explains that the form, the structure, of the world that we are born into is already inborn within us; that is, each of us comes into the world with a virtual image of the world with us. This image then becomes a concrete perception when it is identified with objects in the world; the way that we see the world is largely determined by our collective unconscious. In Jung's words quoted at the head of this chapter, the "form of the world into which he is born is already inborn in him as a virtual image." This account does undermine the notion of a rational subject, the transparent "I" of Descartes' cogito. It shows a subject shaped by forces over which she has little control and hardly understands. It also shows the difficulty for the subject in ever having a nonperspectival view of the subject as object. The way that a person sees herself is shaped in large part by the virtual image with which she is born.

This point could raise an incidental question concerning the relationship of the collective unconscious and organizations, whether archetypes shape rituals that are part of organizational life or whether organizations themselves have unconscious drives.[87] Aspects of this particular question have interested some organization theorists.[88] For example, Hubbell has written about four archetypal shadows that affect the behavior of employees. He writes of people "caught in the grip of their unconscious shadow" not choosing to affirm life, but he ends in a positive manner by noting that the power to change ourselves and our organizations lies within each of us.[89] The psychoanalytic organizational literature is divided on the relationship of the individual unconscious and the organization.[90]

The point of the discussion lies elsewhere, however. It centers on the undermining of the transparency of the subject and the nature of reasoning. Recall chapter 3 and the discussion of modernity. Modernity, we noticed there, is the age of the centered subject. It was explained that "what is" is explored in terms of what appears to the individual subject and how knowing can be grounded in that same individual subject. This point was illustrated in terms of Heidegger's view of the emergence of the subject leading to world picturing. One sense in which the self is centered is that the world consists in what the subject pictures. The claim was made that the subject was centered at the Festival of Reason.

SUMMARY

The search for rational meaning in public administration is useful up to a point. But blind spots and contraries do occur because particular interpretations are always open to newer and better interpretations. Interpretations cannot claim a privileged status, such as that intended for scientific statements. A contrary is met when the pursuit of meaning encounters the undermining of reason and rationality. This undermining has been accomplished by a variety of critiques, such as the linguistic. Critical theorists, on the other hand, have attempted to salvage modernity; Habermas, for example, writes of what he considers to be the inevitable triumph of communicative rationality. The critique highlighted in this chapter is the psychological. Freud shows that the notion of an autonomous and rational subject is a fiction. He writes of the influence of powerful unthought forces, such as the death instinct. Jung's analysis goes even further, speaking of the unthought control of transpersonal psychic forces. The claims of reason are weakened as the subject is decentered.

This topic of hermeneutics is the fifth line of development considered for modernist public administration. In each area (particularism, scientism, technologism, enterprise, and hermeneutics), modernist public administration encounters paradoxes and blind spots. The initial general hypothesis stated at the beginning of this study is supported. Along each critical avenue, modernist public administration theory meets walls limiting its capability for explanation and understanding.

9

Postmodernity
The Dialect

The real political task today, at least in so far as it is also concerned with the cultural . . . is to carry forward the resistance that writing offers to established thought, to what has already been done, to what everyone thinks, to what is well known, to what is widely recognized, to what is "readable," to everything which can change its form and make itself acceptable to opinion in general. . . . The name most often given to this is postmodernism.

—Lyotard[1]

If an angel were ever to tell us something about his philosophy, I reckon we would hear many sentences like "2 + 2 = 13."

—Lichtenberg[2]

DIFFERENT PSYCHOLOGICAL TYPES surely tend to be attracted to one set of views more than to another. It may well be that those with strong sensate and judgmental functions (in terms of the Myers-Briggs personality inventory) might be more attracted to modernity. It may be that those with stronger intuitive and perceptive functions are more open to postmodernity. Accountants and engineers might be more likely to prefer modernity; painters and poets—as well as astrologers and flat-earthers— might have more empathy for postmodernity. The moral of this paragraph is not that man is the measure of all things including the acceptability of postmodernity. Rather, it is that we must guard against approaching this topic with our psychological biases showing. No rush should be made to accept postmodernity as gospel or to dismiss it as a mere fad.[3] If we are to succeed in becoming clearer about postmodernity and in using it to learn about public administration theory and bureaucracy, then there is a need for patience.

Examination of postmodernity can reveal much about the language of public bureaucracy. The first step is to explore postmodernity. There are significant variations among postmodern thinkers, but rather than emphasizing them, it seems more important in this chapter to indicate a general direction. The second step, undertaken in the four following chapters, is to treat public administration and bureaucracy in terms of what might be described as aspects of the postmodern situation, that is, imagination, deconstruction, deterritoriality, and alterity.

INTERPRETING POSTMODERNITY

What is postmodernity? Postmodernity should be understood as negating the core mind-set of modernity, as negating the assumptions that have underlain important thinking during the last five centuries. Postmodernity should be interpreted as denying the core pattern of ideas, the Weltanschauung, that constitutes modernity; this denial would include denying the very process of having a Weltanschauung. It would deny the centered subject and the nonprimacy of discourse and deny the foundationalist and epistemological project that has been at the center of philosophizing in modernity. It would deny that the central task is the picturing of the world, denying the value of grounding the subject's knowledge of the world in the subject. It would deny the view of the nature and role of reason implicit in modernity's view of the centered subject. It would deny macrotheory, grand narratives, and macropolitics. It would deny the distinction between reality and appearance. Postmodernity's denial of modernity, as this list implies, is denial in a particular way. It would not permit a denial of modernity in the sense of a return to premodernity. According to postmodernists, we cannot return to the old gods, to the old society where the subject is embedded in a social role and a value context.

These formulations are negativities. Modernity can yield convenient sets of propositions that invite examination in terms of the laws of logic. Postmodernity does not fit into this mold. As Rorty states, "Lack of seriousness, in the sense in which I have just attributed it to Derrida, is simply this refusal to take the standard rules seriously, conjoined with the refusal to give a clear answer to the question, 'Is it the old game played differently, or rather a new game?' "[4] Postmodernity should be seen as an aggregation, as noted in chapter 1, of negativities. It is a rough-and-tumble disorder/order of ideas/nonideas. We must not look for the gems among the dross; the distinction between gems and dross is denied. In the postmodernist view, an orderly and true account of reality is not what we should expect, nor should we expect a disorderly and untrue account, an account of unreality. Derrida himself describes the *vouloir-dire* as metaphysical and therefore unacceptable: "I try to write the question: (what is) meaning to say? Therefore it is necessary in such a space, and guided by such a question, that writing literally mean nothing."[5]

Why is it so difficult to digest postmodernism, one among a number of "post" descriptions, such as postempiricism, postrationalism, poststructuralism, and postindustrialism? One possibility is that postmodernism might be incoherent nonsense. Another alternative is that, imbued with the assumptions of modernity and regarding them as constituting "common sense," we feel a need to understand and justify the claims of postmodernity in terms of modernity. Part of the difficulty in comprehension can be understood if we examine what it would mean for postmodernity to be incoherent nonsense. To be incoherent and nonsensical, a postmodern view (or any other view) would have to fail to meet some set of criteria for coherence and sense; it would have to fall outside the pale of sense and coherence. This understanding fails if postmodernism is recognized as denying a distinction between sense and nonsense and between coherence and incoherence. It fails if postmodernism is recognized to go on to deny that this means only nonsense exists; there is only an intermingling of sense and nonsense. Nevertheless, from the modernist perspective, this explanation is unappealing.

Armed (or burdened) with the baggage of modernity, a helpful way to approach postmodernity is through reflection on the reflexivity problem, the epistemological status of scientific propositions, and the claim that history has ended. For discussion of the reflexivity problem, see chapter 2. Reflexivity was described in terms of each observer seeing through her own perspective (through her own conceptual framework or from her own context), with the reflexivity problem being that no possibility of seeing exists except from a particular perspective. Even the general observation of "no possibility of seeing except from a particular perspective" is seen from a particular perspective: all the observers, in this view, are described as trapped within a perspectival cobweb. All knowledge, in this view, is essentially contextual; it cannot be disentangled from context. The literature arguing against the various skeptical[6] and relativistic positions about knowledge, resulting from this general kind of thinking, is large; it includes Plato arguing against Protagoras.[7] Nevertheless, as that literature suggests, a perspectival or contextual view of the nature of knowledge can hardly be dismissed out of hand.[8] Postmodernism is radical skepticism.

For comment on the status of scientific propositions, see chapter 5. Views of thinkers such as Kuhn, Lakatos, and Feyerabend were noted. Recall, for example, Kuhn, in the first edition of *The Structure of Scientific Revolutions,* writing of scientific paradigm shifts where the thinking between paradigms is described as incommensurable; there is said to be no rational basis for comparisons between paradigms. As Kuhn writes:

> The point-by-point comparison of two successive theories demands a language into which at least the empirical consequences of both can be translated without loss or change. . . . Philosophers have now abandoned hope of achieving any such ideal, but many of them continue to assume that theories can be compared by recourse to a basic vocabulary consisting entirely of words which are attached to nature in ways that are unproblematic and, to the extent necessary, independent of theory. . . . Feyerabend and I have argued at length that no such vocabulary is available. In the transition from one theory to the next words change their meanings or conditions of applicability in subtle ways.[9]

Such examples were used in chapter 5 to support the contention that the epistemological status of scientific propositions is unsure.

Approaching postmodernity through reflection on the idea of the end of history has an advantage in that it emphasizes the consequences of the advent of a "society of generalized communication."[10] A society of generalized communication is one transformed by the accelerated information flows made possible by the mass media, telecommunications, and computer capability; it is one dominated by images. Vattimo argues that this generalized communication has not made society more transparent; instead, it has resulted in an explosion and proliferation of Weltanschauungen: "Instead of self-transparency, we are moving toward the 'fabling of the world.' The images we receive are not simply different interpretations. They rather constitute the very objectivity of the world. There is no unitary reality. The reality of the world is the context for a multiplicity of fablings."[11] The notion of the end of history appeals to the idea that it is no longer possible to construct a unilinear account of historical events. A unilinear account is one that sees history as proceeding toward an end, such as rational improvement. The Enlightenment thinkers, as Vattimo explains, conceptualize the meaning of history in terms of the gradual realization of civilization in the form of Western European man. Because of the society of communication, we are more keenly aware of the many centers of history—the multitude of historical stories from various cultures. No longer can a single unilinear history be constructed that encompasses all these disparate Weltanschauungen or stories. What exists are "only images of the past projected from different points of view. . . . There is no 'History' . . . capable of unifying all other histories."[12] Such totalizing grand narratives as "the liberation of reason from the shadows of mythical knowledge"[13] are no longer possible. "Demythologizing has itself come to be seen as a myth."[14] As Vattimo puts it, the "demythologization of demythologization . . . may be taken as the true moment of transition from the modern to the postmodern."[15]

There is not only no single set of positions that can be said to make up postmodern theory but also no agreed usage of the term *postmodernity*. The word *modernity*, as has been often said, is contained within the term *postmodernity*. Thus, it is natural to suppose that postmodernity bears a relationship to whatever is understood by modernity. But there is a variety of views about the nature of this relationship. The view suggested here is the widely held one that this relationship should be understood as a denial. Others see postmodernity in different terms. For example, postmodernity may be seen as extending the core ideas of modernity or the forces inherent in modernity, working out the implications, and perhaps even ending with a transformed set of basic ideas and/or a transformed society. Jameson, Laclau, and Mouffe might be placed in this category. Frederic Jameson, for example, treats postmodernism as a stage in the unfolding of capitalism,[16] and Mouffe has described his and Laclau's view as both modern and postmodern.[17] Some distinguish between constructive (or revisionary) postmodernism and deconstructive (or eliminative) postmodernism. Constructive postmodernism has been described as including a revision of the modern world view, providing "a new unity"[18] of the scientific, ethical, aesthetic, and religious. It has also been described (almost vacuously) as a condition where community is restored.[19] Deconstructive postmodernism is the account given in this book. As Griffin writes, "From the point of view of deconstructive postmodernists, this constructive postmodernism is still hopelessly wedded to outdated concepts, because it wishes to salvage positive meaning not only for the notions of the human self, historical meaning, and truth as correspondence, which were central to modernity, but also for the premodern notions of a divine reality, cosmic meaning, and an enchanted nature."[20] Postmodernity has been seen by others as some basic set of attitudes that are beyond (meta) modernity, perhaps in the sense of being unrelated (in the way that the librarians are said to have placed Aristotle's metaphysics notes beyond [meta]—next to, on the other side of—the physics notes). Charles Jencks is an example of someone who does not see postmodernity as a reaction to modernity; he describes postmodernism in architecture as "double coding" of the "modern" with some other style.[21] Furthermore, the idea of denying or extending or being beyond can be understood in more than one way. For example, Foster distinguishes a "postmodernism which seeks to deconstruct modernism and resist the status quo and a postmodernism which repudiates the former to celebrate the latter."[22] Frankel claims that the modern-postmodern debate "has in many ways become an explicit debate over the nature of culture and social production in the emerging 'postindustrial' society."[23] No agreement exists regarding who should count as a postmodernist. Some contributors to postmodernity, it has already been suggested, would not describe their views as postmodern or themselves as postmodernists. Michel Foucault avoids the term and the title; Félix Guattari, another significant contributor, attacks postmodernism as cynical and conservative;[24] and Jacques Derrida (see chapter 8) is reluctant to use the term. Even those who would accept the title would offer differences. Jean Baudrillard would not agree with Frederic Jameson's treatment noted above. Baudrillard and others think in terms of a radical break with modernity; Jameson and others seek to use postmodern notions as part of their social theory and politics. If all those who have written of the postmodern are included, the differences would be even wider. See for example, Arnold Toynbee, an early user of the term. Toynbee describes the postmodern in terms of the rise of a new urban working class, other nations, and "post-Christian" religions.[25]

Tracing the roots and history of postmodernity yields an even more varied account. Precursors such as Nietzsche, Heidegger, and Wittgenstein (and the "dark writers of the bourgeoisie," as Habermas called them) can be identified.[26] Madison provides this information and goes further; he characterizes James's pragmatism as a genuine beginning (but one with no follow-up) for postmodernism in philosophy, and he describes the "genuine and real" beginning of postmodern philosophy as occurring in 1900 with Edmund Husserl.[27] In terms of social theory, discussions about a new form of society occurred in the 1950s and 1960s (e.g., Peter Drucker, C. Wright Mills, and Amitai Etzioni). The notion of postmodernity is well established in art history and aesthetic theory; postmodern forms developed in architecture, painting, poetry, and literature in the 1970s and 1980s. For example, literary theorists popularized the notion in the 1960s with criticisms such as those of the institutionalization of high culture.[28] Postmodernity has developed, with debts to the poststructuralists and others, most markedly and splendidly in France. Best and Kellner describe eight Continental writers in their account of postmodern theory: Michel Foucault, Gilles Deleuze, Félix Guattari, Jean Baudrillard, Jean-François Lyotard, Fredric Jameson, Ernesto Laclau, and Chantal Mouffe.[29] They make the decision to exclude the poststructuralists, that is, Jacques Derrida, Julia Kristeva, Roland Barthes, and Jacques Lacan. Postmodernity became of general interest in the social sciences only in the 1980s in the United States.

Whether a temporal break occurs between modernity and postmodernity, as Baudrillard and others would suppose, raises issues similar to those discussed in chapter 3. On the one hand, is it conceivable that modernity will last indefinitely? Is it not odd to think it impossible that we are entering, or have entered, a completely new era? Some might find supporting evidence for an historical break in some events, say, in the turbulence of the twentieth century, in the galloping world and city populations, or in the possible emergence of a post-Western era as the Pacific Rim grows more significant. An alternative is to see modernity and postmodernity as simultaneous. For example, it is possible to see postmodernity as representing the claim, as noted above, for limits having been reached in philosophy and social theory; thus, Lyotard can say that it is impossible for modernity to realize "the emancipation of humanity from poverty, ignorance, prejudice, and the absence of enjoyment."[30] Chapter 3, as another example, noted the possibility of viewing the modern and the postmodern as contrary tendencies of the human condition and of the group situations we encounter; that is, the modern and the postmodern are sometimes seen as simultaneous. The postmodern would find a resonating chord in the poetic sides of our nature; the modern would refer to our rational sides. Recall Nietzsche's Dionysian and Apollonian contrast mentioned in chapter 3. The contrast would be between the unsayability and the sayability of rationality, against and for a rationality that assumes that all can be explained clearly and that only rational explanations are true. Modernism and postmodernism might then be tendencies or processes in which we participate and that participate in us.

Postmodernity and modernity can be understood as existing synchronically or diachronically, that is, either simultaneously or at specific time periods. Intertextuality encounters a similar choice about temporality. Plett points out that intertextuality chooses to use two opposite perspectives. The synchronic regards all texts as existing simultaneously, and the diachronic adopts a historical approach.[31] This distinction can be blurred in some historical periodizing, it will be noticed. Ihab Hassan, for example, sees postmodernism going back to the 1930s or even the 1890s: "[A] 'period' is not generally a period at all; it is rather a diachronic and synchronic construct."[32]

Postmodernity can be seen as a matter of figural time. Lyotard, as noted in chapter 3, holds that the postmodern can occur before the modern: "A work can become modern only if it is first postmodern. Postmodernism thus understood is not modernism at its end but in the nascent state, and this state is constant."[33] Lyotard's view is that the postmodern indicates a temporal aporia, a time gap characterized by an event. An event, for him, is a happening that is so distinctive that it cannot be understood as merely a moment of time without losing its distinctiveness; it cannot be understood at the time because it changes the frame of reference of discourse. The enactment of the U.S. Constitution might be an example of such an event. As Lyotard puts it, "I made use of the word 'postmodern': it was but a provocative way to put the struggle in the foreground of the field of knowledge. Postmodernity is not a new age, it is the rewriting of some features modernity had tried or pretended to gain, particularly in founding its legitimation upon the purpose of the general emancipation of mankind. But such a rewriting . . . was for a long time active in modernity itself."[34]

HYPERREALITY

What is Baudrillard's hyperreality? Recall the statement made earlier in this chapter that the postmodern denies the distinction between reality and appearance. As Baudrillard writes, hyperreality "manages to efface even this contradiction between the real and the imaginary. Unreality no longer resides in the dream or fantasy, or in the beyond, but in the real's hallucinatory resemblance to itself."[35] Hyperreality is a merging of the real and the unreal as the real is transformed in the realm of simulation. This doctrine can be best expressed, like other postmodern ideas, in terms of negativities. In postmodernity, reality is not privileged. No dividing line exists between the real and the unreal, not even the assurance that comes from this positive statement. As Baudrillard writes, "Illusion is no longer possible, because the real is no longer possible."[36] He also states, "All appearances conspire to combat meaning, to uproot meaning, whether intentional or not."[37]

For Baudrillard, hyperreality is the result of implosions between entities formerly distinct. Hyperrealism is the "meticulous reduplication of the real, preferable through another reproductive medium, such as photography."[38] Hyperreality is a world, as he has explained, of simulacra without referents. It functions "entirely within the realm of simulation."[39] The whole of political, social, historical, and economic reality "is incorporated into the simulative dimension of hyperrealism."[40] Elsewhere, he expresses the idea in reverse manner. As he writes, "Today it is the quotidian reality in its entirety—political, social, historical and economic—that from now on incorporates the simulatory dimension of hyperrealism."[41] For him, all has imploded; all dividing lines are sucked inward. Simulations come to be more real than real. The experience and the foundation of the real disappear. The strength of this claim is paralleled by Baudrillard's view that the end of modernity marks the end of history. Baudrillard's view is that the modern-postmodern divide marks the crossing of the greatest chasm in the history of the universe—the change from truth to the end of truth. Baudrillard holds that the human race has dropped out of history.[42] For him, we have, without realizing it, left reality behind. But reality is "not extinguished."[43] The real becomes "not only that which can be reproduced, but that which is already reproduced; the hyperreal."[44] Reality "itself is hyperreality."[45]

Hyperreality is a difficult doctrine, just as are all the doctrines—or nondoctrines—of postmodernism. If hyperreality is understood not to be absurd, we should have no difficulty understanding as not absurd any other claims made for postmodernity. It would follow (if this verb is allowed) almost trivially that a foundationist and epistemological project would be pointless, as would a picturing of the world. The nature and role of reason could not be the same, and the modernist views of truth, system, coherence, and rationality would be denied. The notion of the end of history would also seem easier to understand. For such reasons, it is helpful to examine what can be said for the "reasonableness" of the hyperreality doctrine, although some postmodernists may have no special wish for reasonableness.

First, it may help to recognize the difficulty of defining and applying the term *real*. People do differ radically regarding what should be counted as real. For example, an idealist could say that the real is what is mind or spirit, a materialist could say that the real is the material, and so on.[46] Attempt a mind experiment. Look at what is around you and contemplate or imagine what is real and what is not real; do that first on the assumption of idealism and second on the assumption of materialism. Try some difficult cases. Are possibilities real? Are options real? Are future events real? Is the imaginary real? It is debatable whether possibilities are real, for example. Buchler states that for "the most part, philosophers have not known how they should use 'existence' or 'being' or 'reality' when confronted by problems concerning, for example, the relation between possibility and actuality."[47]

Thinkers differ not only regarding what should be classified as real but also regarding what the idea of real means. It is unclear whether the real refers to the furniture, or the ultimate furniture, of the universe. Does reality include the appearance of this word processor, or the word processor regardless of its appearance to me, or the chemical elements or the atomic particles that make up the word processor? It is also unclear whether the real refers to the existent. McTaggart thought it did—almost. He describes reality as "an indefinable characteristic, of which it can be said that whatever is, is real."[48] He states that even if there should be anything real that is nonexistent (such as possibilities), it would be of no practical interest. For Bradley, on the other hand, the real and the existent are not synonymous. He considers time and space to be unreal, for instance, but he writes that both exist: "Time and space are mere appearance, and the result is quite certain. Both, on the other hand, exist; and both must somehow in some way belong to our Absolute."[49] The situation is even more complex. For example, some would say that there are degrees of reality; others would deny this. Bradley and McTaggart, respectively, are examples of major thinkers taking these different positions.

A general description of the real can be given, but it is unclear how it can be defined. For example, Bertrand Russell offers a general description when he writes,

"When I talk about reality as I am now doing, I can best explain what I mean by saying that I mean everything you would have to mention in a complete description of the world; that will convey to you what I mean."[50] But all that Russell's comment achieves is to defer the problem; for example, what is a "complete description of the world"? A general description is not a definition. On the matter of definition, McTaggart argues that the "proposition 'whatever is, is real,' although true, does not help us to define reality, or to determine it in any other way, because in 'whatever is' the 'is' involves being, and being is the same as reality."[51]

For some thinkers, such as Moore, the real is a matter of common sense. In "A Defence of Common Sense," Moore takes the position that we have a "common sense view of the world" that is made up of propositions that we know to be true.[52] We know them (he thinks) with assurance. This view does suffer from the disadvantage that it represents more a statement of faith than an argument. For others, there is no single meaning of the word *real*. For example, J. L. Austin thinks that, although it is a normal word, *real* lacks a "single, specifiable, always-the-same meaning."[53] He describes it as substantive-hungry (in the sense that to say that X is real you have to know what X is) and as a "trouser word" (in the sense that not real is more basic to understanding *real*). He also describes *real* as a dimension word (a word in a group of other words, such as *artificial* and *genuine*) and as an "adjuster word" (providing exceptions to normal categories).

Second, it may help to recall that postmodernists would deny that reality is substance (because they would say that the very notion of substance is a metaphysical myth), and they would deny that the universe should be examined in terms of sets of opposites such as material-immaterial, becoming-being, and contingent-necessary. Descartes's idea of a finite substance is, "Everything in which there resides immediately, as in a subject, or by means of which there exists anything that we perceive, i.e., any property, quality, or attribute, of which we have a real idea, is called a substance."[54] The notion of substance has had various meanings during its long history, but the idea that one can distinguish between a thing and a thing's properties seems hard to sustain. For instance, as the English empiricists such as Berkeley and Hume say, it is hard to think about a substratum that has no properties or qualities.[55]

How, then, can we distinguish appearance from reality? The most respectable arguments can be advanced for utterly divergent answers. The philosopher F. H. Bradley was mentioned earlier. In one reading, appearances are things that are self-contradictory/self-discrepant/inconsistent.[56] The "Appearance" section of his *Appearance and Reality* is divided into primary and secondary qualities; substance and adjective; relation and quality; space and time; motion and its change and perception; causation; activity; things; the meanings of self; the reality of self; phenomenalism; and things-in-themselves. For Bradley, all of these appearances are self-contradictory, and the last two are not even appearances. According to Bradley, all relations are mere appearances because he holds that the idea of a relation involves a contradiction. Consider Bradley's reality. As Timo Airaksinen states, "Bradley's leading idea is that there is something which covers, or is, everything which is, namely some kind of prime totality, which in the true Hegelian manner is that infinite complex which has nothing outside itself. That totality is an 'immediate' unity."[57] On the other hand, we find Bertrand Russell arguing that the notion of a totality of facts leads to a contradiction.[58]

The point here is not merely that reality is a slippery topic but also that talk about appearance and reality tends to be addictive. Talking about the distinction tends to suggest that a distinction exists (even if one does not). We are heirs to a long tradition of such distinguishing. It goes back beyond the beginning of philosophizing. The ancient philosophers continued the search for the real that underlies the world of appearance. The word *continued* is used because we know of primitive religions and poets in the business of pointing out the reality behind the appearance, the gods and goddesses behind the thunder, the divine behind the earthquake and the burning bush; the Orphic and Homer are examples.[59] The Milesians sought the essential reality; Thales said water, Anaximander said the unbounded, and Anaximenes said air. Heraclitus said fire, and Pythagoras said numbers. Plato distinguished between the world of the Forms and the world of becoming, which only exists because it participates, in some manner, in the world of the Forms. The search for substance, for what accounts for the being and the unity of things, continued. (As indicated earlier, the notion of substance has been subjected to important critiques during recent centuries.) The distinction between appearance and reality is often thought to be Hegel's leading principle. We are heirs to all this history, heirs to the work of subsequent philosophers and scientists, heirs to the mechanical universe of modernity, and heirs to all the talk about the real in contemporary religions and in society. Perhaps we in modernity, it could be argued, have slipped into an unquestioning acceptance that a reality exists that is distinct from appearance. Such a disposition would make it harder to process Baudrillard's hyperreality claim.

Third, it may help to consider some cases where the distinction between appearance and reality seems especially blurred. One question is, Does it not seem that, over the years, the dividing line between what seems to be real and what seems unreal has become progressively more difficult to draw? Another question is, Could we not imagine a situation where it is impossible to draw any such dividing lines? Baudrillard could give many examples where the sign without the signified is "more real" than any signified, and he could point to the images or signs on the television, in the movies, in the way we talk, and in other aspects of everyday life. Advertising provides many examples. For example, Baudrillard asks us to imagine that, in a city that has been stripped of all its signs, the word GARAP appears on the walls.[60] It is a pure signifier without a signified. People wonder about it. It is discussed, interpreted, and consumed; people come to read meaning in, and to believe in, GARAP. For Baudrillard this illustrates the hyperreal.

Baudrillard could point to the status of signs, the merging of meaning and media, on the evening news and in political life. Viewers who have access to different national news programs (e.g., the American network news, Turner Broadcasting, and the Moscow Evening News) see, in a sense, a different reality on different news channels. Consider how the reality of the 1992 political conventions changed for those who switched between C-Span (with no intervening commentators) and the network channels (with many intervening commentators). Consider how an event becomes an event by being reported on television or in a newspaper. The political reporting of major newspapers, such as the *Washington Post* or the *New York Times,* is an example. Baudrillard could point to the images on the soap operas and in the movies. He could point to the hyperreality of the characters who do not represent persons of flesh and blood, such as Mr. Spock and Dirty Harry. Viewers become involved in characters' lives, rejoicing with their successes and empathizing with their troubles. The soap opera character becomes real. It is not enough to dismiss these situations as things the unsophisticated do. Is it not a mark of sophistication to be able to become involved in movies or plays or operas, suspending our disbelief and treating the stories and the characters as real?

The postmodernist asks us to consider how the ideal is often more real than the real. The ideal figure for a model is . . . The ideal weight for a man is . . . The ideal diet is . . . The ideal vacation is . . . The ideal way to spend Christmas is . . . The ideal time to go to bed is . . . Does not our language reflect a tendency to think of the ideal as really real? She is a real lady; he is a real man; he is a real soldier; she is a real artist. Consider now Baudrillard's estimate of Disneyland as the "idealized transposition of a contradictory real";[61] "Disneyland is there to conceal the fact that it is the 'real' country, all of 'real' America, which *is* Disneyland."[62]

The signs and images in other aspects of everyday life could be given as examples. Baudrillard was impressed by the hypermodern when he visited California.[63] He might have found the signs and symbols easier to notice in the relatively unfamiliar American Southwest. Much of familiar daily living is performed in an automatic way, as when a driver suddenly starts and realizes that she has been driving for many miles without thinking about it. If attention is focused on noticing hyperreality, then it is easier to notice the hyperreality of the signs and symbols encountered even in everyday life. The noticing may not occur at the conscious level. The notes for this chapter give excerpts of an account of a journey through the Southwest, which may encourage readers to try and come into contact with the hyperreality of the symbols and images they encounter.[64] By becoming conscious of the surrealism of images and symbols that appear or are felt through fiction or some shocking experience, perhaps Baudrillard's insights can be shared in various everyday settings. They can also be sought in public administration settings.

Because such surreal experiences are private, they cannot constitute any kind of proof, of course. Nevertheless, it is possible to appreciate how Baudrillard could have sensed hyperreality in California, even if we have difficulty in processing the appreciation. Moore, as a philosopher, thought it sufficient "proof" of external reality (proof of the existence of entities outside one's own mind) merely to wave his hands.[65] The assumption behind the waving of the hand is that "common sense" is a sufficient guide. Baudrillard justifiably might have objected to such a proof. He could well have questioned whether common sense is an adequate guide, whether a proof of reality is as simple as a wave of the hand. "There are more things in heaven and earth, Horatio, / Than are dreamt of in your philosophy." Surely, Hamlet is right. Such uncommonsensical findings as those of relativity and subatomic physics suggest that common sense, valuable as it is, sometimes can be nonsense.

THE KNOWLEDGE TURN

Come the postmodern turn, fundamental change can be expected in the conduct of all social and other inquiries. The study of public administration will change no less, as subsequent chapters explain. Radical change is to be expected in a world that denies the core pattern of ideas that constitutes modernity. As has just been discussed, postmodernity denies such fundamental assumptions as the distinction between reality and appearance, and it denies the character of reason implied in modernity's view of the centered subject. Change will occur in both the structure and character of the social and all other sciences.

Postmodernity contemplates the collapse of the boundaries between the scientific, the aesthetic, and the normative. Postmodernity denies, as chapter 12 will discuss, the boundaries between academic disciplines and the hierarchy of knowledge. There will be no economics, no psychology, no physics. Postmodernity also denies the ideals of truth, rational, system, and coherence. Consequently, no sciences of economics, psychology, and physics will exist. Scientific statements lose their privileged epistemological status. Science becomes discourse, subject to the deconstruction discussed in chapter 10.

Theorizing itself ends in postmodernity because postmodernity passes beyond history and theory. Yet discourse continues, and exciting possibilities for thinking occur. For example, a mingling of discourse can permit the figurative and the aesthetic to afford us additional possibilities for self-creation and creation. This idea of "self-creation," as Richard Rorty calls it, runs against the Cartesian and commonsensical notion that we look inside ourselves and discern a self. As Rorty writes, we must "see human beings as generators of new descriptions rather than beings one hopes to be able to describe accurately."[66]

The differences between postmodernist and modernist discourse are suggested by considering, in part, two lists that were drawn up by Ihab Hassan and that Margaret Rose interprets as having been intended by Hassan as "contrasting characteristics for 'Modernism' and 'Postmodernism.'" The items omitted from the lists are indicated in the notes.[67]

Modernism	Postmodernism
Form (conjunctive, closed)	Antiform (disjunctive, open)
Purpose	Play

Design	Chance
Hierarchy	Anarchy
Mastery/Logos	Exhaustion/Silence
Art Object/Finished Work	Process/Performance/Happening
Distance	Participation
Creation/Totalization	Decreation/Deconstruction
Synthesis	Antithesis
Presence	Absence
Centering	Dispersal
Signified	Signifier
Narrative	Antinarrative
God the Father	The Holy Ghost
Symptom	Desire
Origin/Cause	Différence—Différance/Trace[68]
Metaphysics	Irony
Determinacy	Indeterminacy
Transcendence	Immanence

Rose's gloss on this list should be noted. She observes that "the view of post-modernism given here is still one which Jencks for one will read as 'late modern' rather than as post-modern, and because, as with other 'late-modernisms,' it extends the language and categories of modernism rather than adding some new, or even older, meanings."[69]

When the new lens of postmodernity is turned to that patch of terrain that used to be public administration's, the problematics, as another example of the possibilities, could be expected to change. It is hard to avoid speaking in this representational and modernist way, as though the theory would change but the facts would remain. Modernist public administration and other facts are constituted in distinctive ways (e.g., separating private and public, media and bureau, politics and administration, reality and unreality). Take an isolated part of this terrain as an instance; modernist public administration theory would speak in terms of press relations as if the press were outside the getting things done through people. The problematics created in the postmodern situation, even the nature of problematizing itself, would radically change.

What in this postmodern era would be the relevant actions, if any, that would be valued for the purpose of public administration discourse? What are some distinctive interests on which the relevant postmodern discourse would focus? A parallel question about modernist public administration theory might be, What underlying lines of theoretical development would be valued? A set of answers has been offered in chapters 4 through 8 in this book. A parallel question about modernist public administration practice might be, What are the functions of the public administrator? One celebrated answer, although much criticized and corrected, was the acronym POSDCORB.[70]

It is to be expected that questions about the postmodern situation, the questions at the beginning of the previous paragraph, would yield different answers. They are discussed in subsequent chapters under four headings: imagination, deconstruction, deterritorialization, and alterity. Others may include other features, such as the aesthetic of the sublime or (what some postmodernists describe as the opposite of rationalization) dedifferentiation; the four headings included seem to me to be of special significance for bureaucracy. The order of the discussion could have been different.

SUMMARY

Descriptions of the nature of postmodernity vary even more than those about modernity. Postmodernity can be seen, variously, in diachronic or in synchronic terms. Viewing postmodernity as an historical epoch, some say that we have entered a new era. Understood as a tendency coexisting with modernity, postmodernity can be seen as one of the contrary tendencies in human nature and in the human condition. For example, there could be a contrast between the unsayability (postmodernity) and the sayability (modernity) of rationality. Postmodernism is skepticism, properly understood.

Postmodernity negates the core mind-set of modernity. It denies the centered subject, the foundationalist and epistemological project, the nature and role of reason, macrotheory, grand narratives, and macropolitics. It speaks of the end of history, and it denies the distinction between reality and appearance.

Hyperreality is a critical idea in postmodernity. It is the merging of the real and the unreal as the real is transformed in simulation. Hyperreality can be better understood if we consider, first, the difficulty in defining the term *real* and, second, the postmodernist's (and others') denial that reality is a substance. Understanding can also be facilitated if cases are examined where the distinction between reality and appearance is especially blurred.

In postmodernity, fundamental change can be expected in the conduct of all social and other forms of inquiries. The listing of some of the differences between modernity and postmodernity suggests the radical change in the intellectual climate. Social sciences and action programs as they are presently constituted will terminate. Theorizing, as we know it, will end. The scientific components of all disciplines will become discourse, open to deconstruction.

The radical changes described for all inquiries will apply no less to the study of public administration, as the following four chapters discuss. This discussion is conducted by examining four distinctive interests on which the postmodern discourse focuses: imagination, deconstruction, deterritorialization, and alterity.

10

Postmodernity
Imagination

> The reality of Paris at the end of May 1968 conformed less to the categories of existence preceding May . . . than to the activated imaginations of the movement. . . . The May events . . . established however briefly a new type of social reality where living human energy and not things were predominant. . . . [H]uman imagination will be freed to take giant steps in constructing a better world. "All Power to the Imagination," written everywhere in May 1968, will become inscribed in the lives and institutions of future generations.
>
> —Katsiaficas[1]

IMAGINIZATION; TO IMAGINIZE. This term, italicized when written in this chapter in order to distinguish it from other usages of the same word, is used to symbolize the first of the four aspects of postmodernity to be discussed.[2] *Imaginization* suggests a divergence from Weber's notion of the primary characteristic of modernity, a divergence from rationalization. This departure does not mean that reason should be banished. It does not mean what the classical public administration theorists mean by vision. What it is intended to suggest is that as modernity's autonomous spheres implode and as the aesthetic, the scientific, and the normative lose their exclusive internal logics, *imaginization* should be a dominating part of the new thinking and action dynamic. In modernity, the imagination has been dominant in only one of the spheres, the aesthetic; in postmodernity, it will not be so walled off and contained.

Imaginization would have a parallel pervasive and catalytic effect on society in postmodernity as rationalization has in modernity. Modernity's rationalization extended more and more throughout society, bringing more and more under the domain of rationality. The basis of science, technology, and modernist interpretation is rationality. Other features play important roles, but they are subordinate because all is subject to the judging, the checking, of rationality. Postmodernity's *imaginization,* in a parallel fashion, can be expected to spread through society. Individuals in society, and elements of society, might try to give imagination the central role in their interrelationships and in their lives that the modernists previously gave to rationality.

The postmodern perspective stresses the importance of images and imaging, and it emphasizes the place and significance of the image without referent. Images (understood in the wide sense, discussed below) have always had great importance, but that significance has never been greater than in the postmodern situation. So, as *imaginization* develops, the role of the imagination can be anticipated to play an increasingly important role not only in the context of discovery but also in what will be explained as the context of justification. Generally, imagination has been seen as secondary in the Western tradition. Imagination plays, and always has played, a large part in our day-to-day lives; even actuaries and accountants make secondary use of their imaginations. But the more dramatic products of the imagination seem to have been confined mainly to the arts, an area that we tend to marginalize; rationalization, on the other hand, has produced important economic and scientific miracles. This point can be seen more readily if the context of discovery is distinguished from the context of justification; the inputs that are used in the discovery of scientific information (or the production of a work of art) can be different from those used in justifying the scientific information (or in evaluating the work of art). Inevitably, we are prejudiced by these facts about the economic and scientific fields, especially in the context of justification. The imagination tends to be uncomfortable for a variety of reasons. It is multidimensional and resistant to being captured in neat rationalistic categories. Talking about imagination seems to tend toward trying to say the unsayable or at least toward saying the unfamiliar. For instance, some who talk about the imagination (say, Carl Jung) have also been fascinated by the Eastern tradition.[3] Additionally, the imagination is uncomfortable not only because it is a side of ourselves that requires more elucidation but also because we tend to associate it with untruth, lack of control, and even madness. The imagination discussed in this chapter is not intended to denote Schwärmerei, the vacuous enthusiasm to which Immanuel Kant objected. Imagination is not a prescription for promoting idle daydreaming nor, as it is sometimes indelicately called, scientific wild-eyed guessing (S.W.A.G.).

Some may quibble with Sartre's explanation of the possibilities of imagination. They may suppose that Sartre has gone too far if they interpret him as ascribing blame to the dominant classes, powerful though their effects might be. Sartre underlines that a primary role for the imagination can result in life-changing liberation and a realization that human potential exceeds, in an important sense, the rational. Sartre interprets the 1968 student formula "All power to the imagination" to mean "the area of the possible is much more vast than the dominant classes have accustomed us to believe."[4]

If *imaginization* does play a permeative role in postmodernity (parallel to rationalization in modernity), there are implications for public administration practice and for public administration thinking—and implications for the basic project of public administration. See chapter 2 for an account of the view of NASPAA on the nature of the public administration discipline. For example, NASPAA describes a prime characteristic of the field as "creative pluralism," and it speaks of four "waves of innovation." The first wave includes the aim of establishing public administration as a field of specialized professional competence; the subsequent waves are the public affairs, public policy, and public management movements. A change of paradigms suggests the possibility of a change in "fundamental" project. As long as any such project of public administration is still needed in postmodernity, it would suggest an increased emphasis on developing administrators with greater relevant imaginative capacities. Nevertheless, the change implied is unlikely to consist of a simple shift in objectives, emphasizing some topics (say, nonorthodox organization theory) and deemphasizing other topics (say, technical topics such as budgeting). It suggests a sea change, including the possibility of the eventual abandonment of thinking in terms of such projects. Considering the project of public administration before examining the other aspects of postmodernity (those discussed in chapters 11 through 13) would be premature. Focusing on the role of the imagination alone provides an inadequate perspective on these changes in public administration practice and in the public administration project. Needed also will be the shifts indicated by deconstruction, deterritorialization, and alterity. We will return to this project of public administration, then, in chapter 13. There it will be suggested that postmodernity underlines the importance of, and radically develops the notion of, creative pluralism. It also suggests an orientation to what is explained and described as antiadministration. The latter term will be discussed in chapter 13, where it will be explained as intending to represent a manner of administering that is radically antibureaucratic. This method will involve administering that at the same time works against critical features of the Weberian rationalistic model of bureaucratic activity.[5]

In the modernist situation, rationalization for the manager was both internal and external. The manager extended rationality within, and by means of, the bureaucracy. Of course, there were exceptions (e.g., leaders who operated on a nonrationalizing basis), but the general rule was to judge actions in terms of their rationality, to act rationally, and to induce subordinate managers and operatives to act rationally. In the new situation, leaders and managers might strive to manage, with imagination taking the leading role; they might extend responsibility for imagining to subordinates and to others. Changes might be expected in the business of developing such leaders. Thinkers might think even more about imagining.

Where is the alternative, rationalization, leading us? What should be said about the nature of *imaginization*? What can be said about the imagination and the public manager? This chapter will consider these questions.

THE END OF RATIONALIZATION

Where is the alternative, rationalization, leading? By way of an answer, consider this parable; that is, consider the results of modernity's rationalization of, and through, bureaucracy by the example of the following specification analysis sheet. Consider this moral tale, an example unimportant in itself. Consider that this sheet at one point governed the purchase of chilled and frozen hot dogs by the U.S. Department of Defense. Many other similar examples, possibly beyond number, can be found elsewhere in U.S. and other governmental hierarchies.

The 32-page specification begins by "incorporating by reference" within the present specification a number of other specifications and standards: those relating to "Spices, Ground and Whole"; "Spice Flavorings, Soluble"; "Cans, Metal, 28 Gauge and Lighter"; "Box, Fiberboard"; "Canned Subsistence Items, Packaging and Packing of"; "Preservation, Packaging and Packing Levels"; and "Marking for Domestic Shipment (Civilian Agencies)." On the next page, it tells us that to sell frankfurters under this specification the supplier also needs to consult some additional specifications and standards: "Labelling of Metal Cans for Subsistence Items"; "Packaging and Packing, Labeling and Marking, of Meat Cuts and Sausage Products (Chilled or Frozen) for Domestic or Overseas Shipment"; "Marking for Shipment and Storage"; "Federal Food, Drug and Cosmetic Act and General Regulations for its Enforcement"; "Regulations Governing the Meat Inspection of the U.S. Department of Agriculture"; "Official Methods of Analysis of the Association of Official Agricultural Chemists"; and "The Journal of the American Oil Chemists' Society." Thus, the initial document was multiplied.

Turn through several pages of bureaucratese to the requirements for the finished product. After the first five requirements, we read:

6. There shall be no foreign material (e.g. dirt, insect, insect part, wood glass or metal).
7. There shall be no foreign color (e.g. green, black, purple or light grey).
8. Style A links shall not be pinkish-red to red (artificially colored).
9. Style B links shall be pinkish-red to red (artificially colored).
10. Ten links of Type I product shall weigh 20 to 27 ounces (6 to 8 size), 16 to 19-7/8 ounces (8 to 10 size), or 13 to 15-7/8 ounces (10 to 12 size).
11. Ten links of Type II and III product shall weigh 18 to 23 ounces (8/lb size) or 15 to 17 ounces (10/lb size).
12. A link shall not be split or ruptured more than 1/4 inch.
13. A link shall not retain all or part of an artificial casing.
14. A link shall not have a cut or broken end.
15. A link shall not have a fat cap or streak.
16. The right-hand surface resulting from bisecting a link lengthwise shall not have a bone particle greater than 1/4 inch in any dimension.
17. The right-hand surface resulting from bisecting a link lengthwise shall not have a pocket of air, fat gelatin, or water greater than 1/4 inch in any dimension.
18. The right-hand surface resulting from bisecting a link lengthwise shall not

have more than 3 pieces of material (cartilage, ligament, tendon or connective tissue) greater than 1/4-inch in any dimension that will not break up when subjected to pressure from the flat side of a spatula.

19. The product shall contain not more than 30 percent fat.

20. Type III product, a link shall not have a surface which requires more than 2.5 pounds of force to pierce (see 4.4.1).

21. Type III product in a can, an ice cube measuring 1-inch or less along each edge in which a certified green food coloring (see 5.1.1.1.1.) has been encapsulated shall be on top of the product.

This excerpt is enough to give the general flavor; much, much more is available. For example, we read items such as the following: "The tin coating weights shall be determined by any method specified in PPP-C-96"; "The container shall be a fiberboard box, constructed, closed and strapped in accordance with type I or II, class 2, grade 3, style RSC, of PPP-D-636"; and "The product packaged in accordance with 5.1.2. shall be packed in accordance with 5.2.2."

Picture it; the specification really does include a sketch of the compression device for testing the surface resistance of frankfurters. As item 4.4.1. of the specification explains,

A Hunter, or equivalent mechanical force gauge, equipped with a wedge-shaped bit as illustrated . . . and a holding-at-maximum indicator, shall be securely supported in a vertical position. The equipped force gauge shall be placed in a compression device (see figure . . .) which has been calibrated to move at the uniform rate of 1 inch per minute. A frankfurter chilled to between 40 and 50 (degrees) F. shall be firmly held against a platform of the mechanical compression device. The gauge shall be so aligned that the long edge of the blade on the bit is at right angles to the major axis of the frankfurter, and, as the gauge is moved at the prescribed rate, contact with the surface of the frankfurter shall be made at the point near the central vertical plane. The maximum force required to pierce the outer surface of the frankfurter shall be recorded (see item 20 of Table III).

It is appreciated that the military must have adequate hot dogs. Furthermore, the situation is more complex; bureaucracies function within political, social, and economic contexts and constraints, just as they act on these contexts and just as they impose their own constraints. Of course, powerful rationalizations for rationality exist.

Most of us can tell a lot of these bureaucracy "war stories," and a number of the stories have an even clearer moral dimension. The frankfurter specification and related stories should not be trivialized as, for example, mere matters of subculture or of efficiency. Consider the procedure for the humane execution of prisoners. To avoid the human difficulties of electrocution and the gas chamber, some states have the condemned prisoners executed by painless lethal injection. In addition, to avoid having the prisoners soil the gurney, the states had also administered (1992 data) rectal stoppers and catheters. A case is reported of a dead body with his broken-off catheter being returned to the widow. Consider the bureaucrats who rationally developed and executed plans for the extermination of ethnic and other groups. Raul Hilberg, in his *The Destruction of the European Jews,* documented that the assault on European Jewry was performed through a vast bureaucratic machine, the coordinated work of thousands of public servants.[6] They used their bureaucratic skills "to get things done through people." For example, he describes how one bureaucrat, allowed to transport Jews of mixed marriages only on grounds other than their ethnicity, got the job done by using the loophole that the victims had omitted their middle names on their food ration cards.

THE IMAGINAL

What should be said about the nature of imagination? The image—the allegory, the metaphor, the picture, the parable, for example—has always played an important role in thinking and understanding. One of the most celebrated expressions of philosophical thought is an allegory, that is, Plato's allegory of the cave. A central metaphor in economic thinking is that of the invisible hand, just as for much of modernist science it was the metaphor of the universe as a machine. A new picture of space and time is the Einstein-Minkowskian picture of spacetime. The parable is at the heart of religious and ethical thinking such as that offered in the New Testament. Even the specification analysis sheet discussed above can be seen as a parable about the effects of rationalization. The effects of the imagination have never been confined to literature.

Imagination is understood here to be concerned with images but only where *images* is interpreted in a wide sense. *Imaginization* is not the same as visualization, for example, and imagining is not limited to visual images. Imagination is also concerned with the other senses; for example, we can imagine smells and sounds. Imagination is not limited to the experiential; for example, we can also imagine the nonexistent. Imagination is not limited to the senses, and it is not limited to things. The question of the precise nature of imagination has a substantial literature, but these disagreements do not need to be settled or even discussed at length for the purposes of this chapter. For example, some people associate imagination with intuition.[7] *Image* is used here in the sense of *possibility.* These possibilities can be created out of whole cloth, however. As White puts it, "Great thinkers are often imaginative thinkers because they can free themselves from the rut of the actual and ride on the uncharted trails of the possible."[8]

Creating images has long been recognized as a way to think and create. The power of imaging varies by culture and time in history. Sometimes it is repressed strongly (the Puritans and the Amish may be examples). It has also been long recognized that images have power over an audience and over the image creators themselves. Ordinary language reflects these aspects of images. When we say that someone has a poor self-image, we do not mean the person should change himself but that he should change his image, the picture or the conception of the possibilities for himself.

Postmodernity can be said to be the time of imagining and of imagining without referents. Recall the discussion in chapters 1 and 9 of Baudrillard's hyperreality; for him, the barrier between the real and the appearance has imploded. Images and imagination have always been used to examine and to communicate ideas about what is, what might be, what ought to be, and what will never be. Postmodernity emphasizes the power of imaging without referents. Public administrationists and all who wish to have a societal effect should recognize the power of referentless imagery. A postmodern perspective is that the image creates and is part of what is.

As stated earlier, the role of the imagination has tended to be secondary in much of the Western tradition; imagination has been seen as neither an independent nor the primary phenomenon. (The exceptions should be acknowledged, however. Imagination has played, and continues to play, a large part in everyday life, and it is dominant in the arts. Some thinkers would give imagination the primary role in knowing. The romantics, for example, considered imagination to be primary.) Consider views offered by philosophers such as Aristotle, Hume, and Kant. Aristotle is characterized as placing imagination between perception and intellect, and the role of the imaginative faculty is to transform the impressions into a thought. In Hume, image also has this secondary role, enabling us, for example, to repicture impressions and to think about things no longer present. In Kant's account of cognition, all knowledge is derived from imaginative synthesis. Sherover notes, "There are, then, not two elements in [Kant's] cognition but three: pure intuition, the power of imaginative synthesis, and the understanding. But, as Heidegger points out, it is imaginative synthesis that is central; in pure imagination, pure intuition and pure thought meet together in a common 'overlap' and are able to be fused into the unity of the cognitional act."[9]

Perhaps Jung would be an example of one who treats the work of the imagination as independent. For instance, he states, "Every psychic process is an image and an imagining" and elsewhere says, "The image is an expression of the unconscious as well as the conscious situation of the moment."[10] Here the image is not treated as representing, as in a memory, an afterimage or a reflection; it is treated as autonomous. As Avens explains it, the Jungian position is closer to the Eastern view: "The Eastern attitude toward images is embodied in the Taoistic principle of action through non-action. . . . For example, in the Eastern systems of meditation one is advised to watch the psychomental flow without interfering with it or getting attached to its content. . . . In Jung's opinion, the Eastern way . . . is superior to our rationalistic disavowal of images."[11] Avens goes on to contrast this view with what he perceives as the position of Freudian psychoanalysis, which sees beyond the image to the "real": "Images and symbols are but signs of repressed and mainly sexual content."[12]

For an example of one who believes the imagination to be primary, we can turn to John Keats. Keats, as would be expected from his *Ode on a Grecian Urn,* holds that what the mind seizes as beauty is true. "Beauty is truth, truth beauty,—that is all / Ye know on earth, and all ye need to know." Chambliss tells us that Keats accepted the worth of consecutive reasoning, and he quotes one of Keats's letters questioning the relative worth of poetry as against philosophy. Chambliss goes on to say, "In striving to temper his imagination with reason, he gave expression to a poetry which is a celebration of the idea that imagination works best when it is informed by reason."[13]

The imagination is not seen in the Western tradition as a valid justification for an account of reality, as was suggested earlier. (It is not denied that aesthetic consideration plays a limited part in justification, e.g., through application of Ockham's razor.) Consider science, for example. With exceptions (e.g., see chapters 5 and 8), the scientific method is widely accepted as a basis for justifying a view of reality. The scientific method is regarded as providing privileged information, and this view gives the justifying role to the rational. In postmodernity, the justifying role can be expected to change. Imagination can be anticipated to be increasingly included.

IMAGINATION AND PUBLIC ADMINISTRATION

The postmodern primacy of the image and the possibility of using the hyper-reality of images to create is a major implication of the postmodern perspective for those with an interest in public administration and similar concerns. In a sense, the image precedes any referent, if there is a referent; the image is prior to, and independent of, any referent. Another major implication, as the walling off of the aesthetic ends, is the emerging and growing role of imagination in public administration and other knowledge and action areas in the context of justification.

The value and possibilities of imaging in public administration and similar areas have been discussed, and advocated, in much recent and contemporary organization theory and management. Much of this organization and management thinking has gone beyond the issue of imagination; a discussion of qualitative research and nonorthodox organization theory, for instance, is included in chapter 12. But valuable work has been conducted in these areas on aspects of imagination, and this work and emphasis will be illustrated here by focusing on the contribution of Gareth Morgan. Other examples, of course, are available.

Morgan has published on what he calls "imaginization."[14] This term is the same word used in this chapter, but the meaning is different in important ways. *Imaginization* as we intend it here is the mirror image in postmodernity of modernity's tendency to rationalization. Morgan uses the term to mean the "art of creative management."[15] He summarizes his concept as entailing five points: "improving our abilities to see and understand situations in new ways,"[16] "finding new images for new ways of organizing,"[17] creating "shared understandings,"[18] bringing about "personal empowerment,"[19] and "developing capacities for continuous self-organization."[20]

Morgan's consideration of imaginization seems limited not only to organizations but also to visualization.

Morgan privileges visual images and visual image making as ways to improve organization and management; that is, he believes that such images and metaphors can be used to effect changes in management style, organizational design, management and facilitation of change, development of teamwork, and rethinking products and services. He describes, for instance, how managers and other organizational members can start by visualizing the organization as a spider plant and then use the power of visualization to create new space to empower decentralized units to become more autonomous and self-organizing. The "metaphors of the moment" and images he discusses include animals (such as termites and amoebae), plants, and inanimate objects. He explains how such visual images can be used to create metaphors where "key messages are lived" and where people can go beyond the imaging process. He believes that the capacity for imagination is an "innate skill,"[21] and he wants to show how it can be used in a more systematic manner. His idea is a "logical" extension of the advice given to the person with a poor self-image: visualize and then realize the image you want. At one point, in fact, Morgan explains that as individuals, "we frequently get trapped by images of ourselves and our role and, as a result, lock ourselves into inappropriate modes of behavior."[22]

The field of related writing on organization and management is crowded, and some of these writings have attracted considerable attention. Morgan's work, as he explains, has links with research on a sizeable literature regarding "the need for more creative, intuitive, empowered approaches to management" and links with research on the literature "exploring the challenges facing modern organizations as we move from a mechanistic to an information-based world."[23] Morgan believes that, collectively, these writings present a challenge that his conception of imaginization helps us to meet. He writes, "Collectively, these writings challenge us to recognize that we are leaving the age of organized organizations and are moving into an era where we need to learn how to facilitate and encourage processes of self-organization that allow 'organized' activity to evolve and flow with the change."[24]

As the means of addressing the challenge, others might prefer different words to stress essentially similar goals. Intuition is an idea favored by some. Thomas Peters and Robert Waterman are among those who value intuition: "It is probably only the intuitive leap that will let us solve problems in the complex world."[25] Weston Agor, one of the writers referenced by Morgan, has written about the idea of intuition in management, and his work includes editing a book on the nature of intuition, the importance of intuition in leadership and management, the testing of intuitive ability, how to use intuition in decision making to increase productivity, and how to develop intuitive powers.[26]

Critics express difficulty in getting behind the air of Schwärmerei and intellectual looseness that some organization and management publications transmit. For example, they find it disconcerting to encounter what they consider to be an extravagance of phrasing. Seven topics in a recent publication on "the new paradigm in business"[27], although it contained interesting material, read as follows: "Redefinitions of corporate wealth," "Labor as trash," "The new kind of company with a new kind of thinking," "The age of light," "Foundation for a new world order," "Approaching the millennium," and "Rebuilding the spaceship while it is still in flight."[28] Even Morgan opts to make some of his points with cartoon figures.[29] Regarding the matter of style, some would claim that a need exists to stir the audience or that the material demands the treatment given. Regarding substance, some contemporary organization and management theorists might believe that, as discussed in chapter 9, they encounter the postmodernist difficulty of trying to say the unsayable.

The question can be raised whether there can be a satisfactory study of imagination confined within the context of organization and management theory. This question may come to mind again in chapter 12 when qualitative inquiry and nonorthodox organization theory are discussed. For instance, the nonpositivist methodology of constructivist (or naturalistic) inquiry may seem to owe much to the nature of the terrain dealt with by organization theory. In other words, the terrain of organization theory may be such (mushy, as the quantitative research advocates might put it) that it does not encourage the use of rigorous quantitative methodology in order to yield interesting results. Morgan certainly has no wish to limit the application; his "imaginization" is a "way of thinking."[30] Nevertheless, the purpose and the setting of the ideas are clear enough. It is reflected in a set of cartoons that are labeled "organization is imaginization." The first page of the introduction in bold letters defines imaginization as "the art of creative management."

The point here is that an adequate understanding of large societal issues may not be possible from within the confines of a particular and narrow social science specialty. The point is not to make the absurd claim that the work of organization or management theorists is bad or wrong. It is, rather, to claim that perhaps no one can provide adequate understandings until the process of deterritorializing, described in chapter 12, is undertaken. Perhaps we are all confined to developing the equivalent of a horseless carriage instead of a car. (It will be recalled that in the early days of the automobile, manufacturers made cars that looked a lot like horseless carriages.) Morgan himself put the point well in his drawing of a pig. The drawing shows a pig surrounded by a butcher, an artist, a wolf, a farmer, a veterinarian, a philosopher, a Muslim, and a small child, and the caption underneath the picture asks, "What is the pig?" Morgan explains, "for the wolf, the pig is food; for the Muslim, it's an unclean animal," and so on. As he adds, "The precise meaning and significance of the pig will vary according to the frame of reference through which it is viewed. Each frame opens or closes a horizon of understanding."[31] Consider now the effects of Morgan's research protocol. Morgan characterizes the protocol of what he calls his "action learning" research method as "a loose quasi-ethnographic style of research."[32] This frame of reference is used to look at any problem or pig. The point is that the postmodern perspective may be difficult to realize from within the subject specialty "cubicles" designed by modernity. It is even harder from some cubicles than from some others. At this point, let us leave consideration of Gareth Morgan and turn to *imaginization* as it is conceptualized in this chapter.

Imaginization, as has been noted, is understood here as the mirror image of rationalization. It is seen as the permeative force of postmodernity. What should be said about the nature and implications of this understanding of *imaginization* in the case of public administration? From a negative viewpoint, *imaginization* is an administrative spirit that does not rely on making rules and following procedures, as in modernity. From a positive viewpoint, *imaginization* is an administrative spirit that gives a primary role to the development of the use of the imagination. A function of public administration thinking should be to explore such characteristics.

The Negative Viewpoint

Consider the claim that *imaginization* would be an administrative spirit that does not rely on making rules and following procedures, both in interactions with the public and in internal operations. The acts of making rules and following procedures are prime instruments of modernity's rationalization; through them, rationality is extended throughout society and throughout the administering process itself.

The acts of making rules and following procedures dominate not only the output but also the input mechanisms of modernist public agencies. On the output side, examples are the specification analysis sheet (discussed earlier) and the Internal Revenue Service's tax code. On the input side, consider human resources development; the essence of civil service is reliance on rules. Consider resources management; the essence of budgeting and of accounting is reliance on procedures. Modernity's rationalizing rule making is fecund; it begets, and facilitates the begetting of, other rules. It amounts to what can be called "rulism," administration through overreliance on rules.

The roots of rationalization lie deep in the nature of modernity and in its antecedents. Washington muckrakers could produce volumes on volumes of examples of the ill effects of the application of "rational" principles and of the effects of rational systems having lives of their own. Nevertheless, the exposés make little difference because the rationalizing motif remains operative. The mind-set through which the modernist sees the world suggests the advantages of rationalization; we see that we can be rewarded by our adherence to rationalization (e.g., in bigger and better economies and in more creature comforts). We see it as fulfilling our inheritance. Long before modernity, the Western inheritance had been largely rule oriented. The dominant religious faiths have been rule based, for example. The first five books of the Bible and the Ten Commandments have set the Western tone, a tone well pursued by the genius of our legal tradition. The political systems of countries such as the United States are built on adherence to carefully constructed sets of rules. The Enlightenment's Thomas Jefferson had a well-known fascination with clocks, for instance, and he and others designed a government (as God had designed the world, William Paley might want to say) with a procedural precision that one would expect in clock making.

The change contemplated in imagination, steering away from procedural rule making, is clearly fundamental. No bureaucracy by itself could effect such a revolution unless society itself were revolutionized in a parallel way. The way in which the society expects and requires the administrative process to operate would need corresponding adjustments. The operation of the legislative branch in the United States would require radical readjustment, for example. A minor instance is the making of laws that leave significant parts of the program to be developed by the administrative process (i.e., framing a law with the understanding that the program design is incomplete until it is supplemented by a set of administrative regulations). Another example is the legal system, a societal enterprise given to rule making; it would have to cease requiring administrative rules and procedures. In the interim, however, is public administration thinking about *imaginization* precluded?

Consider the sanitation service. It is imagined that some principles of garbage collection would still be necessary in city X. For example, certain principles govern the handling of dangerous items such as acids or radioactive materials. There seem to be laws of nature (whether or not they are timeless truths), and there are the principles of how the work will be done. It is expected that sanitation supervisors would still give instructions, but three-ring binders stuffed with procedures are not essential to carrying out these principles. Consider the fire service. Again, principles are required. Better and worse ways of fighting fires exist, and we need to rely on prompt action in emergency and dangerous situations. Nevertheless, we do not need to rely on sets of procedural rules. Consider a more difficult case, the police. The activities of the police to maintain order must respect the requirements of law. But, given a suitable legal environment, it cannot be supposed that the only way in which this process can be conducted requires the procedural method of management. (The rules and procedures in large U.S. police agencies are so multiplicitous that it is hard to see how they all could be understood and executed by the street officer. The fact that such rules have many purposes makes this condition hardly less bizarre.)

How could a governmental entity possibly operate in a non-rule-based manner? Of course, it does look extremely difficult, but, as discussed earlier, it is unrealistic to expect that radical changes should be either easy or obvious. In addition, it will be recalled that proposals that seem impossible in one framework can become possible in another. Is it not similar to the kind of difficulty we would encounter if we tried to develop a sports program for children? A lot of organization and rules would seem to be required. No, look instead at the vast amount of independent, unregulated play that children engage in by themselves. At one time, and probably it is the same now, there were two types of children's games: the adult-led and supervised games such as institutional football and the child-dominated and non-rationalized motley of games that children played (e.g., marbles, hopscotch, and tic-tac-toe). It is true that regulated play, like a sort of Gresham's law, can drive out unregulated play; little league baseball can drive out sandlot play. But anarchistic arrangements can develop if not stifled by the rationalization. The suggestion here is that *imaginization* can fill the need in public administration no less than in children's play.

This games example is open to the possible objection that it is speaking of the unnecessary rules and regulations. It is true that the example is about the rules and regulations that the administration of a sport imposes; administration is the center of interest in this chapter. Some may say that games themselves are nothing but sets of rules, that even games such as pétanque (boules as seen in the villages of France's Midi), although apparently free of overregulation, are rule governed and that a game without rules might be considered to have the rule, "There shall be no rules." It is hard to imagine how far *imaginization* can go in the postmodern society, but the suggestion is plausible that it can go further than we can now imagine. In the example of games, games are not just sets of rules; games are games, activities with recreational purposes. When rules are stripped away, the result is a changed activity. Consider contemporary tennis. Professional tournaments require rules and procedures to be executed by at least an umpire, lines officials, and ballpersons; they also require stands, commentators, and hot dog vendors. Many of these rules and procedures seem required by the economics rather than by the nature of the game. Beyond these factors, could games be designed so that the rules would be secondary to the playing in the sense that imagination is subordinate to reason in scientific work? The answer is affirmative, but it is difficult to imagine an *imaginizing* society from within a rationalizing mind-set.

Imaginization would be an administrative spirit that relies less on the merely rational—quite different, of course, from relying on the irrational because the irrational and the nonrational are not synonymous terms. Modernity's rationalization makes use of instrumental rationality, means-ends generalizations that are calculated to yield optimal results. This reliance has yielded benefits, but we should remind ourselves of the shortcomings. These shortcomings include not only difficulties in the working out of rationality in governmental bureaucracy but also in the treatment accorded to individuals. In bureaucracies, agency reliance primarily on rationalization inevitably results in a bureau wanting to acquire more than optimal resources for rationalization. Recall the discussion in chapter 7 of the supply and demand for bureaucratic output; recall, for instance, that the substantial oversupply and distortion of resource use is inevitable where there is no meaningful "effective demand" measure. In such a circumstance and for the public choice reasons discussed in that chapter, it would be "irrational" for an agency not to acquire more than an optimal supply of resources of rationalization. Because rationalization is so prominent among the criteria for bureaucratic effectiveness,[33] it is inevitable that a rational bureau manager should overstock on the resources that yield rational information. There is a "rational" pressure tending toward a proliferation of specialists and subspecialists in governmental bureaucracies. This is not to deny the existence, perhaps, of "psychological" pressure toward the same overstocking. Having more information and specialists helps in reducing uncertainty, for example, and bureaus have been described as attaching importance to the reduction of uncertainty. As Scott writes, "Organizations and individuals are forever seeking to reduce uncertainty."[34]

Instrumental rationality has resulted in human costs for customers and bureaucrats. For customers, a trade-off can exist between being treated fairly and being treated as an end (rather than as a means only). This point may seem odd because in a sense customers are treated as ends (e.g., the person who qualifies for food stamps is provided with food stamps). Nevertheless, rationalization insists that each person should be treated according to the rational rule (i.e., as a means toward compliance with the rule). Because of the unchecked character of rationalization, this approach does lead to some human problems. Consider the current welfare system or the volumes of regulations foisted on small businesses. Customers are put into categories or boxes. From the rationalizing viewpoint, they cease to be full human beings; they become abstractions in the form of cases. Rationalization will only permit deviation to satisfy the unique needs of customers who do not fit that particular rule if another rule covers the case at issue.

At first hearing, the phrase "administrative spirit" seems to be an oxymoron; matters of administration and matters of spirit seem incompatible. The reason for this appearance is that administration is taken as virtually synonymous with rationalizing. Such living by rules and procedures is seen as subordinating what is deemed the essence of spirituality to the dead hand of rationality. Fairly or not, it is seen as subordinating the person to the inanimate, subordinating the human to the inhuman, and perhaps even subordinating the hot juice of spirituality to the cold "no" of rationality. It is also seen as justified on the grounds of necessity and of productive programmatic results.

The Positive Viewpoint

On the positive side, what could it mean to claim that *imaginization* is an administrative spirit that gives a primary role to the development of the use of the imagination? This new role for imagination can be explored under at least two kinds of headings: those connotations pointing to the particularism of circumstances and those suggesting the universalism of imaging. The predominance of the imaginal does not entail the nonuse of the rational, just as the modernist ascendancy of rationality did not exclude imagination from scientific discovery. Nevertheless, the net

effect of *imaginization* on theorizing about, and on thinking about, public administration and other events would be a shift toward the poetic. This shift is implied, as
was suggested earlier, by the implosion in the postmodern situation of the barrier
between the aesthetic and the nonaesthetic spheres.

Thinkers sometimes speak of reformulated attitudes toward knowing. Two are
mentioned as a preface to thinking about how public administration "facts" can be
"approached" in a more poetic manner. These views are offered, respectively, by
Merleau-Ponty and by Deleuze and Guattari. For example, in *The Visible and the
Invisible,* Merleau-Ponty writes of reflection, intuition, and dialectic being incompatible with his ontology.[35] They must become, respectively, hyperreflection, auscul-
tation in depth, and hyperdialectic. Hyperreflection is radically self-critical; it must
question its own operation and adequacy. As Patrick Burke describes it, ausculta-
tion or palpation in depth "requires a different kind of intuition than that of the
pure gaze of a wordless subject that flattens the world; rather one that is an opening
out of the self from and upon the abyssal depths of the world, and which expresses
the turning in of the world upon itself."[36] The hyperdialectic, according to Burke,
"criticizes itself and surpasses itself as a separate statement." He explains,

> Philosophy must join the "ambiguous movement of self-manifestation . . . at the
> heart of Being itself." Thus, the hyperdialectic is that labyrinthian thought of laby-
> rinthian Being, of the Being that cannot be positively intuited or reflected through a
> positive judgment, but which thought must follow into the night without knowing
> the route in advance or whether it is indeed traversable, and along which and in
> terms of which thought discovers its own inherent logic of reversibility beneath
> reflection and intuition and the imperative of noncontradiction.[37]

There is more to seeing events in the world as a poem—or of seeing the world as a
poem—than looking at postmodernity as if it were still modernity. Although Merleau-Ponty is writing of the ultimate nature of things, the idea is relevant to our
present interest because there are no postmodern subject-matter empires.

Deleuze and Guattari write of "schizoanalysis."[38] Schizoanalysis speaks in terms
of removing the rationalistic, institutional, and other discourse impediments to the
flows of the unconscious and desires, and it speaks of decentering modern identities and of dissolving the ego and superego. Schizoanalysis also has positive tasks.
For example, the "first positive task consists of discovering in a subject the nature,
formation, or the functioning of *his* desiring-machines, independently of any interpretations."[39] Another and related task is "to reach the investments of unconscious
desire of the social field, insofar as they are differentiated from the preconscious
investments of interest."[40] Schizoanalysis seeks to liberate the body from its intellectual, social, and subjectified chains; Deleuze and Guattari wish to deterritorialize
the body and therefore understanding. We will return to schizoanalysis and these
authors in chapters 12 and 13.

Starting from the perspective of particularism, two trends seem clear. The first trend is the mushrooming of the supply of particulars and particular circumstances. It is not just that the population of countries is increasing, that a great Shakespeare is 1 in 4 million, whereas a mere Hemingway is 1 in 150 million. It is not just that a given population increase leads to an even greater increase of interactions between particulars (and thus particular circumstances); recall from elementary statistics that the number of pairs or other combinations of integers is greatly increased by the addition of even one more integer. With increases in all forms of mobility (physical, economic, social, and political) and with other changes, such as technological, the number of circumstances per person has escalated even further. Our grandfathers' careers were more likely to be settled and fixed as they followed their fathers' foot-steps. Each of our great-grandsons' careers is likely to be a kaleidoscope of unre-lated careers because it is doubtful whether these great-grandsons will be able to follow their mothers' or their fathers' footsteps.

The second trend is a mushrooming in the capacity to record, process, examine, and judge particulars. The radical character and dimensions of the information pro-cessing revolution are changing the world, but the revolution involves more than merely computers or information; it is a revolution in the processing of particulars.

Absent the second trend, the first trend might result in a multiplication of rules and procedures. Such rules, even if completely apposite and complementary, suffer from disadvantages, such as becoming reified and resting on the assumption that other things are equal (i.e., no special circumstances vitiate the working of the rule). These disadvantages would lead to a large increase in snafu results and surely a much larger sense of alienation between governed and governing. Present the second trend, these same results still will occur unless new ways of coping are developed. The increasing data processing capability may permit the dealing with particulars without the intermediation of rules and regulations. It is important to recognize that rules and regulations are essentially decision rules for coping with particular cases and with aspects of the total societal situation. The speculation here is that particulars can be analyzed directly, without the intermediation of rules. A com-mon strategy is to think of data processing that will produce information on a mul-titude of cases that then will be treated in accordance with a set of rules. This new development is not like that; it permits human interaction directly with the particu-lar situation.

Consider illustrations from a game, Foucault, and Plato. It is possible to play chess by calculation, by what is sometimes called "by hand," or by a combination of methods. A player can calculate the consequences of alternative candidate moves, applying decision rules to the options. A player can use other rules, such as principles about the opening (e.g., tucking the king away, bringing the rooks onto open files, not developing the queen too soon, controlling the middle squares, and not uglify-ing the pawn structure). The player can also "know" what to do; it is as if one played with the hand. The latter need not be explained in such grand terms as intuition or an additional ability beyond the five senses. It could be that the brain is rapidly processing sets of future positions, perhaps even millions among those with especially "gifted" hands.[41] It could be that unconsciously the brain is evaluating sets of alternative particular positions, perhaps not even using decision rules. Even if this is not the case in chess, it could be the case in administering a nation. It could be the process of government not to develop and administer rules but to cope with the needs of particular people.

For the second illustration, let us turn again to Foucault's study of "governmentality."[42] Foucault holds that modern governmental rationality is about individualizing and about totalizing. A parallel can be drawn between individualizing and particulars, about what it is for an individual to be governed. Totalizing can be considered as parallel to the attitude that leads to rule making, about what it is for a society or population to be governed. Foucault distinguishes between the shepherd game and the city game. The shepherd game concerns pastoral power, and it appeals to the way that the shepherd is concerned for the welfare of each of the sheep. The city game refers to the business of making laws and administering laws to groups.

We can also turn to Plato for the distinction between the particular and the universal aspects of administering. Plato distinguishes between the best form of government where the true statesman is one whose rule is flexible and focuses on the individual case, and this approach can be seen as approximating the particular. The rule of law, suggesting the universal approach, is a next best operation. As Skemp puts it in the introduction to his translation of the *Statesman,* "The best government is lawless. It is guided by the true statesman whose rule is flexible and can be adapted to each individual case. . . . The best government then is independent of law. Statesmanship is an art just as painting is. A good state can no more be produced and maintained by laws than a good picture can be painted by formulas for mixing colors."[43] In fairness, it should be added that Colin Gordon reports that Foucault thinks Plato denies that the ruler's art is like the shepherd who cares for the individual sheep in his flock: "Plato's dialogue, *The Statesman,* concerning the nature of the art of government, discusses the possibility that the ruler's art is like the shepherd's who cares for each individual sheep in his flock. In Plato, this idea is dismissed as impracticable: a ruler's knowledge and attentiveness could never extend so far as to minister to each individual: 'only a god could act thus.' "[44] Nevertheless, the point here is to give meaning to the distinction in the case of imaging between particular and universal.

Data processing capability can depersonalize society. Some feel this depersonalization when they hear of an individual fighting with the machine processes to correct some inadvertent systems error in a telephone bill or credit check. For others, depersonalization could be exemplified by the machine that calls the home to tell the individual about the advantages of Brand X or it could be the machines that control the launching of nuclear war. The common characteristic of these systems seems to be that they are rule driven, applying rules to individual situations. This depersonalization will escalate as the powers of data processing jump. An alternative is a strategy of imaging that deals directly with the individual case. This alternative can focus, as postmodernism indicates, on micropolitics.

From the universal perspective, imaging is connected in part with the unfreezing, or freeing, of one's interpretive lenses. We can constitute (or see) the public administration world, discourse involving public administration, through the lens of modernist public administration theory. We could constitute (or see) it differently through other lenses. Foucault's "governmentality," as chapter 4 claimed, would provide a different perspective. Gordon explains that Foucault defines government as "the conduct of conduct," and he writes of the "government of one's self and of others" as follows: "Government as an activity could concern the relation between self and self, private interpersonal relations involving some form of control or guidance, relations within social institutions and communities and, finally, relations concerned with the exercise of political sovereignty."[45] If we see budgeting through the lens of governmentality, we see a different text than if we see it through the lens of modernist public administration theory; if we see it successively through both lens, we see a third text. Add yet other lenses. The reader will recognize this description as that (see chapter 2) of the reflexive language paradigm.

All such postmodern imaging takes place within the context of the transpolitical. As Jean Baudrillard writes,

> The transpolitical is the transparency and the obscenity of all structures in a destructured universe, the transparency and obscenity of change in a dehistoricized universe, the transparency and obscenity of information in a defactualized universe, the transparency and obscenity of space in the promiscuity of networks, the transparency and obscenity of the social in the masses, of the political in terror, of the body in obesity and genetic cloning. . . . The end of the scene of history, the end of the scene of the political, the end of the scene of the phantasm, the end of the scene of the body—it is the irruption of the obscene. The end of secrecy—it is the irruption of transparency.[46]

Baudrillard goes on later to write, "The transpolitical is also this: the passage from growth to excrescence, from finality to hypertely, from organic equilibria to cancerous metastases. It is the locus of catastrophe, and no longer of crisis. Here things rush headlong to the rhythm of technology, including 'soft' and psychedelic technologies, which take us even further from all reality, all history, all destiny."[47]

Such imaging also implies a step away from a critical feature of the rationalistic model of bureaucratic structure contemplated by Max Weber. It implies a step away from the bureaucracy seen as a rational organization bound together by rules. A prime characteristic of Weber's notion of bureaucratic structure was described as "a continuous organization of official functions bound by rules."[48] Etzioni explains what Weber means as follows: "Rules save effort by obviating the need for deriving a new solution for every problem and case; they facilitate standardization and equality of treatment of many cases. These advantages are impossible if each client is treated as a unique case, as an individual."[49] *Imaginization* erodes a critical ingredient of Weberian rationalist bureaucracy.

In the new postmodern situation, when the rigid subject-matter distinctions have been obliterated, discussion will turn to deconstructing relevant image texts. The next chapter describes this deconstruction in more detail.

SUMMARY

Imaginization is the word used to suggest a primary characteristic of postmodernity, a characteristic that steps away from critical features of the Weberian rationalistic model of bureaucratic structure. *Imaginization* has a catalytic effect in postmodernity parallel to the role Weber describes for rationalization in modernity. As the autonomous spheres implode, the dominance of imagination will be no longer confined to the aesthetic, and imagination can be expected to play a larger role in the scientific and the normative spheres. The imagination will play a larger role not only in the context of discovery but also in the context of justification. In modernity, imagination plays a secondary role; in postmodernity, rationalization still plays a role, but a shift toward the poetic would occur. One's interpretive lenses would unfreeze.

This movement has critical consequences for those concerned with public administration, including any project of public administration. It is suggested that such a project will move toward what is described in chapter 13 as antiadministration. Leaders and managers would strive to manage, with imagination taking the leading role; they would extend responsibility for imagining to subordinates and others. Individuals would give imagination the central role in their interrelationships and in their lives. On the negative side, imagination is an administrative spirit that does not rely on modernist acts of making rules and following procedures. Examples can be given of the unfortunate consequences of such reliance. One given in this chapter is that bureaucracies relying primarily on rationalization, if they act rationally, will overinvest in information production, that is, specialists and subspecialists. Another is that customers are always treated as the means toward compliance with a rule (or rules).

Imagination and creativity have been discussed by organization and management theorists. The work of Gareth Morgan is discussed as an example of this literature. His recent publication is intended to show managers and others how visualization can be used to effect desired organizational and management results.

On the positive side, imagination is the administrative spirit that gives the primary role to the development of the imaginal. Imagination can be described as dealing with *image,* where the latter term is understood in a wide sense. The development of the imaginal can be facilitated by new capabilities, especially in a situation where population growth means that the number of particulars will be increasing and the number of particular situations consequently will be increasing exponentially. Data processing may be developed, for example, so that particulars can be analyzed directly rather than through decision rules. Foucault's and Plato's comments should be noted. Foucault distinguishes between the shepherd game (concern for the welfare of each sheep) and the city game (making laws and administering laws to groups). Plato is quoted as writing that the best government is lawless and that the true statesman is one whose rule is adapted to each individual case. In postmodernity, this development will take place in a new context, one that Baudrillard calls the transpolitical.

Discussion of imagination only begins the description of the view from the lens of postmodernity, but it is suggested that this discussion has already implied the possibility of going beyond modernist public administration theory. The description continues with a consideration of deconstruction.

11

Postmodernity
Deconstruction

> If deconstruction takes place everywhere it (ça) takes place, where there is something (and is not therefore limited to meaning or to the text in the current and bookish sense of the word), we shall still have to think through what is happening in our world, in modernity, at the time when deconstruction is becoming a motif, with its word, its privileged themes, its mobile strategy, etc. I have no simple and formalizable response to this question.... I would not even dare to say ... that we are in an "epoch" of being-in-deconstruction.
>
> —Derrida[1]

DECONSTRUCTION IS NEITHER a method nor even an operation; it is neither an analysis nor a critique. Derrida complains that the methodological metaphor has been applied to deconstruction, particularly in the United States. For him, it is not enough to deny this, nor to say that each deconstructive "event" is "singular" like "an idiom or a signature." As he puts it,

> Deconstruction is not a method and cannot be transformed into one.... It is true that in certain circles (university or cultural, especially in the United States) the technical and methodological "metaphor" that seems necessarily attached to the very word "deconstruction" has been able to seduce or lead astray.... It is not enough to say that deconstruction could not be reduced to some methodological instrumentality or to a set of rules and transposable procedures.... It must also be made clear that deconstruction is not even an act or an operation.[2]

Deconstruction is not an analysis because it is not a "regression toward a simple element" and because values such as analysis are also deconstructible. Deconstruction "is not an analysis in particular because the dismantling of a structure is not a regression toward a simple element, toward an indissoluble origin. These values, like that of analysis, are themselves philosophemes subject to deconstruction."[3]

What, then, is deconstruction? With regard to public administration in the postmodern situation, how, then, can deconstruction be understood as a valued activity? This chapter will address these two questions in turn. The first section gives an account of deconstruction. The second section explores implications for public administration. It suggests that bureaucratic deconstruction can be used to dismantle narratives that constitute the underpinnings of modernist public administration theory and practice.[4] Bureaucratic deconstruction can also be used to dismantle narratives constructed in postmodernity. Grand narratives are the accounts that are thought to explain the development of history, and Hegel's and Marx's (the march of history being explained by the workings of, respectively, the Absolute Spirit and economic factors) are often given as examples. An Enlightenment grand narrative is that rationalization equals human progress. Public administration theory and practice are also underpinned by certain narratives. Two examples are chosen here. One narrative is that *the* goal for public administration theory should be objectivity. A second narrative is that efficiency is a viable goal for public administration practice. One narrative is illustrative of a modernist underpinning of theory, and the other is an example of a grounding of much practice. Certainly, alternative examples of narratives could have been selected.

Why is it desirable to remove the modernist underpinnings, the modernist narratives, of public administration? Solutions founded on illusions can surely make problems worse; erroneous approaches can impede the development of better remedies. Formaini is one who claims that "scientific" public policy is a myth. His claim is that "scientifically based (i.e. justified) public policy, a dream that has grown ever larger since the Enlightenment and that, perhaps, has reached its apogee toward the close of our own century, is a myth, a theoretical illusion."[5] He argues that the twin techniques of risk assessment and cost-benefit analysis, on which we currently rely, are "completely incapable of generating the certain answers we desire."[6] His claim is that the illusion stands in the way of developing more effective public policy. Guba and Lincoln are among those who deny that "time- and context-free generalizations are possible."[7] Denial of these and other positivist axioms has value for the postpositivist because the axioms can be seen as constituting the underpinnings of scientific social research and of classical organization theory. Denial has value in the sense that it encourages, at least, the development of constructivist (or naturalistic) inquiry and nonorthodox organization theory, developments discussed in chapter 12. Bureaucratic deconstruction can also be directed at postmodern narratives, such as the account of naturalistic inquiry and the narratives in nonorthodox organization theory. Again, this approach is positive in putting such accounts in perspective and in facilitating new accounts. But, as will become clearer by the end of this chapter, deconstruction is more than a mere critique or a mere analysis.

Deconstruction, like postmodernism, is a difficult word. A joke, perhaps repeated more than it should be, asks "What's the difference between the Mafia and a deconstructionist?" The answer is, "A deconstructionist makes you an offer you can't understand."[8] This claim is an exaggeration; the offer is merely difficult to understand. We should start from recognition of that difficulty. We should also start by recalling that the postmodern claim about deconstruction is serious. Deconstruction includes the idea, as Lyotard reminds us, of the reduction of science to discourse.[9] In this view, science has no surer epistemological status than literature. Deconstruction, understood in this way, is considered to be a valuable activity.

QU'EST-CE QUE C'EST QUE ÇA?

Deconstruction can be considered against the background of structuralism. Structuralism is concerned with identifying and examining the "rules" that underlie language and cultures. Ferdinand de Saussure, the founder of structuralism, is interested in exploring the deep structures of the language system. His focus is not on particular languages (*parole*) but on language as a whole (*langue*).[10] He compares the approach with being interested not in the patterns of moves in particular chess games but in the underlying structural rules of any chess game. In the case of the language system, he is concerned with how such rules produce meanings. For him, the working of the linguistic system as a whole is prior to the working of particular signs in generating meaning. Language is a system that predetermines our ways of understanding and experiencing the world; for him, reality is constructed by language. Others apply the structuralist approach to cultural and other areas. Claude Lévi-Strauss uses it to study the "rules" that underlie cultural myths, for example.[11] Jacques Lacan attempts to decode the unconscious,[12] and Roland Barthes examines the signs of mass media and popular culture.[13] Derrida would reject such projects. For him, there are no explanatory rules or conventions. There are no underlying rules governing the activity of signifiers. He would also deny the existence of any firm meanings; meanings are continually changing. The aims of deconstruction include denying that a definite interpretation of texts is possible. It also includes exposing the multiple meanings in texts and showing that the signifiers are in free play.[14] One of the deconstructive aims, it can be said, is "to subvert the authoritarian claim to definitive knowledge."[15]

What, more precisely, is deconstruction? To begin answering this question, we must appreciate not only the reasons for the opaqueness and complexity of deconstruction but also must think through whether simplifying steps should be sought. In terms of opaqueness, we can note the problem of providing a dictionary-like definition, the relationship of deconstruction to other words used by postmodernists, and the characterizations of some critical "notions." In terms of avoiding simplification, we can consider the nature of a simplifying option and establish the loss involved in taking that step.

Asking for a dictionary-like definition of deconstruction is like asking for a square circle because deconstruction (for Derrida) denies the possibility of such definitions. If X entails the claim that X cannot be defined, there is difficulty in blithely going ahead and specifying a definition of X. Let us establish that this point is indeed understood as an issue by postmodernists. As Derrida writes, "[All] sentences of the type 'deconstruction is x' or 'deconstruction is not X' a priori miss the point, which is to say that they are at least false. As you know, one of the principal things at stake in what is called in my texts 'deconstruction' is precisely the delimiting of ontology and above all of the third person present indicative: S is P."[16] Derrida's view is that deconstruction deconstructs itself. As he puts it, "[T]he difficulty of defining and therefore also of translating the word 'deconstruction' stems from the fact that all the predicates, all the defining concepts, all the lexical significations, and even the syntactic significations, which seem at one moment to lend themselves to this definition or to that translation, are also deconstructed or deconstructible, directly or otherwise, etc. And that goes for the very word, the very unity of the word deconstruction, as for every word."[17]

A Derridean move, in this circumstance, is to note the connection of deconstruction with other words. Deconstruction (for Derrida) must be considered in a context of other words. Increasing the complexity even more is the fact that these other words must also be considered in relationship to deconstruction and to one another. Ask the meaning, and the questioner is told that the value is determined by certain other unfamiliar words. Ask the meaning of one of the unfamiliar words, and the questioner is told that the value is determined by the first word and the remainder of the set of unfamiliar words. Writing about deconstruction, Derrida states,

> For me, ... the word has interest only within a certain context, where it replaces and lets itself be determined by such other words as "écriture," "trace," "différance," "supplément," "hymen," "pharmakon," "marge," "entame," "parergon," etc. By definition, the list can never be closed, and I have cited only names, which is inadequate and done only for reasons of economy. In fact I should have cited the sentences and the interlinking of sentences which in turn determine these names in some of my texts.[18]

Speaking about différance (one of these words), Derrida says,

> [D]ifférance finds itself enmeshed in the work that pulls it through a chain of other "concepts," other "words," other textual configurations. Perhaps later I will have occasion to indicate why ... and why room had to be left for their insistence (for example, gram, reserve, incision, trace, spacing, blank—sens blanc, sang blanc, sans blanc, cent blancs, semblant—supplement, pharmakon, margin-mark-march, etc.). By definition the list has no taxonomic closure, and even less does it constitute a lexicon.[19]

Derrida thinks the vouloir-dire hopelessly metaphysical: "The word 'deconstruction,' like all other words, acquires its value only from its inscription in a chain of possible substitutions, in what is too blithely called a 'context'."[20]

Some of the characterizations of key postmodern notions are difficult. Consider différance, created by Derrida by changing the e to a in the ordinary French word différence. Gayle Ormiston quotes Derrida as saying that the difference between différence and différance "cannot be heard, and we shall see in what respects it is also beyond the order of understanding."[21] Ormiston goes on to write, "Derrida's différance is untranslatable, undefinable, unthinkable. Différance cannot be thought by any ontology, nor can it be elevated to a master-word, master-concept, or master-key."[22] Thinking about the unthinkable is not impossible, like thinking without thinking would be. It is forbidding, however. Consider deconstruction. Derrida's "Letter to a Japanese Friend" explains that deconstruction obtains its value "only from its inscription in a chain of possible substitutions."[23] Derrida then exclaims, "What deconstruction is not? everything of course. What is deconstruction? nothing of course."[24]

For Derrida, writing (which is neither speaking nor the result of speech nor the opposite of speech) is différance, the inscription of différance. Différance, neither a concept nor even a word, is spacing. It is pharmakon, which could injure or help. Writing is also the inscription of signature that leaves traces. The task of producing examples of the obscure from Derrida's writings is not hard.

Faced with a parallel difficulty of having to say the unsayable, Ludwig Wittgenstein adopts his ladder strategy: "My propositions serve as elucidations in the following way: anyone who understands me eventually recognizes them as nonsensical, when he has used them—as steps—to climb up beyond them. (He must, so to speak, throw away the ladder after he has climbed up it.) He must transcend these propositions, and then he will see the world aright."[25] If a person believes that nothing outside language exists and if that person wants to make statements from a language-free perspective, she is faced with the difficulty of having to say the unsayable; the reader will recall the discussion on perspectivism in chapter 2. For Derrida, there is no "outside" of language. The Wittgensteinian ladder option is to say it anyway but then to issue a disclaimer such as that in the *Tractatus*. Derrida flirts with a form of the ladder option; for example, he tells Houdebine and Scarpetta, "If there were a definition of différance, it would be precisely the limit, the interruption, the destruction of the Hegelian relève wherever it operates."[26] But, Derrida has resisted.

If he were to choose a ladder option, Derrida might say that deconstruction is essentially a special kind of critique or critical analysis. Having established that we understand, he would then point out that speaking of "X being essentially Y" and the ideas of a critique or a critical analysis are nonsense. He would say that what he has just said must be abandoned, transcended, deconstructed. It will be noticed that these disclaimers are not trivial, not at all to be compared with disclaimers such as warning labels on cigarette packages or on supermarket food cartons. Wittgenstein writes that his own propositions are "nonsensical" and that they must be transcended if the reader wishes to see the world aright.[27] Nonsense is such a common word that we tend to need to remind ourselves that it means gibberish or gobbledegook.

Two preliminary points should be made about any loss that would follow from imitating Wittgenstein's ladder strategy. First, we must remember the obvious fact that Wittgenstein's and Derrida's places in the development of thought, as well as their views, differ. For example, Derrida's antecedents, including Wittgenstein's philosophy, may constitute an event, in Lyotard's sense, that would change the frame for subsequent thinkers like Derrida. In this sense, what is or is not appropriate for Wittgenstein may or may not be appropriate for Derrida. Second, any loss sustained from imitating the ladder strategy would have several facets for Derrida. One is the hazard that, wishing to overcome metaphysics, Derrida's very method of overcoming metaphysics must avoid simply creating another metaphysics, and use of the ladder strategy might entail falling into this trap. The logic here can perhaps be illustrated with an example: if we want to say that all arguments are wrong, we cannot argue for that position. In Derrida's words, "Now, even in aggressions or transgressions, we are consorting with a code to which metaphysics is tied irreducibly, such that every transgressive gesture reencloses us—precisely by giving us a hold on the closure of metaphysics—within this closure."[28]

Let us limit our focus to only part of the loss, and to do so let us specify a goal that Derrida (because he considered that no outside of language exists) would consider nonsensical. The goal is to explore "the world aright." Following use of the ladder strategy, can we explore "the world aright"? Arguably, it is now more productive to play with the limits, that is, to work with the consequences of a situation when there can be no more picturing of the world, to play in the postmodern situation. As Derrida says to Henri Ronse, "I try to keep myself at the limit of philosophical discourse."[29] Later in the same interview, Derrida says,

> I try to write the question: (what is) the meaning to say? Therefore it is necessary in such a space, and guided by such a question, that writing literally means nothing. Not that it is absurd in the way that absurdity has always been in solidarity with metaphysical meaning. It simply tempts itself, tenders itself, attempts to keep itself at the point of the exhaustion of meaning. To risk meaning nothing is to start to play, and first to enter into the play of différance which prevents any word, any concept, any major enunciation from coming to summarize and to govern.[30]

As Derrida himself adds, this "meaning to say nothing," this refusal of the ladder strategy, as it were, is uncomfortable: "To be entangled in hundreds of pages of a writing simultaneously insistent and elliptical, imprinting, as you saw, even its erasures, carrying off each concept into an interminable chain of differences, surrounding or confusing itself with so many precautions, references, notes, citations, collages, supplements—this 'meaning-to-say-nothing' is not, as you will agree, the most assured of exercises."[31] Avoidance of a ladder strategy is awkward and irritating, but the idea is that this avoidance permits the exploration at the limits of philosophical discourse.

If deconstruction is seen as a critique or an interpretation of a text, it is a critique with a difference. It does not pretend to offer a correct critique or interpretation; at the same time it does not present either an incorrect or one person's estimate of the truth interpretation. Meaning or value, for Derrida, is determined completely within the language. It is determined only by differences from other units in the language. Language does not, to repeat, refer to anything outside of itself. No decidable meaning, then, exists. Meaning, according to Derrida, is "infinite implication, the indefinite referral of signifier to signified."[32] For Derrida, there is no meaning "in" the texts; there is nothing but texts.

Deconstruction is a "strategy without finality."[33] This statement seems reasonable if there is no decidable meaning; "for Derrida, writing always leads to more writing, and more, and still more."[34] After the text has been deconstructed, the deconstruction, as suggested above, turns on itself and deconstructs itself: "[T]he enterprise of deconstruction always in a certain way falls prey to its own work."[35] To give an illustration from the early computer-friendly generation: Pacman gobbles up the other little images, then gobbles up himself, then gobbles up whatever he used to gobble up himself, then gobbles up "whatever he used to gobble up whatever he used to gobble up himself," and so on ad infinitum.

This Pacman example (an irritating one from the modernist perspective) leads us to the equally irritating notion of play. Derrida accepts the notion of play. Like children's play, deconstructive play is both aimless and not aimless. It is aimless because it does not aim for truth or ultimate meaning and because it rejects the meaning of standards. According to Christopher Norris, "Deconstructive rigor—if we are to use that term—belongs to a discourse which can only question all standard, regulative notions of logical consistency."[36] It is also not aimless. Derrida writes that free play (*le jeu*) "is the disruption of presence."[37] He speaks of "a kind of general strategy of deconstruction. The latter is to avoid both simply neutralizing the binary oppositions of metaphysics and simply residing within the closed field of these oppositions, thereby confirming it."[38] This statement may bring to mind the earlier discussion of Wittgenstein's ladder. The deconstructive play discovers a text's blind spots, bringing out the author's metaphysical and epistemological assumptions. As Derrida states, deconstruction "attacks not only the internal edifice, both semantic and formal of philosophemes, but also . . . its extrinsic conditions of practice: the historical forms of its pedagogy, the social, economic or political structures of this pedagogical institution."[39]

Let us risk using the ladder. Deconstruction can be seen as deconstructing the narratives that make up texts, both modern and postmodern texts. An emphasis is typically placed on deconstructing the undergirdings, the narratives, that are and were constitutive of modernity and to move beyond that removal. Some of these undergirdings have histories prior to modernity (e.g., the oppositions that are constitutive of metaphysics). This deconstruction can be seen (to recall earlier discussions of Heidegger) as part of the working out of not seeing the world as a picture, of not picturing the world. On these lines, we would expect Lyotard to write that deconstruction is concerned with a questioning of the authorial point of view and the privileged order of valorization.[40] We would expect a commitment to open textuality. We would expect all the other characteristics of deconstruction discussed in this chapter. Deconstruction is a reading and rereading of texts in recognition of the postmodern situation at the limits that include recognizing and abandoning the basic underpinnings of modernity.

Deconstruction is a reading that accepts that the sign in the text has no referents. If this point is recognized, it is clearer why Derrida would not define *deconstruction* and why he has to speak of differences between it and other words. The sign in postmodernity can serve different functions (e.g., to conceal the absence of reality or simply to be its own simulacrum). Nevertheless, one thing it cannot do is refer to underlying reality; as Gertrude Stein might have said about the city she left, there is no "there" there. Baudrillard writes in this way of the "precession of simulacra":

> Abstraction today is no longer that of the map, the double, the mirror or the concept. Simulation is no longer that of a territory, a referential being or a substance. It is the generation by models of a real without origin or reality: a hyperreal. The territory no longer precedes the map, nor survives it. Henceforth, it is the map that precedes the territory—precession of simulacra—it is the map that engenders the territory.[41]

By contrast, the sign in modernity refers to an underlying reality. The referring can fulfill different functions, such as reflecting, counterfeiting, and masking. In reflecting, the sign "carries" its meaning. For Baudrillard, counterfeiting and fashion were born with the Renaissance, when the order changed and the universe became "disenchanted." Marxism and Freudianism are examples where the referent is seen as concealing—the masking of the real by, respectively, commodification and the unconscious. Deconstruction, on the other hand, is the reading and rereading of texts in recognition that (to adapt Baudrillard's phrase) "the simulacrum is never that which conceals the truth—it is the truth that conceals that there is none." Now, let us swiftly kick away the ladder.

BUREAUCRATIC DECONSTRUCTION

Continuing now with a consideration of public administration in the postmodern situation, how can the deconstruction of texts be understood as a valued activity? Bureaucratic deconstruction aims to dissect the narratives that underlie modernist projects and that are interwoven in postmodern accounts. It aims to show the narratives as lacking; it also aims to show that the dissections themselves are unsatisfactory. It was noted at the beginning of this chapter that a modernist grand narrative can be an explanation of societal development, a description of the motive force that underlies the development of history; an example offered was the Enlightenment's equation of rationalization with human progress. The modernist narratives of public administration are more limited, but they are related to the Enlightenment's modernist grand narrative. Examples were also given of postmodern narratives.[42]

One value of a deconstruction that deconstructs itself can be suggested intuitively by an example from public administration. From a modernist perspective, the idea seems self-defeating. Such a study methodology, evidencing both a critique about something and the conclusion that the study methodology can be questioned, would be considered a weak or unacceptable study. Nevertheless, it will be recalled that postmodernity allows no epistemologically privileged discourse, a surer way to the truth that the positivist considers possible through use of "the" scientific method. Postmodernity is postpositivist; "science" is like any other discourse. An example of the disutility of privileged discourse is provided by administrative reports; the administrative study and the organization and methods study may be among the examples.[43] A general experience is that such professional administrative reports are often extremely valuable. For example, one might propose a certain number of sensible organizational changes or a certain commonsensical allocation of police and fire personnel. An equally general experience is that the report would have been equally useful if it had made a different set of recommendations, perhaps offering a different sensible alternative for organization or a different commonsensical public safety deployment. Neither such a set of conclusions nor an administrative study method is privileged. Some will respond by saying that this statement applies only to certain kinds of reports, but that argument is to agree with the point being made. A danger would exist if the administrative recommendations and the method were regarded as being not merely sensible but somehow epistemologically privileged. Sometimes, people do treat a commonsense set of administrative recommendations as set in stone; that view is a disutility that requires, as it were, Pacman.

The first example of bureaucratic deconstruction is directed toward the public administration "grand" narrative that "the" goal for the development of public administration theory should be objectivity, and the strategy chosen is to focus on a particular "theoretical" text. The second addresses the "grand" narrative that efficiency should be the objective of public administration practice. This example relates to a "text" that is, arguably, as much part of cultural practice as at the heart of much theory: the concept of efficiency. Other narratives could have been chosen, such as a variant of the efficiency narrative that states that the model for effective government is business.

The term *text* in this context should be understood in its broadest and fullest sense. In terms of broadness, the term should be understood to include the products of all forms of language and action. Texts relating to public administration or to anything else are more than documents. We know that speech is read, for example; this idea is suggested when radio operators say, "I read you loud and clear." As computers and televisions continue influencing our lives, new forms of language may appear. It was a radical moment, symbolized perhaps by the cleft between the talk-

ing Socrates and the writing Plato, when writing assumed its role in human living. In a 1993 televised convocation speech, Prince Charles twice referred to the
contents of the Library of Congress being stored on a computer disc as small as a
hand.[44] This "unscholarly" citing of a television program rather than a document
is given to underscore a point made by many people. Is not a radically new form
of language developing? Texts in the present context would include not only all
of these language forms but also public administration and other actions. Actions,
situations, and people are read. Life is indeed literature; life's actions constitute a
book, a text.[45] In terms of fullness, the double sense of text should be understood.
This point is brought out by Ronse in one of his questions to Derrida: "In your essays at least two meanings of the word 'writing' are discernible: the accepted meaning, which opposes (phonetic) writing to the speech that it allegedly represents (but
you show that there is no purely phonetic writing), and a more radical meaning that
determines writing in general, before any tie to what glossematics calls an 'expres-
sive substance'; this more radical meaning would be the common root of writing
and speech."[46]

Three preliminary caveats should be given here. First, deconstruction cannot
be translated into bureaucratese, specifying the steps for executing the deconstructive method. Recall the opening lines of this chapter: "Deconstruction is neither a
method nor even an operation; it is neither an analysis nor a critique." This answer
may cause disappointment when seen from the mind-set of modernist public administration theory, but it is unreasonable to require play to be nonplay.

Second, it is not clear that deconstruction by itself, that is, apart from imaginization, deterritorialization, and alterity, can be made to yield a satisfying response
to the question on the value of deconstruction for public administration. Third, it
is inappropriate to hold deconstruction to an unreasonable binary brilliancy test,
meaning that deconstruction must be either brilliant (brilliance including the notion of being novel in all respects) or a fraud. Absent brilliance, an assumption of
such a test is that no third position exists and that deconstruction must be, so the
notion goes, fraudulent. On the contrary, deconstruction is not a chess game; it is for
plodders.

The first candidate for bureaucratic deconstruction, then, is a "grand" narrative
that equates good public administration theory with objectivity; it equates better
theory with more objectivity. The deconstructive strategy selected here is to consider the authorship of Simon's *Administrative Behavior.* We start by trespassing in
the area of critical theory. One aim of the strategy is to suggest that forces beyond
Herbert Simon's control shaped the authorship of the contents. A picture should
emerge that points away from objectivity and suggests that any other theoretical
work in public administration is open to similar lines of deconstruction. It is suggested that Simon's book was written in the context of other texts and that its un-

derstanding is shaped by the presence of later texts; that is, Simon's text is what will be explained as a text within a series of texts. Because no method is epistemologically privileged, clearly other deconstructive strategies could have been used.

Who authored Herbert A. Simon's *Administrative Behavior?*[47] Who was the author, the decision maker who decided the content of *Administrative Behavior?* A correct answer is Herbert A. Simon. The question sounds silly because the answer seems obvious. Nevertheless, perhaps the answer is not quite so straightforward. In fact, the list of coauthors and coauthoring forces is immense, as it is for any other book. Consider the text in terms of two chains, or lines, of inquiry (although of course others exist).

As a first line of inquiry, we may begin by asking about the objectives and constraints of the managers of the Macmillan Publishing Company (The Free Press Division) when they codetermined that the company would publish *Administrative Behavior.* Really, it is more than merely publishing; it is also a matter of choices about production volume and marketing strategy. This line of inquiry is exciting because it might lead to questions about who and what determines, or sets parameters for, a publisher's objectives and constraints; this might lead to questions regarding who or what in the socio-politico-economic environment sets parameters and motivation for the company's decisions, and so on. This inquiry might lead to interesting analyses about how, say, the market and consumerism shape the character of what is published as a marketable book on a public administration topic. It might lead to analyses of the working of the economic system, of which that authoring was a part. Various views will be encountered, including the narrative that speaks of the influence of the dominant class in society. One of these narratives is represented by Gramsci's idea of "hegemony," expressing the advantaged position of dominant social groups in establishing the propositions that make up what society considers to be "common sense."[48] Both books and writers are commodified (see definition given earlier in this chapter), one in the marketplace and the other in the academic and other marketplaces. We are led to the work of Marx (never a Peoria favorite), the critical theorists, and others on the commodification of discourse and then beyond to those critical of Marx and the critical theorists. This step is important, partly because it suggests that public administration theory, no less than a single book, is itself commodified.

Along these lines, one might argue that, like a book, public administration is a commodity that is subject to market forces, developed within the framework of being packaged for sale and bought for a price. Its general features, its shape and character, are delimited by its commodification. If a theorist subscribed to Marxist analysis, to take only one instance, would a work using that analysis be well received (sell)? Would that theorist's career thrive (sell)? The naturalness of the demand with which we started—for an example of how deconstruction can be of any practical significance—also reflects this commodification. Public administration theory is bought, or not bought, by bureaucracies and governmental officials. Without support from governments and bureaucrats, for example, university suppliers of public administration credentials, competing with departments supplying alternative credentials such as those in other social sciences or in the humanities, would lose their customers (students). Without support from bureaucratic funding sources, suppliers of public administration theory and (taking one way of looking at it) applied public administration theory would have less of a market for their consulting and research wares. Of course, other systems and entities exert demands: public universities must respond to legislative demands for the utility of the product. On the supply side, the product is designed to reflect not only its own commodification but also the commodification of the university, the commodification of social science, and the commodification of science. All these forces incline public administration theory toward short-run payoff, and the forces are intensified because of competition from competing credentialing sources. Public Administration Theory is a special case in this respect of the society analyzed by the critical theorists of, say, the Frankfurt school, which uses Marxist categories such as commodification and exchange. Horkheimer and Adorno write that the "individual is wholly devalued in relation to the economic powers, which at the same time press the control of society over nature to hitherto unsuspected heights."[49] The commodification of public administration is such a powerful limit, it seems, that we tend to internalize the short-term utility imperative. The requirement for utility seems natural.

Who authored Herbert A. Simon's *Administrative Behavior?* Let us consider a second line of inquiry. Three points appear from a reading of the text. First, the text is written within a context of other texts, and the text responds to those texts. Consider as examples the texts of the logical positivists and of Chester Barnard. Simon states what he supposes to be the connection between the logical positivist texts and his text: "[T]he conclusions reached by a particular school of modern philosophy—logical positivism—will be accepted as a starting point, and their implications for the theory of decisions examined."[50] In the footnote on that page, Simon lists what he believes to be the seven relevant logical positivist texts: *Foundations of the Theory of Signs* by Charles W. Morris, *Foundations of Logic and Mathematics* by Rudolf Carnap, *The Logic of Modern Physics* by P. W. Bridgman, "Testability and Meaning" by Carnap, *The Logical Syntax of Language* by Carnap, *Language, Truth and Logic* by Alfred J. Ayer, and *Beyond Conscience* by T. V. Smith. Simon's text surely can be seen as a partial response to a reading (direct, indirect through others, or both) of these texts. A "reading" is stressed because a reading in the earlier part of this century, when logical positivism was in vogue, might be different from a reading at a later time when the popularity of logical positivism has (rightly or wrongly) declined. Simon's text does not engage the texts about logical positivism closely in the sense that it does not challenge ideas or add supporting argumentation; it uses them to support a study of decision-making processes. Simon's text accepts as a given what is described as the critical conclusion of the logical positivist texts (i.e., about the distinction between facts and values). Considering subsequent related texts, any such acceptance at the present time would be different; the text written later would have had to have justified the acceptance differently. No statement is made about whether the slope of the chain is upward or downward, but Simon's text is a response to the other texts in a chain of texts.

This placing in a chain is also seen in the relationship of Simon's text to Barnard's text. Simon's text does engage the latter more intimately. The text specifically acknowledges the debt to Barnard and to Barnard's text: "To Mr. Chester Barnard I owe a special debt: first, for his own book *The Functions of the Executive,* which has been a major influence upon my thinking about administration; secondly, for the extremely careful critical review he gave the preliminary version of the book; and finally for his Foreword to the present edition."[51] By a more intimate engagement is meant that Simon's text interrelates with ideas read in Barnard's text on equal terms. For instance, Simon's text discusses the "zone of acceptance."[52] As is acknowledged in the Simon text, this term involves changing the name of the "zone of indifference" described on page 169 of Barnard's text.[53] It bears repeating that this text is a response in a chain of texts. The response of Simon's text to Barnard's text was one molded by the reading of Barnard's text that was possible in the context of the chain of texts that had occurred. If made half a century later, the response might have been different because other texts would have joined the chain.

Some may experience a negative reaction to a privileging of texts over authors (i.e., making the points about texts instead of authors). Thinking about the primacy of discourse is easier if one can think of texts as having, as it were, lives of their own. Some writers do experience a separation after a time between themselves and their texts. They can read at random from one of their texts, and it can seem as if the text were written by someone else.

Who authored Herbert A. Simon's *Administrative Behavior?* The second point that emerges from a reading of Simon is that his text is also a response to the rationalization and other dynamics that constitute the texts of modernity. This response is reflected in the preface and in the content. The preface expresses the hope that the text will be of use to "individuals concerned with the science of administration," to "practical administrators" and to students; the first mention reflects scientism and the second technologism. Rationalization is part of the warp and woof of the text. For example, a major theme of the text is that participation in organizations makes it possible to attain greater rationality and that the character of the organizational environment determines the extent of the rationality; objective rationality is the ideal. Simon states, "The need for an administrative theory resides in the fact that there are practical limits to human rationality, and that these limits are not static, but depend upon the organizational environment in which the individual's decision takes place."[54] We can also again mention satisficing, which speaks of the "rationality" of choosing (as explained in chapter 3) the first satisfactory option rather than making the optimal choice. Significant parameters of the decisions about the content of *Administrative Behavior* were, then, already made by the texts that constitute modernity. More than that, much of the content was established by these same texts. Is it too poetic to say that modernity was the coauthor, perhaps even the first author?

A third point that emerges from a reading of Simon's text is the role of the reader (of the responding text) as the attacher of meaning to the text, as happens with any text. The meaning that is read would be conditioned by the place of this reader in the chain of texts. The question, "Other things being equal, how would Simon of *Administrative Behavior* read Barnard of *The Functions of the Executive* in 1993?" is nonsensical. The two texts seem bound to their places in the chain of discourse between texts, and the birth of other responding texts between 1945 and 1993 makes it impossible that "other things" ever could be equal. This example, and perhaps the earlier discussion, may have the disadvantage of appearing to privilege dates and to suggest that texts do have inherent meaning. Authors do not have the power to entrap meaning in a text at a particular point of time.

Let us pursue this. Consider an example where the text appears different to different readers. Contrast Argyris's reading of *Administrative Behavior* with Simon's reading of *Administrative Behavior*. Argyris reads Simon's rationality as excluding self-actualizing: "Professor Simon continues, as his title states, to make rationality and self-actualization mutually exclusive."[55] Simon reads Simon differently: "If there is a danger that the 'or' in the title of my reply to Argyris may be interpreted as exclusive rather than inclusive, I am more than happy to accept 'and' or even 'and/or'."[56] The "reply" cited is, "Organization Man: Rational or Self-Actualizing?"[57] Now, this difference is not trivial when it comes to a reading of *Administrative Behavior*. Consider Argyris's comment against Simon: "Reason, for me, is not, and never has been, a shackle of freedom. Reason is a foundation for my view of interpersonal competence acquisition (Argyris, 1968). . . . It is the design and administration of organizations that do not encourage the discussion of emotions and emotionally loaded substantive issues (when they are relevant) that is the shackle."[58] Argyris's reading is that rational man organizational theories such as Simon's are inadequate and that "a more complex and humanistic model of man and more normative research are required."[59] One of Simon's major objections is that he reads Argyris as creating "a straw man called 'rational man organizational theory,' which allegedly ignores motivational and emotive aspects of human behavior." Later, continuing his reply, Simon writes, "To which I can only answer with the punchline of an ancient joke: 'Vas you dere Charlie (or Chris)?"[60] Nevertheless, of course, these readers' readings of Simon's text do overlap in places. For example, Argyris reads the text as "brilliant" and a "classic."[61]

We have now sketched the beginnings of an analysis of the question, "Who authored Herbert A. Simon's *Administrative Behavior?*" The inquiry started along two lines. One showed that we could look at the text in the chain of forces and choices (other texts, as we have described *text*) that culminate in the associated publishing and distribution decisions; the other showed that we could examine the printed text in terms of a chain of other published texts. I have no interest here in pursuing these or similar analyses beyond the point of suggesting that such lines of analysis are useful. If it is appropriate to think of theory as a lens through which the public administration world can be pictured (or of theory as participating in constituting that world), a minimal judgment is that such analyses would seem to be lens cleaners—or lens changers.

The second candidate for bureaucratic deconstruction, it will be recalled, is the narrative that efficiency is a viable goal for public administration practice. The objective in the present discussion is to suggest how such a deconstructive strategy could be pursued, rather than to carry the strategy as far as it can go. It is also suggested that parallel concepts, such as effectiveness, could be subjected to similar deconstructive analyses.

Why should we be concerned with deconstructing efficiency? Two reasons are suggested. First, practitioners have long shown a concern for efficiency in bureaucratic reform. The latest major manifestation of this concern is Vice-President Albert Gore's national performance review report. This reform report does not view efficiency as "the" administrative value, as arguably the earlier Grace Commission and important early public administration reformers did. Nevertheless, as the preface to the report makes clear, efficiency is a major concern: "The Clinton administration believes it is time for a new customer service contract with the American people, a new guarantee of effective, efficient, and responsive government."[62] Second, it is unclear how effective the efficiency concept has been, and can be, in achieving efficiency. The results problem is sometimes thought to lie with the politicians and bureaucrats, and we have such disagreements as those between the bureaucrat bashers and the bashers of the bureaucrat bashers; that is, it can be considered to be the context. Alternatively, the problem can be thought to lie with the method chosen. A lesson suggested by Downs and Larkey, for example, is what they call "a grand-strategy problem": "One problem with many past reforms is that they have taken a comprehensive, strategic approach. They have usually been directed at all agencies or all programs in the target government and have been aimed at the highest-level decision."[63] Another alternative is that the problem lies in the nature of the concept, in our theory of efficiency; the concept of efficiency is itself inefficient. Yet again, perhaps the problem lies in all three areas.

The strategy adopted (of the alternatives available) could have three elements. First, it could be reiterated that the concept of efficiency is a social construction, and it could be contended that this understanding has important consequences. Second, it could be suggested that the social construction of the concept of efficiency is culturally relative to the aims of the modernist world. Efficiency has been culturally determined to be an ineluctable moral concept and a concept of a particular shape, it can be explained. Third, it could be argued that, as such a moral concept, efficiency is regrettable. Each of these lines of argument are discussed below.

Such a criticism would be in the tradition of significant public administrationist opposition to the predominance of the efficiency value. Arguably, *efficiency* is a concept that, along with the reciprocals, does constitute a criterion widely considered critical by practitioners and others for evaluating practice. Nevertheless, the concept has been discounted in some administrative theory, such as New Public Administration, and other opponents can argue that more important priorities exist, such as meeting the public interest. With regard to opponents, Simon states, "Criticisms of 'efficiency' as a guide to administration have been frequent and vociferous."[64] Simon refers to examples cited by Marshall Dimock, and he proceeds to give his responses to the criticisms.[65] Waldo also refers to Dimock, quoting his criticism that efficiency "is a mendicant—it begs the question until the auditor can discover the particular connotations the user has in mind."[66] Simon's own view in *Administrative Behavior* is that the "criterion of efficiency as applied to administrative decisions is strictly analogous to the concept of maximization of utility in economic theory."[67]

The first element of the suggested deconstructive strategy is to emphasize that the concept of efficiency is a social construction. In *The Administrative State*, Dwight Waldo proposes a formula that will be considered in discussing the second and third elements, for mediating between the objective and the normative interpretations of efficiency. He writes, "We propose this formula: the descriptive or objective notion of efficiency is valid and useful, but only within a framework of consciously held values."[68] Does an "objective" notion of efficiency exist? Yes, one certainly does in the sense that such a notion is an objective feature of the social world in which we live; the notion is not subjective insofar as it is a feature of the social environment in which public administrators work. There is no such objective notion in the sense that efficiency is a given, part of the furniture of the world. Clearly, efficiency was created by society. It is a social construction in the sense discussed in chapter 2.

This point could seem to be quibbling, especially if one accepts a logocentric view of the term *efficiency;* that is, it can seem like hairsplitting if, contrary to Saussure and those in his tradition, one views language as mere nomenclature.[69] Saussure explains that not only does each language produce a different set of signifiers but also it produces a different set of signifieds. Signifiers, as discussed above, are words such as *efficient, effective,* and *responsive;* they are among the signifiers or words used in the first paragraph of the preface of the Gore report discussed above. Signifieds are whatever the signifiers signify. A logocentric view is that language should attempt to be as transparent as possible so that it does not distort the understanding of the entities that lie behind the medium of language; that is, the signifiers should not distort the signifieds that are supposed to exist independently of the signifiers. Saussure's view is different.[70] As Culler goes on to explain, Saussure has indicated that each language has "a distinctive and thus 'arbitrary' way of organizing the world into concepts or categories."[71] Culler gives as an example the English distinction between a river and a stream, and he points out that the French words *fleuve* and *rivière* divide the conceptual plane differently.[72] Later he shows how the semantic field for *Kunst* changed in Middle High German between about 1200 and 1300: "At an early stage (Kunst) was a higher, courtly knowledge or competence, as opposed to lower, more technical skills ('List'), and a partial accomplishment as opposed to the synoptic wisdom of 'Wisheit.' In a later stage the two major oppositions which defined it were different: mundane versus spiritual ('Wisheit') and technical ('Wissen') versus non-technical. What we have are two different organizations of a semantic field."[73] He adds that an explanation of what happened to *Kunst* "would have to refer to nonlinguistic factors or causes (social changes, psychological processes, etc.) whose effects happened to have repercussions for the semantic system."[74] The concept, or set of concepts, represented by the modern word *efficiency* should not be regarded as a given. It can be misleading to think in terms of an objective notion of efficiency.

It deserves reemphasis that there are possible worlds (worlds that could be) that do not contain *efficiency*. An example might be the ideal world sketched in Plato's *Republic;* the reference here is not to the world in which Plato lived but only to the world he created. It will be recalled that we are speaking of a state where there is a firm division between the three classes and there are four cardinal virtues. A virtue shared by the artisans is temperance, and the virtue that serves as a balance among all three classes is justice. These arrangements seem to slice up well enough the spectrum of conceptual possibilities without the notion of efficiency. Contemporary examples may well exist of societies without the notion of efficiency. Consider Iran, for instance. Amin Alimard, a colleague and former dean of the School of Economics and Political Science at the National University in Teheran, notes in a personal communication of March 19, 1994, that the Iranian word for *efficiency* (*kara-ee*) was coined in the 1950s. The coining was done by modifying a word (*karamad,* meaning efficiency and applied to farming) found in Persian literature of more than seven hundred years ago. He reports that there was no concept of efficiency represented in Farsi in the intervening period. With the exception of the limited use for farming, he explains that the concept of efficiency was not used.

A consequence of the social construction of efficiency is that we as a society have considerable latitude in shaping and reshaping the signified.[75] In an interview, Waldo explains the development of his views on efficiency:

> In the beginning I came at efficiency with the instincts or biases of the humanist. That is, I was critical of the uncritical and crude way it was often used, and even of the idea that it is *the* central value in administration—an idea carefully developed by Luther Gulick. Along the way, so to speak, I had second thoughts. Efficiency could be overplayed, used loosely or dishonestly, but it is—how to put it?—a relevant consideration in many decisions and very central in some. I concluded that considerations of efficiency were relevant to the attainment of liberal or humane values.[76]

As a society, we can aim to go the other way; there is possibly a world where efficiency is not part of the signified.

The second element of the suggested deconstructive strategy is to point out that the social construction of the concept of efficiency is culturally relative. It can be argued that the concept arose from our culture and that it is shaped by the culture. It is shaped, as is explained below, both as a normative imperative and as a normative imperative directed at a particular treatment of society. It is an appropriate value, in its current form, for a society shaped by the Enlightenment ideals of modernity. As chapter 3 discussed, the modernist mind-set has included the equation of increasing rationalization with ever-increasing human progress and happiness. In such circumstances, it makes sense to value an optimal input-output ratio; efficiency in working toward increasing human happiness is itself rational.

Efficiency was valued in premodernity, but it is even more useful in a society organized in the relatively freewheeling manner of market enterprise.[77] Arguably, efficiency becomes such a valued activity for purposes of control in circumstances where the market is structured in terms of decentralized decision making. In the free enterprise system, the motivation assumed by mainstream microeconomics is the optimization of utility, and this translates into an appropriate relationship between inputs and output. In more straightforward terms, there is a need to control the activities of others in business enterprise and to value the efficiency of business associates. Where it is conceptualized as achieving the organization's ends in an optimal fashion (doing what one is told), efficiency is admired and rewarded by the owner, by the owner's business associates, and by customers. This conception could have reinforced the special "historical" motives for political leaders to control their bureaucracies. Some governmental leaders (for example, King Frederick the Great) have had special reasons to emphasize the value of doing what one is told. Deeper and perhaps more fundamental motivations for efficiency do exist, of course; for instance, children who "do what they are told" are often praised by their parents, and this surely has psychoanalytical consequences. Efficiency is a means of control that is consistent with the aims of modernist (and other) private and public enterprise. Efficiency is, as it were, not simply a matter of efficiency.

Efficiency, it is suggested, is part of the language of social control—the set of directive words, phrases, and sentences that are intended to make things happen in the future. As Hayakawa explains his view, society is a network of mutual agreements, a vast network consisting "essentially of statements about future events which we are supposed, with our own efforts, to bring about."[78] Efficiency is an example of what Hayakawa would call a "directive with collective sanction."[79] Hayakawa does not include (nor does he exclude) efficiency; instead, his examples are constitutions, legal contracts, oaths of office, marriage vows, confirmation exercises, and initiations. He explains that such directive utterances can show any or all of seven features. In its own way, efficiency shows at least five of these features. A first is the use of words or forms of expression that have affective connotations. In legal documents and weddings, for example, it is the use of archaic language (e.g., wilt thou? and to whit). In the case of efficiency, it is both the use of numbers and the use of numbers associated with the "scientific" or "technological" precision of the coefficient of efficiency of a machine. Numbers can carry affective weight in a scientifically oriented society; this particular use of numbers carries the additional affective clout of association with the spectacular success of the technology of machines that was noted earlier. A second is the fear of punishment. Inefficiency typically is punished (e.g., in pay adjustments, in profit and loss statements, and in lowered respect and admiration). A third is preliminary disciplines, such as training courses. A fourth is "feasting, dancing and other joyous manifestations."[80] This relates back to the second item, and a small example might be the celebration of pay raises to the extent that they are said to be tied to efficiency ratings. A fifth is frequent repetition. There is a drumbeat of repetition about efficiency, evidenced in the United States not only in the long history of efficiency commissions but also in the way that governmental administration is discussed. Efficiency is in this way a cultural ritual, a part of our modernist cultural text.

Efficiency is ineluctably a normative concept, an ethical precept. That efficiency is a powerful moral phenomenon is recognized no less than by Waldo. Waldo points out that the term, generally regarded as descriptive, became "in fact invested with moral significance. To a considerable extent the exaltation of efficiency must be regarded as the secularization, materialization, of the Protestant conscience. The tenet of efficiency is an article in the faith of 'muscular Christianity.' "[81] As Downs and Larkey put it, "Efficiency ranks with motherhood, apple pie, citizen participation, and balanced budgets as a fundamental American value."[82]

The opposition to the value of efficiency by some public administrationists was noted earlier, but it is not clear whether any opponent would wish to deny the enduring cultural force of the notion; we are eager for efficiency—at least in others. Without dismissing the opposition, it can be repeated that *efficiency* is a concept that carries significant normative weight in modernist society. It does so in the sense that, used as an adjective in describing administrative practice, it is typically taken to be a commendation and a mark of approval. Ordinarily, for instance, it would seem odd to remark, "That unit is admirable because it is inefficient." Admiration for efficiency is a strong cultural phenomenon, as may be reflected in admiration for the "efficiency" of the enemy in war situations.

The point was made earlier that efficiency is a concept that incorporates significant cultural baggage; it is a normative imperative directed at a particular treatment of society. Cultural or social attitudes shape the form of the concept—and of the form of reciprocal concepts, such as waste. Consider the different attitudes toward the private and the public sectors; the discussion in chapter 7 regarding the differing attitudes toward duplication will be recalled. Some would hold that, although public efficiency (or waste) is of concern, efficiency (or waste) in private enterprise is not a public concern. How should we interpret a statistical claim that, say, 90 percent of restaurants go out of business? Despite any views about ill effects such as the trauma caused to employees and others, most would say that what restaurant owners do with their own money is their business. "Mind your own business" is an attitude that in this case helps shape the social construction of waste in such a way that private waste is seen as different from public waste. Perhaps, or perhaps not, the table should be tilted in this way. One consequence is that comparisons of efficiency across the two sectors are affected; in such a situation, government is the only sector that can be inefficient. As Nagatani puts it, "Of the two categories of bureaucracies, governmental and private/corporate, the latter has largely escaped attack by successfully personifying itself. (Corporations call themselves legal persons.) Government bureaucracy has consequently come to bear the brunt of criticism, hatred and ridicule."[83] Later we will consider another of Nagatani's examples, showing that the different assignment of responsibilities between the private and the public sectors shape our notion of efficiency.

Efficiency should not be interpreted as merely a straightforward formula or ratio. Waldo seems to make this interpretation in proposing his formula that "the descriptive or objective notion of efficiency is valid and useful, but only within a framework of consciously held values."[84] Efficiency, for him, can be measured only in terms of purpose, a frame of reference. He proposes a hierarchy of purposes in mediating between what he calls the normative and descriptive aspects of efficiency. He explains that efficiency can be measured at various "levels" of human purposes, with the purposes being essentially the same at lower levels and showing greater disparity at the higher levels: "[As] long as the frame of reference is made clear, studies of 'efficiency' in public administration are possible and useful."[85]

Waldo was unduly optimistic, it is suggested, about the feasibility of separating the descriptive and the normative understandings of efficiency. Because it is so powerful a cultural tenet, efficiency accepted as merely "a" value within a framework of purposes tends in practice to be accepted as sufficient justification in most frameworks. Some frameworks of purpose are so deviant that mere efficiency is not accepted as moral justification; the Nuremberg and later military trials are examples. Nevertheless, the tendency for efficiency to serve as justification is clear in less dramatic, but important, bureaucratic situations (e.g., "I am just doing my job").

The third element of the suggested deconstructive strategy is to argue that, as a moral concept, efficiency is regrettable. A line of argument available here is to appeal to the idea that a normative ideal should encourage only desirable behavior. How can a person take seriously a normative injunction that requires her to do something undesirable? It is suggested that efficiency is such an equivocal concept that it inevitably encourages some undesirable behavior. If efficiency is a normative ideal, some varieties of meaning give conflicting normative endorsements.

Cases do exist in which efficiency is undesirable. If efficiency is defined as choosing the optimal method for realizing a certain stated goal or goals, then efficiency can be undesirable whenever the goals are undesirable. In that situation, inefficiency may be considered desirable if it resulted in, say, better outcomes. Chapter 10 gave an example about the World War II death camps. In such cases we might be comfortable saying, "X was magnificent because he chose to be inefficient." Nevertheless, the case is not clear. What could be admired might not be the inefficiency itself but rather the courage in subverting orders or even the "efficiency" that was displayed in this subversion. If X were inefficient without a studied intent of subverting the program's purposes, it is unlikely that X would be commended. Certainly, cases can be imagined where inefficiency in achieving evil purposes might result in even more evil; for instance, the inefficiency of the clumsy torturer's assistant may or may not increase the victim's suffering. Nevertheless, the point remains that situations exist where efficiency is undesirable.

Part of the problem regarding efficiency is obvious, but its full significance can be ignored. The obvious part of the problem is that efficiency is usually defined in public administration as taking whatever ends are proposed by the organization as givens; efficiency in this case is expressed as the relationship of the input to the output defined by the organization. The obvious part of the significance is reflected in questions raised in the politics-administration dichotomy, discussed in chapter 4. It is also reflected in the conceptualization of the nature of a science. If public administration is purely instrumental (focusing, say, on the idea of getting things done through people or the idea of decision making), greater public administration efficiency can be undesirable. On the one hand, it could be argued that Herbert Simon in *Administrative Behavior* glides over this difficulty when he writes that it "may be freely admitted that efficiency, as a scientific problem, is concerned chiefly with 'means,' and that 'efficient' service may be efficient with respect to any of a wide variety of ends. But merely to recognize that the process of valuation lies outside the scope of science, and that the adaptation of mean to ends is the only element of the decisional problem that has a factual solution, is not to admit any indifference to the ends which efficiency serves."[86] On the other hand, Simon has available the argument that science is one thing and that its uses are another. An analogy could be drawn with, say, nuclear physics, noting that physicists determine how to make the weapons and that society decides whether to mass produce and use them. Such an evaluation of efficiency leads to consideration of the general notion of value-free science. It raises the issue of whether public administration in particular should be constructed as ethics-free, and we return to difficulties about ethics such as those discussed in chapter 5.

Efficiency is an ambiguous word, as public administrationists have recognized. It can apply to entities as diverse as movements or to individual acts. Thus, Schiesl describes the politics of efficiency that shaped the American municipal reform movement, where governmental efficiency "tended to be defined as the promotion of economic growth and development" and where the movement for governmental efficiency turned on the three key concepts of nonpartisanship, a strong executive, and the politics-administration dichotomy.[87] Waldo writes of seven or eight dictionary meanings, which he believes reduce to two "fundamental meanings." He describes efficiency in public administration literature as "a synonym for 'competent,' 'productive,' 'capable.' "[88]

Alternative conceptualizations of *efficiency* raise difficulties where efficient behavior is valued. Mainstream economic theory recognizes definitions of efficiency other than the firm's input-output ratio, a ratio equivalent to the one discussed for public administration, where the output is set by the organization. It recognizes conceptualizations other than X-inefficiency, a concept noted in chapter 5.[89] Pareto efficiency is an example of an output-presupposing conceptualization of efficiency; one that speaks in terms of maximizing societal utility is another. In the first case, there is economic inefficiency, in a broad sense, if any one person in a society can be made better off without making anyone worse off.[90] In the second case, society's resources, in a broad sense, are considered to be used efficiently if society's production possibilities are realized. Chapter 5 suggested that fundamental difficulties exist in specifying economic justice.[91] Nevertheless, it remains the case that neither the Pareto nor the utility maximization conceptualization of efficiency can be considered to guarantee a just outcome; that is, the results can be unjust.

Efficiency is a social construction, ambiguous in that it displays varieties of meaning. This idea may be seen more readily, as in the earlier example, by examining efficiency as a reciprocal of waste;[92] that is, it is taken that the amount of waste is a measure of the amount of inefficiency. That *waste* and thus *efficiency* are ambiguous terms can be seen in four respects. We are approaching this matter from the private sector perspective, with the claim that clear parallels to the public sector situation exist.

First, note the large numbers of categories that could be considered waste in the private sector, and note that some people would disagree about these categories being counted as waste. Such a situation is no less true in the public sector. A distinction has been drawn, for instance, between demand-side and supply-side waste.[93] Demand-side waste is understood as the failure to operate the economy at full capacity. Some would say that this type of waste is not waste to the firm; others would say that it might be waste to society but that it is a qualitatively differently kind of waste. Examples of forms of supply-side waste, the inefficient use of input resources, range from varieties of corporate welfare (such as excessive executive compensation, wasting resources on those mergers that are unproductive, fraudulent practices, and governmental tax breaks and bailouts) to environmental (environmental denigration, neighborhood deterioration effects, making dangerous products, discrimination, worker injuries, and product differentiation and nonprice competition through advertising), and to bureaucratic inefficiencies.[94] Some people would disagree with the inclusion of some (or even all) of these items. For instance, some would say that fraudulent practices are not wasteful; after all, cannot organized crime be efficiently, or inefficiently, run? As another instance, some would say that the idea of *dangerous* is too slippery to permit inclusion of dangerous products. As another example, some might argue that nothing is wasteful about securing product differentiation through advertising if the results include greatly increased sales and profits. There is microwaste, as when consumers pay too much for, say, house repairs;[95] and there is macrowaste, represented by the economy not moving in directions it should go. Some might say that a consumer (assuming that the consumer is neither mentally deficient nor declining in years) paying too much for house repairs is a matter of consumer choice; it is, they might say, a matter of bad judgment and not waste. Waste can be considered as producing the wrong products, misusing scarce resources, and underusing available resources. But some might regard the notion of "wrong products" produced in a free society to be incoherent.

Second, what is waste, in both the private and the public sectors, from one viewpoint is not necessarily waste from another. What is not waste to the private company may be waste to society, for example. Thus, Dowd can speak of "the immense amount of land, capital, and natural resources chronically wasted (in military and restricted agricultural and industrial production, planned obsolescence, advertising and packing and so forth) and those left idle (uncultivated acreage, closed factories, and mines) and the most important of them, under and unemployed labor."[96] None of these examples need be waste from the perspective of the individual firm.

Third, the allocation of waste between categories can be constructed and reconstructed and can occur in both the private and public sectors; it can be seen in terms of whether costs are internalized in the private sector, for example. The cost of repairing the land disfigured by strip mining can be internalized as a cost to the firm, or it can be externalized as a cost to society; the decision about the extent of the internalization affects the efficiency calculations of the firm and its operations. As another example, labor costs are socially constructed; for instance, health care costs can be internalized and be borne by the employers, or they can be externalized and assumed by the individual, society, or both.[97]

Fourth, the ambiguity of waste statements is suggested by the fact that, when waste is assessed on an input-output basis, the extent of the waste is a function of the difficulty of attaining the output. When the high-jump bar is lowered from 10 feet to 5 feet and when other things are equal, the efficiency of the jumpers is likely to increase. Nonetheless, if the jumpers jump as high in both circumstances, are the jumpers really more efficient in the second circumstance? On a micro level, federal and other managers required to develop annual personnel performance contracts against which their performance will be evaluated at the end of the year know that it is unwise to set goals so high that their efficiency ratings suffer. On the macro level, the allocation of responsibilities between the public and private sectors is such that the "high-jump bar" for the public sector has been set relatively higher. As Nagatani writes about the allocation, the "civil services are burdened with responsibilities far in excess of their capabilities."[98] The "higher bar" includes governmental bureaucracy being responsible for the health and growth of the economy; despite the scale of their economic activity and despite their interest, even the largest firms have no responsibility for more than their own company's welfare. Nagatani claims that, rather than shoulder a larger part of government's responsibility for the health of the economy, "[E]xperience shows that random individualistic lobbying is the best strategy by which to prey on the public purse. . . . Governments today, in effect, run a free, no-fault insurance against business casualties in various guises; tax laws allow extensive carry-overs and carry-backs of losses in addition to the many special tax credits and deferrals for business investment and R and D expenditures; unemployment insurance and other welfare programs support the workers whom business releases as it sees fit."[99]

Efficiency, being equivocal, is more than merely inefficient. When interpreted in a normative sense and as a method of control, it is crude and can be misleading; when not interpreted in a normative sense (to the extent that this is possible in our culture), it is a trivial statistic. The equivocal character of efficiency can be further recognized by considering Coleman's claim that the concept of the efficiency of an economic system is defined "only" within a particular distribution of resources. Coleman calls this particular distribution "a particular constitutional allocation of rights and resources,"[100] and he explains that if "in a given system, with a given constitutional allocation, all externalities are internalized and transaction costs are reduced to zero, the system has achieved efficiency. But if rights are allocated differently, to persons with different interests, the 'efficient' outcomes of the system may differ, even in the absence of transaction costs."[101] One of Coleman's examples relates to Germany's 1976 codetermination law. The codetermination law, providing new rights to workers, requires that half of the members of a board of directors must be employee representatives and that workers' councils should be created. Coleman reports that, before the law's enactment, the Adam Opel organization (a subsidiary of General Motors) made the decision to locate a plant to manufacture a new small car in Spain. The outcome of locating the car in Germany (a likely outcome, if the decision had been made after the 1976 law) "might have been more efficient for the firm under the new constitutional allocation of rights, and the Spanish location more efficient under the old allocation."[102]

Deconstructive strategies should themselves be deconstructed. The reason they can be deconstructed is that the strategies are themselves narratives. For instance, a narrative interwoven in the second example might be that "normative ideals should not be equivocal." The public administration parallel, drawn above with the nature of some or all administrative reports, can be extended to claim that such a second deconstruction can fit with administrative experience. Even a deconstruction of the deconstruction of the deconstruction might be useful in the administrative study case. Imagine that the administrative study results (viewed as a deconstruction of administrative practice) are useful if the results are treated as epistemologically compelling (e.g., carrying authority because they are "scientific"). The deconstruction of the deconstruction might be compared with pursuing the notion that the administrative study can be questioned. Note that it was suggested above that an alternative set of recommendations might well have been equally compelling. The deconstruction of the deconstruction of the deconstruction, in this example, might be compared with opposing the claim that the fact the study's recommendations are not scientific means that they are not compelling.

Privatization may also serve as an example and was discussed in chapter 7. In a sense, privatization is a literal deconstruction of bureaucracy. The rationale for privatization, it will be recalled, includes the claim that governmental bureaucracy is more inefficient than a private enterprise bureaucracy. The public choice results were noted, suggesting that a rational public manager will fail to supply an optimal output. The argument was noted that supply pressures, combined with an absence of effective demand restraints, will necessarily yield inappropriate outputs. The fact of bloatedness is suggested in a number of models (such as Downs's and Migué' and Bélanger's); the massive scale of the oversizing of governmental bureaucracy is suggested in Niskanen's model to be twice the optimal output. Assuming that Niskanen's model "reflects reality," a modernist prescription might be to cut back to half the output and to privatize from the remainder.

Privatization, presented as such a "grand" narrative or as "the" solution, invites bureaucratic deconstruction. In a sense, this deconstruction can be seen as a deconstruction of a deconstruction. One strategy of this deconstructive iteration might be based on the argument, offered in chapter 7, that privatization has limits as a policy. Inefficiency in governmental administration, it was suggested, depends not only on the absence of effective demand but also on the existence of monopoly and oligopoly powers; that is, it depends not only on the demand side but also on supply characteristics of public sector operations. If the privatization establishes private sector monopolies and oligopolies administering former governmental programs, the result also will be inefficient. To the extent that private sector managers pursue their self-interest more vigorously than do public sector managers, the privatized entity will exacerbate this inefficiency. Another strategy for this deconstructive iteration might take the line that one such rational consideration is inevitably confounded by another. The inevitability of conflicts could be described between the economizing motive of privatization and other motivations, such as the wish for equity. A privatized jail program might (or might not) be more economical, for instance; it could be imagined how, urged by profit considerations, questions of equity might tend to be slighted. A profit-seeking enterprise might wish to adopt business strategies to maintain only the least costly prisoners or the least costly services. Other strategies for this deconstructive iteration are also available.[103]

Faced with a barrage of argument that could be developed within such a framework, a deconstruction of the deconstruction of the deconstruction may well seem useful to the administrator or policy maker. This deconstruction might have the worthy aim of helping the policy maker arrive at more informed decisions about radically downsizing and privatizing a bloated bureaucracy. Both the privatization example and the administrative study example may help to make clearer how several iterations of deconstruction could be useful. On the other hand, it is harder to see how an infinite series of deconstructions could be useful because administrators and others live in a finite world. The practical point is that administrators need not wait for the infinite series to be completed; they are practitioners, not unused to partial information, to uncertainties, and even to the world not always being as we would like it to be. Nevertheless, that practical point, it could be said, does not change the situation; it does not change the theoretical point. The theoretical point is that such an infinite series of deconstructions reflects the postmodern perspective that no underlying reality exists. Modernist interpretations understand signs as referring to the real; they would assume that the text has inherent meaning that can be interpreted. Deconstruction takes it that no underlying reality exists, that this text has no inherent meaning, and that the meaning is undecidable. Nothing but signs exist.

Nevertheless, some would argue that an infinite number of deconstructive iterations need not be taken as a litmus test of postmodernity. Chapter 8 reported the view that Hans-Georg Gadamer, for instance, is a postmodernist.[104] Madison singles out three of Gadamer's central theses: "to understand is in fact to interpret, . . . all understanding is essentially bound up with language, [and] . . . the understanding of a text is inseparable from its application."[105] Madison states that, unlike Derrida's contention that meaning is undecidable, Gadamer's view is that determining meaning is inexhaustible. He quotes Gadamer's *Truth and Method* ("the discovery of the true meaning of a text or a work of art is never finished; it is in fact an infinite process"). His interpretation of Gadamer is that determining meaning is possible because "readers are always particular individuals existing in particular situations, in the light of which and by application to which the text assumes, by means of what Gadamer calls a 'fusion of horizons,' a particular decidable meaning."[106] He also claims, "Unlike 'undecidability,' 'inexhaustibility' points not to the eternal vanity of all human endeavors but, rather, to the limitless possibility of interrogation, expression and understanding."[107] When Gadamer and Derrida held their first public academic meeting at the Goethe Institute in Paris in April 1981, there was much anticipation. As might be expected, Derrida says at that meeting that he finds Gadamer's notion of "the lived experience" as the context of interpretation to be "problematical."[108] But they avoid their disagreements. Dallmayr calls it a "non-dialog," and Gadamer for one accepts this description.[109] We will follow that lead.

Who authored Herbert A. Simon's *Administrative Behavior?* We should pursue such deconstructions for at least two reasons, even if texts have no underlying referents. For two reasons we would not wish to say that if there is no underlying reality, there is nothing real to discuss. The first reason concerns the world we inhabit, and the second concerns seduction.

First, if we live in a "world" where the real and the unreal have imploded and where the "world" is a flux of images, our analyses must be shaped accordingly. If the Roman Empire has collapsed, we can be nostalgic for Rome but we can no longer look to Rome. We must deconstruct the pretenses; we must adjust to the situation where we must cope with trying to say the unsayable. The environment and character of politics and government have changed in important ways during the last fifty years. Government, politics, and bureaucracy are awash in a flux of images, for example. The question has been raised as to why public policy is now subjected to politics run like show business, complete with celebrity building.[110] The postmodern suggestion is that any activity must be crafted in a context where not only the line dividing politics and show business has collapsed but also where the wall between images and living is no longer there. In such circumstances, it is not sensible to strive to return to an age that has gone; it is more prudent to understand where we are.

In what kind of world does the reader of Simon's *Administrative Behavior* live? This question is important not only for the argument being advanced but also for readers attracted to Gadamer's view that describes readers (quoted above) "as particular individuals in particular situations, in the light of which and by application to which the text assumes . . . a particular, decidable meaning."[111] A postmodern response can point to Jean Baudrillard on the system of objects.[112] Chapter 9 noted Baudrillard's comment on the hyperreality of GARAP, a sign without a signifier.[113] Baudrillard continues on that theme by pointing to the need for objects of consumption to become signs. The suggestion is that advertising is required to make objects into signs so that they can become successful objects of consumption:

> Actually, in our highly competitive system, few products are able to maintain any technical superiority for long. They must be invested with overtones to individualize them; they must be endowed with richness of associations and imagery; they must have many levels of meaning, if we expect them to be top sellers, if we hope that they will achieve the emotional attachment which shows up as brand loyalty.[114]

> In order to become object of consumption, the object must become sign; . . . a-signed arbitrarily and non-coherently to this concrete relation, yet obtaining its coherence, and consequently its meaning, from an abstract and systematic relation to all other object-signs. . . . The conversion of the object to a systematized status of signs entails a concomitant modification in the human relation, which become a relation of consumption.[115]

We also deal with bureaucracy in a context of signs without signified. Recall the question noted several paragraphs ago: Why is public policy subjected to politics run like show business, complete with celebrity building?

Simon's *Administrative Behavior* is firmly set (as Simon would be the first to agree) in the frame of modernity that takes the reality principle for granted; the concern is to improve the production of the real, to match means to ends in a rational manner to achieve real results. His referent is reality; he is within the ambit of the reality principle. Now comes postmodernity and with it the end of the reality principle. Baudrillard and others now see the power of production replaced by seduction. For Baudrillard, seduction is the "world's elementary dynamic."[116] For him, seduction is stronger than power because it "envelops" the real process of power and the order of production. Seduction is not part of the real; it is, for him, that which lets appearance circulate as a secret and "that which extracts meaning from discourse and detracts it from its truth."[117] Simon's *Administrative Behavior* does not bear on the world of seduction, nor does mainstream public administration theory. The failure of those following the reality principle to recognize the role of appearances and of seduction needs a reality check.

Deconstruction can be imagined to play a role (not a fixed role) for us because we and bureaucracy are part of the swirl of images and appearances. Deconstruction might be used in coping with the narratives, without "real" referents, thrown up by images. Part of the problem is that appearances are not taken seriously enough; we tend to trivialize them, attempting to sweep them aside in order to get at what is supposed to be the real. This failure to take appearances as seriously as they deserve is as applicable to modern public administration theory as it may be to other disciplines. Baudrillard would include psychoanalysis and social theory in general in the latter category. As he writes,

> Appearances, which are not at all frivolous, are the site of play and chance taking the site of a passion for diversion—to seduce signs is here far more important than the emergence of any truth. Interpretation overlooks and obliterates this aspect of appearances in its search for hidden meaning. This is why interpretation is so characteristically opposed to seduction, and why every interpretive discourse is so unappealing. The havoc interpretation wreaks in the domain of appearances is incalculable, and its privileged quest for hidden meanings may be profoundly mistaken.[118]

Baudrillard explains that the seductive action is contrary to the workings of the psychoanalytic distinction between manifest and latent discourse: "In seduction, conversely, it is somehow the manifest discourse, the most 'superficial' aspect of discourse, which acts upon the underlying prohibition (conscious or unconscious) in order to nullify it and to substitute for it the charms and traps of appearances."[119]

The hyperreality, the work of seduction and signs without referents, has been widely described in terms of economics, politics, and culture. For example, the lack of referent for exchange value has been discussed.[120] Vertigo does tend to result when one tries to identify the referent for the value of a pet rock—and, even more, to see economic theory as rhetoric, as McCloskey (see chapter 7) and others describe. A clear case of referent-free narratives are those generated in the economic sphere by the images of advertising: "put a tiger in your tank," or "the tea that dares to be known by its good taste alone." Numerous examples have been offered for political behavior. Luke speaks of national electronic politics, nuclear deterrence, and the masses as neither subject nor object.[121] Politics is an activity engulfed by such narratives; for instance, some television images create narrative imperatives for politicians. We need to get into the habit of seeing instances of hyperreality. We can recognize why the Persian Gulf War, for instance, seemed to some of us to have relatively few casualties; we never saw media images of the Iraqi dead. Many have written of the postmodern situation in culture.[122] As we sit in front of the television, it is hard to remember how dominated we are by images. It is hard because we are so used to images such as commercial advertisements that they seem part of nature.

Seduction, images, and signs without referents can also be seen, although less dramatically, as constituting the public administration world. Lying, manipulation, and covering up are no less a part of management, leadership, and the other functions of macrolevel public administration than they are part of politics. Deceit plays no less a part in dealing with superiors, subordinates, and the public; saying one thing and doing another is not at all extraordinary. The "C. Y. A." memorandum or conversation is routine for the seasoned administrator. Breaking the rules (rules for which we hold others accountable) in order to get a desired goal may be even the mark of the gutsy leader, someone who gets things done through people. Defending one's own turf, at the expense of the whole, is the norm. Doing favors (say, legal extra attention to reported problems) for politicians and the more powerful is also usual. All this behavior can be avoided if one administers a small unit or a backwater agency, but imaging without referents is normal in large-scale administration. The macromanager acts like a politician, although he or she might call it something different, such as leadership.

Such actions are officially condemned, and they should be. They are also condemned because another image that many share is that even worse than doing such things is being caught doing such things. Because of this disapproval, such actions tend to be denied, otherwise justified, repressed, or displaced. They are denied, for instance, in official codes of ethics. They are otherwise justified, for example, in such terms as "for the good of the service" or even "for the public interest." They are repressed and forgotten, often contributing to the cynicism and ennui that afflict too many bureaucrats. They can be displaced and renamed in terms of public relations, customer relations, or congressional relations services. Readers working in a significant capacity in government can probably provide even better examples on the basis of their own experiences. A problem in reading theoretical writings is that the theorist will usually appeal to larger issues, such as Watergate or the arms race. Practitioners do not need the examples; they have lived them or seen them in others.

A difficulty with the account just offered is that it gives the impression that imaging without referents is bad; this implication was not intended. This issue of using images with no referents has a long history. For example, the issue appears in the ideal society of Plato's *Republic*.[123] The grand "white lie," the myth of the metals, is designed to develop loyalty to Plato's ideal state by having people believe that the rulers have gold in their veins, the auxiliaries have silver, and the artisans have only iron and bronze. Much, perhaps most, imaging without referents is not bad if one is willing to allow "white lies"—or allow a consequentialist ethics that calculates the net gain from the results. When he declared that his people would fight on the beaches and landing grounds and fields and streets and hills and that "we shall never surrender," Winston Churchill was imaging. It was great imaging, and we rightly consider him a great leader for such exaggerations that were part of his job as war leader. When asked whether today's uproar in Central Park was a riot and when he knows that an affirmation will lead to a riot tomorrow, the Borough of Manhattan police commander knows that it is part of his job to misstate, "Oh no, it was just a case of high jinx." George Orwell's 1984 newspeak has long been here, but we are trapped by modernity and are sometimes afraid to explore.

Does the unacceptability of this newspeak image of the public servant shed any light on the tenacity of the image of the public servant as inefficient? Simon's *Administrative Behavior* and mainstream public administration theory and practice have certainly reflected a great interest in efficiency; it is an interest that many in politics and among the public share. Perhaps it is safer to focus on the efficiency problem. Perhaps public administrationists and others are unconsciously using that concern to cover the larger and more uncertain issues of dealing with images, a set of issues with ramifications for our understanding of politics and for possible revision of the American understanding of our political institutions. Baudrillard refers to the necessity for the Soviets to immortalize Stalinism in order to protect themselves from recognizing that the revolution was hollow: "The Revolution is alive only in the fact that everyone is opposed to it, especially that mimetic and parodic double, Stalinism. Stalinism is immortal because it will always be there to hide the fact that the Revolution, the truth of the Revolution, doesn't exist. It thus restores hope. 'The people,' says Rivarol, 'did not want the Revolution, they only wanted the spectacle.' This is the only way to preserve the seduction of the Revolution, rather than nullifying it in its truth."[124]

Deconstruction has a playful quality that is at odds with the seriousness of a modernist downstairs operation such as public administration. The reference here (using Dwight Waldo's metaphor) is to the social practice of the owner and his family (translated as politicians) living upstairs in the house while the set of household servants (translated as public servants) work and live downstairs. Unlike interpretation, deconstruction does not promise the "truth." It pokes over the images, tweaking out assorted insights. Reinforced by the seriousness that is felt by any downstairs servant, public administration theory will appeal to the nostalgia of an age that may have disappeared:

> When the real is no longer what it used to be, nostalgia assumes its full meaning. There is a proliferation of myths of origin and signs of reality; of second-hand

truth, objectivity and authenticity. There is an escalation of the true, of the lived experience; a resurrection of the figurative where the object and substance have disappeared. And there is panic-stricken production of the real and the referential, above and parallel to the panic of material production. This is how simulation appears in the phase that concerns us: a strategy of the real, neo-real and hyper-real.[125]

It is unfortunately the case that servants sometimes feel more nostalgia than do their masters and mistresses for the old days that meant their servitude. That prejudice ought to be excised.

SUMMARY

Deconstruction is hard to understand partly because it does not fit into neat modernist pigeonholes and because it tries to avoid the trap of using descriptions that support the very understandings against which it is directed. As Derrida makes clear, it is neither a method nor even an operation; it is neither an analysis nor a critique. A ladder option is proposed to facilitate a description of deconstruction, and it is explained why use of this option is not basically satisfactory. This difficulty should be expected in postmodernity, which includes denial of the range of reason and denial that all is sayable.

Deconstructing modern and postmodern texts deconstructs narratives. Modernist texts are deconstructed, for example, to remove the narrative undergirdings that are constitutive of modernity and to move beyond that removal. It is a reading of a special sort, one that itself must be subjected to deconstruction. Deconstruction does not offer a correct interpretation, nor does it offer an incorrect interpretation. Meaning, for the postmodernist, is determined completely within the language.

Bureaucratic deconstruction, it is suggested, can be used to dismantle narratives that constitute the underpinnings of modernist public administration theory and practice. It can also be used to dismantle narratives constructed in postmodernity. Grand narratives are the forces that account for the development of history; an example is the Enlightenment view that rationalization equals human progress. Public administration theory and practice are also underpinned by certain narratives. Two examples are examined in the chapter. One concerns the relationship of public administration theory with objectivity, and the strategy chosen for this deconstruction is a questioning of the authorship of Herbert Simon's *Administrative Behavior.* A second narrative is that efficiency is a viable goal for public administration practice. One narrative is illustrative of a modernist underpinning of theory, and the other is an example of a grounding of much practice. The iterative character of deconstruction is illustrated in terms of two public administration examples: administrative studies and privatization.

Such deconstruction permits better appreciation of texts in the particular conditions of the postmodern situation. This postmodern situation is where the real and appearance have imploded, where bureaucracy is part of the swirl of images and appearances, where the world of production has been replaced by the world of seduction, and where public policy is subjected to politics run like show business. Seduction, images, and signs without referents constitute the postmodern administrative world. Lying, manipulation, and covering up, it is argued, are as much part of bureaucratic management and leadership as they are a part of politics. It is noted that deceiving and breaking rules in order to get desired results may be the mark of the courageous manager and that doing favors for the politicians and the powerful is the norm. How to deal with such newspeak features of administration and with images is a central concern for administrators. Nostalgia for the old ways, although normal, is not helpful. Appearances have to be taken seriously; they should be deconstructed.

12

Postmodernity
Deterritorialization

> The first great movement of deterritorialization appears with the overcoding
> performed by the despotic State. But it is as nothing compared to the other great
> movement, the one that will be brought about by the decoding of flows.
>
> —Deleuze and Guattari[1]

POSTMODERNITY PROMISES A transformation in the form of thinking and of the business structure of thinking. The transformation applies to public administration no less than to all other specialties and disciplines. *Deterritorializing* is a concept that can be used to characterize a leading feature of this change. As explained more fully later, *deterritorialization* means removal of the coding or grid that is imposed on the study of issues and situations by the way that thinking is conducted and the way that the business of thinking is structured.

Deterritorializing and territorializing are terms used by Deleuze and Guattari in their analysis of psychoanalysis and schizoanalysis. (A reference was made to Deleuze and Guattari's schizoanalysis in chapter 10, and we will return to it in the next chapter.) In their analysis, Deleuze and Guattari write of the coding that shapes and confines desires and libidinal flows; their explanation is in terms of the coding of psychoanalysis that, in their view, produces the subject who conforms to modern societal requirements. The nature of psychoanalytic theory and practice is territorialized in such a way that the treated subject is the kind of being who is "appropriate" for modern society. Deleuze and Guattari go on to explain that the first task of the revolutionary is to break from the grip of this code; all coding confines thinking. Writing of Oedipus, "the figure of power as such," they advise that this task is to learn from the psychotic how to shake off the effects of power and to initiate a politics of desire free from all beliefs. As Seem continues to summarize it, such "a politics dissolves the mystifications of power through the kindling, on all levels, of anti-oedipal forces—the schizzes flows—forces that escape coding, scramble the codes, and flee in all directions: orphans (no daddy-mommy-me), atheists (no beliefs), and nomads (no habits, no territories)."[2] Modernist sciences and action disciplines, such as public administration theory, can surely be seen as participants in such a territorializing process. Deterritorializing is the decoding and liberating, a process that can be expected in postmodernity to yield desiring persons. Deterritorializing removes the code that has been imposed: "It should therefore be said that one can never go far enough in the direction of deterritorialization: you haven't seen anything yet—an irreversible process."[3]

The study of public administration is deterritorialized in postmodernity, as indicated, in the sense that an attempt is made to remove the code that shapes the way that the seeing is performed. This code or grid is made up of such elements as, first, the character of thinking that is possible and, second, the organizational or business structure of the discipline.

CHARACTER OF THINKING

The radical nature of the transformation in the character of thinking was suggested in the discussion in chapters 9 and 11 of the change occurring between modernity and postmodernity in the conditions and prospects for knowledge. Postmodernists such as Derrida speak of knowledge entirely in terms of texts. For them, there is nothing outside the texts, and the purpose of writing is more writing. For those holding that nothing outside texts exists, it is no shock that Baudrillard should write of postmodernity as the breakdown in the distinction between reality and appearance or that he should write of loss of meaning. We may begin to approach this idea of loss of meaning, in a situation where the distinction between real and appearance is abandoned, by recalling our consciousness of how individual words can lose meanings for us. For instance, the words "kill" and "love" can lose meaning after years of cable movie watching; with extensive use, swear words can lose meaning. The notion that we have reached the end of history may be even more shocking for modernist public administration thinkers because the pressure to produce something new—to go forward up the Enlightenment hill of progress—is a fundamental modernist motif. The metanarratives, such as the emancipation of humanity, are rejected by postmodernity. There is also a rejection of totalizing thought such as can be found in systems theory. Lyotard and others write of the inevitable pluralism of language games and of the local character of all discourse. All this bewildering variety and more betokens radical change in thinking, but it does not signal the end of thinking.

For one thing, in postmodernity the scientific component of public administration, like all scientific activity, becomes discourse. The modern refers to a "science that legitimates itself with reference to metadiscourse ... making an explicit appeal to some grand narrative, such as the dialectics of the Spirit, the hermeneutics of meaning, the emancipation of the rational or working subject, the creation of wealth ... [or] the rule of consensus between the sender and the addressee of the statement."[4] The "status of knowledge is altered as societies enter what is known as the postindustrial age and cultures enter what is known as the postmodern age."[5] Science does become discourse, and it can be treated in a deconstructionist manner. Science becomes just another text, open to the deconstruction discussed in chapter 11. Public administration "theorizing," even if it remains as a recognizable entity, changes from the directions discussed in chapters 4 through 8.

Attempts at a postpositivist approach to thinking have been developed in organization theory and in constructivist (or naturalistic) inquiry. The naturalistic method has been developed and applied in a variety of other areas, such as social work.[6] A significant literature now exists to support claims for a "new story" as paradigmatic shifts are seen in "the organizational theory paradigm and in the inquiry or empirical paradigm";[7] it can be explored by focusing on work by Yvonna Lincoln and Egon Guba. Others might opt to consider other terms and representatives.[8] The work in nonorthodox organization theory and naturalistic inquiry is an example of developments affecting public administration where serious attempts are being made to step further away from the Weberian and rationalist conception of bureaucratic structure and to develop a technique of inquiry that denies the privileged epistemological status of scientific propositions. This significant deterritorializing is described in this subsection; the next subsection describes how the deterritorializing may proceed much further as the tendencies of postmodernity continue to emerge.

Lincoln and Guba describe a progression in eras and paradigms from the prepositivist through the positivist to the postpositivist.[9] The prepositivist era, seen as stretching from Aristotle to just before Hume, is described, unfortunately, as offering no "provocative acts and ideas" and "simply a precursor to the more exciting period that followed."[10] They define the positivist era as "a family of philosophies characterized by an extremely positive evaluation of science and scientific method," and they see it as beginning in the early nineteenth century and receiving its "most powerful advocates" in the twentieth century in the logical positivists.[11] Postpositivism is described as having basic tenets that are "virtually the reverse of those that characterized positivism."[12] In describing the paradigm and in discussing the revolution that they believe is occurring in organization theory and inquiry, Lincoln discusses with approval "seven radical moves in the 'map' of reality with which most of Western society operates."[13] The seven moves are shifts from the simple to the complex, from hierarchy to heterarchy, from the mechanistic to the holographic, from the determinate to the indeterminate, from direct or linear causality to mutual causality, from the assembled to the morphogenic, and from the objective to the perspectival.[14]

The "emerging paradigms in organization theory and research" are characterized as a progression from orthodoxy derived from Max Weber, through the neoorthodox, and then to the nonorthodox paradigm.[15] Clark describes the orthodox in terms of the items to the left of the seven moves just listed, and he explains that the dominant theoretical paradigm in organizational theory includes theories characterized by "the element of conscious, foresightful action reasonably autonomously constructed to achieve some action or goal."[16] He reproduces Pfeffer's chart, and under the heading of "purposive, intentional goal-directed, rational" are listed expectancy theory, goal setting, needs theories and job design, political theories, structural contingency theory, market features/transaction costs, and Marxist or class perspectives. Clark's contention is that the classical paradigm was so powerful that the diversity of organizational perspectives that developed from 1950 to 1975 were merely modifications of the unchallenged classical paradigm.[17] At the time of his article, however, Clark considered the period of denial to be well advanced.[18]

Nonorthodox organizational theorists are described as presenting challenges to "goals, rationality, sequence, causality, and purposive behavior" and as "beginning to offer alternative views that deny rather than modify the classical view."[19] In describing the nonorthodox paradigm, the debt to Karl Weick is acknowledged, and Clark might well have included the "grook" with which Weick ends his *Social Psychology of Organizing:*

Our choicest plans
have fallen through.
Our airiest castles
tumbled over,
because of lines we neatly drew
and later neatly
stumbled over.[20]

As Clark explains it, the movement to the nonorthodox paradigm has consisted of shifts in the seven characteristics. For example, Clark emphasizes that the "objective of the nonorthodox position is to nurture complexity and eschew simplicity."[21] Writing of the move from hierarchy to heterarchy, he indicates that it is more realistic to think in such terms as goals being discovered by acting, action preceding intent, solutions searching for problems, and subordinates specifying "spheres of work to superordinates."[22] On the shift to an image of the holograph, Clark claims that the mechanical metaphor is under "deadly attack" because its survival depends on "rationality, sequence and calculability. . . . The nonorthodox theorists point us toward disorderliness in studying and understanding organizations," and they argue that to "continue to accept linear causality seems to many organizational theorists to be insisting upon unwarranted simplicity."[23] The morphogenesis in nonorthodoxy is illustrated by Lincoln as the process of the creation of planets and stars from galactic garbage—"elements that are in part identifiable, but whose identity give no clue as to what the new configuration will be like."[24] The other shift is that away from objectivity in investigation, methods, and processes. As Lincoln writes, "Objectivity as a pursuit in empirical investigations turns out to be a chimera, a Holy Grail, an illusion, and a snare."[25]

Organizations in this view are not seen as rational, monolithic, and basically stable. This view is in marked contrast to the picture of the organization presented by Herbert Simon in his *Administrative Behavior,* the organization that permits individuals to be more rational than they otherwise would be. According to Weick, "There is less rationality than meets the eye. Organizations are segmented rather than monolithic. Stable segments in organizations are quite small. Connections among segments have variable strength. Connections of variable strength produce ambiguity."[26] These themes are among those discussed by Weick with regard to the new paradigm of organizational theory, a paradigm he sees as an "alternative to the rational bureaucratic model of organization."[27] As Weick puts it, "These newer proposals . . . do not claim that order is completely absent (from organizations). Organizations may be anarchies, but they are organized anarchies. Organizations may be loosely coupled systems. Organizations may resort to garbage can decision making, but garbage cans have borders that impose some structure."[28]

The naturalistic or constructivist paradigm, the particular postpositivist paradigm for inquiry that Lincoln and Guba present, has five axioms. (The terminology should be explained first, however. Lincoln and Guba first used the term *naturalistic,* but they later decided they preferred the label *constructivist.*[29] Either term is satisfactory, and *naturalistic* is used more widely here.) Lincoln and Guba's axioms are not "grounded," and consequently criticisms of the axioms may not be as relevant as they otherwise would be; that is, Lincoln and Guba believe that their choice of axioms can be arbitrary. As they explain, "Axioms (basic beliefs) are arbitrary and may be assumed for any reason, even if only for the 'sake of the game.' "[30] The first axiom of the naturalistic paradigm is that "realities are multiple, constructed and holistic," as contrasted with the positivist paradigm, which contemplates a reality that is "single, tangible and fragmentable."[31] Guba refers to this statement as ontological,[32] and an objection can be made that, given his objectives, it seems unnecessary to claim that reality is multiple. Presumably, Guba would want to argue that because, for example, a widely held and false belief exists that senility is inevitable in old age,[33] there are two realities: the reality of the false belief and the reality of the "truth" about old age. This view is opposed to the idea that there is one reality containing two contrary beliefs. (If A looks at a horse and thinks it beautiful and B looks at the same horse and thinks it ugly, is it necessary to say that there are two horses?) In response, Guba could appeal to Baudrillard's doctrine that denies the distinction between reality and appearance. Images in postmodernity, he might say, cannot be considered "mere" appearances.

Another naturalistic or constructivist axiom that may cause difficulties is the contention that "inquiry is value-bound,"[34] contrasted with the positivist aim for value-free inquiry. Disagreement has occurred regarding the extent to which organizational theory is, in fact, ideological. Clegg and Dunkerley are among those arguing that organization is largely ideological, with an ideology identifiable in business schools. In their view, the ideology supports capitalism and represents organizations as shaped by technology that is rational. Lex Donaldson rejects Clegg and Dunkerley's claims, and gives the following view: "Contrary to the claims of its detractors there is nothing inherently ideological in such work. . . . Moreover, even if such occasional use were established this would not be sufficient grounds for classifying organizational analysis as simply an ideology."[35] Nevertheless, it can be repeated that inquiries claiming to be value-free inevitably incorporate values, if only the value of being value-free. As noted in chapter 6, mainstream economics is an example, and it is not trivial to adopt as a value that questions of economic justice should be excluded from economic analysis. On the other hand, it is difficult for a conservative (liberal) to accept that studies should incorporate liberal (conservative) values. As Lincoln and Guba explain, "[The] realization that values can and do influence inquiry in so many ways is more than a little anxiety-producing. There are those who, on finally being persuaded that values do have influence, are inclined to despair that inquiry can have any utility, since it seemingly can yield little more than opinions. We prefer to say that it yields constructions that also have value dimensions, and such constructions are useful even if they are not absolute."[36] Lincoln and Guba hold that it is better to be openly, rather than covertly, ideological. They also claim that it is better to recognize the ideological nature of inquiry; for them, "inquiry always—repeat, always—serves some social agenda."[37] Caught in what chapter 2 called the perspectival cobweb, this view also applies to their own inquiry; it must also serve some social agenda.

The other three axioms of the naturalistic or constructivist paradigm relate to the relationship of the knower to the known, the possibility of generalization, and the possibility of causal linkages. The naturalistic paradigm holds that "the knower and known are interactive and inseparable," compared with the positivist view where the knower and known are independent.[38] The naturalistic paradigm permits "only time- and context-bound working hypotheses" (or what are called "ideographic statements"), compared with the positivist aim of producing time- and context-free generalizations (or nomothetic statements).[39] The remaining naturalistic axiom is, "All entities are in a state of mutual simultaneous shaping, so that it is impossible to distinguish causes from effect."[40] This idea contrasts with the positivist view that states, "[T]here are real causes, temporally precedent to or simultaneous with their effects."[41]

From these axioms, Lincoln and Guba deduce fourteen characteristics of operational naturalistic inquiry. At first sight, this list of characteristics seems to invite a charge of inconsistency because one of the characteristics they "deduce" is that the naturalist prefers inductive data analysis to deductive data analysis. Nevertheless, no inconsistency exists if the characteristic is merely a preference and if the preference refers only to data analysis. Lincoln and Guba claim that these fourteen characteristics are justified "by their logical dependence on the axioms that undergird the paradigm, and . . . by their coherence and interdependence."[42] They go on to claim, "These fourteen characteristics display a synergism such that, once one is selected, the others more or less follow."[43] The fourteen characteristics are as follows[44]:

1. Natural setting. Conduct research in the natural setting or context. One reason is that the writers hold that "realities are wholes that cannot be understood in isolation from their contexts."

2. Human instrument. Use humans as the primary data-gathering instruments, as opposed to, say, paper-and-pencil instruments.

3. Utilization of tacit knowledge. Regard tacit (intuitive, felt) knowledge as legitimate, in addition to propositional knowledge.

4. Qualitative methods. Choose "qualitative methods over quantitative (although not exclusively) because they are more adaptable to dealing with multiple (and less aggregatable) realities."

5. Purposive sampling. Avoid random or representative sampling. One reason is that the writers hold that the researcher thereby "increases the scope or range of data expressed."

6. Inductive data analysis. One reason why the writers prefer inductive data analysis is that it "is more likely to identify the multiple realities to be found in those data."

7. Grounded theory. Prefer that "the guiding substantive theory emerge from ... the data."

8. Emergent design. Allow the research design "to emerge (flow, cascade, unfold) rather than to construct it preordinately (a priori)."

9. Negotiated outcomes. Negotiate "meanings and interpretations with the human sources from which the data have chiefly been drawn." One reason is, "It is their construction of reality that the inquirer seeks to reconstruct."

10. Case study reporting mode. Prefer the "case study reporting mode (over the scientific or technical report)."

11. Ideographic interpretation. Interpret data and conclusions "ideographically (in terms of the particulars of the case) rather than nomothetically (in terms of lawlike generalizations)."

12. Tentative application. Be hesitant about applying the findings broadly.

13. Focused-determined boundaries. Set boundaries to the inquiry "on the basis of the emergent focus (problems for research, evaluands for evaluation, and policy options for policy analysis)."

14. Special criteria for trustworthiness. The "conventional trustworthiness criteria (internal and external validity, reliability, and objectivity) are inconsistent with the axioms and procedures of naturalistic inquiry."

Where it seems appropriate, selected reasons are included above, but it should be noted that Lincoln and Guba provide many other explanations. For instance, the emergent design characteristic is justified in the following way:

N elects to allow the research design to emerge . . . rather than to construct it pre-ordinately (a priori) because it is inconceivable that enough could be known ahead of time about the many multiple realities to devise the design adequately; because what emerges as a function of the interaction between the inquirer and the phenomenon is largely unpredictable in advance; because the inquirer cannot know sufficiently well the patterns of mutual shaping that are likely to exist; and because the various value systems involved (including the inquirer's own) interact in unpredictable ways to influence the outcome.[45]

Lincoln and Guba give a rationale for each operational characteristic in terms of each of the five axioms.

The picture presented by this review of selected developments in organizational theory shows an attempt to examine bureaucracy in models that reject hierarchical[46] and other elements of the Weberian rationalistic model. The Weberian definition of bureaucracy, it will be recalled, can be described in terms of a "fixed division of labor among participants, a hierarchy of offices, a set of general rules which govern performance, a separation of personal from official property and rights, selection of personnel on the basis of technical qualifications and employment viewed as a career by participants."[47] The postpositivist picture opens a vista of the "antiorganization," the postmodern corporate arrangement that differs from the vertically integrated mass production hierarchy symbolized by the Ford Corporation. As Cooke writes, "The model of organization of the Fordist corporation, hierarchized, bureaucratized, divisional, task-specified, and spatially decomposed, has come under attack in the contemporary management literature. What is being rejected is the 'mechanical picture' of the organization . . . in favor of something called 'anti-organization.' "[48] Cooke describes antiorganization in four terms. Internally, the postmodern corporation provides greater decentralized autonomy through internal competition (a strategy he credits to Xerox and then to Philips and IBM) and derigidifies the organization through such methods as abandoning the hierarchy in favor of the matrix structure and temporary team arrangements. Externally, the postmodern corporation is described as developing strategic alliances and vertical disintegration such as is evidenced in Toyota City, Japan. The culture of incorporation, represented by Japanese business methods and symbolized by a manager sitting on a production line, is part of this description.[49] So is the greater flexibility made possible by computer-aided design and computer-controlled machine tools, the latter encouraging programmable assembly rather than mere mass production. As Borgmann points out, "The paradigmatically postmodern firm is a small group of well-educated people, eager and alert to find market openings and to fill them quickly with high-quality goods and services. Informed cooperation is second nature here, a necessity of prosperity."[50]

The greater office flexibility that Cooke describes[51] for the postmodern corporation is of immediate significance for public enterprise still limited by what in chapter 10 was described as civil service rulism. The flexibility is both functional and numerical. Functional flexibility contemplates multiskilled technical employees, a change represented by the modifications effected by word processing in the work for lower-level managers and professionals. (For instance, secretaries can now write contracts of a recurring nature.) Numerical flexibility refers to the greater use of part-time and temporary employees, the latter including those who are self-employed, those who are on short-term contracts, and those who are consultants.[52]

The picture offered by the description of the development of constructivist or naturalistic inquiries also shows a serious movement toward abandoning the pursuit of the scientific. Constructivist or naturalistic inquiry is an attempt to work out an approach for examining issues in a context that accepts the postmodern contention that scientific propositions constitute only one form of discourse, one that is not privileged in the sense of providing results that give greater epistemological assurance of truth than nonscientific discourse. Together, the developments in organization theory and naturalistic inquiry represent important attempts at deterritorializing. These attempts will be taken further when changes are effected in the "business of thinking," the topic of the next section.

THE BUSINESS STRUCTURE OF THINKING

How will deterritorialization affect the organizational structure, the business structure, of thinking about public administration? First, the organizational structure of the business of thinking is a powerful force encoding—territorializing—the character of that thought. Deterritorializing will liberate that thinking. Second, the deterritorializing will not lead to a restoration of any unity of knowledge. Third, the deterritorializing expected in postmodernity will implode boundaries between disciplines. These three issues are explored in this section as we examine how the public administration turf may be affected.

The impact of the organizational structure on the character of public administration thinking can be illustrated by the following two examples. To repeat: this impact is an encoding or territorializing. First, the very fact of dividing the social science turf into disciplines tends to induce the various specialists to see problems in terms of the particular divisions that are used. As was noted in chapters 2 and 10, the organization theorist sees organizational problems, the economist sees economic problems, the sociologist sees sociological problems, and so on. This example is not trivial. Relatively few persons are able to look at societal issues with a background that ranges across all relevant disciplines. Most social science disciplines are trapped within the code maintained by that discipline. This point can be made clearer by considering what is required to change a discipline. Keynes, in *The General Theory of Employment, Interest and Money,* provides a model for advancing a discipline; he was able to change the nature of economics not only because his ideas were apposite but also because he wrote in the then-language of economists. If Keynes had expressed the same ideas in a language foreign to mainstream economics, it is less likely that the ideas would have been taken seriously by professional economists.

The point can also be made clear by recalling that adherence to a particular method produces tendencies toward blind spots, and particular disciplines tend to be limited to a set of methodologies. It may be asked, for instance, whether the preference for the inductive in the naturalistic or constructivist method (discussed earlier) does not limit opportunities for the insights that could be obtained from use of a deductive approach. As an example, consider the insights available from transaction cost economics. In transaction cost economics (or markets and hierarchies), "markets and firms are seen as alternative instruments for completing a related set of transactions. Whether transactions will be executed across markets or within a firm depends on the relative efficiency of each instrument, given the transactional characteristics. The Markets and Hierarchies approach attempts to explain which kind of transactions will be coordinated across markets and within firms respectively."[53] As Williamson writes, "The markets and hierarchies approach attempts to identify a set of environmental factors which together with a related set of human factors explain the circumstances under which complex contingent claims contracts will be costly to write, execute and enforce."[54] With a naturalistic approach, would it not be more difficult to reach the insights available from transaction cost economics?

Second, critical theory can be used to provide another example of the power of the organization of the business of thinking to encode the nature of thinking, that is, in terms of discourse being commodified and alienated from its producer. It was used as part of the discussion of Herbert Simon's *Administrative Behavior* in chapter 11; the general point deserves repetition. Also, it will be recalled that a claim that organization theory has been commodified was noted earlier. A similar claim can be made that mainstream economic theory is a commodity that receives support from the dominant groups and others favoring a laissez-faire economic system. (It might be more direct to use the word "bought" instead of "receives support from," but "bought" is such an emotive word.) It must be wondrously pleasing for those who benefit the most from the laissez-faire system to have the support of mainstream economic theory, justifying the pursuit of sheer self-interest. It must be pleasing to have scholars demonstrating that, with appropriate attention to such issues as market failures and the business cycle, nothing need interfere with the laissez-faire system because an invisible hand ensures that each individual trying to gouge his neighbor is actually contributing toward making the entire community better off— that is, better off than it would have been if each person had actually tried to make that community better off. Public administration theory may be coded as a commodity, a commodity of such a nature that it receives support from the dominant groups. Public administration theory is useful to such a set of groups if it encodes the ways of thinking about public administration as, say, a theory of downstairs work and a theory of how to function better at getting things done. It makes sense to support a way of looking at things that can make the servants work more effectively and efficiently; that is a commodity that deserves upstairs support. The successful commodification tends to alienate the product from the producer in that the latter must make intellectual contributions that fit in with the code represented by the commodity. If the commodity is public administration theory and if this commodity encodes as acceptable a certain way of looking at public administration issues, then the producer of public administration theory is limited in terms of the commodity that she can sell. Expressed another way, public administration has become territorialized.

Will deterritorialization of the business structure of thinking lead to a restoration of the unity of knowledge? The radical character of the postmodern transformation in the business of thinking is suggested by the claim that modernity's conceptual framework for knowledge building is abandoned in postmodernity. The direction of this change can be noted by considering Deleuze and Guattari's contrast between the arborescent and the rhizomatic models of knowledge.[55] The arborescent description reflects the fact that knowledge in the Western tradition is conceptualized in the form of a tree; arborescent means having the characteristics or form of a tree. Knowledge is divided in a hierarchical manner into branches and subbranches. There is an essential rootedness of knowledge, and there is a unity of knowledge. We may have a sense that this metaphor is not holding when we see philosophy slipping from the trunk to a branch in the form of a special science, erecting its own wall against the encroachment of outsiders. Nevertheless, tribute is paid to the tree metaphor when we try to shore it up by wishing that philosophy would regain its place in the trunk. Deleuze and Guattari contrast this model with the rhizomatic, the latter being one way of thinking about knowledge in postmodernity. A rhizome in botany is a rootlike and typically horizonal stem that grows along or under the ground and sends out roots below and stems above. Deleuze and Guattari write of a rhizome in their earlier study of Kafka: "This work is a rhizome, a burrow. The castle has multiple entrances whose rules of usage and whose functions aren't very well known. The hotel in *Amerika* has innumerable main doors and side doors that innumerable guards watch over; it even has exits and entrances without doors."[56] The rhizomatic decenters information into divergent languages; it destroys roots and binaries; it produces multiplicities of differences.

Increasing specialization and the proliferation of specialties, as suggested in chapter 4, are characteristics of modernity. The trends accelerated in the nineteenth century. Klein has described the "modern connotation of disciplinarity" as a nineteenth-century product and links it with "the evolution of the modern natural sciences, the general 'scientification' of knowledge, the industrial revolution, technological advancements, and agrarian agitation."[57] Klein also points out that, as modern universities developed, disciplinarity was encouraged by industries demanding specialists, by disciplines recruiting students, and by more expensive instrumentation in some fields. As Flexner writes, "The history of the curriculum in American higher education has been one of increasing diversification and specialization."[58] The situation is now atomized. The rhetoric that academia is (as it were) in a wormhole-type condition has some substance, with each specialty being a wormhole within which the specialists can work not only with little reference to many (if any) other relevant wormholes but also without knowing of the existence of those wormholes burrowing through the same piece of turf. The situation is also complex and uneven. This is suggested by the distinctions that have been drawn, for example, between highly codified and less codified fields, high- and low-paradigm fields, narrow and broad specialisms, restricted and configurational sciences, consensual and nonconsensual fields, and federated and nonfederated disciplines.[59] For instance, physics is categorized as high paradigm, and sociology is seen as low paradigm. The fact that ranges, rather than dichotomies, exist is suggested by attempting to classify public administration as less codified, broad, configurational, consensual, and nonfederated. The prospects for a modernist holistic view appear small even in one sector of knowledge such as social science, in view of the present balkanization of social science specialties.

A proliferation not only of specialties but also of interdisciplinary attempts has occurred, the latter being countermovements that have given rise to what has been termed an interdisciplinary archipelago.[60] Throughout the modern period, concerns have been expressed regarding the fragmentation of knowledge and there have been calls to restore the lost unity; Bacon, Descartes, the French encyclopedists, Kant, Hegel, and Comte were among those reported to be the concerned.[61] Nevertheless, the twentieth century has seen the development of a rich variety of attempts at interdisciplinarity. For histories of these attempts, see writers such as Klein and Flexner, who were cited earlier in this chapter. Interdisciplinarity has been applied to the functional aspects of disciplines such as general education, professional education, the training of researchers, basic research, and applied research. The pattern of development has varied among countries, and the motivations have been diverse; they have dealt variously with the needs of students, teachers and researchers, university systems, and scientific interests.[62] An account of developments in the United States and elsewhere would include descriptions of national and other organizations (such as the Social Science Research Council in the 1920s, the 1948 Foundation for Integrative Education, and the National Science Foundation's programs) and of the relatively few but significant interdisciplinary universities (such as East Anglia and Wisconsin at Green Bay). It would include descriptions of externally driven developments (for example, those resulting from World War II such as the Manhattan Project), and of internally driven developments (for example, those resulting from synthetic theories such as structuralism and general systems theory). The 1960s and 1970s saw especially wide interest and support for interdisciplinarity.

The literature has grown. As Klein reports, "Chubin, Rossini, and Porter found the literature on interdisciplinary problem-focused research is just over thirty years old, dating from a 1951 paper. . . . After 1969, however, the literature grew significantly; doubling from 1969 to 1972, then   growing 120 percent from 1973 to 1977, and an additional 95 percent from 1978 to 1982."[63] The nature of the literature has also changed: "Since 1970 scholars have been paying closer attention to the problems of designing and managing interdisciplinary curricula and research projects, the practical and philosophical consequences of relations between different disciplines, the dynamics of interdisciplinary problem-solving, and the nature of interdisciplinary theory and method. The momentum is undeniable."[64]

The main interest of those concerned with restoring the lost unity of knowledge would lie in transdisciplinarity. According to Little and Haas, "A transdisciplinary science is one that cross-cuts several traditional sciences, while at the same time providing synthesis, integration, and greater understanding of a body of knowledge."[65] Even the number of terms and meanings have proliferated, as it were, because interdisciplinarity can have a range of meanings. A suggestion at a 1970 Centre for Educational Research and Innovation conference in Nice was to recognize the following: a discipline is conceptualized as a "specific body of teachable knowledge with its own background of education, training, methods and content areas"; multidisciplinarity is seen as a "juxtaposition of various disciplines, sometimes with no apparent connection"; pluridisciplinarity is understood as the juxtaposition of related disciplines, such as mathematics and physics; and interdisciplinarity is taken as describing interaction between two or more disciplines.[66] The report continues, "This interaction may range from simple communication of ideas to the mutual integration of organizing concepts, methodology, procedures, epistemology, terminology, data, and the organization of research and education in a fairly large field." Transdisciplinarity is reserved for "a common system of axioms for a set of disciplines."[67] An example of the latter is human population biology: "The theoretical perspectives and training experiences that are held in common among human population biologists are based in evolutionary biology, genetics, statistical expression of human variation, adaptation to the environment, an understanding of the human life cycle, and a commitment to learning how the interaction of human behavior and biology contributes to individual and population adaptability."[68] Materials science is another example; it is "an emerging syncretic discipline hybridizing metallurgy, ceramics, solid-state physics, and chemistry. [It is] a new academic discipline . . . emerging by fusion instead of fission."[69] Nevertheless, the message of postmodernism to an attempt at restoring overarching transdisciplinary unity is that the attempt is misguided. Knowledge is a rhizome.

In a situation where the arborescent metaphor of knowledge is abandoned, it is to be expected that the structure and turf of public administration will cease to exist in their present forms. So will each of the special social sciences and each of the action subjects. With no ordered branches, there will be no separate disciplines. A mingling together, a merging into the rhizomatic, will occur.

Chapter 9 noted that the effects of postmodernity would be felt by all disciplines, not merely public administration. Barry Smart writes on the effect of postmodernity on sociology:

> For empirical sociology the objective needs must become to seek a "new social application of its skills ... or new skills" (1988:119) to combat the declining requirement from the State for social management knowledge. The second category, "interpreting sociology," takes two forms, one of which retains a vestige of social relevance in that it is concerned to enrich one's own tradition by rendering "alien" forms and experiences comprehensible, a product for which Bauman implies potential customers may still exist. The second variant of "interpreting sociology" is presented as making a virtue out of necessity, the decline in social demand for sociology providing an opportunity for, and legitimation of, a retreat into a self-serving disinterested patrol of one's own patch. The final form is that of a sociology of postmodernism which remains committed to a notion of social relevance and seeks to make the "opaque transparent," a strategy which given the withdrawal of the State from the field effectively constitutes sociological discourse as a potentialy critical and/or "subjective force"—this is the familiar figure of an emancipatory sociology.[70]

Some details in this account seem wrong. For one thing, it is unclear how "patrol of one's own patch" could occur in the postmodern situation where the patch ownership system would end; postmodernity would mean the end of the elbowing-out manner of studying what we modernists call "social" problems. Smart quotes Bauman with approval, "[S]ociology's postmodern crisis ... cannot be met by the strategy of 'business as usual,' for the game and the customers have changed."[71] Nevertheless, the scope and character of the change will be more profound than merely a shutting down of specialties, more than a matter of base closings. The nature of the knowledge activity will change as thinking is deterritorialized.

In postmodernity, public administration theory as it is presently constituted withers away. The age of artificial academic boundaries would be gone.[72] As Foster mentions, "Postmodernism encourages the view that various fields and specialties are strategies and conventions whereby reality is divided up, the result of power struggles between groups. Postmodernism is committed to think in terms sensitive to difference, a skepticism about autonomous spheres or separate fields of experts."[73]

Postmodernity means deterritorializing in more than the sense that academic boundaries will implode. It means the end of public administration theory and theorizing as they are known. It means the end of the kind of theorizing that is part of modernity. Postmodernity is often characterized as meaning the end of the logocentric metaphysics of presence. It is described as the end of representationism, the end of a world existing to be represented by the subject. It is described as abandoning such grand narratives as those of reason and spirit. It is described as both the end of philosophy and the end of history.

The walls would be gone; the commodity would be gone. So too would bureaucracies as we know them. In the world of texts, there would be a multiplicity of writers, but thinking would be of a rhizoid, nonlinear, nomadic type. It would be a world deterritorialized. We would not have a distinct language of public administration theory.

Deterritorializing the public administration "patch" can be approached from another avenue, that is, by considering Foucault's comments on critique. *Critique* is an attitude that values what Foucault describes as "the art of not being governed." Foucault explains that it is the movement by which the subject has the right to discover the truth through "an art of voluntary insubordination, of thoughtful disobedience."[74] Foucault traces his idea of critique from the Reformation dissenters, through the critics of absolutism, to the Enlightenment thinkers, and beyond. For him, such critique develops the Enlightenment injunction to rely on one's own reason. It is an "absolute skepticism toward all concepts" inherited from others. Miller gives the following account of this notion:

> After Kant, it is indeed Nietzsche who perhaps came closest to describing "the problem of enlightenment" as Foucault himself understood it. Philosophers, Nietzsche had written some one hundred years after Kant's essay, "must no longer accept concepts as a gift, nor merely purify and polish them, but first make and create them, present them and make them convincing. Hitherto one has generally trusted one's concepts as if they were a wonderful dowry from some sort of wonderland." But this trust must be replaced by mistrust: "What is needed above all"—and this is where the Nietzschean "will to know" finds its true vocation—"is an absolute skepticism toward all concepts" Hence "critique."[75]

The subject uses her own reason to such an extent that all inherited concepts are rejected; the subject, refusing to be subjected, rejects all grids. In other words, the thinking is deterritorialized.

These prospects are very disconcerting to the modernist public administration view, a view that has a predilection for the structure of the known, the pragmatic and the predictable—a predilection for modernity. Thus, it is salutary to be reminded that the arborescent model of knowledge might not have been the optimal; that is, even better results might be achieved with another system. A comparison can be drawn for this purpose between the academic tree of knowledge (the modernist arborescent model) and the structure for providing physicians' services. Driven by such forces as those of the economic system and of medical opportunities, physicians have become more and more specialized. Among the many difficulties is that the patient, who chooses what she and the insurance company can afford, is encouraged to self-diagnose and choose among the specialists; relatively too few physicians specialize in general or family practice. The arborescent model for structuring social science knowledge takes the principle of the physician's system even further. It provides for specialists: public administrationists, educationalists, sociologists, economists, social workers, urban studies specialists, leisure scientists, criminal justicians, and so on. But, except for mavericks, there is no equivalent in academe—or in the model—of the specialists in general practice. The holistic approach is not pursued.

The word *enceinte* can be appropriated to symbolize the dilemma that faces the modern knowledge establishment, the business of knowing, in the face of the postmodernity. *Enceinte* is a word taken from the French that has at least two meanings. As an adjective, it means pregnant. As a noun, it means wall or fortification or the area protected by the fortification. At the point of tension between the modern and the postmodern, enceinte symbolizes the dilemma as the organized structure of knowing implodes. Each branch of knowledge, each specialization, is pregnant with a bewildering and too heavy volume of intellectual results; in addition, there are specializations within specializations, each pregnant with documents and results. The galloping acceleration of knowledge is going beyond the capacity for coping in the old ways, and the new ways are not yet clear. Each specialty knows too much, even in the social sciences. Each specialization is also a fortified area within which specialists protect their turf. The defenses are not merely social, aided by associations and accrediting agencies. They are also linguistic; ideas can penetrate only if they are put in the right form, in the right words. It is true that public administration and the other social action disciplines are more porous than the more established subjects, but the walls are still there. We want to be pregnant with results; we want our walls.

SUMMARY

All knowledge in postmodernity is deterritorialized in terms of character and organization. This situation applies no less to public administration than to other disciplines. The grids or codes of assumptions that are imposed on our understanding are removed.

Deterritorialization will be realized when the implications of entering postpositivist circumstances are recognized for thinking and for inquiries. The character of thinking will change when science is regarded as one discourse among many discourses. In the postmodern situation, scientific inquiry will lose its status as a provider of epistemologically privileged information. This point is illustrated by examining some postpositivist work now being undertaken in terms of organization theory and constructivist (or naturalistic) inquiry.

Changes in the business of thinking will carry the deterritorialization process further. The limitations of the territorializing grip need to be appreciated. Postmodernism regards interdisciplinary and transdisciplinary attempts to regain a lost unity of knowledge to be misguided. However, postmodernity does spell the end of disciplinary autonomy as the age of artificial academic boundaries finishes. The structure of public administration collapses as the walls between disciplines and specialties fall. Such organizational changes are suggested by Deleuze and Guattari's contrast between the arborescent and the rhizomatic models. The modernist tree model, contemplating the unity and rootedness of knowledge, divides knowledge in a hierarchical way into branches and subbranches. The rhizomatic model decenters information, destroys roots, and produces multiplicities of differences.

Public administration and all other disciplines are deterritorialized in postmodernity in the sense that the character of study changes. The conditions and possibilities for knowledge change. Postmodernity means the end of the logocentric metaphysics of presence. "Theorizing" as it is known terminates because postmodernity means the end of representationism, the end of grand narratives, and the end of history. As many postmodernists write, there is no meaning outside of the texts.

New circumstances do arise in what was the public administration field. Some developments in organization theory and in the economy may suggest questions in terms of understanding nonhierarchical and debureaucratized arrangements. The implications of critiques concerning the art of not being governed stand as another example.

13

Postmodernity
Alterity

Deconstruction is justice.
—Derrida[1]

Deconstruction, while seeming not to "address" the problem of justice, has done nothing but address it, if only obliquely, unable to do so directly.
—Derrida[2]

From the idea that the self is not given to us, I think that there is only one practical consequence; we have to create ourselves as a work of art.
—Foucault[3]

I would say that *Anti-Oedipus* (may its authors forgive me) is a book of ethics, the first book of ethics to be written in France in quite a long time.
—Foucault[4]

BECAUSE IT IS integral to the public administration act, the critical implications of the postmodern attitude toward alterity must be teased out. Alterity concerns the "moral other," and clearly every administrative act directly or indirectly affects another person, for example, a client, a subordinate, a superior, or a bystander. The "other" in modernist Western philosophy has been largely an epistemological issue, included in terms such as "the problem of other minds" or "the issue of intersubjectivity." As Johnson adds, "The term 'alterity' shifts the philosophic concern away from the 'epistemic other' to the concrete 'moral other' of practices—political, cultural, linguistic, artistic, and religious. This is consistent with the movement from the concerns of modern philosophy of knowledge to the more decentered philosophies of post-modernism."[5] Absent an efficiency motivation, the moral question becomes more relevant for the administrator; that is, if the obligation cannot be captured in the requirement of being merely efficient, what should the motivation be? How should an administrator behave in relationship to others?

The upshot of the implications of postmodern ethical attitudes for public administration is summarized in the slogan "antiadministration." That is, it is suggested

227

that postmodern ethical attitudes imply that any administration should carry out its programs, but it should do so in a spirit where administrative capabilities are simultaneously directed at negativing administrative-bureaucratic power. What this antiadministration means can be understood by considering the following highlighting of the suggestions made in this chapter. This overview compresses the information; discussion of the rationale, the specifics, and the terminology can be found in the balance of the text. The account in this chapter starts with Foucault's injunction against what he calls the "fascism in us all."[6] Starting by explaining this attitude, the chapter selects for discussion four characteristics of the postmodern view toward alterity. These characteristics are an openness to the other, a preference for diversity, an opposition to metanarratives, and an opposition to the established order. Derrida's claim that "deconstruction is justice," it is indicated, can be read as implying claims about each of these characteristics.[7] An "openness to the other" has implications that cumulatively can be expressed under the heading "antiadministration." It will be explained that openness does more than imply that the practice of public administration should be so constructed and executed that it is antiauthoritarian; it should do more than introduce service-oriented attitudes. Openness is described as implying that an administration should seek to open all of its decision making to communities. The text explains that openness also suggests the need for substantial anarchism. Paralleling such anarchism, it is noted, should be a development of micropolitics in the form of local community action.

The second characteristic of the postmodern view of alterity is the preference for diversity. This characteristic does suggest a preference for incorporating a spectrum of perspectives. Furthermore, this chapter will explain that this characteristic suggests that antiadministration takes such forms as opposing what is described as administrative boxism, that is, stereotyping employees and citizens in organizational and category boxes. The opposition to metanarratives implies antiadministration in the sense that the administrator is endorsed as deconstructor of metanarratives and unrealistic foundations. It is argued that the administrator should deconstruct the mystical foundation of administrative authority, showing public administration to be a kind of "violence" without ground. This characteristic would also encourage the development of what is explained as an administration that favors tentativeness. The fourth feature is the imperative to be opposed to existing institutions. Antiadministration is reflected in what is claimed to be the feasibility of an "antiinstitutional" agency.

Chapter 10 promised that we would return to the issue of the changes that postmodernity might mean for the project of public administration. It is suggested that these changes mean that administration should aim to conduct its functions in a way that we are calling antiadministrative. Such an antiadministrative attitude would aim toward a diminishment of the scope and role of administration and the administrator. The implications of chapters 10 through 13 show approaches toward this end; each is directed toward antiadministration. Chapter 10 suggests that imaginization might mean a shift toward the imaginal. If the purpose of generating a cadre of administrators were still valid, it was indicated that the cadre would be developed to focus on the skills and opportunities offered by imagination. It can be added that a goal of this cadre should be antiadministration. Chapter 11 suggests that such a project of public administration should stress deconstructive opportunities and skills. This effort would include deconstructing the narrative that underlies the idea of any such public administration project; it would include deconstructing the narrative that imaginization equals human progress; also, it would include deconstructing the narrative of antiadministration. Chapter 12 suggests that all study and all practice should be deterritorialized. This effort would imply that those who still administer should conduct a never-ending battle to shake off the limits of conceptual grids and that the discipline of public administration, like any other specialty, constitutes one such grid. The practices of administration also constitute a grid for the practitioner. The postmodern administrator is likely to be one who is skilled in practicing and developing the implications of antiadministration. To the extent that administrators exist, postmodernity seems to lead the project of public administration toward a radical emphasis and development of the NASPAA notion of creative pluralism. Such a development would be in the direction of the attitudes of the reflexive language paradigm and would be directed toward antiadministration.

ANTIFASCISM

Ethics and postmodernity at first sight seem strange bedfellows, and this idea is reflected in Foucault's "may its authors forgive me" side comment quoted at the head of this chapter. The idea is also encouraged by Baudrillard's notion of the fractal stage, where value has no referent. White writes of Derrida in the 1980s as attempting "to show more clearly the sense of 'ethical-political responsibility' that is compatible with deconstruction."[8] It is true that much in postmodernism is cynical and deterministic. Although its interests do not lie primarily in the ethical, much of postmodernity has a moral engine, and postmodernity has moral implications for alterity. Foucault's explanation of why and how *Anti-Oedipus* should be seen as a book of ethics gives a response to this concern about postmodernity and ethics:

> How does one keep oneself from being fascist, even (especially) when one believes oneself to be a revolutionary militant? How do we rid our speech and our acts, our hearts and our pleasures, of fascism? How do we ferret out the fascism that is ingrained in our behavior? The Christian moralists sought out the traces of the flesh lodged deep within the soul. Deleuze and Guattari, for their part, pursue the slightest traces of fascism in the body. Paying a modest tribute to Saint Francis de Sales, one might say that *Anti-Oedipus* is an *Introduction to the Non-Fascist Life.*[9]

This example is open to the objection about Foucault's credentials to be considered a postmodernist. The title of one of Baudrillard's works will be recalled: *Forget Foucault.* It is also an objection that can be made about Deleuze and Guattari. For example, Guattari has criticized postmodernism as conservative and cynical.[10] Nevertheless, postmodernity is not tidy; these authors can be read as postmodernists.

Postmodern ethics appear unfamiliar. They are not the activist, missionary, or insistent positions that, with our medieval and postmedieval Christian past, we take to be usual. It is more as Foucault sees Greek ethics: a matter closely tied to aesthetics and most closely tied to self-definition. Postmodernism opposes totalizing claims. However, it emphasizes rejection of macrotheory, rationality, consensus, and social system. It does lean toward fragmentation, difference, heterogeneity, the implosion of boundaries, and the abandonment of the canonical. It tends to a focus toward the self. It has interesting points to make that relate to particular subtopics such as feminism and populism. It has much that we can use as input for examining our lives, for determining the attitude toward alterity. It has input for a postmodern view of the administrator.

Listen to some postmodern ethical injunctions derived by Foucault from *Anti-Oedipus.* The phrase "public administration" could be substituted for the word "political" wherever it occurs in these injunctions. Each of the injunctions seems to say something of operational significance to the public administrator. Consider the injunction, "Do not become enamored of power." It could be translated, "Do not become enamored of control."

In his introduction to *Anti-Oedipus,* Foucault explains that living counter to all forms of fascism entails some principles. He writes that, if he "were to make this great book into a manual or guide to everyday life," he would summarize its ideas in seven principles:

- Free political action from all unitary and totalizing paranoia.
- Develop action, thought, desires by proliferation, juxtaposition, and disjunction, and not by subdivision and pyramidal hierarchization.
- Withdraw allegiance from the old categories of the Negative (law, limit, castration, lack, lacuna), which Western thought has so long held sacred as a form of power and an access to reality. Prefer what is positive and multiple, difference over uniformity, flows over unities, mobile arrangements over systems.
- Do not think that one has to be sad in order to be militant, even though the thing one is fighting is abominable.
- Do not use thought to ground a political practice in Truth; nor political action to discredit, as mere speculation, a line of thought.
- Do not demand of politics that it restore the "rights" of the individual, as philosophy has defined them. The individual is the product of power. What is needed is to "de-individualize" by means of multiplication and displacement, diverse combinations. The group must not be the organic bond uniting hierarchized individuals, but a constant generator of de-individualization.
- Do not become enamored of power.[11]

People easily can become offended if they believe they are being accused of fascism, especially English-speaking peoples who are used to supposing that it is a malady confined only to one country—and not theirs. An alternative phrase (something such as "urge to power") is less likely than the word "fascism" to raise resistances. It might have been better to have found another term if use of the word "fascism" raises resistances unnecessarily. By his term, Foucault means "the fascism in us all, in our heads and in our everyday behavior, the fascism that causes us to love power, to desire the very thing that dominates and exploits us."[12] Nevertheless, Foucault uses the term "fascism," and so we should not shy away from it. Foucault has summarized this list by writing in terms of eradicating fascism, and we can extend his thought by describing it as the fascism that we carry into our choice of becoming an administrator and that is further encouraged by the practice of administering others. "How do we rid our speech and our acts, our hearts and our pleasures, of fascism? How do we ferret out the fascism that is ingrained in our behavior?"[13]

OPENNESS

What are some of the distinctive characteristics of the antifascism that is a prominent feature of a postmodern view of alterity? The first of the four characteristics to be discussed is "openness to the other." This openness is considered here in terms of postmodern writings that speak of the nonprivileged status of "my" text, the decanonization of textual traditions, and the self-design motivation of ethical actions.

Individually and collectively, as will be indicated, these features have implications for public administration practices and procedures, for decision making, for the structural relationship between an administration and its publics, and for the ethical motivation of administrators. Openness to others implies, for one thing, that the practice of public administration should be so constructed and executed that it is antiauthoritarian. Practices, procedures, and conduct, it would imply, should be contrary to the spirit described by Etzioni as characteristic of the 1950s. As Etzioni writes,

> In the fifties we had a clear set of values that spoke to most Americans, most of the time, with a firm voice. These values were often discriminatory. . . . They were also at least a bit authoritarian. When your doctor told you that you needed surgery, you did not even think of asking for a second opinion. When your boss ordered you around at work, you did not mention that the Japanese invite their workers to participate in decision making. When your priest, labor leader, or father spoke, he spoke with authority. Indeed, often such figures of authority expected unquestioning obedience.[14]

It will be suggested that openness to others, taken seriously, goes far in reshaping bureaucracy.

Deconstruction, which reminds us of the nonprivileged status of "my text" and the "other's text," carries in part the same sense as Foucault's injunction against the fascism in all of us. "Deconstruction is justice," as Derrida writes.[15] (As an aside, the context of Derrida's sentence is, "Justice in itself, if such a thing exists, outside or beyond law, is not deconstructible. No more than deconstruction itself, if such a thing exists. Deconstruction is justice.") In other words, none of what Foucault terms fascism should exist in the relationship between one and the other; in no sense does my text have meaning that should prevail over the reader's and vice versa. Derrida can be understood as indicating that our alterity (justice being an issue of moral relationship with the other) should be practiced in the same endlessly tentative, open-ended manner as would be conducted in a deconstructive reading.

Deconstruction does not privilege texts or ways of speaking. Consider whole languages. Todorov tells us of Columbus's statement after first meeting the Indians: "If it please Our Lord, at the moment of my departure I shall take from this place six of them to Your Highnesses, so that they may learn to speak."[16] This example is not an isolated situation. Other languages, such as those spoken by people from Africa, are marginalized by being characterized as pidgin English. Yiddish is described by Frakes as having been regarded during the Enlightenment and at other times as corrupt and corrupting, sometimes as a dialect, a pidgin-like corruption, or even a lexical misnomer.[17] As Frakes explains it,

> The case is in fact easy to make: not because Yiddish is a corrupt, bastardized language, but because such cases are by definition easy to make: it is simply the stuff of comparative historical linguistics, especially as conceived in the late nineteenth and early twentieth centuries. . . . Such studies abound for the "bastardization" of Anglo-Saxon in the centuries after the Norman Conquest, for the "bastardization" of Norwegian in the period of Danish domination . . . or the "bastardization" of Maltese, etc. But rarely, if ever, is the hybridization of these languages actually termed "bastardization." . . . The marginalization of Yiddish as the language of the other . . . had a long tradition in non-Jewish European letters before the period in question here, i.e. before the period of "modern" literary and linguistic analysis.[18]

Nevertheless, recall that *texts* is a term used to designate not only whole languages and not only texts within languages. Lives are also texts or narratives.

Because texts or narratives do not have implanted meanings and because the authorial point of view is deconstructed, the postmodern attitude encourages openness to other texts. Lyotard characterizes the attempted domination of one text by another as excess.[19] The form of alterity, for Lyotard, can be set by free contractual arrangements. In situations not governed by such arrangements, Lyotard's justice means recognizing "the autonomy, the specificity of the various untranslatable and mutually interconnected language games; with one rule which would nevertheless be a universal rule: 'let play continue . . . and let us play in peace.' "[20] Lyotard's general statement has all the lack of specificity characteristic of propositions such as the golden rule; "play in peace" is open to a range of interpretations. Most other postmodern thinkers have not been even that specific. The variation in activity that could be counted as altruism is significantly wide, ranging from mere respect to active indulgence.[21] Lyotard's prescription does leave open the question of what action might be required.

A limited step toward acting with openness toward other texts is made with such reforms and gestures as seeking for public agencies what can be variously called a customer orientation, a service orientation, or a helping attitude. Shortcomings can be seen in the performance of various administrative arrangements to achieve these and similar purposes. A hope always exists that the current fad will be an exception, and the advocates of steps such as total quality management can argue this point. Nevertheless, as discussed in chapter 6, administrative history has a record of eventual failures for plans that at their inception seemed so promising and popular. The reasons for this history of failures include the fact that the reforms do not go far enough. The real customers of an agency are not those who line up at the service windows; rather, the real customer is the legislature or other body that sponsors and funds the agency. The customer-oriented improvement plans are inclined to fail because the improvements are designed within the context of the same basic situation of power inequality between the bureaucracy and the customer. A swimming against the situation's natural tide would be required for the improvement project to succeed. One way of conceptualizing this inequality is to understand it as a switch from nonbenevolent to benevolent paternalism—benevolent but still paternal at root. Another way to conceptualize it is to understand the inequality as a bureaucratic monopoly remaining a monopoly but trying to make its customers happy (and also more supportive). The attempt to develop such improvement plans is laudable, but the improvements cannot be expected to endure. An agency wishing to realize an "open text" attitude must do more to achieve it. It should seek to decanonize its tradition.

Postmodernism expresses the wish to decanonize established intellectual and cultural traditions. The Western philosophical tradition is one, starting from Thales and going through texts such as those of Plato, Aristotle, Descartes, Spinoza, Leibniz, Hume, Kant, and Hegel. The Western literary tradition is another, including in the English case the tradition that includes Chaucer, Milton, Shakespeare, Swift, Keats, Coleridge, Byron, and Dickens. In postmodernity, there is no privileged status for any texts. In the same way, there is no privileged status for nonliterary texts, such as works of art; there can be no high culture of art. It is discomforting to think that some of these traditions could not be privileged.

The cost of privileging traditions of texts has been high in terms of denying the excluded and of limiting ourselves to the established sets of texts. Consider the economics canon. This canon includes the classical economists, the neoclassical economists, the Keynesians, and beyond. The upshot of using this canon is that mainstream economic theory essentially does economics in only one basic way. Excluded are minor strains such as the institutionalists, the Marxists, and those who emphasize human capital. Excluded are those who would see the work of the economists as economic philosophers rather than as mainstream "economic physicists" and "number crunchers." Excluded from economic policy making are the alternatives not captured in the numbers or in those particular numbers. (For instance, it will be recalled that the gross national product does not include all that we value, such as environmental integrity.) Excluded from economic science is a real sense of history that does not squeeze Adam Smith into a narrow category that he himself would not recognize. Those who are excluded experience a loss, and the mainstream loses from their exclusion.

The cost of texts being canonized in action subjects such as public administration theory appears less because the discipline is not as well defined or as developed as, say, economics. But, consider the modernist tradition described in chapters 3 through 8. One way of interpreting that information is to see modernistic rationalization as a straightjacket, as a limiting force. Its achievements, like the entire Enlightenment project, are notable. Nevertheless, regardless of the positive aspects, it seems defensible to hold that the problems of bureaucracy remain. The purpose here is not to point out the limitations of modernist public administration theory; it is merely to indicate that discussing decanonizing series of texts such as those in the established public administration tradition is not unreasonable.

It is suggested that the public administrator can seek to decanonize her practice. Postmodern practice would not privilege reliance on expertise in policy making and in administration; that is, agencies can expose their texts, their manner of thinking and deciding, to the texts of citizens. Many in government have attempted to expose the bureaucracy to influence from outsiders. There have been important attempts to share some decision making, but there have been relatively few genuine attempts to share decision making throughout an administrative agency. The Model Cities program is one example of an attempt to include citizen participation in the administrative decision-making process. Nevertheless, citizen participation in this program was an activity that was confined largely to cooptation, consultation, and social education (or therapy). Success in developing community power proved more difficult.

Decanonizing public administration practice, in the sense of opening all aspects of decision making to communities, is suggested by postmodernity. This effort would favor the attitude represented by a theory of citizen participation based on community power. It goes further than cooptation, whereby agencies seek to build citizen constituencies to protect projects. It goes further than consultation, whereby agencies inform citizens and gather their ideas. It goes further than education and social therapy that trains citizens and develops their self-confidence. A community power strategy involves a fundamental redistribution of governmental power in favor of the community. This idea was conceptualized in the Model Cities program as consisting of two basic approaches. One approach of the community power strategy aimed at upgrading the responsiveness of governmental institutions; the other was directed toward establishing independent political power bases in the community. As a Model Cities management package put it,

One approach aims at making local governmental institutions more responsive and democratic. This approach usually involves the inclusion of citizens on joint policy boards. A formally negotiated sharing of power takes place between the community and those officially responsible for the program. The other approach aims at establishing independent political power bases in low-income areas. This approach assumes that only by controlling every aspect of the program or institution can a community receive its just share of resources. The establishment of independent neighborhood corporations and citizen control is the goal.[22]

Such decanonization of public administration practice can be easily said; its revolutionary impact can be gauged by thinking through what decanonization of practice would mean in functional areas such as intelligence gathering and police work.[23]

This sharing of decision making, although difficult, can be facilitated by organizational changes. Arguably, such features as hierarchy, because of the inherent power-over element, are less conducive to such sharing than is a flat organization. Arguably, the nonorthodox organization theory, discussed in chapter 12, is more conducive to such sharing of decision making. Centralized and hierarchical decision making, that is, centralized government, is less conducive.

The motivation that should guide postmodern bureaucracy in this decanonization and other processes is implied by Foucault; an inspiration would come not only from the external imposition of a citizen participation requirement (as in the Model Cities case) but also from the self-designing activity of the bureaucracy itself. The suggestion seems strange; it involves the idea that the bureaucracy should develop such community involvement as part of the process of developing itself as a work of art. Let us turn to Foucault for an indication of what this activity means.

Foucault does write of alterity by implication, but his focus is on the "I." (The quotation at the head of this chapter will be recalled.) Foucault in his "On the Genealogy of Ethics" says that, recognizing that the self is not given, we must create ourselves as a work of art; that is, we are both art object and artist.[24] Our natures and our ways of acting are not determined for us, and thus we have the radical freedom to design ourselves in the way that we might create an art object. Foucault explains how this self-creation differs from Sartrian existentialism: "I think that from the theoretical point of view, Sartre avoids the idea of self as something which is given to us, but through the moral notion of authenticity, he turns his back on the idea that we have to be ourselves—to be truly our true self. I think that the only acceptable practical consequence of what Sartre has said is to link his theoretical insight to the practice of creativity—and not of authenticity."[25] He redraws the contrast between his position and Sartre's. Sartre, he explains, refers the work of creation to a relationship to oneself that has the form of authenticity or inauthenticity. Foucault explains that he does not require the relationship of the author to himself. On the contrary, he "should relate the kind of relation one has to oneself to a creative activity."[26] The creation of the self—the choice of text that will constitute me—is radical. It is not a question of discovering my "real self," of knowing myself.

Consider the relationship between aesthetic and anaesthetic;[27] one concerns the sense of the beautiful and the other concerns the loss of senses. We can get a better sense of what Foucault means by looking at his comments on the ethics of the Greeks and others in his "On the Genealogy of Ethics." Foucault is not recommending that we return to the Greeks. Nevertheless, he explains that the principal aim of Greek ethics is aesthetic and that Greek ethics are a matter of choice for an elite few. The reason for the choice is "the will to live a beautiful life, and to leave to others memories of a beautiful existence."[28] No one is obliged to behave in prescribed ways. Rather, each accepts obligations for the beauty of existence; it is a personal choice. He contrasts this type of ethics with an ethics aimed at normalizing the population. He points out that in our society, art is related only to objects and not to individuals or to life; it is a specialized activity performed by specialists called artists. Foucault asks, "But couldn't everyone's life become a work of art? Why should the lamp or the house be an art object, but not our life?"[29]

The self-creation that results from our act of self-creating has clear implications for alterity. Now we are in a better position to understand Foucault's notion of the nature of the fascism in each of us. It is something that relates to the "I"; it is in our heads and in our everyday behavior. Foucault describes it, as noted earlier, as the "fascism in us all, in our heads and in our everyday behavior, the fascism that causes us to love power, to desire the very thing that dominates and exploits us."[30] The fascist self is an ugly self, an unaesthetic self.

The Foucauldian route to alterity raises questions. For one thing, it tends to center the subject—to privilege the "I." It privileges the "I" not in the same way but in a sense similar to the way that the positively expressed Christian and negatively expressed Confucian golden and silver rules privilege the "I." Do (do not) to others as you would that they should (should not) do to you; whether the ugly, the beautiful, the saintly, or the fascist, I (*moi*) choose what I (*moi*) think that the other should choose (in my view) to do to me (*moi*). Some thinkers, such as Kant, have suggested that, to avoid sanctioning the bad, the golden rule needs a sense of the good. In the same way, this chapter's reading takes the Foucauldian comments on fascism as an equivalent to the "sense of the good," a view of the aesthetic. Also, this Foucauldian route to alterity seems to take the dichotomy between the "I" and the "other" as a given. Can the I-thou relationship here be interpreted as a fundamental opposition, an opposition that can be paralleled with the other metaphysical oppositions (such as that between appearance and reality) against which postmodernity argues?

An advantage of Deleuze and Guattari's view in *Anti-Oedipus,* the book Foucault enthusiastically praises, is that it overcomes any possibility of such difficulties. Deleuze and Guattari write of the destruction of the ego to delimit the dynamic unconscious. They would liberate the body and decenter the subject. As they write,

> The task of schizoanalysis is that of tirelessly taking apart egos and their presuppositions liberating the prepersonal singularities they enclose and repress; mobilizing the flows they would be capable of transmitting, receiving or intercepting;

establishing always further and more sharply the schizzes and the breaks well below conditions of identity; and assembling the desiring machines that countersect everyone and group everyone with others.[31]

This decentering has important consequences for alterity. These consequences can be illustrated by referring to a distinction that Ülker Gökberk draws in thinking about *Ausländerliteratur* and about the interaction of Western culture with the non-Western other. The attitude of comparative literature exists, an attitude similar to that Mosher reflected when writing about the limited value of cross-cultural studies (see chapter 4). In that I-thou relationship, the "I" is privileged. Then we see the type of "postcultural" attitude encountered by writers such as Conrad and Kafka, writers who achieve writing greatness in their nonnative languages. Gökberk quotes Clifford, who explains that Conrad became a great writer in English, his third language: "His life of writing, of constantly becoming an English writer, offers a paradigm for ethnographic subjectivity; it enacts a structure of feeling continuously involved in translation among languages, a consciousness deeply aware of the arbitrariness of conventions, a new secular relativism."[32] Gökberk believes that this interpretation of Conrad demonstrates why "exile—in writing—can serve as a most productive paradigm for the awareness of relativity or alterity."[33] Deleuze and Guattari, as Gökberk explains, also describe this liberating effect of exteriority to language in their study of Kafka. Derrida uses the same language in speaking of justice. As he says, "To address oneself to the other in the language of the other is, it seems, the condition of all possible justice."[34] He writes that this condition implies the need for the use of the same idiom in a language in which all affected persons are competent, such as the lawmakers, the judged and the judge, the witnesses, and other bystanders. He adds, "And however slight or subtle the difference of competence in the mastery of the idiom is here, the violence of an injustice has begun when all the members of a community do not share the same idiom throughout."[35]

A decentering of the subject has similar implications for the public administrator, thrust by the nature of her work into a position that tends to be centered. Consider the implications for bureaucratese in the writing and reading of bureaucratic texts. In their study of Kafka, Deleuze and Guattari ask, "How many people today live in a language that is not their own? Or no longer, or not yet, even know their own and know poorly the major language that they are forced to serve?"[36] A carpenter completing an income tax form is not writing, that is, entering the numbers and responding to the instructions, in her own language. The carpenter may not know the major language, the language of bureaucratese, that she is forced to serve. Later in the same paragraph, Deleuze and Guattari have a question that could be asked of the centered public administrator or could be posed to the income tax official: "How to become a nomad and an immigrant and a gypsy in relation to one's own language?"[37] Translating to this situation: how can the public administrator become an outsider to her own language, the language of public administration theory and of bureaucratese? Deleuze and Guattari give Kafka's answer, where it might be fantasized that the "baby" is the language of modernist public administration theory and the "tightrope" is postmodernity: "Kafka answers: steal the baby from its crib, walk the tightrope."

Involving citizens in the decision-making process is not enough for genuine openness to others. The latter also implies a motivation to involve communities not only in executing programs that come down from above but also in helping them to do what they want, even when their wishes conflict with the "program from above" or the administrator's professional judgment. Much more facilitation of anarchism would be the order of the day. The example was given in chapter 7 of how, even today, much police work is conducted on an anarchistic basis by citizens themselves. The question that was asked, it will be recalled, is why people queue for buses (where they do). The striking point from the maintenance of order point of view is that they line up of their own volition; they self-police. It is in such a sense that an antiadministration administration, downsizing as it went, would seek to facilitate anarchistic arrangements in the execution of objectives. However, if only in terms of quantity, a radical anarchism would be needed; such anarchism is a logical development for antiadministration.

Paralleling such an anarchism would have to be a development of micropolitics in the form of local community action. Local citizen empowerment would be an ideal; centralized and hierarchical decision making, it has been suggested, is incompatible with postmodernity. The bureaucracy cannot retreat from responsibility until the communities, in their diverse ways, are willing to pick up the slack. Communities would have to be willing to make decisions now left to others, such as governmental and private enterprise bureaucracies; for instance, the levels and shapes of governmental service would be determined at the local level. It is unclear whether such a community empowerment process would take the form as that proposed by communitarians such as Etzioni. Of the changes he sees necessary for "shoring up the moral, social and political environment," Etzioni considers change of heart to be the most basic; renewal of social bonds and reform of public life are the others. As he writes, change of heart "is the most basic. Without stronger moral voices, public authorities are overburdened and markets don't work. Without moral commitments, people act without any consideration for each other. In recent years too many of us have been reluctant to lay moral claims on one another. It is a mistaken notion that just because we desire to be free from governmental controls we should also be free from responsibilities to the commons, indifferent to the community."[38] Openness to others requires not only changes in the bureaucracy but also changes in society.

DIVERSITY

A second characteristic of the postmodern view of alterity is the preference for a diversity of texts. Deconstruction, emphasizing that no privileged meaning exists, leads quite naturally to the plurality and multiplicity of texts. Lyotard, to take a different example, has written of the imperative for a multitude of narratives and for abandonment of the authorial point of view. The latter would tend toward heterogeneity and listening.[39]

The public administration discipline has been engaged in issues of diversity. There is disagreement about the relationship of achievements to needs; it is a volatile subject. On the practical side and responding to the political environment, noticeable (although some say "too few") changes have occurred in such respects as personnel practices and results. The police can be taken as a symbol; the percentages of African-Americans and women in policing, including in the higher ranks, have grown substantially in the past quarter century in the United States. Compared with the political impetus, the contributions generated from within public administration theory probably will be judged to be small. Some contributions have indeed been made, however. New Public Administration, for example, emphasized the value of representation, and public administrators have assisted in developing plans for various agencies, such as Model Cities (as noted above) and social welfare organizations, that attempted citizen involvement in administration. Public administration is a context where analysis of ancient and real wrongs—some of the issues of feminism, color, and the physically challenged, for instance—can be facilitated by the use of the insights available from discussions of postmodernity. On the negative side, some people interested in such diversity issues report finding the lack of totalizing categories in postmodernism a hindrance. Nancy Fraser, a scholar who describes herself as a feminist, is an example (see citation below).

On the positive side, consider the matter of people as texts. My life is a text; I am a text. So is your life; so are you. Nevertheless, it is not a text that can be read in one way; it is not a text that can be put into a neat category. The text that is A might be read in certain ways by A's partner; she can read A as an x or as a y. It can be read in different ways by A's children, by A's colleagues, and so on. Each will try to put A's text into a category for intellectual processing purposes. But A knows that her text cannot be neatly pigeonholed. The same is true for, say, the category of "woman." Nancy Fraser and others point out that no one is simply a woman because social identities are plural, discursively constructed in historical contexts, and changeable over time. As Fraser writes,

> Thus, no one is simply a woman; one is rather, for example, a white, Jewish, middle-class woman, a philosopher, a lesbian, a socialist, and a mother. Moreover, since everyone acts in a plurality of contexts, the different descriptions comprising any individual's social identity fade in and out of focus. Thus, one is not always a woman in the same degree; in some contexts, one's womanhood figures centrally in the set of descriptions under which one acts; in others, it is peripheral or latent. Finally, it is not the case the people's social identities are constructed once and for all and definitively fixed.[40]

Thus, she can point out that one use of a theory of discourse for feminist politics is in understanding "social identities in their full socio-cultural complexity, thus in demystifying static, single variable, essentialist views of gender identity."[41] On this line, it is untrue to say of someone, "She was all woman," just as it is untrue to say of someone, "He is all man."

Such understanding of people has relevance for the ethics of public administration theory and practice. Work specialization can be defended in modern bureaucracy in efficiency and effectiveness terms.[42] Nevertheless, part of the curse of bureaucracy is the tendency to box (boxism) or stereotype, that is, the way that bureaucrats, despite the organizational humanism movement, are considered primarily as members of organizational and category boxes. In a large bureaucracy, the person hired into the account clerk 2 category henceforth is regarded as having all the capabilities and limitations of an account clerk 2; an incumbent is expected to become what the box designates, with the exception that she might develop at some point into an account clerk 3. An economist is an economist is an economist; she is not an artist except in her spare time. Looking at people and programs in the context where organizational units are primary is boxism, and a symptom of boxism can be seen when a reorganization sets out not to eliminate internal organizational barriers but to shuffle these barriers. Boxism has also been called stereotyping, a term borrowed from the acting business. John Wayne's roles might have led him to be stereotyped as a macho man, for example. In the same way, an account clerk is an account clerk is an account clerk. Postmodernity may be seen as providing light both on the ethics and the effectiveness of such administrative boxism. The natural tendency of modernist administration has tended toward such boxism; the tendency of the antiadministration of postmodernity will be to break the boxes.

OPPOSITION TO METANARRATIVES

The third characteristic of the postmodern view of alterity selected for discussion is addressed in terms of postmodernity's opposition to metanarratives. Postmodernity can be seen as "incredulity toward metanarratives."[43] Examples of metanarratives are the grand narratives and narratives discussed in chapter 11. Metanarratives include the ultimate sources of justification for modernity's projects. Because of the opposition to metanarratives, no foundation for justice can be established, and no fundamental and mystical grip for ethics can exist. The main burden of metaethics throughout its history has been to consider the foundations, the ultimate justification, for ethics. For the postmodernist, the search is futile; for him or her, the establishment of unquestioned grounds is harmful. As Derrida writes, "[N]ever to yield on this point, constantly to maintain an interrogation of the origin, grounds and limits of our conceptual, theoretical or normative apparatus surrounding justice is on deconstruction's part anything but a neutralization of an interest in justice, an insensitivity toward justice."[44] To be ungrounded is not to be degraded; for the postmodernist, phony grounding is debilitating, and there is an imperative to face things as they are.

Wyschogrod distinguishes an ethic that appeals to alterity and one that "leans" on some view of the good. She writes that a strand of postmodernism "is that of alterity, an old word used for otherness, that is generally used to refer to the otherness of persons."[45] Pointing out that an ethics that offers no foundation could be taken as useless, she asks whether postmodern ethics must not "offer some point d'appui, some anchorage that could guide moral deliberation and choice?" Her answer is to offer alterity but to deny that the "other" is a conceptual anchor: "To answer the question about whether postmodernism requires some point d'appui, this Other, the touchstone of moral existence, is not a conceptual anchorage but a living force."[46]

Because of the opposition to metanarratives and mystical foundations, deconstruction—and genealogy—is justice in the sense that it winkles out supposed anchorages or foundations. The mystical foundation of authority is of importance to some modernist public administration thinkers. As indicated in chapter 5, some speak of the ethical obligation of administrators to obey the law. Some think of administration as founded in the obligation to discharge the public interest or to execute the will of the elected representatives of the people. What this thinking has in common is the urge to ground, to specify the unquestioned basis. Deconstruction would demystify these and other foundations, showing the act of public administration to be violence without ground. As Derrida comments about the law, "Since the origin of authority, the foundation or ground, can't by definition rest on anything but themselves, they are themselves a violence without ground."[47]

An activist imposition of a notion of justice on another is repugnant to Derrida: "Justice remains, is yet, to come, à venir, it has an [sic], it is à-venir, the very dimension of events irreducibly to come." Later Derrida adds, "Justice as the experience of alterity is unpresentable."[48] More emphasis is placed on avoiding injustice than on providing justice. This attitude is also reflected in the opposition to reducing justice and ethics to rules. This element was seen in Foucault's view of self-creation as a work of art. It is also clear in Derrida's discussion of law. He writes of "justice that exceeds law and calculation, . . . [an] unpresentable (that exceeds the determinable)."[49]

Public administration influenced by these attitudes would be less concerned to impose just solutions, less concerned to find the applicable rule. The simple imposition of just solutions and rules, seen in this way, is a undesirable form of violence; it is an enforcement of the meaning of one text on another. As Derrida states, " 'Perhaps,' one must always say perhaps for justice."[50] Cannot a distinction be drawn between a public administration concerned with enforcing justice and one concerned with eliminating injustice? Skepticism about this point is understandable. Like the positive and negative versions of the golden rule, eliminating injustice and enforcing justice seem to be logically equivalent. Nevertheless, the connotations are different, and, when it comes to the pragmatic world of administration, the effects of the differences in connotation might lead to substantially different results. A police force setting out to enforce justice, for example, might be supposed to be more likely to execute street delinquents in Rio de Janeiro and to give criminals the third degree; an agency oriented to eliminating injustices might be expected to have an imperative toward the micropolitics of removing the unfair. A similar argument could be developed for the idea of tentativeness. The present method of administration tends to avoid any tentativeness. Police, for example, are oriented toward taking charge of situations; a similar claim could be made for administration in functional areas such as tax collection, foreign affairs, street repairs, and environmental protection. Administrators are oriented toward taking charge through application not only of their programmatic but also of their administrative or managerial expertise. This "taking charge" element is reflected, for instance, in the standard job description of the program manager as the person who directs, coordinates, and controls all the activities and personnel of the assigned program. How could an administration be developed that would operate on a tentative basis? This situation is not straightforward; for instance, it is not enough to say that administrators will become mere information coordinators rather than directors. That issue is not one that currently concerns public administration theory; perhaps it should. It would be an aspect of antiadministration.

THE ESTABLISHED ORDER

A fourth characteristic of postmodernity and alterity is the opposition in Derrida and other postmodernists (such as Lyotard) to established institutions and practices of justice. This opposition is associated with a preference for opposing injustice rather than advocating justice. Derrida states that we cannot speak directly about justice, nor can we experience it. Continuing one of the gobbets at the head of this chapter: "Obliquely, as at this very moment, in which I'm preparing to demonstrate that one cannot speak directly about justice, theorize or objectivize, say 'this is just' and even less 'I am just,' without immediately betraying justice, if not law."[51] The opposition to established institutional practices is reflected in the reaction to the events of 1968, and the opposition to the traditional moral theorists is reflected in various writings.[52]

Postmodernity is often characterized as a neoconservative force, it should be added. Habermas contrasts his own rational progressive thought with what he sees as the neoconservatism of Foucault, Deleuze, and Lyotard. They merit this title, in his view, because they can present no theoretical justification for an alternative to the status quo of contemporary capitalism. The postmodern avenue is micropolitics and a firm unwillingness (as noted earlier) to rely on metanarratives. It has a preference for community initiatives, for instance, rather than for national solutions.

Administrative agencies are by their character in favor of administrative institutions. Certainly, there are exceptions. For instance, armies actually fight one another, and agents of noncompatible regimes can be despised (e.g., dictatorships by those in democracies). Nevertheless, tax enforcement agencies from one part of the world have a bond with all other such agencies; the same is true for firefighting agencies, endangered species agencies, corrections agencies, diplomatic agencies, and so on. The institutional tends to favor the institutional and its own program, other things being equal. But, what would the administrative world look like if there were a moral imperative to be antiinstitutional?

Such an antipractitioner attitude might be illustrated by Thomas Szasz's well-known publication of *The Myth of Mental Illness.* Szasz, a professor of psychiatry, makes the thesis of his book, "Mental illness is a myth."[53] He writes, "It seemed to me that although the notion of mental illness made good historical sense—stemming as it does from the historical identity of medicine and psychiatry—it makes no rational sense."[54] As a reviewer puts it, this psychiatrist has probably "done more than any other man to alert the American public to the potential dangers of an excessively psychiatrized society."[55] It would be helpful to develop a similar "anti" attitude at the institutional level. Such an attitude would be directed against the institution's program, parallel to Szasz. Additionally, it would be directed against itself as an institution and against all similar institutions, thus achieving an antiinstitutional institution.

How could such an antiinstitutional activity work? One strategy might be to focus on a latent intent, especially where that intent is control. In view of Foucault's injunction against the fascism in us all, control is an apposite choice. Consider a social work agency, for example. An "anti" attitude might be developed by reacting against the standard notion that, paraphrasing a definition developed by the National Association of Social Workers, social work is the professional activity of enhancing and restoring the capacity for social functioning, that is, to help individuals and groups in terms of bio-psycho-social development and functioning. Rather, these professionals would stress the possibility of a latent intent underlying this manifest goal. They would react in the spirit of Thomas Szasz's criticism of the concept of mental illness and the deterritorializing criticism directed against psychiatric practice in Deleuze and Guattari's *Anti-Oedipus.*[56] They might even focus on how social work practice can be used indirectly by the power group in society (or by society in general) as a method of controlling deviant individuals and groups;[57] that is, social workers can be misused for the purpose of maintaining order. These professionals might see the attempts to produce appropriate or normal individual and societal behavior, similar to the *Anti-Oedipus* charges against psychiatry, as amounting to a form of policing or social control. Normalization can be seen not only as helping but also as controlling.[58] In such a way, it may be possible to develop an antiprogram and an antiinstitutional attitude while still providing services, but the suggestion is that the character of the service would inevitably be modified by the "anti" attitude. The notion of "professionals" has been stressed in this example not only because social workers are professionals but also because the development and execution of the specifics of "anti" practice would take courageous professionalism. A variety of other examples could be given, such as the control involved in the socialization process of education.

How would corrections agencies tend to behave if they suspected correctional operations and agencies? How would tax managers tend to operate if their moral predisposition was to suspect the institution of taxing and all taxing agencies? How would diplomats tend to behave if they felt a moral imperative against the institution of diplomacy? Such a postmodern emphasis would give institutions a different emphasis toward alterity.

This partial account of postmodernity in terms of alterity stresses the playful, the tentative, and the open features. This choice was made because these aspects have special significance for deepening understanding of the language of public administration. Other postmodern attitudes could have been emphasized, however. One is the strand that tends toward the pessimistic, toward the abyss. By no means are all postmodern attitudes confined to postmodernists. Thus, a movement toward the pessimistic occurs in Schopenhauer's world; a movement toward the abyss occurs in Freud's notion of the death instinct. A postmodern attitude includes a keen sense of the negativity of the human condition; it embraces that condition. This attitude leads to ethical features that put a premium on a seeking of the vertigo encountered at the yawn of the abyss.

SUMMARY

Postmodernity does suggest a moral stance, and this stance has relevance for bureaucracy in postmodernity. The upshot of the implications for public administration of postmodern ethical attitudes is summarized in the slogan "antiadministration."

Postmodernity suggests that changes should occur in any project of public administration. These changes stem from the fact that any postmodern administration should aim to conduct its functions in a way that we have called antiadministrative. Nevertheless, no prescription can be given because this too must be open to deconstruction. The implications of chapters 10 through 13 show the approaches that should be directed toward this antiadministration. Chapter 10 suggests that imaginization might mean a shift toward the imaginal, and a goal of this effort should include antiadministration. Chapter 11 suggests that such a project should stress deconstructive opportunities and skills. This project would include deconstructing the narrative that imaginization equals human progress. Chapter 12 suggests that all study and all practice should be deterritorialized. The discipline of public administration, like any other specialty, constitutes a grid. The postmodern administrator is likely to be one who is skilled in practicing and developing the implications of antiadministration. Postmodernity seems to point any such project of public administration toward a radical emphasis and development of the NASPAA notion of creative pluralism. Such a development would be in the direction of the attitudes of the reflexive language paradigm and directed toward antiadministration.

The nature of antiadministration is explained by discussing four features of the postmodern attitude toward alterity. These features are an openness to the "other," a preference for diversity, an opposition to metanarratives, and opposition to the established order. The account in this chapter starts with an explanation of Foucault's provocative injunction against what he calls the "fascism in us all."

An openness to the other, the first feature, is described as implying that the practice of public administration should be so constructed and carried out that it is antiauthoritarian; it also implies encouragement of service-oriented attitudes. It is described as implying that administration should seek to open all of its decision making to communities and that it should not impose the categories of the bureaucratic text on others. It also suggests the need for substantial anarchism, accompanied by the development of micropolitics in the form of local community action.

The second feature consists of a preference for diversity and the recognition that no privileged meaning exists. A public administration application is seeking to avoid boxism and stereotyping. The third feature is the opposition to metanarratives. The opposition to metanarratives implies antiadministration in the sense that the administrator is deconstructor of metanarratives and unrealistic foundations. Opposition to metanarratives implies that there can be no foundation for justice, no fundamental moral grip. An application for public administration thinking would be to explore the practical relevance of distinguishing between enforcing justice and eliminating injustice. It is also asked whether an administration could be developed that would operate on a tentative basis.

The fourth feature is the imperative to be opposed to existing institutions. Most administrations are by their character in favor of administrative institutions. The feasibility of developing an antiinstitutional method of administration is discussed.

Imagination, deconstruction, deterritorialization, and alterity have now been explored. Taking these four aspects together indicates that indeed an opportunity exists to take thinking about public administration beyond the limits imposed by the modernist mind-set.

14

Epilogue

THE REFLEXIVE LANGUAGE paradigm has been applied in this study to the postmodern and the modern frameworks in order to struggle away from a unidimensional and distorted understanding of public bureaucracy and public administration, away from an understanding that comes naturally to each of us. Looking at bureaucracy through such diametrically contrasting lenses as modernity and postmodernity, when the examination is reflexive and when the social construction of public administration "facts" is recognized, provides more than merely two views. Taken together, the perspectives provide a deeper understanding both of the process of thinking about public administration and of the practice of bureaucracy. Use of these contexts (or lenses) can help us shake some of the deep-seated prejudices of our era. Thus, we have spoken of a language paradigm, where modernity and postmodernity are the dialects. Recall chapter 2 for an introduction to the paradigm.

It is a modernist, but not necessarily invalid, prejudice to take a "which one is right?" approach. This approach is to ask which of the alternatives (modernity or postmodernity) is the true historical context and then to draw conclusions for the study of public bureaucracy. The logic is as follows: if postmodernity is right (or nonsense), what used to be public administration theory is now X (or just as it was before). Nevertheless, on a similar basis, it would be helpful to leave open the possibility that it is not an either-or situation, that we have always lived in a situation that contains both modern and postmodern characteristics. Recall chapters 3 and 9 for accounts of modernity and postmodernity.

Whether the modernity-postmodernity perspectives are a matter of historical epochs or a matter of different tendencies of the human situation, the contention in this book has been that the mind-sets of modernity and postmodernity provide useful lenses for observing the socially constructed phenomena of public administration. The existence of multiple lenses does imply that there can be multiple perceptions, and recognizing differences in perceptions is important. Nevertheless, it does not entail that multiple realities exist. We have no need to rush headlong to a supposed new reality. "Going beyond" modernity does mean recognizing the dead ends to which modernity leads, but the benefits of "going beyond" modernity do not imply abandoning all the insights and contributions achieved by the mind-set of modernity. If modernity is understood in terms of the mind-set of an era, it was the leading edge of what can be considered that most brilliant of eras; it would be short-sighted to deny completely its characteristic discourses. The reflexive language paradigm requires, as was discussed in chapter 2, only that the thinking be in terms of "as if." It is suggested that use of the paradigm can materially strengthen the language of public administration.

Four reflections should be made about the present study, although in no sense are they intended to summarize the text. Summaries may be found at the ends of the various chapters. The first two reflections concern the dialect of modernist public administration theory, and they suggest that the loose general hypothesis discussed in chapter 2 proved to be a useful (if not the only) way of looking at modernist public administration theory. The third reflection relates to the dialect of postmodernity, and the fourth concerns the language of public administration.

First, modernist public administration theory, as it is, is facing crippling dead ends. What it has produced and what more it can offer should be valued; it can yield more. But modernist public administration as science, as technology, as enterprise, and as interpretation—by themselves—encounter dead ends against which public administration theory continues to push. The modernist epistemological project has proven problematic, and the modernist dialect of public administration is limiting. Recall chapters 3, 5, 6, 7, and 8.

Second, American public administration theory is further shackled by its particularism. Certainly it has yielded significant results, but American public administration theory is confined by its adjectives. Recall chapter 4.

Third, the postmodern perspective offers the prospects and the discomforts of a revolution in the character of thinking about public bureaucracy. It is a perspective that requires thinking through the consequences of a world (and of a public administration) without certainties, without false illusions. The thinking can be seen as a kind of therapy, if one wishes. Nevertheless, the therapy, or thinking, is revolutionary because it requires each analysand to make her own journey and because it leads to no further certainties, no further false illusions; for the postmodernist, there is no meaning outside the text. Recall the context that includes hyperreality and a loss of metanarratives and meaning. The postmodern perspective has little appeal for the impatient thinker, for the dichotomous thinker, or for the thinker who favors *Cliffs Notes*. It does suggest important, although difficult, insights for the language of public administration. These tentative insights concern the nature of the public administration context and the character of important functions concerning imagination, deconstruction, deterritorialization, and alterity. See chapters 9, 10, 11, 12, and 13. The postmodern lens tends to add flesh to the idea of debureaucratization, to the notion of antiadministration.

Finally, the language of public administration, as distinct from its modernist manifestation, does not face dead ends. Theorists are not likely to find the path beyond the clear dead-ends, however, unless the deep-seated hold of modernist prejudices can be loosened. In a period of multiple discourse, it was discussed how no text is privileged. Neither modernity's nor postmodernity's texts need be denied; on the contrary, their contributions should be appropriately understood.

The study and practice of public administration can become a more aware (more self-aware) thinking activity. To do so, it would seem helpful for theorists to become more aware by reaching further into other areas—further into philosophy, deeper into social theory, more agilely into economics, for example. That effort is always useful. Nevertheless, the main need is the awareness that could come from loosening the grip of our unconscious mind-sets. Thinking can be pushed further by using, and then by transcending, what we have called the reflexive language paradigm. The language in which we think can be assumed to shape the world that we see, and our best hope for escaping (if we can) may be through a multiple use of dialects that are sufficiently different. Public administration thinking might then have more chance of becoming what we have always wanted it to be. A transmogrification could occur.

Notes

Chapter 1. Introduction

1. As another example, see William K. C. Guthrie, *The Greek Philosophers: From Thales to Aristotle* (New York: Harper and Row, 1975), 4–11. Guthrie explains (p. 4) that "to understand [Ancient] Greek ways of thinking without some knowledge of the Greek language is not easy. Language and thought are inextricably interwoven, and interact on one another. Words have a history and associations, which for those who use them contribute an important part of the meaning, not least because their effect is unconsciously felt rather than intellectually apprehended." Guthrie illustrates this point (pp. 5–11) by discussing selected Greek words. Examples can also be added about the relationship between syntax and thinking. For example, see Bertrand Russell, *A History of Western Philosophy* (New York: Simon and Schuster, 1972). Russell is commenting on Aristotle's metaphysics and on the distinction between things and qualities. Russell writes (p. 164), "The true ground of the distinction (between things and qualities) is, in fact, linguistic; it is derived from syntax. There are proper names, adjectives and relation-words; we may say 'John is wise, James is foolish, John is taller than James.' . . . Metaphysicians, ever since Aristotle, have interpreted these syntactical differences metaphysically; John and James are substances, wisdom and folly are universals. (Relation-words were ignored or misinterpreted.)"

2. Ludwig Wittgenstein, *Philosophical Investigations,* trans. G. E. M. Anscombe (New York: Macmillan, 1958), 3.

3. This paraphrases Wittgenstein when he writes, "Here the term 'language-game' is meant to bring into prominence the fact that the speaking of language is part of an activity, or a form of life" (Wittgenstein, *Philosophical Investigations,* 11).

4. Widely held negative characterizations of public bureaucracy have been disputed, it should be noted. For example, see Gary L. Wamsley, et al., *Refounding Public Administration* (Newbury Park, Calif.: Sage, 1990), 33. The authors write, "Thus our political culture has come to include a pernicious mythology concerning the public sector and public administrators which needs to be corrected before the American dialogue can enter a new and meaningful phase." Among the seven supporting items they list, one is that "[m]ost clients of bureaucracy are not dissatisfied; in fact the vast majority of them are very pleased with the services and treatment received." Also see Charles and William Beard, "The Case for Bureaucracy," *Scribner's Magazine* 93, no. 4 (1933): 209–14, reprinted in *Public Administration Review* 46, no. 2 (1986): 107–12; and Beverly A. Cigler and Heidi L. Neiswender, " 'Bureaucracy' in the Introductory American Government Textbook," *Public Administration Review* 51, no. 5 (1991): 442–50. Relying on Richard J. Stillman, *The American Bureaucracy* (Chicago: Nelson Hall, 1987), Cigler and Neiswender provide an objection to the "textbook view," listing eight most often repeated bureaucratic myths in bureaucracy chapters in introductory American gov-

ernment textbooks. These myths are that bureaucracy is the problem with the U.S. government; government bureaucracy is overwhelmingly large and monolithic; bureaucrats stay on forever; bureaucracy grows relentlessly; bureaucracy is all-powerful and out of control; governmental bureaucracy is inefficient and wastes resources; bureaucrats are unrepresentative of the U.S. population; and bureaucracy produces only red tape. Cigler and Neiswender note (p. 448) that "it is clear that many of the introductory American government textbooks perpetuate the so-called myths. . . . Just as Stillman and others must provide empirical data to support arguments, so too must textbook authors."

5. For an account of the scope of public administration and public bureaucracy, see the introductory comments in chapter 2 and the discussion in chapter 7.

6. See Hans-Georg Gadamer, *Truth and Method* (New York: Seabury Press, 1975), 91. Gadamer comments, "It is more important that play itself contains its own, even sacred, seriousness. Yet, in the attitude of play, all these purposive relations which determine active and caring existence have not simply disappeared, but in a curious way acquire a different quality."

7. Alvin Toffler, *The Third Wave* (New York: William Morrow, 1980); John Naisbitt, *Megatrends: Ten New Directions Transforming Our Lives* (New York: Warner Books, 1982).

8. René Descartes, *Discourse on Method and Meditations on First Philosophy*, 3rd ed., trans. Donald A. Cress (Indianapolis: Hackett Publishing Co., 1993), 35.

9. Edward Shils, *Tradition* (Chicago: University of Chicago Press, 1981), 291.

10. Rogers Brubaker, *The Limits of Rationality: An Essay on the Social and Moral Thought of Max Weber* (London: George Allen and Unwin, 1984).

11. Stephen A. Tyler, *The Unspeakable: Discourse, Dialogue and Rhetoric in the Postmodern World* (Madison: University of Wisconsin Press, 1987), 3, acknowledging William V. Spanos and Robert Magliola.

12. Baudrillard gives Disneyland as an illustration of his claim. See Jean Baudrillard, "Simulacra and Simulation," in *Jean Baudrillard: Selected Writings*, ed. Mark Poster (Stanford: Stanford University, 1988), 172. As Baudrillard writes, "Disneyland is presented as imaginary in order to make us believe that the rest is real, when in fact all of Los Angeles and the America surrounding it are no longer real, but of the order of the hyperreal and of simulation."

13. Jean Baudrillard, "Game with Vestiges," *On the Beach* 5, no. 1 (1984): 24.

14. Max Horkheimer and Theodor Adorno, *Dialect of Enlightenment* (New York: Seabury, 1972), xiv.

15. As we proceed, it should become clearer why it is beside the point that sooner or later the term *postmodernity* as a label will surely pass out of fashion.

16. For a 1960s publication that contains a forecast of continuing urban disorders, see David J. Farmer, *Civil Disorder Control: A Planning Program of Municipal Coordination and Cooperation* (Chicago: Public Administration Service, 1968), 1.

17. Governmental size is discussed in chapter 4. As a percentage of gross domestic product, for example, general governmental expenditures increased between 1960 and 1985 for all countries in the Organization for Economic Cooperation and Development.

18. See Cigler and Neiswender, " 'Bureaucracy' in the American Government Introductory Textbook," 449. In their analysis of introductory American government textbooks, Cigler and Neiswender conclude, "In general, bureaucrat-bashing of the permanent career bureaucrat has increased in texts published since 1985 as evidenced in the use of unflattering cartoons." See also Aaron Wildavsky, "Ubiquitous Anomie: Public Service in an Era of Ideological Dissensus," *Public Administration Review* 48, no. 4 (1988): 753. Wildavsky writes,

"In a little piece on leadership, Irving Spitzberg, Jr. writes about the 'ubiquitous anomie . . . throughout the federal service.' That seems to describe the situation pretty well. Things are bad and are unlikely to get better." Wildavsky goes on to give his diagnosis.

19. For a discussion of the meaning of "Kafkaesque," see Frederick R. Karl, *Franz Kafka: Representative Man* (New York: Ticknor and Fields, 1991), 757–60. As Karl explains (p. 757), "Kafka has lent his name to an entire range of meanings that help interpret the appalling history of the later twentieth century. . . . For *Kafkaesque* at its most meaningful and exalted denotes a world that has its own rules, its own guidelines, its own form of behavior that cannot be amenable to the human will. *Kafkaesque,* in fact, seems to denote a will of its own, and it is, apparently, destructive of human endeavors. Clearly, it runs counter to human directions or goals or aims, and it serves as a form of bedevilment. *Kafkaesque* in our century has replaced the now old-fashioned *fate* or *destiny* or even *circumstance* and *happenstance.*" Karl adds (p. 759), "Kafkaesque need not be completely inhuman or negative. For Kafka himself, the adjective described conditions that brought out the Sisyphus-like qualities in himself. . . . After his death, and in the development of the adjective, we have turned the word into 'the way of the world.' And since that way has been so negative, we find *Kafkaesque* a denial, or else the definition of a region waiting to entrap us." For the claim that the term *Kafkaesque* has been widely "used and abused" in the United States, see Johannes Urzidil, *There Goes Kafka* (Detroit: Wayne State University Press, 1968), 30–31. Urzidil complains (p. 31) that after 1941, "The name had become a general designation for the psychological problems of the individual within certain groups troubled by all kinds of insecurities and by unattainable or inadequately comprehended religiosity." The term *Kafkaesque* in the present text is used in the "most meaningful" sense noted by Karl.

Chapter 2. Method: Reflexive Interpretation

1. Gadamer, *Truth and Method,* 432.

2. Friedrich Nietzsche, *The Will to Power,* trans. Walter Kaufmann and R. J. Hollingdale (New York: Vintage Books, 1968), 283.

3. See Anthony Giddens, *New Rules of Sociological Method* (London: Hutchinson, 1976); Andrew Sayer, *Method in Social Science: A Realist Approach* (New York: Routledge, 1992). Giddens and Sayer also describe social science in terms of a double hermeneutic.

4. For a view of "play," see chapter 1, note 6, and "play as the clue to ontological explanation" in Gadamer, *Truth and Method,* 91–119.

5. Karl Popper, *Objective Knowledge* (London: Oxford University Press, 1972).

6. Francis H. Bradley, *Principles of Logic* (Oxford: Oxford University Press), 2–3.

7. Jean Marsh, *The Illuminated Language of Flowers* (New York: Holt, Rinehart and Winston, 1978), 14.

8. The rose, in itself, has no meaning. In the same way, the marks on the page "rose" have no intrinsic meaning. Consider the following series of marks on a page. "Esel mögen Spreu lieber als Gold" in John Sallis and Kenneth Maly, *Heraclitean Fragments: A Companion Volume to the Heidegger/Fink Seminar on Heraclitus* (University: University of Alabama Press, 1980), 6. These marks on the page translate a set of Greek signs attributed by Aristotle to Heraclitus. The marks or signs themselves have no meaning, except the meaning that society through its shared language gives to them. Consider another translation, "Do nke ys pre ferst rawt ogo ld." When the reader who shares the English language sees the meaning, the meaning is not in the gibberish; we have given the gibberish meaning. Public administration and social entities are no different; they are essentially hermeneutic entities.

9. Herbert A. Simon, *Administrative Behavior: A Study of Decision-Making Processes in Administrative Organization* (New York: Free Press, 1945), 130–31.

10. Lester Thurow, *Head to Head: The Coming Economic Battle Among Japan, Europe and America* (New York: William Morrow, 1992), chap. 2.

11. For example, see Peter L. Berger and Thomas Luckman, *The Social Construction of Reality: A Treatise in the Sociology of Knowledge* (Garden City, N.Y.: Doubleday, 1966).

12. See Luther Gulick, "Notes on the Theory of Organization," in *Papers on the Science of Administration,* ed. Luther Gulick and L. Urwick (New York: Institute of Public Administration, 1937), 13. In this 1937 text, Gulick seems to be conceptualizing the role of the chief executive as internal to the organization. For example, he defines (p. 13) "co-ordinating" (the CO in POSDCORB) as "the all important duty of interrelating the various parts of the work." He defines "reporting" (the R in POSDCORB) as "keeping those to whom the executive is responsible informed as to what is going on, which thus includes keeping himself and his subordinates informed through records, research and inspection." The reading could have expanded later (e.g., when the military applied POSDCORB during World War II).

13. For example, see Gerald D. Nash, *Perspectives on Administration: The Vistas of History* (Berkeley: Institute of Governmental Studies, 1969), 29–30. Nash writes, "A perusal of White's administrative histories reveals that they were written primarily from a POSDCORB orientation. A comparison of the table of contents of his text in *Public Administration,* published in 1926, with his books, *The Federalists* (1948) or the *Jeffersonians* (1951) reveals similarities. White applied the same framework to the analysis of contemporary administration and to past events. Thus, he was concerned with the operation of the presidency as an institution, with the functioning of the executive departments, and with the civil service. Yet, by the time he reached the third volume in the series, White himself apparently found his POSDCORB frame of reference too restrictive."

14. It would be misleading to suggest that this tradition reached its end with Hume. We can point to the logical positivists, for example.

15. Immanuel Kant, *Critique of Pure Reason,* trans. Norman Kemp Smith (New York: St. Martin's Press, 1965).

16. See J. J. Smart, "Space," *The Encyclopedia of Philosophy* (New York: Macmillan, 1967), 506–07. As Smart puts it, "[I]n his *Critique of Pure Reason,* Kant argued against both a naive absolute theory of space and a relational view. He held that space is something merely subjective (or 'phenomenal') wherein in thought we arrange nonspatial 'things-in-themselves.' He was led to this view partly by the thought that certain antinomies or contradictions are unavoidable as long as we think of space and time as objectively real." For an account of the development of Kant's views on space, see such publications as Christopher Browne Garnett, *The Kantian Philosophy of Space* (Port Washington, N.Y.: Kennikat Press, 1965).

17. Arthur J. Minton and Thomas A. Shipka, *Philosophy: Paradox and Discovery* (New York: McGraw-Hill, 1990), 3–4.

18. Marcus von Senden, *Space and Sight* (New York: Free Press, 1960).

19. Perhaps the active role of the subject also could be illustrated by presenting objects like Jastrow's celebrated duck-rabbit, Hill's old-lady–young-lady, and Necker's cube. At times, Jastrow's drawing of the duck-rabbit is seen as a duck; at other times, it is seen as a rabbit. The duck (and the rabbit), it has been remarked, could not be recognized as a duck (and a rabbit) unless the observer previously knew what a duck (and a rabbit) is. Reading about the geometry of vesica pisces can make one see objects not before noticed; the Episcopalian shield and the flag of Guam look different in light of what Robert Lawlor calls "sacred geometry." See Robert Lawlor, *Sacred Geometry: Philosophy and Practice* (New York: Thomas and Hudson,

1989). Also consider novels, plays, and life. Characters and people inflict and suffer this harm and that joy because their general attitudes to the world shape what they see. The generous personality, for instance, might see in others generosity that vicious persons take to be viciousness. See Herman Melville, *Billy Budd and Other Stories* (New York: Penguin, 1986). Consider Billy Budd's language. Consider Captain the Honorable Edward Fairfax Vere's language, his world view. With a language that included concepts bred by the discontent among the sailors at Spithead and the more serious outbreaks in the fleet at the Nore, Captain Vere saw Billy Budd's right arm striking Claggart as an act requiring a prompt drumhead court: "Struck dead by an angel of God. Yet the angel must hang." The surgeon saw a different picture. Melville writes (p. 352), "Whether Captain Vere, as the surgeon professionally and privately surmised, was really the sudden victim of any degree of aberration, everyone must determine for himself as this narrative may afford."

20. See, for example, Steven Rhoads, *The Economist's View of the World: Governments, Markets and Public Policy* (New York: Cambridge University Press, 1985) for one account.

21. Richard M. Ebeling, "What is a Price? Explanation and Understanding," in *Economics and Hermeneutics,* ed. Don Lavoie (New York: Routledge, 1990), 191.

22. See Georg Hegel, *Wissenchaft der Logik,* vol. 5, quoted in Anthony Manser, *Bradley's Logic* (Totowa, N.J.: Barnes and Noble, 1983), 34. Hegel writes, "The forms of thought are, in the first instance, displayed and stored in human language. . . . In all that becomes something inner for man, such as a thought or idea, into all that he makes his own, language has penetrated. . . . [L]ogic is his natural element, indeed his own peculiar nature. If nature as such, the physical work, is contrasted with the mental sphere, then logic must be said to be something above nature which permeates every relation of man to nature, his sensation, intuition, desire, need, instinct and by doing so transforms it into something human." Of course, views differ regarding the relationship of language to cognitive ability. For example, see Philip Lieberman, *The Biology and Evolution of Language* (Cambridge: Harvard University Press, 1984), 95–96. Lieberman notes the views of Bronowski, Humboldt, Whorf, and Cassirer. He writes (pp. 95–96), "Bronowski's position is actually not the extreme one in the philosophical debate, since he in essence argues that there is a cognitive base present in human beings, and possibly in other animals, which language builds on and enhances." Lieberman describes Humbolt's view (1836) as "more extreme": "Humboldt's view, which takes expression in recent theories like that of Whorf (1956) is that 'man lives with his objects chiefly . . . as language presents them to him. By the same process whereby he spins language out of his own being, he ensnares himself in it; and each language draws a magic circle round the people to which it belongs, a circle from which there is no escape save by stepping out of it into another.' In this view, which Cassirer develops in a richer manner than either Humboldt or Whorf, human thought, culture, and language all form a matrix that defines the quality of the human condition. However, the deepest level of this matrix is linguistic. Cassirer thus claims that reason and logic follow from language."

23. Berger and Luckman, *The Social Construction of Reality,* 172–73.

24. See Jürgen Habermas, *Knowledge and Human Interest* (London: Heinemen, 1971) for his distinction between empirical-analytical, interpretive, and critical analytic forms.

25. Renata Tesch, *Qualitative Research* (New York: Falmer Press, 1990), 59–67.

26. For an account of the hermeneutic tradition from Ast to Ricoeur, see publications such as Gayle L. Ormiston and Alan D. Schrift, *The Hermeneutic Tradition* (New York: State University of New York, 1990). For an account of the use of hermeneutics in the social science, see publications such as Zygmunt Bauman, *Hermeneutics and Social Science: Approaches to Understanding* (London: Hutchinson, 1978). Bauman discusses the hermeneutic contribu-

tions of Karl Marx, Max Weber, Karl Mannheim, Edmund Husserl, Talcott Parsons, Martin Heidegger, and Alfred Schutz. For a description of three strands of contemporary hermeneutics, see Josef Bleicher, *Contemporary Hermeneutics: Hermeneutics as Method, Philosophy and Critique* (London: Routledge and Kegan Paul, 1980). Bleicher distinguishes hermeneutical theory, seeking objectivism; hermeneutic philosophy, aiming not at methodological procedures "but at the explication and phenomenological description of human Dasein in its temporality and historicality"; and critical hermeneutics.

27. For an account of forms of the "liar paradox" and attempts at refutation, see Richard L. Kirkham, *Theories of Truth: A Critical Introduction* (Cambridge: MIT Press, 1992), 271–306. As Kirkham notes (p. 271), saying that someone is a liar "is not to say that everything he says is a lie." He summarizes his account (p. 306), "We have seen that the language-levels response can solve both the Liar and the Strengthened Liar paradoxes for artificial languages, but it can solve neither for natural languages. The approach of truth-value gaps can solve the Liar Paradox for both artificial and natural languages, but it cannot solve the Strengthened Liar for either. Neither can the approach truth-value gluts, save at risk of unintelligibility. The situational-semantics approach solves both paradoxes for both kinds of languages, but only if we accept the impossibility of talking about the whole world."

28. See David J. Farmer, *Being in Time: The Nature of Time in Light of McTaggart's Paradox* (Lanham, Md.: University Press of America, 1990), 5, for a similar account and also for the Synge illustration.

29. John L. Synge, *Talking about Relativity* (Amsterdam: North Holland, 1970), 16–19.

30. Ibid., 16.

31. Ibid., 17.

32. Ibid., 18.

33. Martin Heidegger, *On the Way to Language,* trans. Peter D. Hertz (New York: Harper and Row, 1971), 134.

34. Ludwig Wittgenstein, *Tractatus Logico-Philosophicus,* trans. D. F. Pears and B. F. McGuinness (London: Routledge and Kegan Paul, 1961), 5, 6.

35. For an account of other reasons, see for example George A. Morgan, *What Nietzsche Means* (New York: Harper and Row, 1941), 14–20. Morgan (p. 16) writes, "One reason for [Nietzsche's] use of the aphoristic style was that it kept his real meaning from those unfit to grasp it."

36. Hilary Lawson, *Reflexivity: The Post-modern Predicament* (London: Hutchinson, 1985), 28–29.

37. Ibid., 10–11.

38. For example, see Ralph P. Hummel, "Stories Managers Tell: Why They Are as Valid as Science," *Public Administration Review* 51, no. 1 (1991): 31–41; Charles T. Goodsell, "Administration as Ritual," *Public Administration Review* 49, no. 2 (1989): 161–66.

39. For example, see Gadamer, *Truth and Method;* Hans-Georg Gadamer, "The Hermeneutics of Suspicion," in *Hermeneutics,* ed. Gary Shapiro and Alan Sica (Amherst: University of Massachusetts Press, 1984); Hans-Georg Gadamer, "Text and Interpretation," in *Dialogue and Deconstruction,* ed. Diane Michelfelder and Richard Palmer (Albany: SUNY Press, 1989), 21–71.

40. Anthony Weston, *A Rulebook for Argument* (Indianapolis: Hackett, 1992).

41. Sigmund Freud, *The Interpretation of Dreams* (New York: Modern Library, 1978).

42. Robert B. Denhardt, *Theories of Public Organization* (Monterey, Calif.: Brooks/Cole, 1984), 32–36.

43. Willard V. Quine, *The Ways of Paradox and Other Essays* (Cambridge: Harvard University Press, 1976), 1.

44. Ibid., 1.

45. Ibid., 5. As Quine writes, "It establishes that some tacit and trusted pattern of reasoning must be made explicit and henceforth be avoided or revised."

46. William Kneale and Martha Kneale, *The Development of Logic,* 2nd ed. (Oxford: Clarendon Press, 1984), 56.

47. See Farmer, *Being in Time,* 69–77, for a discussion of such implicit assumptions and for discussion in particular of the law of noncontradiction.

48. Howard McCurdy, *Public Administration: A Bibliography* (Washington, D.C.: American University, 1975), 9.

49. Ibid., 9.

50. See Brack Brown, "The Search for Public Administration: Roads Not Followed," *Public Administration Review* 49, no. 2 (1989): 216. Brown comments, "Billions of dollars annually and tens of thousands of professionals are engaged in managing public activity beneath the seas, above the earth, and around the globe. The armed forces consume the largest single portion of United States national expenditures, and still public administration practically ignores the uniformed military. This huge component of public administration has never even been the subject of a chapter in a basic textbook." Gulick surely did not have the military in mind when he incorrectly stated, "[I]f government does it, it is 'public administration.' " See Luther H. Gulick, "Reflections on Public Administration, Past and Present," *Public Administration Review* 50, no. 6 (1990): 602.

51. For an account of the major role of the American Society for Public Administration (ASPA) in the development of American public administration, see Darrell L. Pugh, "ASPA's History: A Prologue!" *Public Administration Review* 45, no. 4 (1985): 475–84. Pugh's article also discusses the withdrawals from ASPA in 1970 and in 1976, respectively, of the National Association of Schools of Public Affairs and Administration (NASPAA) and the National Academy of Public Administration (NAPA).

52. NASPAA Ad Hoc Committee, *Report of the Ad Hoc Committee on the Future of Public Service Education and Accreditation* (Chicago: NASPAA, April 12, 1992).

53. Dwight Waldo, "Education for Public Administration in the Seventies," in *American Public Administration: Past, Present and Future,* ed. Frederick C. Mosher (University: University of Alabama Press, 1975), 181; and Dwight Waldo, "Introduction: Retrospect and Prospect," *The Administrative State: A Study of the Political Theory of American Public Administration,* 2nd ed. (New York: Holmes and Meier, 1984), lx.

54. NASPAA Ad Hoc Committee, *Report of the Ad Hoc Committee.*

55. Ibid.

Chapter 3. Modernity: The Dialect

1. Max Weber, *The Protestant Ethic and the Spirit of Capitalism,* trans. Talcott Parsons (New York: Scribner, 1958), 16.

2. Talcott Parsons, Introduction, in Weber, *The Protestant Ethic and the Spirit of Capitalism,* 26.

3. Scott Lash, "Modernity or Modernism? Weber and Contemporary Social Theory," in *Max Weber, Rationality and Modernity,* ed. Scott Lash and Sam Whimster (London: Allen and Unwin, 1987), 355–77.

4. Ibid., 355.

5. Jürgen Habermas, "Modernity: An Incomplete Project," in *The Anti-Aesthetic: Essays on Postmodern Culture,* ed. Hal Foster (Port Townsend, Wash.: Bay Press, 1983), 9.

6. Ibid., 9.

7. Thomas Carlyle, *The French Revolution: A History* (London: Chapman and Hall, 1837), 653–54.

8. Ibid., 654.

9. Ernest F. Henderson, *Symbol and Satire in the French Revolution* (New York: G. P. Putnam's Sons, 1912), 406.

10. Mona Ozouf, *Festivals and the French Revolution* (Cambridge: Harvard University Press, 1988).

11. Lynn Hunt, Preface, in Ozouf, *Festivals and the French Revolution,* ix.

12. Wider understandings of the term *Enlightenment* have also been offered. For example, see Lucien Goldman, *The Philosophy of the Enlightenment: The Christian Burgess and the Enlightenment* (Cambridge: MIT Press, 1973), 5.

13. Horkheimer and Adorno, *Dialectic of Enlightenment.*

14. Max Weber, "Science as Vocation," in *From Max Weber,* ed. Hans H. Gerth and C. Wright Mills (New York: Oxford University Press, 1946), 148.

15. Jean-François Lyotard, *The Postmodern Condition: A Report on Knowledge,* trans. G. Bennington and B. Massumi (Minneapolis: University of Minnesota, 1984).

16. See Crane Brinton, "Enlightenment," in *The Encyclopedia of Philosophy,* ed. Paul Edwards (New York: Macmillan, 1967), 524, for this quotation from the entry under "philosophe" in Diderot's encyclopedia.

17. Peter Gay, trans., *Voltaire: Philosophical Dictionary* (New York: Basic Books, 1962), 122–23. In the previous lines, Voltaire had written, "Do you want to know why your arm and foot obey your will, and why your liver doesn't? Do you seek to know how thought forms itself in your puny understanding, and the infant in the uterus of that woman? . . . Your colleagues have written ten thousand volumes on the subject. . . . But what is that substance at bottom? And what is this thing you've called spirit, from the Latin word meaning breath, unable to do better because you know nothing about it. . . . And yet you have taken your degrees and you are covered with fur, and your cap is too, and they call you master. . . . Montaigne's motto was 'What do I know?' and yours is 'What don't I know?' "

18. Immanuel Kant, "What is Enlightenment?" in *Kant on History,* ed. Lewis White Beck (Indianapolis: Library of Liberal Arts, 1963).

19. Henderson, *Symbol and Satire in the French Revolution,* 405.

20. Ibid., plate 166, 407.

21. Gary B. Madison, *The Hermeneutics of Postmodernity: Figures and Themes* (Bloomington: Indiana University Press, 1988), x.

22. Hans Blumenberg, *Legitimacy of the Modern Age,* trans. Robert M. Wallace (Cambridge: MIT Press, 1985), 75.

23. Martin Heidegger, "The Age of the World Picture," in *The Question Concerning Technology and Other Essays,* trans. William Lovitt (New York: Harper and Row, 1977), 128–29.

24. Ibid., 132.

25. Jürgen Habermas, "Modernity: An Incomplete Project," 9.

26. Ibid.

27. See Horkheimer and Adorno, *Dialectic of Enlightenment;* also see Max Horkheimer, *Eclipse of Reason* (New York: Seabury, 1974).

28. Jean Baudrillard, *America,* trans. Chris Turner (London: Verso, 1989), 77.

29. Weber, *The Protestant Ethic and the Spirit of Capitalism.*

30. Max Weber, *Economy and Society,* ed. Guenther Roth and Claus Wittich (Berkeley: University of California Press, 1968), 975.

31. David Kolb, *The Critique of Pure Modernity: Hegel, Heidegger and After* (Chicago: University of Chicago Press, 1986), 13.

32. Sigmund Freud, *Civilization and its Discontents,* trans. James Strachey (New York: Norton, 1961).

33. Frank H. Knight, *The Ethics of Competition and Other Essays,* ed. Milton Friedman, Homer Jones, George Stigler, and Allen Wallis (New York: Books For Libraries Press, 1935).

34. For example, see Alasdair MacIntyre, *After Virtue: A Study in Moral Theory* (Notre Dame: University of Notre Dame Press, 1981).

35. Terry L. Cooper and N. Dale Wright, eds., *Exemplary Public Administrators: Character and Leadership in Government* (San Francisco: Jossey-Bass, 1992), 7.

36. Weber writes of "the distinctiveness of Western and especially of Modern Western rationalism" in *The Protestant Ethic and the Spirit of Capitalism,* 26.

37. Max Weber, *The Methodology of the Social Sciences,* ed. Edward A Shils and Henry A. Finch (New York: Free Press, 1949), 16.

38. Ibid.

39. Stephen P. Turner and Regis A. Factor, *Max Weber and the Dispute over Reason and Value* (London: Routledge and Kegan Paul, 1984), 57.

40. James G. March, *Decisions and Organizations* (Oxford: Basil Blackwell, 1988), 15.

41. See, for example, Simon, *Administrative Behavior;* and James G. March and Herbert Simon, *Organizations* (New York: Wiley, 1958).

42. Richard M. Cyert and James G. March, *A Behavioral Theory of the Firm* (Englewood Cliffs, N.J.: Prentice-Hall, 1963).

43. See, for example, Charles Lindblom, "The Science of 'Muddling Through,' " *Public Administration Review* 29, no. 2 (1969): 316–25; and in other publications in 1961, 1963, 1965, and 1979.

44. Amitai Etzioni, "Mixed Scanning Revisited," *Public Administration Review* 46, no. 1 (1986): 8.

45. Amitai Etzioni, "Mixed Scanning: A 'Third' Approach to Decision-Making," *Public Administration Review* 47, no. 6 (1987): 385.

46. For an example in a functional area other than budgeting, see Graham Allison, *Essence of Decision* (Boston: Little, Brown, 1971). Allison analyzes foreign policy decision making during the Cuban Missile Crisis, and he uses three models for this purpose. One model considers the nation as a rational actor, the second focuses on organizational processes, and the third analyzes the decision making in terms of bureaucratic politics.

47. Aaron Wildavsky, *The Politics of the Budgetary Process* (Boston: Little, Brown, 1964), and in other publications.

48. See Gordon Leff, *The Dissolution of the Medieval Outlook: An Essay on Intellectual and Spiritual Change in the Fourteenth Century* (New York: New York University Press, 1976), 2–5. He writes (p. 2), "What we call an outlook is an abstraction or more strictly a set of abstractions formed from our idea of the ideas, attitudes, and beliefs of different individuals or groups." Later (pp. 4–5), he adds, "Hence there is not—or only exceptionally—a single view of reality governing all understanding. What we identify as an outlook is rather a certain framework of commonly held absolute presuppositions about the meaning of reality—as they concern God, man, nature, society, the universe—mediated in varying degrees of coherence

and articulateness by the conceptual worlds coming within it. Which in a formative sense means those of theologians and the physicists and the other intellectual agents rather than of the peasants and those who are the recipients."

49. Anthony J. Cascardi, *The Subject of Modernity* (New York: Cambridge University Press, 1992), 2.

50. Marshall Berman, *All That is Solid Melts into Air: The Experience of Modernity* (New York: Simon and Schuster, 1982).

51. See Max Horkheimer and Theodor W. Adorno, *Dialectic of Enlightenment,* trans. John Cumming (New York: Herder and Herder, 1972), 43 ff.

52. Weber, "Author's Introduction," *The Protestant Ethic and the Spirit of Capitalism.* As Schluchter writes, "Like capitalism, rationalism is for Weber not limited to the modern West." Wolfgang Schluchter, *The Rise of Western Rationalism: Max Weber's Developmental History* (Berkeley: University of California Press, 1982), 9.

53. See Leff, *The Dissolution of the Medieval Outlook,* 4. Leff writes that an "outlook is not uniformly diffused and does not follow a single direction."

54. Eugen Weber, *In the Western Tradition,* videorecording, Fred Barzyk, producer (Santa Barbara: Intellimation, 1989).

55. Margaret A. Rose, *The Post-Modern and the Post-Industrial* (Cambridge: Cambridge University Press, 1991), 5.

56. Lyotard, *The Postmodern Condition,* 79.

57. Boris Frankel, *The Post-Industrial Utopians* (Cambridge: Polity, 1987), 10.

58. See Dwight Waldo, *Public Administration in a Time of Turbulence* (Scranton: Chandler Publishing, 1971), 270–73. Waldo writes (p. 270), "Written deeply into the human condition is a duality and in some measure an antagonism between two tendencies, two potentials. One of these is signified by such terms as reason, rationalism, cognition, logic, classicism; the other by such terms as faith, emotion, intuition, feeling, passion. Western history can be, and to a large extent is, written in terms of the relative dominance of one over the other and of the particular 'mixes' that occur: the Apollonian and Dionysian cults, the Age of Faith, the Enlightenment, the classical and romantic periods, the doctrine of the Two-Fold Truth, the struggle between science and theology, and so forth." A little later in this book published in 1971, he states (p. 271) that "the proposition that we are now in a period in which the Dionysian is ascendant, in ardent contest with the Apollonian, would seem to require no proof."

59. For an account of different conceptions of Nietzsche's Apollonian-Dionysian relationship, see Joan Stambaugh, *The Problem of Time in Nietzsche* (London: Associated University Presses, 1987), 19–37. She writes, for example (p. 26), that we "have two different conceptions of the Apollinian and the Dionysian: (1) the Apollinian and the Dionysian as two equally primordial forces of art, and (2) the Dionysian as the primal unity that produces the Apollinian world of appearance. In both conceptions Nietzsche speaks of a contradiction." See also Carl G. Jung, *Psychological Types,* trans. H. Godwin Baynes (New York: Harcourt Brace, 1923), chap. 3, for consideration of Nietzsche's contrast of the Apollonian and the Dionysian in *The Birth of Tragedy.*

60. Thomas Gould, *Platonic Love* (New York: Free Press of Glencoe, 1963), 38. Gould continues, "The realms of Apollo, therefore, included science, philosophy, politics, business, and those of the arts which revealed order in the world about us. But Dionysus was invoked by drink, sex, religious ecstasy, and the wilder sorts of music and dance." Later, Gould adds (p. 39), "To speak of Apollo and Dionysus is to risk accusations of dilettantism from most scholars today."

61. For a view of the split brain, see Herbert A. Simon, "Making Management Decisions:

The Role of Intuition and Emotion," *Academy of Management Executive* 1, no. 1 (1987): 60–61 (reprinted in Weston H. Agor, *Intuition in Organizations: Leading and Managing Productively* [Newbury Park, Calif.: Sage, 1989], 26–27). Simon writes, "Physiological research on 'spilt brains'—brains in which the corpus callosum, which connects the two hemispheres of the cerebrum, has been severed—has provided encouragement to the idea of two qualitatively different kinds of decision making—the analytical, corresponding to Barnard's 'logical,' and the intuitive or creative, corresponding to his 'non-logical.' . . . The more romantic versions of the split-brain doctrine extrapolate this evidence into two polar forms of thought labeled above as analytical and creative. . . . The evidence for this romantic extrapolation does not derive from the physiological research. . . . For our purposes, it is the differences in behavior, and not the differences in the hemispheres, that are important. Reference to the two hemispheres is a red herring."

62. Freud, *Interpretation of Dreams.*

63. McTaggart's argument against the existence of time can be countered, in my view, by distinguishing ontology and predication, by denying that what is the case can be always said. McTaggart was not alert to the distinction between ontology and predication, and he did not distinguish between time as a concern for ontology and time as a subject for predication. He believed that, for the ontological property of being present to be as it is, it is necessary to be able to predicate that property. See Farmer, *Being in Time,* 173–79.

Chapter 4. Modernity: Limits of Particularism

1. Mosher, *American Public Administration,* 7–8.

2. John F. D'Amico, "Manuscripts," in *The Cambridge History of Renaissance Philosophy,* ed. Charles B. Schmitt, Quentin Skinner, and Eckhard Kessler (Cambridge: Cambridge University Press, 1988), 27. Some specialization occurred before this time, of course. For example, see Leff, *The Dissolution of the Medieval Outlook,* 10–11. Leff claims that greater advances were made in the fourteenth century in mathematics, physical theory, and logic than at any other time in the Middle Ages. He continues, "Although the independent development of these and other branches of knowledge goes back in some cases—notably logic—to the twelfth century they attained a new identity in the fourteenth century. . . . While many of the leading figures, such as Bradwardine, Buridan, and Nicholas of Oresme were also philosophers or theologians or ecclesiastics, or all three, many seem to have devoted themselves wholly to scientific or logical problems."

3. Robert A. Dahl, "The Science of Public Administration: Three Problems," *Public Administration Review* 7, no. 1 (1947): 1–11.

4. Stephen P. Turner and Regis Factor, *Max Weber and the Dispute over Reason and Value,* 49, quoting Max Weber, *Max Weber: Selections in Translation,* ed. W. G. Runciman (Cambridge: Cambridge University Press, 1978), 223.

5. NASPAA Ad Hoc Committee, *Report of the Ad Hoc Committee.*

6. Khiyong Lan and David H. Rosenbloom, "Public Administration in Transition?" *Public Administration Review* 52, no. 6 (1992): 535.

7. Mosher, *American Public Administration,* 7–8. Mosher writes, "With only a few minor exceptions—some paragraphs by Hamilton in *The Federalist* papers, some interesting observations by de Tocqueville, some rhetorical complaints by Lincoln and other political leaders—the subject as one for science, study or generalization was largely ignored in the century following the drafting of the Constitution. As a profession, it did not exist. In intellectual terms, it was picked up by a scattering of scholars in the late nineteenth and early twentieth

centuries—Wilson, Goodnow and others—and they drew on European literature and examples. But, as the article by the Stones in this volume makes clear, the real origins of public administration lay in the cities, especially the big ones."

8. Ibid., 8.

9. Ibid., 9.

10. Ibid.

11. Ibid., 10.

12. John A. Rohr, "The Constitutional World of Woodrow Wilson," in *Politics and Administration: Woodrow Wilson and the Study of Public Administration,* ed. Jack Rabin and James S. Bowman (New York: Marcel Dekker, 1984), 44.

13. See Richard J. Stillman, "The Constitutional Bicentennial and the Centennial of the American Administrative State," *Public Administration Review* 47, no. 1 (1987): 4–5. As Stillman comments, "The Constitution of 1787 radically altered the basis of political order and hence changed the world for the better. . . . The Constitution reflects a unique institutional order, a 'Novus Ordo Seculorum,' according to the motto on the U.S. Seal. . . . The 'New Order of the Ages' was a genuine 'first' in the advancement of the science of government. It was boldly an American original which ranks ahead of even such U.S. technological 'firsts' as splitting the atom or landing men on the moon. The new constitutional order also formulated possibly the most difficult government to administer with its ample internal checks and balances, strictly enumerated legislative powers, specified individual rights, limited institutional functions, decentralized authority and representative governance. No action before—and few since—have tried to order their governmental affairs in this manner and then make them work."

14. The undermining has been limited, nevertheless. See Eleanor V. Laudicina, "A Thousand Flowers Blooming: Recent Texts in Public Administration," *Public Administration Review* 47, no. 3 (1987): 275. Laudicina comments (in her review of seven texts), "Some serious gaps remain, however. Among the most glaring is the absence of a comparative perspective. Unless instructors choose to include a supplemental text such as Thornhill's, most students in introductory courses would know only the American model." See also Brach Brown, "The Search for Public Administration," 215. Brown comments, "Fourth, from Wilson to Dahl to the present, the injunction to be cross-cultural and international in perspective and research has been largely ignored."

15. Ferrel Heady, "Issues in Comparative and International Administration," in *Handbook of Public Administration,* ed. Jack Rabin, W. Bartley Hildreth, and Gerald J. Miller (New York: Marcel Dekker, 1989), 501.

16. George M. Guess, "Comparative and International Administration," in *Handbook of Public Administration,* ed. Rabin, Hildreth, and Miller, 477–97.

17. Ibid., 493.

18. Ferrel Heady, "Issues in Comparative and International Administration," 499.

19. Dwight Waldo, *The Enterprise of Public Administration* (Novato, Calif.: Chandler and Sharp, 1980), 10.

20. Ibid.

21. Ibid., 11.

22. See Dwight Waldo's letter in "Waldo on Wilson," *Public Administration Review* 48, no. 4 (1988): 834–35. Waldo adds (p. 834), "For me it is a matter of regret that the history of administration during the four or five millennia of civilization is so underdeveloped or fragmented. Of course, there are good treatments of this or that era, institution, or regime. But

administrative history has not been, in general and as such, a 'field' for the historians. Above all we lack grand comparative-synoptic treatments of this aspect of the human endeavor."

23. Daniel W. Martin, "Déjà Vu: French Antecedents of American Public Administration," *Public Administration Review* 47, no. 4 (1987): 297.

24. Daniel W. Martin, *The Guide to the Foundations of Public Administration* (New York: Marcel Dekker, 1989), 3–24.

25. Martin, "Déjà Vu: French Antecedents of American Public Administration," 298–301.

26. William A. Niskanen, *Bureaucracy and Representative Government* (Chicago: Aldine-Atherton, 1971).

27. Ibid.

28. See Patrick Dunleavy, *Democracy, Bureaucracy and Public Choice* (Hemel Hempstead, U. K.: Harvester Wheatsheaf, 1991).

29. Thurow, *Head to Head*, 260.

30. James Miller, *The Passion of Michel Foucault* (New York: Simon and Schuster, 1993), 299. As Miller evaluates governmentality (p. 301), "The disposition of forces described at the end of [Foucault's] research into 'governmentality' is essentially the same as that described in the pages of *Discipline and Punish*. On the one side stands an all but omnipotent machine of government, meticulously designed to etch the Law into 'the very grain of the individual'; while on the other side stands the solitary human being, its instinct for freedom pushed back, incarcerated, and 'finally able to vent itself only on itself'—just as [Nietzsche's] *Genealogy of Morals* had suggested." See also Arnold I. Davidson, "Ethics as ascetics: Foucault, the history of ethics, and ancient thought," in *The Cambridge Companion to Foucault*, ed. Gary Gutting (New York: Cambridge University Press, 1994), 118–19.

31. See Lynton K. Caldwell, *The Administrative Theories of Hamilton and Jefferson: Their Contribution to Thought on Public Administration* (New York: Russell and Russell, 1964). See also others such as Leonard D. White, *The Jeffersonians: A Study in Administrative History* (New York: Macmillan, 1951). White writes (p. 4), for example, "Apart from disposing of particular cases there is hardly a reference in [Jefferson's] public or private papers to the management of the public business, a silence that contrasts impressively with the constant aphorisms of George Washington and the prolific propositions of Alexander Hamilton on the art and practice of administration."

32. See Alan Williams, *The Police of Paris 1718–1789* (Baton Rouge: Louisiana State University Press, 1979), 8. Williams states that Robert Estienne in his 1539 dictionary defined *police* as the "government of a republic." He quotes Robert Cotgrave as defining the word in his 1611 dictionary as "civil government"; and he writes that Nicolas Delamare stated in 1720 that the word is "still often understood to mean government." Williams comments (pp. 8 and 9), "In each of these definitions . . . police stands as a synonym for governance or, one might say, for the act of control." He adds (p. 8) that during the seventeenth century the term had "begun to assume a more limited sense, one that came gradually to predominate." For an account of the use of the term in England in the eighteenth century, see Stanley H. Palmer, *Police and Protest in England and Ireland 1780–1850* (Cambridge: Cambridge University Press, 1988), 69. Palmer (p. 69) remarks that the "word itself was strange to Englishmen." He continues, "When Englishmen did use the word, they were referring to the general regulation or government, the morals or economy, of a city of country. The French word derived from the Greek *polis*. . . . In England, Adam Smith noted in 1793, the imported French word 'properly signified the policy of civil government, but now means the regulation of the inferior parts of

government, viz.: cleanliness, security (the modern definition), and cheapness or plenty (i.e., the police of grain). William Blackstone in 1765 detected the same trend toward a narrower definition."

33. Cesare Marchese di Beccaria, *Elementi di economia pubblica* (Milan: University of Milan, 1804), 22–23, quoted in Pasquale Pasquino, "Theatrum Politicum: The Genealogy of Capital—Police and the State of Prosperity," in *The Foucault Effect: Studies in Governmentality,* ed. Graham Burchell, Colin Gordon, and Peter Miller (Chicago: University of Chicago Press, 1991), 109.

34. Pasquino, "Theatrum Politicum," 108. According to Pasquino, the "science of police is . . . the culmination of a whole vast literature . . . which traverses the whole of the modern period, accompanying and supporting the construction of the social order we have known since the century of the Enlightenment."

35. The chair in law and police was subsequently held by William Nelson, Robert Nelson, and then James Semple.

36. Charles T. Cullen, "St. George Tucker and Law in Virginia" Ph.D. diss., University of Virginia, 1971), 202.

37. Ibid., 172. For information that George Wythe and St. George Tucker taught a William and Mary course on "Law and Police," see also "Original Records of the Phi Beta Kappa Society," *William and Mary College Quarterly Historical Magazine* 4, no. 2 (1896): 264. I am indebted to a number of my graduate students for alerting me to these and some of the other references on this topic of police.

38. Lester Thurow, *Head to Head,* 261.

39. Additional examples of such blind spots can be given. For example, some might argue that, although there are literatures on both topics and although there has been some limited legislation, those in the United States concerned with crime control have blind spots when it comes to issues such as gun control and the propensity to violence.

40. For example, see Gerald E. Caiden, "Dealing with Administrative Corruption," in *Handbook of Administrative Ethics,* ed. Terry L. Cooper (New York: Marcel Dekker, 1994).

41. See, for example, Paul H. Appleby, *Big Democracy* (New York: Russell and Russell, 1970), 11–27.

42. John A. Rohr, *Ethics for Bureaucrats: An Essay on Law and Values* (New York: Marcel Dekker, 1989).

43. McCurdy, *Public Administration: A Bibliography;* and Aurora Payad, *Organization Behavior in American Public Administration: An Annotated Bibliography* (New York: Garland Publishing, 1986).

44. Knapp Commission to Investigate Allegations of Police Corruption and the City's Anti-Corruption Procedures, *Commission Report* (New York: George Braziller, 1973), 6.

45. Ibid., 68.

46. See Nina Duchaine, *The Literature of Police Corruption* (New York: John Jay Press, 1979). Meanwhile, the same room in which the Knapp Commission held its hearings was the site of a 1993 corruption hearing on the New York City Police Department.

47. Orlando W. Wilson and Roy McLaren, *Police Administration* (New York: McGraw-Hill, 1978).

48. Knapp Commission, *Commission Report,* 68 and 5, respectively.

49. The Dimocks' comment, "[T]here is substantial agreement on the definition of public administration among those who have written basic treatises in the field." Marshall E. Dimock and Gladys O. Dimock, *Public Administration* (New York: Rinehart and Co., 1953), 3.

The Dimocks quote James M. Pfiffner as stating that administration "consists of getting the work of government done by coordinating the efforts of people so that they work together to accomplish their set tasks." In the same paragraph, the Dimocks quote W. F. Willoughby, Leonard D. White, and Luther Gulick.

50. Dennis C. Mueller, *Public Choice II* (New York: Cambridge University Press, 1989), 322–47.

51. Ibid., 344.

52. Ibid.

53. For summaries of the literature on these topics, see Martin, *The Guide to the Foundations of Public Administration,* 37–181.

54. See, for example, Jürgen Habermas, *The Structural Transformation of the Public Sphere: An Inquiry into a Category of Bourgeois Society,* trans. Thomas Burger and Frederick Lawrence (Cambridge: MIT Press, 1989). Robert Denhardt also gives this example in a different context. See Denhardt, *Theories of Public Organization,* 169–70. Denhardt cites Jürgen Habermas, "The Public Sphere," *New German Critique* 3 (1974): 49–55.

55. Habermas, *The Structural Transformation of the Public Sphere,* 195.

56. Paul A. Samuelson and William D. Nordhaus, *Economics,* 13th ed. (New York: McGraw-Hill, 1989).

57. H. George Frederickson, "Finding the Public in Public Administration," in *Executive Leadership in the Public Service,* ed. Robert B. Denhardt and William H. Stewart (Tuscaloosa: University of Alabama Press, 1992), 32.

58. Ibid., 24.

59. H. George Frederickson, "Toward a Theory of the Public for Public Administration," *Administration and Society* 22, no. 4 (1991): 395.

60. For one view of public interest, for example, see Glendon Schubert, *The Public Interest: A Critique of the Theory of a Political Concept* (Glencoe: Free Press of Glencoe, 1960). Schubert writes (p. 223), "It may be somewhat difficult for some readers to accept the conclusion that there is no public-interest theory worthy of the name and that the concept itself is significant primarily as a datum of politics. As such, it may sometimes fulfill a 'hair shirt' function. . . . [I]t may also be nothing more than a label attached indiscriminately to a miscellany of particular compromises of the moment." For another view, see Richard E. Flatham, *The Public Interest: An Essay Concerning the Normative Discourse of Politics* (New York: John Wiley and Sons, 1966). Flatham's study of public interest uses not only what he calls the "standard materials and methods of political study" (p. x) but also ordinary language philosophy.

61. Frederickson, "Toward a Theory of the Public for Public Administration," 408. He writes that the "first requisite for a general theory of the public for public administration is that it must be based on the Constitution." For a discussion of such a one-nation view of public administration, see "The American Element" section in this chapter. In the next paragraph, Frederickson explains, "Because the Constitution is a piece of paper, its legitimacy derives from the act of the sovereign people breathing life into it. . . . The [government] officials are controlled by a principle above majority decisions, that principle being the constitutional order. The primary moral obligation is that the public administrator be the guardian and guarantor of the founding values to every citizen." For a discussion of the moral grip such as is implied here, see the section on "The Ethical Enterprise" in chapter 5.

62. Ibid., 410.

63. Robert L. Heilbroner, *The Nature and Logic of Capitalism* (New York: W. W. Norton, 1985), 123. Heilbroner goes on (pp. 123–24) to write, "Emissaries are exchanged as personnel

move from one sphere to the other; treaties are negotiated as laws; spheres of influence are defined and recognized as policy." Heilbroner agrees (e.g., p. 143) that a realm of business and a realm of the state exist, but he points out (p. 104), "It is . . . a profound mistake to conceive of capitalism as being in essence a 'private' economic system."

64. Warren J. Samuels, "Some Fundamentals of the Economic Role of the State," *Journal of Economic Issues* 23, no. 2 (1989): 432. See also Heilbroner, *The Nature and Logic of Capitalism*, 122. Heilbroner comments, "Laissez faire was never intended to signify that there was to be no 'interference' by government within the economic realm."

65. McCurdy, *Public Administration: A Bibliography.*

66. Martin, *Guide to the Foundations of Public Administration.*

67. Rabin, Hildreth, and Miller, eds., *Handbook of Public Administration.*

68. Michael M. Harmon and Richard T. Mayer, *Organization Theory for Public Administration* (Boston: Little, Brown, 1986).

69. NASPAA Ad Hoc Committee, *Report of the Ad Hoc Committee.*

70. For example, Uveges and Keller name each of the decades since the "foundation." See Joseph A. Uveges and Lawrence F. Keller, "The First One Hundred Years of American Public Administration: The Study and Practice of Public Management in American Life," in *Handbook of Public Administration,* ed. Rabin, Hildreth, and Miller, 1–42.

71. Rachelle A. Dorfman, ed., *Paradigms of Clinical Social Work* (New York: Brunner/Mazel, 1988).

72. See Lionel Robbins, *An Essay on the Nature and Significance of Economic Science* (London: Macmillan, 1962).

73. Hans Falck considers a similar issue in the context of social work. See Hans S. Falck, *American Social Work: Finding the Center* (Richmond: School of Social Work, Virginia Commonwealth University, 1993), 4. Falck makes a distinction between a claim for uniqueness and a claim for centrality, arguing that the proper concern in social work is to find the center. As he writes, "Centrality is defined as any characteristic or set of characteristics which is necessary for something to be what it claims to be; and without which it cannot be it. It refers to core conditions. It is distinguished from claims to uniqueness which by experience tend to compare social work to other professions, and calls attention instead to what makes social work, social work."

74. For another view on whether Wilson is responsible for the politics-administration dichotomy, see Paul P. Van Riper, "The Politics-Administration Dichotomy: Concept or Reality," in *Politics and Administration: Woodrow Wilson and the Study of Public Administration,* ed. Rabin and Bowman, 203–18.

75. Martin distinguishes two versions of the politics-administration dichotomy. He argues that Wilson's ideas progressed "until, by about 1890–91, Wilson had completely abandoned the unique purpose of his dichotomy and had adopted the European version being used by his contemporaries." See Daniel W. Martin, "The Fading Legacy of Woodrow Wilson," *Public Administration Review* 48, no. 2 (1988): 633.

76. Woodrow Wilson, *The Study of Public Administration* (Washington, D.C.: Public Affairs Press, 1955), 13.

77. See Jameson W. Doig, "If I See a Murderous Fellow Sharpening a Knife Cleverly . . . ," in *Politics and Administration: Woodrow Wilson and the Study of Public Administration,* ed. Rabin and Bowman, 177.

78. For example, see Harvey Leibenstein, "Long-Run Welfare Criteria," in *The Public Economy of Urban Communities,* ed. Julius Margolis (Baltimore: Johns Hopkins Press, 1965), 539–57.

Chapter 5. Modernity: Limits of Scientism

1. Kenneth J. Gergen, *Toward Transformation in Social Knowledge* (New York: Springer-Verlag, 1982), 12.

2. Paul Feyerabend, *Against Method* (London: New Left Books, 1975), 51.

3. Simon, *Administrative Behavior,* 253.

4. Gulick and Urwick, eds., *Papers on the Science of Administration.*

5. See Robert K. Whelan, "Data Administration and Research Methods in Public Administration," in *Handbook of Public Administration,* ed. Rabin, Hildreth, and Miller, 658.

6. James L. Perry and Kenneth L. Kramer, "Research Methodology in the 'Public Administration Review,' 1975–1984," *Public Administration Review* 46, no. 3 (1986): 215–26.

7. Robert A. Stallings and James M. Ferris, "Public Administration Research: Work in PAR, 1940–1984," *Public Administration Review* 48, no. 1 (1988): 583–84. Stallings and Ferris explain (p. 583), "Research is still dominated by efforts to conceptualize researchable problems, delineate possible areas of inquiry, and describe objects for study. Little causal analysis or theory testing has taken place over the years, and causal analysis, while significantly more frequent now than in previous decades, comprise only a small proportion of current research. . . . Interestingly, research using the case study approach has been even less frequently reported in the PAR over the years than has that using multivariate statistical methods. It remains to be seen whether the recent resurgence of both types of research is part of a random pattern or the beginning of new research directions in the field."

8. Robert K. Whelan, "Data Administration and Research Methods in Public Administration," 687.

9. Samuel J. Yaeger, "Classic Methods in Public Administration Research," in *Handbook of Public Administration,* ed. Rabin, Hildreth, and Miller, 683–793.

10. For the claim that a consensus does exist in recent developments in the philosophy of science, see Richard Boyd, Philip Gasper, and J. D. Trout, *The Philosophy of Science* (Boston: MIT Press, 1991). The introduction states (p. xiii), "It will be apparent that the new consensus is much more complex than that achieved in late positivism. In part this is simply a reflection of the fact that there is no doctrinal consensus but rather a consensus that identifies three distinct alternative general approaches—scientific realism, neo-Kantian constructivism, and post-positivist empiricism—as the major competitors." For one view of the value of any existence of a consensus, see John O. Wisdom, *Challengeability in Modern Science* (Aldershot, U. K.: Gower, 1987), 16. Wisdom comments, "In my opinion hardly anyone in this scientific age knows what the nature of science is, and this includes not only those who are aware of science through weekly magazines, but also philosophers and scientists themselves. It may come as a surprise to most scientists to hear that there are competing views of the nature of science sponsored by exalted scientists."

11. See The Committee on Standards of Official Conduct, *House Ethics Manual* (Washington, D.C.: USGPO, 1992).

12. Donald N. McCloskey, *The Rhetoric of Economics* (Madison: University of Wisconsin Press, 1985).

13. Simon, *Administrative Behavior,* 253.

14. The Committee on Standards of Official Conduct, *House Ethics Manual,* v.

15. Simon, *Administrative Behavior,* 122.

16. Ibid., 61.

17. Ibid., 45.

18. Ibid., xvii.

19. McCloskey, *The Rhetoric of Economics,* 6.

20. Ibid., 7–8.

21. Ibid.

22. See Simon, *Administrative Behavior,* 43, for his comment on logical positivism.

23. The present section discusses this difficulty in terms of science understood as induction. Wider, and other, arguments are also available. For example, see Wisdom, *Challengeability in Modern Science,* 39. Wisdom writes, "My aim is to show that all three of the standard philosophies of science that have been current in this century fail to solve the problem of the data-theory gap and that observationalism is a fundamental assumption of them all." These three standard philosophies are induction, instrumentalism, and conventionalism. Instrumentalism is "the doctrine that scientific theory is only a tool, only an instrument, for calculation or prediction" (p. 18). Conventionalism regards a scientific theory "as a pattern, drawn not because it reflects reality but because it brings order of some sort into our observations; and this order or pattern is conventional, because, if it does not produce adequate order, we can modify the pattern to make it usable. In effect, theoretical terms on this view have no denotation" (p. 21).

24. John Stuart Mill, *A System of Logic, Ratiocinative and Inductive,* ed. J. M. Robson (Toronto: University of Toronto Press, 1974).

25. Rudolf Carnap, *The Logical Structure of the World,* 2nd ed., trans. Rolf George (Hamburg: Meiner, 1961).

26. David Hume, *A Treatise of Human Nature* (Oxford: Clarendon Press, 1978), 134.

27. Ibid., 89.

28. Karl Popper, *The Logic of Scientific Discovery* (New York: Harper, 1959).

29. Ibid.

30. See R. Ariew, "The Duhem Thesis," *British Journal for the Philosophy of Science* 35 (1984): 313–25.

31. David Oldroyd, *The Arch of Knowledge* (New York: Methuen, 1986), 208.

32. For the grue-bleen paradox, see Nelson Goodman, *Fact, Fiction, and Forecast* (Indianapolis: Bobbs-Merrill, 1965), 63–126. For a discussion of the grue-bleen and three other paradoxes about induction, see Jonathan L. Cohen, *An Introduction to the Philosophy of Induction and Probability* (Oxford: Clarendon Press, 1989), 197–203.

33. For a discussion of the theory-laden character of observations, for example, see Wisdom, *Challengeability in Modern Science,* 71–104.

34. Popper, *The Logic of Scientific Discovery,* 121.

35. Ibid., 82.

36. Ibid., 273.

37. See, for example, Imre Lakatos, "Falsification and the Methodology of Scientific Research Programmes," in *Criticism and the Growth of Knowledge,* ed. Imre Lakatos and Alan Musgrave (Cambridge: Cambridge University Press, 1970), 91–196.

38. Thomas Kuhn, *The Structure of Scientific Revolutions,* 2nd ed. (Chicago: University of Chicago Press, 1970).

39. Feyerabend, *Against Method.*

40. Ibid., 51.

41. Carol W. Lewis, *The Ethics Challenge in Public Service: A Problem-Solving Guide* (San Francisco: Jossey-Bass, 1991), 7.

42. Ibid., 6.

43. Terry L. Cooper, *The Responsible Administrator: An Approach to Ethics for the Administrative Role* (San Francisco: Jossey-Bass, 1990), xii.

44. John Rawls, *A Theory of Justice* (Cambridge: Harvard University Press, 1971).

45. Robert Nozick, *Anarchy, State and Utopia* (New York: Basic Books, 1974).

46. Joyce Hendricks, "Ethics," in *Reflection on Philosophy: Introductory Essays,* ed. Leemon McHenry and Frederick Adams (New York: St. Martin's Press, 1993), 82.

47. Weber, *Methodology of the Social Sciences,* 57.

48. Kathryn G. Denhardt, *The Ethics of Public Service: Resolving Moral Dilemmas in Public Organizations* (New York: Greenwood Press, 1991), viii.

49. For discussion of the relation of reason and value, for example, see E. J. Bond, *Reason and Value* (New York: Cambridge University Press, 1983). As the publisher's blurb on Bond's book puts it, "The relations between reason, motivation and value present problems which, though ancient, remain intractable. If values are objective and rational how can they move us, and if they are dependent on our contingent desires how can they be rational?"

50. Lewis, *The Ethics Challenge in Public Service,* 32. This point is not to deny that she is in good company in her conclusion; see Plato's *Crito,* for example, in Edith Hamilton and Huntington Cairns, *The Collected Dialogues of Plato* (Princeton: Princeton University Press, 1961), 27–39; and many later philosophers.

51. Lewis, *The Ethics Challenge in Public Service,* 35.

52. Ibid., 38.

53. Ibid., 39.

54. Charles Dickens, *Oliver Twist,* chapter 51.

55. Herbert J. Storing, "Slavery and the Moral Foundations of the American Republic," in *The Moral Foundations of the American Republic,* ed. Robert H. Horwitz (Charlottesville: University Press of Virginia, 1977), 222.

56. Denhardt, *The Ethics of Public Service,* 8, 23, and 26. As another example, the model titled "After Cooper" differs from the "After Rohr" model in the following three respects: the phrase "at least to the extent that the decisions are legitimately made at that level of the organization" is added to the first sentence; the phrase "and recognition of the goals of the organization" is added to the third sentence; and the phrase "within the organization" is inserted after the ninth word in the fourth sentence. A key sentence for the present purpose thus reads, "An administrator should be ready to adapt decision standards to these changes, always reflecting a commitment to the core values of our society and recognition of the goals of the organization."

57. Ibid., 35.

58. William L. Morrow, *Public Administration: Politics and the Political System* (New York: Random House, 1975), 13–19.

59. For discussion of such values, see, for example, Mary J. McCormick, *Enduring Values in a Changing Society* (New York: Family Service Association of America, 1975), 13 ff. Yet other values have been discussed; see, for example, Byron E. Shafer, *Is America Different?* (Oxford: Clarendon Press, 1991).

60. Arbitrariness may also be suggested by the fact that values change. For instance, see David K. Hart and William G. Scott, "The Organizational Imperative," *Administration and Society* 7, no. 3 (1975): 259–60. Hart and Scott report, "American values have undergone a massive change. The pluralistic forces that shaped our national character have withered away and the collective strivings of our society have been consolidated into a single social invention: modern organizations. They are vast, complex, technologically based administrative systems which synthesize clusters of resources into rationally functioning wholes. In contemporary America, the needs of organization overwhelm all other considerations, whether those of family, religion, art, science, law, or the individual."

61. Plato's *Euthyphro,* 10a, in *The Collected Dialogues of Plato,* 178. Lane Cooper's translation reads, "Is what is holy holy because the gods approve it, or do they approve it because it is holy?"

62. Ruth Benedict, "Anthropology and the Abnormal," *The Journal of General Psychology* 10 (1934): 59–82.

63. Kolb, *The Critique of Pure Modernity,* 14.

64. James Rachels, *The Elements of Moral Philosophy* (New York: Random House, 1986).

65. For a collection of texts on Verstehen, see Marcello Truzzi, *Verstehen: Subjective Understanding in the Social Sciences* (Reading, Mass.: Addison-Wesley, 1974).

66. Jürgen Habermas, *The Theory of Communicative Action,* vol. 1, *Reason and the Rationalization of Society,* trans. Thomas McCarthy (Boston: Beacon Press, 1984), 108.

67. Alexander Rosenberg, *Philosophy of Social Science* (Boulder: Westview Press, 1988), 15 and 22.

68. Ibid., 28–29.

69. Ibid., 49–50.

70. Ibid., 25.

71. Max Weber, *The Methodology of the Social Sciences,* trans. and ed. Edward A Shils and Henry A. Finch (New York: Free Press, 1949).

Chapter 6. Modernity: Limits of Technologism

1. Waldo, *The Enterprise of Public Administration,* 4–5.

2. George Grant, "Technology and Empire," in *Philosophy and Technology,* ed. Carl Mitcham and Robert Mackey (New York: Free Press, 1972), 189.

3. Herbert A. Simon, *The Sciences of the Artificial* (Cambridge: MIT Press, 1969), 53.

4. Lynn White, "The Historical Roots of Our Ecologic Crisis," in *Philosophy and Technology,* ed. Mitcham and Mackey, 261.

5. Waldo, *The Enterprise of Public Administration,* 4–5.

6. Joseph Agassi, "Shifting from Physical to Social Technology," in *Research in Philosophy and Technology,* vol. 1, ed. Paul T. Durbin (Greenwich, Conn.: JAI Press, 1978), 205.

7. Carl Mitcham, "Types of Technology," in *Research in Philosophy and Technology,* ed. Durbin, 232.

8. Herbert A. Simon, "The Proverbs of Administration," *Public Administration Review* 6, no. 6 (1946): 53–67.

9. Office of Technology Assessment, *Computerized Manufacturing Automation: Employment, Education and the Workplace,* OTA-CIT-235 (Washington, D.C.: USGPO, 1984).

10. Theodore Levitt, "Imitative Imitation," *Harvard Business Review* 64, no. 5 (1966): 64.

11. Lynn G. Johnson, *The High-Technology Connection: Academic/Industrial Cooperation for Economic Growth* (Washington, D.C.: Association for the Study of Higher Education, 1984).

12. See Ann R. Markusen, Peter Hall, and Amy Glasmeier, *High Tech America: The What, How, Where, and Why of the Sunrise Industries* (Boston: Allen and Unwin, 1986), 16.

13. Romesh Diwan and Chandana Chakraborty, *High Technology and International Competitiveness* (New York: Praeger, 1991), 29–30.

14. For example, see John J. Stallard et al., *The Electronic Office: A Guide for Managers* (Homewood, Ill.: Dow Jones-Irwin, 1983); Andrew Doswell, *Office Automation: Context, Experience and Future* (Chichester, U. K.: John Wiley, 1990); Dimitris N. Chorafas, *Office Automation: The Productivity Challenge* (Englewood Cliffs, N.J.: Prentice-Hall, 1982).

15. Randy J. Goldfield, *Office Information Technology* (New York: Quorum Books, 1990), 5–6.

16. See Michael M. Crow and R. F. Shangraw, "Public Administration as a Design Science," *Public Administration Review* 49, no. 2 (1989): 153. Shangraw and Crow claim, "While considerable support exists in the literature for the broad notion that public administration comprises design activities, no direct applications of Simon's model appear to exist in public administration." Simon's model is that indicated in Simon, *The Sciences of the Artificial.*

17. Alice Rivlin, *Systematic Thinking for Social Action* (Washington, D.C.: The Brookings Institution, 1972).

18. For the same argument, see David J. Farmer, *Crime Control: The Use and Misuse of Police Resources* (New York: Plenum Press, 1984).

19. For a discussion of the practitioner as theorist, see Denhardt, *Theories of Public Organization,* 176–97.

20. Mitcham, "Types of Technology," 258.

21. Woodrow Wilson, "The Study of Administration," *Political Science Quarterly* 2 (July 1887): 197–222. The Pendleton Civil Service Act was enacted in 1883.

22. Joseph A. Uveges and Lawrence F. Keller, "The First One Hundred Years of American Public Administration: The Study and Practice of Public Management in American Life," in *Handbook of Public Administration,* ed. Rabin, Hildreth, and Miller, 1–42.

23. Mario Bunge, "Epistemology and Methodology III," *Treatise on Basic Philosophy,* vol. 7 (Dordrecht, The Netherlands: R. Reidel, 1985), 220.

24. Lewis Mumford, "Technics and the Nature of Man," in *Philosophy and Technology,* ed. Mitcham and Mackay, 77.

25. Bunge, *Epistemology and Technology,* 1.

26. C. West Churchman, *The Systems Approach* (New York: Dell, 1983).

27. Daniel Katz and Robert L. Kahn, *The Social Psychology of Organizations* (New York: John Wiley, 1966).

28. Bunge, *Epistemology and Technology,* 275.

29. Ibid., 277.

30. Ibid., 276.

31. Daniel Wren, *The Evolution of Management Thought,* 3rd ed. (New York: John Wiley and Sons, 1987).

32. Ibid., 426–27.

33. Conceptualizing public administration as a design science does not require understanding public administration as a machine. Public administration could also be understood as an organism, for example. On distinguishing between a machine and an organism, see Luther Gulick, "The Metaphors of Public Administration," *Public Administration Quarterly* 7, no. 3 (1984): 377. Gulick observes, "To look on government as a machine was once a useful and constructive posture. That was over 50 years ago. Under present conditions, the analogy is both inaccurate and dangerous." He prefers the organism metaphor. See also James L. Garnett, "Operationalizing the Constitution via Administrative Reorganization: Oilcans, Trends and Proverbs," *Public Administration Review* 47, no. 1 (1987): 42. As Garnett points out, "[S]ome consider reorganization more like gardening than engineering or architecture. 'Like gardening, reorganization is not an act, but a process, a continuing job. And like gardening, reorganization is work whose benefits may largely accrue to one's successors.' (Szanton, 1981) Even if the organic view of reorganizing is more appropriate than the mechanistic, greater intentionality promises to yield more benefits to future successors. Gardens need not grow like topsy. Perhaps reorganizers should be emulating genetic engineering to produce new hy-

brids designed for special tasks and needs." The Szanton citation is to Peter Szanton, "So You Want to Reorganize the Government," in *Federal Reorganization: What Have We Learned?* ed. Peter Szanton (Chatham, N.J.: Chatham House, 1981), 24.

34. Frederick W. Taylor, *The Principles of Scientific Management* (New York: Harper, 1911), 130.

35. Mumford, "Technics and the Nature of Man," 81.

36. See Louis Gawthrop, *Public Sector Management, Systems, and Ethics* (Bloomington: Indiana University Press, 1984), 7.

37. Kenneth J. Arrow, *Social Choice and Individual Values,* rev. ed. (New York: John Wiley and Sons, 1963).

38. Ibid., 19.

39. See Kitchen's account of the dangers of the interdisciplinary approach to theory construction in cognitive science in Patricia Kitchen, *Freud's Dream* (Cambridge: MIT Press, 1992).

40. Simon, *The Sciences of the Artificial,* x.

41. A. K. Sen, "Liberty, Unanimity and Rights, *Economica* 43 (August 1976): 217.

42. Simon, *The Sciences of the Artificial.*

43. Simon, *Administrative Behavior,* 252.

44. See Simon, *The Sciences of the Artificial,* x. As he puts it, his "writing on administration, particularly in *Administrative Behavior* and Part IV of *Models of Man,* has sought to answer those questions by showing that the empirical content of the phenomena, the necessities that rise above the contingencies, stems from the inabilities of the behavioral system to adapt perfectly to its environment—from the limits of rationality."

45. Ibid., 52. As Simon writes, "A man, viewed as a behaving system, is quite simple. The apparent complexity of his behavior over time is largely a reflection of the complexity of the environment in which he finds himself."

46. Ibid., 53.

47. Pope Pius XII, *Modern Technology and Peace,* Christmas Message of Pope Pius XII of December 24, 1953 (Washington, D.C.: National Catholic Welfare Conference, 1954), nos. 6–9, note 12.

48. Nicholas Berdyaev, *The Bourgeois Mind and Other Essays* (New York: Sheed and Ward, 1934).

Chapter 7. Modernity: Limits of Enterprise

1. Michael Laver, *The Politics of Private Desires* (New York: Penguin Books, 1981), 72.

2. The Committee on Standards of Official Conduct, *House Ethics Manual,* v.

3. Weber, *The Protestant Ethic and the Spirit of Capitalism,* 17.

4. Ibid., 17. Weber goes on to state, "We will define a capitalistic economic action as one which rests on the expectation of profit by utilization of opportunities for exchange, that is on (formally) peaceful chances of profit."

5. R. H. Tawney, Foreword, in *The Protestant Ethic and the Spirit of Capitalism,* 1, quoting Max Weber, *General Economic History,* trans. Frank H. Knight (Glencoe: Free Press, 1950), 355–56.

6. For example, Gordon Tullock, "Public Choice in Practice," in *Collective Decision Making: Applications from Public Choice Theory,* ed. C. S. Russell (Baltimore: Johns Hopkins University Press, 1979).

7. The Committee on Standards of Official Conduct, *House Ethics Manual,* v.

8. Ibid.

9. Adam Smith, *Inquiry into the Nature and Causes of the Wealth of Nations* (New York: Oxford University Press, 1993). The book was first published in 1776.

10. Nassau Senior, *An Outline of the Science of Political Economy* (New York: A. M. Kelley, 1965). The book was first published in 1836.

11. Smith, *Wealth of Nations.*

12. Lloyd G. Nigro and William D. Richardson, "Self-Interest Properly Understood: The American Character and Public Administration," *Administration and Society* 19, no. 2 (1987): 166.

13. Ibid., 166.

14. Alexis de Tocqueville, *Democracy in America,* ed. J. P. Mayer (Garden City, N.Y.: Doubleday, 1969), 527.

15. Farmer, *Crime Control,* 85–119.

16. As noted in ibid., 102–3.

17. Willard V. Quine, *Quiddities: An Intermittently Philosophical Dictionary* (Cambridge: Harvard University Press, 1987), 3–4.

18. Ibid., 4.

19. Ibid.

20. Ibid.

21. Ibid., 5.

22. Ibid.

23. See Luther Gulick, "The Metaphors of Public Administration," *Public Administration Quarterly* 44, no. 6 (1984): 374. Gulick writes, " 'Businesslike' is the next metaphor designed to take in the unsophisticated. The business universe at this point in history is designed to generate profits and power for the owners and top managers of economic enterprises on the basis of a very short time span. Since the nation state aims at a span of centuries and drives not for economic profits for the owners of capital but at the life, liberty, and happiness of all its people, the fundamental drive should be not to be 'businesslike' but to make business a little more 'government like.' It is desirable to be efficient in the honest business sense but not at the cost of the welfare of the people."

24. For example, see Samuelson and Nordhaus, *Economics.*

25. Anthony Downs, *Inside Bureaucracy* (Boston: Little, Brown, 1967).

26. Niskanen, *Bureaucracy and Representative Government.*

27. Jean-Luc Migué and Gérard Bélanger, "Toward a General Theory of Managerial Discretion," *Public Choice* 17, no. 2 (1974): 27–43. Niskanen himself comments that the Migué-Bélanger model and his own theory should be regarded as "special theories of bureaucratic behavior." See William A. Niskanen, "Comment," *Public Choice* 17, no. 2 (1974): 43.

28. For a summary, see Mueller, *Public Choice II,* chap. 14; and Dunleavy, *Democracy, Bureaucracy and Public Choice.*

29. Heilbroner, *The Nature and Logic of Capitalism,* 36. Chapter 2 of Heilbroner's book includes a discussion of the connection of the "drive to amass capital" with "power," an entity which he characterizes (p. 46) as "not a well-understood aspect of human society." Heilbroner also analyzes the nature of capital, and two of his characterizations are used in the preceding sentence in the text.

30. Martin Landau, "Redundancy, Rationality, and the Problem of Duplication and Overlap," *Public Administration Review* 29, no. 4 (1969): 346–58.

31. Ibid., 348.

32. Ibid., 358.

33. Ibid., 338.

34. Allan W. Lerner, "There Is More Than One Way To Be Redundant," *Administration and Society* 18, no. 3 (1986): 334–59.

35. Landau, "Redundancy, Rationality, and the Problem of Duplication and Overlap," 340.

36. Ibid., 338.

37. Ibid.

38. Samuelson and Nordhaus, *Economics,* 978; see also Landau, "Redundancy, Rationality, and the Problem of Duplication and Overlap," 586–90.

39. Allen Buchanan, "Efficiency Arguments For and Against the Market," in John Arthur and William H. Shaw, *Justice and Economic Distribution,* 2nd ed. (Englewood Cliffs, N.J.: Prentice Hall, 1991), 184–85. Buchanan describes transaction costs as including "costs of bringing goods and services together for exchange, and costs of reaching agreement for exchange, for example, costs of formulating mutually acceptable contracts, and costs of information about potential offers to buy and sell." He describes perfect competition as existing where "no buyer or seller can influence prices by his own independent actions and there is complete freedom to enter and exit the market."

40. Rhoads, *The Economist's View of the World,* 64.

41. Roger Weiss, *The Economic System* (New York: Random House, 1969).

42. Samuelson and Nordhaus, *Economics,* 43–48.

43. For an account of New Classical Macroeconomics, see, for instance, Bennett T. McCallum, "New Classical Macroeconomics: A Sympathetic Account," in *The State of Macroeconomics,* ed. Seppo Honkapohja (Oxford: Basil Blackwell, 1990), 3–32. As Bennett summarizes it (p. 3), "The essential ingredients of New Classical (NC) macroeconomics are (1) adoption of the equilibrium approach to model construction, (2) acceptance of the natural rate hypothesis, (3) a belief in the superiority of policy based on rules, and (4) a strong skepticism regarding the empirical relevance for macroeconomic issues of rational bubble phenomena."

44. Jean-Michel Grandmont, "Keynesian Issues and Economic Theory," in *The State of Macroeconomics,* ed. Honkapohja, 46.

45. See Robert Nozick, "Distributive Justice," *Anarchy, State and Utopia* (New York: Basic Books, 1974), chap. 7.

46. See Gerald A. Cohen, "Labor, Leisure, and a Distinctive Contradiction of Advanced Capitalism," in *Markets and Morals,* ed. Gerald Dworkin, Gordon Bermant and Peter G. Brown (Washington, D.C.: Hemisphere Publishing Co., 1977), 107–36.

47. Gordon Tullock, "Public Choice in Practice."

48. Further distinctions can be drawn. For instance, Kolderie distinguishes between "the privatization of a primary policy decision of government to provide a service" and "the privatization of a secondary decision to produce a service." He considers that the former risks social equity. See Ted Kolderie, "Two Different Concepts of Privatization," *Public Administration Review* 46, no. 4 (1986): 285–91.

49. For a spoof catalog, see Christopher Cerf and Henry Beard, *The Pentagon Catalog* (New York: Workman, 1986).

50. See David E. Osborne and Ted Gaebler, *Reinventing Government: How the Entrepreneurial Spirit is Transforming the Public Sector* (Reading, Mass.: Addison-Wesley, 1992).

51. For example, see Emanuel S. Savas, *Privatization: The Key to Better Government*

(Chatham, N.J.: Chatham House Publishers, 1987); and Harry Hatry, *A Review of Private Approaches for Delivery of Public Services* (Washington, D.C.: Urban Institute Press, 1983).

52. Matthew Holden, " 'Imperialism' in Bureaucracy," *The American Political Science Review* 60, no. 4 (1966): 943–51.

53. Ibid., 950.

54. Vincent Ostrom, *Intellectual Crisis in American Public Administration* (University: University of Alabama Press, 1973).

55. Rabin, Hildreth, and Miller, eds., *Handbook of Public Administration.*

56. Ostrom, *Intellectual Crisis in American Public Administration,* 19.

57. Ibid.

58. Samuelson and Nordhaus, *Economics,* 980–81.

59. Paul A. Samuelson, "The Pure Theory of Public Expenditure," *Review of Economics and Statistics* 36 (November 1954): 387–89.

60. James M. Buchanan, *The Supply and Demand of Public Goods* (Chicago: Rand McNally, 1968), 171–90.

61. Albert Breton, *The Economic Theory of Representative Government* (Chicago: Aldine, 1974).

62. Gordon Tullock, "Public Choice in Practice."

63. Robert Abrams, *Foundations of Political Analysis: An Introduction to the Theory of Collective Choice* (New York: Columbia University Press, 1980).

64. Francis Bacon, *The New Organon and Related Writings* (New York: Bobbs-Merrill Co., 1960), 93.

65. John O. Wisdom, *Philosophy of the Social Sciences: A Metascientific Introduction* (Aldershot U. K.: Avebury, 1986).

66. Alec Cairncross, "Richard T. Ely Lecture," *American Economic Review* 75, no. 2 (1985): 1.

67. Alec Cairncross, *Essays in Economic Management* (London: George Allen and Unwin, 1971), quoted in Cairncross, "Richard T. Ely Lecture," 1.

68. Tullock, "Public Choice in Practice."

69. James M. Buchanan and Gordon Tullock, *The Calculus of Consent* (Ann Arbor: University of Michigan Press, 1962).

70. Tullock, "Public Choice in Practice."

71. Morris P. Fiorina, "Comment," in *Collective Decision Making,* ed. Russell.

72. Russell, ed., *Collective Decision Making.*

73. E. A. Thompson, "A Pareto Optimal Group Decision Process," in *Papers on Non-Market Decision Making,* ed. G. Tullock (Charlottesville: University of Virginia, 1966), 133–40.

74. Arrow, *Social Choice and Individual Values.*

75. Samuelson and Nordhaus, *Economics,* 768.

76. Julie A. Nelson, "Gender, Metaphor, and the Definition of Economics," *Economics and Philosophy* 8, no. 1 (1992): 107.

77. Wisdom, *Philosophy of the Social Sciences 1,* 129.

78. Nelson, "Gender, Metaphor, and the Definition of Economics," 109.

79. Frank H. Knight, "Ethics and the Economic Interpretation," *The Quarterly Journal of Economics* 36 (1922): 454–81; reprinted in *The Ethics of Competition and Other Essays,* ed. Milton Friedman, Homer Jones, George Stigler, and Allen Wallis (Freeport: Books for Libraries Press, 1935).

80. Frank H. Knight, "The Ethics of Competition," *The Quarterly Journal of Economics* 37 (1923): 579; reprinted in *The Ethics of Competition,* ed. Friedman et al., 41.

Chapter 8. Modernity: Limits of Hermeneutics

1. Jürgen Habermas, "Philosophy as Stand-In and Interpreter," in *After Philosophy: End or Transformation?,* ed. Kenneth Baynes, James Bohman, and Thomas McCarthy (Cambridge: MIT Press, 1987), 313.

2. Carl Jung, "Two Essays on Analytical Psychology," *Collected Works,* vol. 7 (New York: Pantheon Press, 1953), 188.

3. Thomas McCarthy, Translator's Introduction, in Habermas, *The Theory of Communicative Action,* xxviii.

4. For example, see Madison, *The Hermeneutics of Postmodernity: Figures and Themes.* The complexity of such issues is suggested in the fact that it has been argued that antifoundationalism has been a major theme from the early stages of Western philosophy. For example, see Tom Rockmore and Beth J. Singer, *Antifoundationalism Old and New* (Philadelphia: Temple University Press, 1992).

5. Robert B. Denhardt, *In the Shadow of Organization* (Lawrence: Regents Press of Kansas, 1981). See the exchange between Kramer and Denhardt on the book: Robert Kramer, "In the Shadow of Death: Robert Denhardt's Theology of Organizational Life," *Administration and Society* 21, no. 3 (1989): 357–79, and Robert B. Denhardt, "Beyond the Shadow," *Administration and Society* 21, no. 3 (1989): 380–83. Resistances can be expected to analyses at this depth. Some might classify comments both on "administration as ritual" and comments on "administration as requiring 'specific attention not only to economics and psychology but also to the relevant aspects of human biology' " as in an intermediate position in terms of analysis level and as more helpful. For the former, see Charles T. Goodsell, "Administration as Ritual," *Public Administration Review* 49, no. 2 (1989): 161–66. For the latter, see Elliot White and Joseph Losco, *Biology and Bureaucracy: Public Administration and Public Policy from the Perspective of Evolutionary, Genetic and Neurobiological Theory* (Lanham, Md.: University Press of America, 1986). The preface of White and Losco's book opens with Gulick's statement that "the new public administration, as a field of knowledge and operation, now requires specific attention not only to economics and psychology, but also to the relevant aspects of human biology."

6. For an account of Hegel's concept of bureaucracy, see M. W. Jackson, "Bureaucracy in Hegel's Political Theory," *Administration and Society* 18, no. 2 (1986): 139–57. For instance, Jackson offers his view (p. 148) that Weber "had a ten-point checklist of the criteria of bureaucracy. For seven of these ten points there is a counterpart in Hegel."

7. Appleby, *Big Democracy.*

8. Harlan Cleveland, "Theses of a New Revolution: The Social Fallout of Science 300 Years After Newton," *Public Administration Review* 48, no. 3 (1988): 685.

9. Ibid.

10. Jay D. White, "On the Growth of Knowledge in Public Administration," *Public Administration Review* 46, no. 1 (1986): 15–24.

11. Howard E. McCurdy and Robert E. Cleary, "A Call for Appropriate Methods," *Public Administration Review* 44, no. 6 (1984): 553–54.

12. White, "On the Growth of Knowledge in Public Administration," 15.

13. Ibid., 22.

14. Wamsley, et al., *Refounding Public Administration,* 20.

15. Ibid., 47–48.

16. Jay D. White, "Response to Michael Harmon," *Public Administration Review* 49, no. 2 (1989).

17. Ibid., 150.

18. Robert B. Denhardt, "Toward a Critical Theory of Public Organization," *Public Administration Review* 41, no. 6 (1981): 628–35.

19. William N. Dunn and Bahman Fozouni, *Toward a Critical Administrative Theory* (Beverly Hills: Sage, 1976).

20. Ralph P. Hummel, *The Bureaucratic Experience*, 3rd ed. (New York: St. Martin's Press, 1987).

21. B. L. Catron and Michael M. Harmon, "Action Theory in Practice: Toward Theory Without Conspiracy," *Public Administration Review* 41, no. 5 (1981): 535–41.

22. Michael M. Harmon, *Action Theory for Public Administration* (New York: Longman, 1981).

23. Jay D. White, "Action Theory and Literary Interpretation," *Administration and Society* 19 (1987): 346–66.

24. White, "On the Growth of Knowledge in Public Administration," 15–24.

25. Denhardt, *Theories of Public Organization.*

26. Michael A. Diamond, "Bureaucracy as Externalized Self-System: A View from the Psychological Interior," *Administration and Society* 16 (August 1984): 195–214.

27. Donald Schon, *The Reflexive Practitioner* (New York: Basic Books, 1983).

28. Chris Argyris and Donald Schon, *Organizational Learning* (Reading, Mass.: Addison-Wesley, 1978).

29. Arthur Felts, "Organizational Communication: A Critical Perspective," *Administration and Society* 23, no. 4 (1992): 495–513.

30. Ann-Marie Rizzo and Dolores Brosnan, "Critical Theory and Communication Dysfunction: The Case of Sexually Ambiguous Behavior," *Administration and Society* 22, no. 1 (1990): 66–85.

31. White, "Action Theory and Literary Interpretation."

32. Harmon and Mayer, *Organization Theory for Public Administration.*

33. *Public Administration Quarterly* 14, no. 1 (1990).

34. Denhardt, *Theories of Public Organization.*

35. Ibid., 163.

36. For example, see Robert Denhardt, "Toward a Critical Theory of Public Organization," 628–35.

37. John Forester, "Critical Theory and Organizational Analysis," in *Beyond Managerial Method: Strategies for Social Research,* ed. Gareth Morgan (Beverly Hills: Sage, 1983).

38. Robert Denhardt and Kathryn G. Denhardt, "Public Administration and the Critique of Domination," *Administration and Society* 11, no. 2 (1979): 107–20; Dunn and Fozouni, *Toward a Critical Administrative Theory;* and Hummel, *The Bureaucratic Experience.*

39. Denhardt, *Theories of Public Organization,* 171.

40. Dunn and Fozouni, *Toward a Critical Administrative Theory.*

41. Hummel, *The Bureaucratic Experience.*

42. Argyris and Schon, *Organizational Learning: A Theory of Action Perspective.*

43. Denhardt, *In the Shadow of Organization.*

44. Harmon, *Action Theory for Public Administration,* 4–7 and passim.

45. Ibid., 4–7.

46. Hummel, *The Bureaucratic Experience*, viii.

47. Ibid.

48. Ibid., vii–viii.

49. Ibid., 181.

50. Ibid., 200.

51. Harmon and Mayer, *Organization Theory for Public Administration*, 302.

52. *Public Administration Quarterly* 14, no. 1 (1990).

53. Ralph Hummel, "The Rise of Managerial Realism: Applied Phenomenology—A Symposium," *Public Administration Quarterly* 14, no. 1 (1990): 4.

54. Ibid., 5–6.

55. Ibid., 5.

56. Michael Harmon, "Applied Phenomenology and Organization," *Public Administration Quarterly* 14, no. 1 (1990): 10.

57. Ibid., 11.

58. Harmon, "Applied Phenomenology and Organization"; Jong S. Jun and William Bruce Storm, "Social Design in Public Problem Solving"; Michael A. Diamond, "Psychological Phenomenology and Organization Analysis"; Ralph P. Hummel, "Managing and the Crisis of Work in the Public Sector"; John Forester, "No Planning or Administration without Phenomenology"; Sandra Fish, "Interpretive Research: A New Way of Viewing Organizational Communication"; Jay D. White, "Phenomenology and Organizational Development," *Public Administration Quarterly* 14, no. 1 (1990).

59. Harmon and Mayer, *Organization Theory for Public Administration*, 292.

60. Ibid.

61. Ibid., 293, quoting Richard Bernstein, *The Restructuring of Social and Political Theory* (Philadelphia: University of Pennsylvania Press, 1978), 138.

62. Harmon and Mayer, *Organization Theory for Public Administration*, 295.

63. Ibid., 296.

64. Ibid., 300, quoting David Silverman, *The Theory of Organisations: A Sociological Framework* (New York: Basic Books, 1971), 126–27.

65. Harmon and Mayer, *Organization Theory for Public Administration*, 306. As Harmon and Mayer report, the expression was coined by Gibson Winter, *Elements for a Social Ethic: The Role of Social Science in Public Policy* (New York: Macmillan, 1966).

66. Denhardt, *Theories of Public Organization*, 171.

67. Ibid.

68. Ibid., 173.

69. Denhardt and Denhardt, "Public Administration and the Critique of Domination," 107–20.

70. Ibid., 111.

71. In Farganis, "A Preface to Critical Theory," *Theory and Society* 2 (1975): 483–508.

72. Denhardt and Denhardt, "Public Administration and the Critique of Domination," 119.

73. Jürgen Habermas, *The Theory of Communicative Action*, vol. 1 and vol. 2, *Lifeworld and System: A Critique of Functionalist Reason*, trans. Thomas McCarthy (Boston: Beacon Press, 1987).

74. Thomas McCarthy, Translator's Introduction, in Habermas, *The Theory of Communicative Action*, vol. 1, x.

75. Habermas, *The Theory of Communicative Action*, vol. 1, 288.

76. See Nietzsche's image of philosophizing with a hammer. For example, see Friedrich Nietzsche, *The Will to Power,* 80. Nietzsche writes, "We hold in reserve many types of philosophy which need to be taught: possibly, the pessimistic type, as a hammer."

77. Michel Foucault, *The Order of Things: An Archaeology of the Human Sciences,* trans. Alan Sheridan-Smith (New York: Random House, 1966).

78. Simon, *Administrative Behavior,* 79.

79. Ibid., 80.

80. For example, see Horkheimer and Adorno, *Dialect of Enlightenment* (New York: Seabury, 1972). For an example of another critique, see Hans S. Falck, *Social Work: The Membership Perspective* (New York: Springer, 1988).

81. Sigmund Freud, *Beyond the Pleasure Principle* (New York: W. W. Norton, 1961).

82. The translation of Trieb presents difficulties. Ernest Jones translates an approximate definition from Freud's *Three Essays of the Theory of Sexuality* as follows: "By an 'instinct' (Trieb) is provisionally to be understood as the psychic representative of an endosomatic, continuously flowing source of stimulation, as contrasted with a stimulus. . . . The concept of instinct is thus one of those lying on the frontier between the mental and physical." Ernest Jones, *The Life and Work of Sigmund Freud,* vol. 2 (New York: Basic Books, 1955), 317. Jones notes on the same page, "The German word Trieb is less committal than the English word 'Instinct,' which definitely implies an inborn and inherited character."

83. Jean Laplanche and Jean Baptiste Pontalis, *The Language of Psycho-Analysis* (New York: W. W. Norton, 1973), 97.

84. Jean Laplanche, *Life and Death in Psychoanalysis* (Baltimore: Johns Hopkins University Press, 1976), 124.

85. Paul Ricoeur, *Freud and Philosophy: An Essay on Interpretation* (New Haven: Yale University Press, 1970), 290.

86. Calvin S. Hall and Gardner Lindzey, *Theories of Personality* (New York: John Wiley, 1957). This paragraph follows the account provided by Hall and Lindzey.

87. Here are some ideas that one class of administrators gave me on this point. Perhaps an agency's collective unconscious can go some way to explain, for example, what we do in coffee breaks, how we talk in the office, how we relate to superiors and to other organizations, and how decision making can result from the organization's previous day's residue. Perhaps it can help to explain the hidden agenda of employees and subcultures, hiring and promotion decisions, the organization's purposes, how the unconscious of the founder still dominates present action, and how organizations will remain true to their pasts. Perhaps it can be used to help managers, for example, in finding ways of allowing employees to let their unconscious processes work on problems.

88. For example, see Michael A. Diamond, "Bureaucracy as Externalized Self-System: A View from the Psychological Interior," *Administration and Society* 16, no. 2 (1984): 195–214; Michael A. Diamond, "Organizational Identity: A Psychological Exploration of Organizational Meaning," *Administration and Society* 20, no. 2 (1988): 166–90; Julianne Mahler, "The Quest for Organizational Meaning: Identifying and Interpreting the Symbolism in Organizational Stories," *Administration and Society* 20, no. 3 (1988): 344–68; Larry Hubbell, "Four Archetypal Shadows: A Look at the Dark Side of Public Organizations," *Administration and Society* 24, no. 2 (1992): 205–23.

89. Hubbell, "Four Archetypal Shadows," 205–23.

90. For a comment on the psychoanalytic organizational literature, for example, see Howell S. Baum, *The Invisible Bureaucracy: The Unconscious in Organizational Problem Solving* (New York: Oxford University Press, 1987). Baum writes (pp. 8–9), "Writers agree that

individual unconscious processes affect actions in organizations and the actions of organizations. However, analysts disagree about the extent to which individual activity in organizations is simply an expression of individual personality and the extent to which it is a creation of the organization. Those who believe that organizations elicit original behavior disagree about whether the organization is a unique social setting or whether what is seen in organizations is generic."

Chapter 9. Postmodernity: The Dialect

1. Jean-François Lyotard, "Interview," *Theory, Culture and Society* 5, no. 2/3 (1988): 302.

2. Lichtenberg, quoted by Theodor W. Adorno, *Against Epistemology: A Metacritique,* trans. Willis Domingo (Cambridge: MIT Press, 1983), 41.

3. Vattimo writes, "Much is said about postmodernity nowadays. So much, in fact, that it has become almost obligatory to distance oneself from the notion, to see it as a fad and to insist on its having been overcome. It is my belief, however, that the term 'postmodern' has a meaning." Gianni Vattimo, *The Transparent Society,* trans. David Webb (Baltimore: Johns Hopkins Press, 1992), 1.

4. Richard Rorty, *Consequences of Pragmatism* (Minneapolis: University of Minneapolis Press, 1982), 98.

5. Jacques Derrida, *Positions,* trans. Alan Bass (Chicago: University of Chicago Press, 1981), 14.

6. Varieties of skepticism occur if only because there are various types of knowledge. For a discussion of sources and forms of relativism, see, for example, Martin Hollis and Steven Lukes, *Rationality and Relativism* (Cambridge: MIT Press, 1982).

7. See Plato's *Theatetus.* As Plato represents Protagoras' position, "[E]ach one of us is a measure of what is and of what is not; but there is all the difference in the world between one man and another just in the very fact that what is and appears to one is different from what is and appears to the other."

8. For an argument that the skeptic can resist refutation if she is determined to do so, see, for example, Nicholas Rescher, *Scepticism: A Critical Reappraisal* (Totowa, N.J.: Rowman and Littlefield, 1980). One way is to deny the possibility of the kind of knowledge needed to develop premises for counterarguments. Rescher writes, "Scepticism is, in a way, irrefutable, at any rate in the sense that the standard and straightforward sorts of refutatory argumentation cannot successfully be deployed against it. Discursive argumentation standardly proceeds from premises and it is clear that scepticism cannot be refuted by counter-argumentation proceeding along such standard lines" (p. 7). He also quotes David Hume's comment, "This sceptical doubt, both with respect to reason and the senses, is a malady, which can never be radically cur'd" (David Hume, *A Treatise of Human Nature,* Book I, Part IV, Sect. II). Rescher argues that, even if radical skepticism is rejected, skepticism about the completeness, correctness, and consistency of our body of knowledge constitutes "elements of truth in skepticism" (pp. 231–50).

9. Thomas S. Kuhn, "Reflections on My Critics," in *Criticism and the Growth of Knowledge,* ed. Imre Lakatos and Alan Musgrave (New York: Cambridge University Press, 1970), 231–78. As noted in chapter 5, Kuhn's position changed in the second edition of *The Structure of Scientific Revolutions.*

10. Vattimo, *The Transparent Society,* 1. Vattimo's writings also argue that disadvantages exist. For example, see Gianni Vattimo, "The End of History," in *Zeitgeist in Babel: The Post-*

modernist Controversy, ed. Ingeborg Hoesterey (Bloomington: Indiana University Press, 1991), 133. Vattimo comments, "The incapacity of postmodern thought to offer a rational critique of the present conditions of society, and, more generally, to provide a basis for any rational discussion, which is the main reason why Habermas disagrees with Lyotard, is clearly related to the fact that, in postmodern thought, the métarécits have been dissolved. The postmodern mind, in the view of Habermas, is incapable of providing the basis for a rational critique because it no longer believes in a possible rational course of history—that is because, for it, the métarécits have been confuted."

11. Ibid., 24.

12. Ibid., 3.

13. Ibid., 39.

14. Ibid.

15. Ibid., 42.

16. Frederic Jameson, "Postmodernism, or the Cultural Logic of Late Capitalism," *New Left Review,* no. 146 (1984): 53–93.

17. Chantal Mouffe, "Towards a Theoretical Interpretation of 'New Social Movements,' " in *Rethinking Marx,* ed. Sakari Hanninen and Leena Paldan (New York: International General/IMMRC, 19), 139–43.

18. David Ray Griffin, et al., *Founders of Constructive Postmodern Philosophy* (Albany: SUNY, 1993), viii.

19. Roger J. Bulger, *Technology, Bureaucracy, and Healing in America: A Postmodern Paradigm* (Iowa City: University of Iowa Press, 1988).

20. Griffin et al., *Founders of Constructive Postmodern Philosophy,* ix.

21. See Charles Jencks, *What Is Post-Modernism?* (New York: St. Martin's Press, 1986). Jencks holds that this combination can be seen in the varieties of postmodern art. See also Charles Jencks, *Post-Modernism: The New Classicism in Art and Architecture* (New York: Rizzoli, 1987), 40. As he writes, "In all the five streams [of painting] we will discuss, classical motifs are mixed with present day elements and filtered through a sensibility which is responsive to the realities of our time. It is this mixture which makes these artists Post-Modern Classicists rather than revivalists or Canonic Classicists." The five streams are labeled "metaphysical classical," "narrative classical," "allegorical classical," "realist classical," and "classical sensibility." Further, Jencks writes of four traditions of postmodern classical architecture. These are fundamentalist classicism, revivalist classicism, urbanist classicism, and eclectic classicism. Including the arts in a discussion of postmodernity adds to the complication not only because of these varieties but also because postmodernism in artistic and literary circles includes "a specific reaction against 'modernism' in the narrow sense of a movement in artistic-literary circles in the late nineteenth and early twentieth centuries" (p. viii).

22. Hal Foster, "Postmodernism: A Preface," in *The Anti-Aesthetic: Essays on Postmodern Culture,* ed. Foster, xi–xii.

23. Boris Frankel, *The Post-Industrial Utopians* (Cambridge: Polity, 1987), 10.

24. Félix Guitarri, "The Postmodern Dead End," *Flash Art,* no. 128 (May–June 1986): 40–41.

25. See Arnold Toynbee, *A Study of History,* vol. 8 (London: Oxford University Press, 1954), 338.

26. Charles Sanders Peirce, William James, Henri Bergson, Alfred North Whitehead, and Charles Hartshorne have been described as the founders of constructive postmodern philosophy. See Griffin et al., *Founders of Constructive Postmodern Philosophy.*

27. Madison, *The Hermeneutics of Postmodernity: Figures and Themes,* xi.

28. See Irving Howe, *Decline of the New* (New York: Harcourt, Brace and World, 1970).

29. Steven Best and Douglas Kellner, *Postmodern Theory* (New York: Guilford Press, 1991).

30. Jean-François Lyotard, "Interview," 302.

31. See Heinrich F. Plett, "Intertextualities," in *Intertextuality* (New York: Walter de Gruyter, 1991), 25–26.

32. Ihab Hassan, "The Question of Postmodernism," *Bucknell Review* 25, no. 2 (1980): 117–26. See also Ihab Hassan, *The Postmodern Turn: Essays in Postmodern Theory and Culture* (Columbus: Ohio State University Press, 1987).

33. Lyotard, *The Postmodern Condition,* 79.

34. Jean-François Lyotard, "Rewriting Modernity," *SubStance* 54 (1987): 8–9.

35. Jean Baudrillard, "Symbolic Exchange and Death," in *Jean Baudrillard: Selected Writings,* 145.

36. Jean Baudrillard, "Simulacra and Simulation," 177.

37. Jean Baudrillard, "On Seduction," in *Jean Baudrillard: Selected Writings,* 150.

38. Baudrillard, "Symbolic Exchange and Death," 144.

39. Ibid.

40. Ibid.

41. Jean Baudrillard, *Simulations* (New York: Semiotext(e), 1983).

42. For example, see Jean Baudrillard, *Forget Foucault* (New York: Semiotext(e), 1987).

43. Baudrillard, "Symbolic Exchange and Death," 146.

44. Ibid.

45. Ibid.

46. Philosophical terms, such as *idealism* and *materialism,* can be understood in various ways. For example, see Sean Sayers, *Reality and Reason: Dialectic and the Theory of Knowledge* (Oxford: Basil Blackwell, 1985), xiv–xv. Sayers comments that the term *materialism* has "been so much abused in recent years that it often seems to mean no more than 'the theory I hold' (whatever that may be). I must stress, therefore, that I will here be using the term in its strict and philosophical sense, to refer to the theory that consciousness does not exist independent of matter and that all reality is ultimately material in nature. Idealism is the opposite of this: it is the view that reality is ultimately ideal in character, and can be seen as a construct or creation of mere ideas, interpretation, or whatever." In terms of realism in epistemology, there are also important distinctions, for example, between direct (or naive) or representative (or "reflection theory") realism. Sayers describes the former as "the view that we are immediately and directly aware of reality through our sensory experience" (p. 4). He characterizes the latter as holding that "we are immediately aware, not of reality, but of appearances, images, sensations, impressions or ideas" (p. 4). In addition, there are sub-varieties.

47. J. Buchler, *Metaphysics of Natural Complexes* (New York: Columbia University Press, 1966), 4.

48. John McTaggart, *The Nature of Existence,* vol. 1 (Cambridge: Cambridge University Press, 1921), 3.

49. Francis Bradley, *Appearance and Reality* (Oxford: Clarendon Press, 1893), 181.

50. Bertrand Russell, "The Philosophy of Logical Atomism," in *The Philosophy of Logical Atomism and Other Essays 1914–19,* ed. John G. Slater (London: George Allen and Unwin, 1986).

51. McTaggart, *The Nature of Existence,* 3.

52. G. E. Moore, "A Defence of Common Sense," in *G. E. Moore: Selected Writings,* ed.

Thomas Baldwin (New York: Routledge, 1993), 106–33. See also Norman Malcolm, "Defending Common Sense," in *Studies in the Philosophy of G. E. Moore,* ed. E. D. Klemke (Chicago: Quadrangle Books, 1969), 200–19.

53. John J. Austin, *Sense and Sensibilia* (Oxford: Clarendon Press, 1962), 64.

54. Descartes, "Reply to Objection 11," *Philosophical Works,* vol. 2, 53.

55. For example, see Charles D. Broad, *Berkeley's Argument about Material Substance* (New York: Haskell House, 1975); and David Hume, *Enquiries Concerning Human Understanding and Concerning the Principles of Morals* (Oxford: Clarendon Press, 1975).

56. Francis H. Bradley, *Appearance and Reality* (Oxford: Clarendon Press, 1930). See also David J. Farmer, "Bradley and McTaggart: A Double Reading," in *Problemi della Pedagogia,* ed. Ornella Bellini (Milan: Marzorati Publishers, 1994), 20–42; and Garrett L. Vander Veer, *Bradley's Metaphysics and the Self* (New Haven: Yale University Press, 1970), 103–13.

57. Timo Airaksinen, *The Ontological Criteria of Reality: A Study of Bradley and McTaggart* (Turku, Finland Turin Yliopisto, 1975), 1.

58. See Farmer, *Being in Time,* 135–38; also see R. M. Sainsbury, *Russell* (London: Routledge and Kegan Paul, 1979), 308ff.

59. See Jonathan Barnes, *Early Greek Philosophy* (New York: Penguin Books, 1987), 50–60. Chapter 1 is titled "Precursors." See also William T. Jones, *The Classical Mind: A History of Western Philosophy* (New York: Harcourt Brace, 1969).

60. Jean Baudrillard, "System of Objects," in *Jean Baudrillard: Selected Writings,* 10.

61. Jean Baudrillard, "Simulacra and Simulation," 172.

62. Ibid., 172.

63. Jean Baudrillard, *America* (London: Verso, 1989).

64. The following are excerpts from an account of two companions driving through the Southwest (from Gregory Farmer, *Travels* [n.p., 1992]): "They sense hyperreality. . . . [T]hey drive through the Mohave Desert. Ten minutes after they had passed through Barstow, they hear on the car radio that ten minutes ago there had been an earthquake and the epicenter had been at Barstow. They learn what had happened to them ten minutes ago. The real earthquake at Barstow had been unreal. . . . Now it is real and frightening, although non-existent.

At night, the Nevada border arrives. On one side of the road is a light-bedecked mansion, announcing a casino and rooms at $24.50 for two. Next to the casino is a light-bedecked state prison. It seems unreal. . . . The first casino-hotel they see in Las Vegas is King Arthur's Court, a real unreal English medieval castle in the middle of something like suburbia and named after a king who never existed. . . .

Next day, they go to the Grand Canyon. That is real; it is so big, so real that it seems unreal. . . . At Memphis, all the motel rooms are sold out to Elvis fans. The city is flooded with people arrived to celebrate the anniversary of the death of the still-living Elvis Presley. For his fans, he is real."

65. See G. E. Moore, "Proof of an External World," in *G. E. Moore: Selected Writings,* ed. Baldwin, 147–70. Moore writes (on pp. 165–66), "I can prove now, for instance, that two human hands exist. How? By holding up my two hands, and saying, as I make a certain gesture with the right hand, 'here is one hand,' and adding, as I make a certain gesture with the left, 'and here is another.' . . . But did I prove just now that two human hands were in existence? I do want to insist that I did; that the proof which I gave was a perfectly rigorous one, and that it is perhaps impossible to give a better or more rigorous proof of anything whatsoever."

66. Richard Rorty, *Philosophy and the Mirror of Nature* (Princeton: Princeton University Press, 1979), 378.

67. Rose, *The Post-Modern and the Post-Industrial*, 49–50, quoting Ihab Hassan, "The Question of Postmodernism," 123. Pairs in Hassan's listing that are omitted from the text in this book are as follows:

Romanticism/Symbolism	Pataphysics/Dadaism
Genre/Boundary	Text/Intertext
Paradigm	Syntagm
Hypotaxis	Parataxis
Metaphor	Metonymy
Selection	Combination
Root/Depth	Rhizome/Surface
Interpretation/Reading	Against Interpretation/Misreading
Lisable (Readerly)	Scriptible (Writerly)
Genital/Phallic	Polymorphous/Androgynous
Paranoia	Schizophrenia

68. For discussion of "différence" and the neologism "différance," see David Wood, "Introduction," David Wood and Robert Bernasconi, *Derrida and Différance* (Evanston, Ill.: Northwestern University Press, 1988), x. Wood writes, "What Derrida attempted . . . was, in his own way, to gather a number of these threads of difference—including Hegel's 'differentiating relation' (differente Beziehung—into a difference with a difference: différance, in which he attempted the fusion of the logical, ontological, and (transcendental) aesthetic values that might be involved in a difference that would not be merely opposed to identity, together with the apparently divergent motifs to be found in Heidegger and in structuralism." The difficulty of the notion is emphasized in Wood's next sentence when he writes, "Putting such weight on one 'word,' to which [Derrida] even denied the status of a word because it essentially contests such idealizations as words, has had its drawbacks."

69. Rose, *The Post-Modern and the Post-Industrial*, 49–50.

70. As noted in chapter 2, POSDCORB stands for planning, organizing, staffing, directing, coordinating, reporting, and budgeting.

Chapter 10. Postmodernity: Imagination

1. George Katsiaficas, *The Imagination of the New Left: A Global Analysis of 1968* (Boston: South End Press, 1987), 7.

2. To distinguish between different uses, *imaginization* used in the sense intended here is underlined in this chapter (but only in this chapter).

3. See Alan Watts, *Psychotherapy East and West* (New York: Random House, 1961), 3. Watts comments, "If we look deeply into such ways of life as Buddhism and Taoism, Vedanta and Yoga, we do not find either philosophy or religion as these are understood in the West. We find something more nearly resembling psychotherapy."

4. Jean-Paul Sartre, *Between Existentialism and Marxism,* trans. John Matthews (London: N.L.B., 1974), 125.

5. For an account of the Weberian view of the elements of rational-legal authority, see Wren, *The Evolution of Management Thought*, 192–96. Wren lists seven elements as having been essential for Weberian rational-legal authority, with the other two types of authority being traditional and charismatic. The elements concern the division of labor, the hierarchical principle, the selection of organization members on the basis of technical qualifications, the

appointment of officials (rather than their election), fixed salaries for career officials, organizational units not being owned by officials, and the administrator being subject to strict rules. The last element is described in these terms: "The administrator would be subject to strict rules, discipline and controls regarding the conduct of his official duties. These rules and controls would be impersonal and uniformly applied in all cases" (p. 195).

6. See also Raul Hilberg, *The Jewish Catastrophe 1933–1945* (New York: Aaron Asher Books/Harper Collins, 1992).

7. For another example, Sartre comments on what he considers to be the monumental error in the study of the imagination during the past three centuries; the error, for him, is to confuse imagining and perceiving, an error resulting from the assumption that images are things. See Jean-Paul Sartre, *Imagination* (Ann Arbor: University of Michigan Press, 1962), 85. As Sartre writes, "The fact of naked intuition is that there are images and perceptions, and we are quite capable of telling them apart."

8. Alan R. White, *The Language of Imagination* (Oxford: Basil Blackwell, 1990), 186.

9. Charles M. Sherover, *Heidegger, Kant and Time* (Bloomington: Indiana University Press, 1971), 65.

10. Carl G. Jung, *The Collected Works of C. G. Jung,* trans. R. F. Hull (Princeton: Princeton University Press, 1967), 6, quoted in Roberts Avens, *Imagination: A Way toward Western Nirvana* (Lanham, Md.: University Press of America, 1979).

11. Avens, *Imagination: A Way Toward Western Nirvana,* 39.

12. Ibid., 38.

13. Joseph J. Chambliss, *Imagination and Reason in Plato, Aristotle, Vico, Rousseau and Keats: An Essay on the Philosophy of Experience* (The Hague: Martinus Nijhoff, 1974), vi.

14. Gareth Morgan, *Imaginization: The Art of Creative Management* (Newbury Park, Calif.: Sage, 1993).

15. Ibid., 1.

16. Ibid., 2.

17. Ibid., 6.

18. Ibid., 11.

19. Ibid., 14.

20. Ibid., 17.

21. Ibid., 265.

22. Ibid., 15.

23. Ibid., 314. Concerning the more creative approach, Morgan references Agor 1989; Block 1987; DeBono 1970; Russell and Evans 1992; and Schon 1963, 1979. Concerning the movement to an information-based world, he refers to Beer 1975; Davis 1987; Hawken 1983; Kanter 1983; himself 1988; Peters 1987, 1992; Reich 1983; and Stacey 1992. He provides other references in the text and in an appendix.

24. Ibid., 314.

25. Thomas J. Peters and Robert H. Waterman, *In Search of Excellence* (New York: Harper and Row, 1982), 63, note 12.

26. Agor, *Intuition in Organizations.*

27. Michael Ray and Alan Rinzler, *The New Paradigm in Business: Emerging Strategies for Leadership and Organizational Change* (New York: Putnam Publishing Group, 1993).

28. The book has twenty-nine headings. Most are conservative, such as "The Art and Practice of the Learning Organization" and "The Five Stages of Corporate Moral Development."

29. Morgan's earlier book, *Riding the Waves of Change,* contained no such cartoons; Gareth Morgan, *Riding the Waves of Change: Developing Managerial Competencies for a Turbulent World* (San Francisco: Jossey-Bass, 1988).

30. Morgan, *Imaginization,* xxix. As Morgan writes, "Imaginization is a way of thinking. It's a way of organizing. It's a key managerial skill. It provides a way of helping people understand and develop their creative potential. It offers a means of finding innovative solutions to difficult problems. And last, but not least, it provides a means of empowering people to trust themselves and find new roles in a world characterized by flux and change."

31. Ibid., 2.

32. Ibid., 300. Morgan lists (p. 301) the five injunctions of his research method as follows: get inside; adopt the role of a learner; map the terrain; identify key themes and interpretations; and confirm, refute, and reformulate throughout.

33. See Richard W. Scott, *Organizations: Rational, Natural and Open Systems,* 2nd ed. (Englewood Cliffs, N.J.: Prentice-Hall, 1987).

34. Ibid., 306. Scott writes, "Uncertainty again! We have asked this concept to bear a heavy burden throughout this volume. Uncertainty is the source of variety and power, and it is the enemy of rationality and planning. Too much uncertainty can cause individuals to seek protection in ritualism and oversimplification of alternatives; too little uncertainty can cause individuals to wither in boredom and alienation."

35. Maurice Merleau-Ponty, *The Visible and the Invisible,* ed. Claude Lefort, trans. Alphonso Lingis (Evanston, Ill.: Northwestern University Press, 1968).

36. Patrick Burke, "Listening at the Abyss," in *Ontology and Alterity in Merleau-Ponty,* ed. Galen A. Johnson and Michael B. Smith (Evanston: Northwestern University Press, 1990), 85.

37. Ibid., 86–87.

38. For example, see Gilles Deleuze and Félix Guattari, *Anti-Oedipus: Capitalism and Schizophrenia,* trans. Robert Hurley, Mark Seem, and Helen Lane (New York: Viking Press, 1977).

39. Ibid., 322.

40. Ibid., 350.

41. See also Herbert A. Simon, "Making Management Decisions: The Role of Intuition and Emotion," *Academy of Management Executive* 1, no. 1, 57–64; reprinted in Agor, *Intuition in Organizations,* 23–39. Simon writes (p. 29) that the difference between the novice and the grandmaster lies in the grandmaster's "knowledge, acquired by long experience, of the kinds of patterns and clusters of pieces that occur on chessboards in the course of games. . . . Associated with each pattern in his or her memory is information about the significance of that pattern." Simon affirms the operation in decision making of intuitive judgement, properly understood. He writes (pp. 25–26) that "many readers of *Administrative Behavior* have concluded that the theory advanced there applies only to 'logical' decision making, not to decisions that involve intuition and judgment. That was certainly not my intent."

42. Miller, *The Passion of Michel Foucault,* 301.

43. J. B. Skemp, Introduction, *Statesman,* in *The Collected Dialogues of Plato,* ed. Edith Hamilton and Huntingdon Cairns (Princeton: Princeton University Press, 1961), 1018–19.

44. Colin Gordon, "Governmental Rationality: An Introduction," in *The Foucault Effect,* ed. Burchell, Gordon, and Miller, 8. But recall Plato's *Republic.*

45. Ibid., 2–3.

46. Jean Baudrillard, "Figures of the Transpolitical," *Revenge of the Crystal: Selected*

Writings on the Modern Object and Its Destiny, trans. Paul Foss and Julian Pefanis (London: Pluto Press, 1990), 163.

47. Ibid.

48. Max Weber, *The Theory of Social and Economic Organization,* ed. Talcott Parsons (New York: Oxford University Press, 1947), quoted in Amitai Etzioni, *Modern Organizations* (Englewood Cliffs, N.J.: Prentice-Hall, 1964), 53. The other six Weberian features described by Etzioni concern the specific sphere of competence, the principle of hierarchy, regulation of the office by technical rules and applied through specialized training, separation of administrative staff from ownership, resources being free from outside control and monopolization by any incumbent, and formulating and recording in writing of acts, decisions, and rules. Etzioni writes (p. 54), "Underlying the whole analysis is a set of principles that follows from the central organizational problem as Weber saw it: The high rationality of the bureaucratic structure is fragile; it needs to be constantly protected against external pressures to safeguard the autonomy required if it is to be kept closely geared to its goals and not others."

49. Etzioni, *Modern Organizations,* 53.

Chapter 11. Postmodernity: Deconstruction

1. Jacques Derrida, "Letter to a Japanese Friend," *Derrida and Différance,* ed. David Wood and Robert Bernasconi (Evanston: Northwestern University Press, 1988), 4.

2. Ibid., 3.

3. Ibid.

4. It is not implied here that Jacques Derrida writes about bureaucratic deconstruction, but it is suggested that Derrida should not disapprove of the notion, as described here, of bureaucratic deconstruction. Similarly, it is not intended (in the next paragraph) to suggest that Formaini, Guba, and Lincoln are known to have subscribed to the idea of deconstruction. On deconstruction, see Richard Rorty, *Essays on Heidegger and others: Philosophical papers* (New York: Cambridge University Press, 1991), 85–86. Rorty distinguishes two senses of "deconstruction." The first sense refers to Derrida's philosophical projects. The second is "a method of reading texts" (p. 85). Rorty notes that the second sense should not be attributed to Derrida, who is contemptuous of the "very idea of method" (p. 85).

5. Robert Formaini, *The Myth of Scientific Public Policy* (New Brunswick, N.J.: Transaction Publishers, 1990), 1. As he states, "Public policy in the United States is debated, analyzed, and implemented within a framework characterized by the acceptance, explicitly or implicitly, of certain assumptions. One of the main assumptions is the objective nature of the reality which surrounds us, along with a subsidiary assumption concerning the ability of our techniques accurately to explore and to control that reality."

6. Ibid., 2.

7. Egon G. Guba and Yvonna S. Lincoln, *Naturalistic Inquiry* (Beverly Hills: Sage, 1985), 37.

8. Quoted by Stephen Woolgar, *Current Anthropology* 29, no. 3 (1988): 430.

9. Lyotard, *The Postmodern Condition,* 618.

10. Ferdinand de Saussure, *Course in General Linguistics,* trans. Wade Baskin (New York: McGraw-Hill, 1966).

11. See, for example, Claude Lévi-Strauss, *Anthropology and Myth: Lectures, 1951–1982* (Oxford: Blackwell, 1987).

12. Ellie Ragland-Sullivan, *Jacques Lacan and the Philosophy of Psychoanalysis* (Urbana, Ill.: University of Illinois Press, 1986).

13. See George R. Wasserman, *Roland Barthes* (Boston: Twayne Publishers, 1981), 58. Wasserman writes, "Though definitions of French Structuralism are often difficult to reconcile with one another, there seems to be at least popular agreement about attaching the term *Structuralist* to four particular Frenchmen: the anthropologist Claude Lévi-Strauss (everyone's first choice), the philosopher Michel Foucault (who angrily rejects the label), the psychologist Jacques Lacan (who is no more pleased with the identification than Foucault), and Roland Barthes (who accepts the term at least as a historical label for the work produced in the late 1950's and 60s)."

14. See Jacques Derrida, *Of Grammatology,* trans. Gayatri Spivak (Baltimore: Johns Hopkins Press, 1976), 73. Also see David Wood, ed., *Derrida: A Critical Reader* (Cambridge: Blackwell, 1992), 172–73.

15. This phrase is taken from Kearney, who is writing about poststructuralism; Richard Kearney, *Modern Movements in European Philosophy* (Manchester, U.K.: Manchester University Press, 1986), 9. Kearney writes, "For post-structuralism, the two main aims of reading texts are: 1) to subvert the authoritarian claim to definitive knowledge and; 2) to give voice to the prohibited desire for jouissance (the very essence of language as surplus of signifier over signified)."

16. Derrida, "Letter to a Japanese Friend," 4.

17. Ibid., 4.

18. Ibid., 4–5.

19. Jacques Derrida, *Positions,* trans. Alan Bass (Chicago: University of Chicago Press, 1981), 40.

20. Derrida, "Letter to a Japanese Friend," 4.

21. Gayle J. Ormiston, "The Economy of Duplicity: Différance," *Derrida and Différance* (Evanston: Northwestern University Press, 1988), 41. Ormiston refers his reader to Derrida's "Passe-Partout."

22. Ibid., 41.

23. Derrida, "Letter to a Japanese Friend," 4.

24. Ibid., 5.

25. Wittgenstein, *Tractatus Logico-Philosophicus,* 74.

26. Derrida, "Interview with Jean-Louis Houdebine and Guy Scarpetta," *Positions,* 40–41.

27. Wittgenstein, *Tractatus Logico-Philosophicus.*

28. Derrida, *Positions,* 12.

29. Ibid., 6.

30. Ibid., 14.

31. Ibid.

32. Jacques Derrida, *Writing and Difference,* trans. Alan Bass (Chicago: University of Chicago Press, 1978), 25.

33. Jacques Derrida, *Dissemination,* trans. B. Johnson (Chicago: University of Chicago Press, 1981), 7.

34. Rorty, *Consequences of Pragmatism,* 94.

35. Jacques Derrida, *Of Grammatology,* trans. G. Spivak (Baltimore: Johns Hopkins University, 1976), 24.

36. Christopher Norris, *Deconstruction, Theory and Practice* (London: Methuen, 1982), 6.

37. Derrida, *Writing and Difference,* 292.

38. Derrida, "Interview with Jean-Louis Houdebine and Guy Scarpetta," 41.

39. Derrida, *The Truth in Painting,* 19.

40. See Norris, *Deconstruction, Theory and Practice,* 106 and 169.

41. Jean Baudrillard, *Simulacra and Simulations,* trans. Paul Foss, Paul Patton, and Philip Beitchman (New York: Semiotext(e), 1983); reprinted in part in "Simulacra and Simulations," 166.

42. These examples were the accounts of naturalistic (or constructivist) inquiry and nonorthodox organization theory. Accounts can be postmodern even if they are not described as such. The adjective *postmodern,* as noted in chapter 1, surely will be replaced by another signifier at some date.

43. For example, see the reports written on behalf of such consulting organizations as Public Administration Service, 1965–1970, and the Jacobs Company (Planning Research Corporation), 1970–1971, including the fifty or so written or coauthored in these periods on behalf of those organizations by me. Both organizations were located in Chicago, Illinois.

44. Prince Charles, "Convocation Speech," *300th Anniversary of the College of William and Mary* (Richmond, Va.: Channel 8, February 13, 1993).

45. For an account of life as a text, see Heidegger, *Being and Time.*

46. Jacques Derrida, "Interview with Henri Ronse," *Positions,* 7.

47. Simon, *Administrative Behavior.*

48. Antonio Gramsci, *Selections from the Prison Notebooks of Antonio Gramsci,* ed. Quinton Hoare and Geoffrey Smith (New York: International Publishers, 1972).

49. Horkheimer and Adorno, *Dialectic of Enlightenment,* xiv.

50. Simon, *Administrative Behavior,* 45.

51. Simon, "Acknowledgements to the First Edition," *Administrative Behavior,* xlix–1.

52. See Simon, *Administrative Behavior,* 12.

53. Ibid.

54. Ibid., 240–41.

55. Chris Argyris, "Organization Man: Rational and Self-Actualizing," *Public Administration Review* 33, no. 4 (1973): 354.

56. Herbert A. Simon, "Communications," *Public Administration Review* 33, no. 4 (1973): 358.

57. In *Public Administration Review* 33, no. 4 (1973): 346.

58. Argyris, "Organization Man: Rational and Self-Actualizing," 356.

59. Chris Argyris, "Some Limits of Rational Man Organizational Theory," *Public Administration Review* 33, no. 3 (1973): 253.

60. Simon, "Communications," 358.

61. Argyris, "Organization Man: Rational and Self-Actualizing," 354.

62. Vice-President Albert Gore, *From Red Tape to Results: Creating a Government that Works Better and Costs Less* (New York: Random House, 1993), i. For comments on the Grace Commission (the January 1984 President's Private Sector Survey on Cost Control in the Federal Government), see George W. Downs and Patrick D. Larkey, *The Search for Government Efficiency: From Hubris to Helplessness* (Philadelphia: Temple University Press, 1986), 217–36. Downs and Larkey write, "If one can get past the gratuitous vilification of the public sector and the childlike faith that the effortless application of standard business methods can quickly bring enormous efficiency gains, there are some helpful prescriptions to be found [in the Grace Commission] that are . . . very much in keeping with the lessons that emerge from our analysis of the experience with earlier efficiency reforms."

63. Downs and Larkey, *The Search for Government Efficiency,* 237–39.

64. Herbert A. Simon, *Administrative Behavior: A Study of Decision-Making Processes in Administrative Organization* (New York: Free Press, 1976), 182.

65. Simon cites Marshall E. Dimock, "The Criteria and Objectives of Public Administration," in *Frontiers of Public Administration*, eds. Gaus, White, and Dimock, 116–33.

66. Dwight Waldo, *The Administrative State: A Study of the Political Theory of American Public Administration* (New York: Ronald Press Company, 1948), 202.

67. Simon, *Administrative Behavior*, 182. Simon's book contains a chapter on the criterion of efficiency; the word *efficiency* has eight lines in the index, and it is the subject of all four of the proverbs or principles.

68. Waldo, *The Administrative State*, 203.

69. For a discussion of Saussure, for example, see Jonathan Culler, *Ferdinand de Saussure* (Ithaca: Cornell University Press, 1976). This paragraph relies heavily on Culler.

70. See chapter 2, note 21.

71. See Culler, *Ferdinand de Saussure*, 33. As Culler writes, "A language does not simply assign arbitrary names to a set of independently existing concepts. . . . [E]ach language produces a different set of signifieds."

72. Ibid., 33–34. As Culler says, "The signified 'river' is opposed to 'stream' solely in terms of size, whereas a 'fleuve' differs from a 'rivière' not because it is necessarily larger but because it flows into the sea, while a rivière does not. In short, 'fleuve' and 'rivière' are not signifieds or concepts of English."

73. Ibid., 55–56.

74. Ibid., 56.

75. See Waldo, *The Administrative State*, 196. Waldo writes, "In recent years there has been a tendency to speak of 'social economy' and 'social efficiency,' and to contrast these expressions with earlier and narrower usages of economy and efficiency." See also Samuel Haber, *Efficiency and Uplift: Scientific Management in the Progressive Era 1890–1920* (Chicago: University of Chicago Press, 1964), x. Haber writes, "At the very center of the efficiency craze was Frederick W. Taylor's program of industrial management. The four meanings of efficiency that the craze brought to view were all contained within Taylor's system."

76. Brack Brown and Richard J. Stillman, *A Search for Public Administration: The Ideas and Career of Dwight Waldo* (College Station: Texas A and M University Press, 1986), 158.

77. Waldo writes, "The word efficiency begins to appear in our language only in the mid- to late eighteenth century. The rise and diffusion of the concept is, I judge, associated with the modern phenomena identified in the preceding paragraph: with the power-driven machine, with economic rationality, with the business ethos, and so forth." See Waldo, "Introduction: Retrospect and Prospect," *The Administrative State*, lii.

78. S. I. Hayakawa, *Language in Thought and Action*, 4th ed. (New York: Harcourt Brace Jovanovich, 1978), 95.

79. Ibid., 96.

80. Ibid., 97.

81. Waldo, *The Administrative State*, 193.

82. Downs and Larkey, *The Search for Government Efficiency*, 237.

83. Keizo Nagatani, *Political Macroeconomics* (Oxford: Clarendon Press, 1989), 53–54.

84. Waldo, *The Administrative State*, 204.

85. Ibid.

86. Simon, *Administrative Behavior*, 184.

87. Martin J. Schiesl, *The Politics of Efficiency: Municipal Administration and Reform in America 1800–1920* (Berkeley: University of California Press, 1977), 2–3.

88. Waldo, *The Administrative State,* 201.

89. Also see Harvey Leibenstein, *General X-Efficiency Theory and Economic Development* (New York: Oxford University Press, 1978). Leibenstein describes "X-inefficiency" in a narrow and a broader sense. Of the narrow sense, he writes (p. 17), "When an input is not used effectively, the difference between the actual output and the maximum output attributable to that input is a measure of the degree of X-inefficiency. In this context X-efficiency is to be contrasted with allocative efficiency, the latter being the form of efficiency commonly considered in neoclassical economics."

90. For a discussion of Pareto optimality, see Abrams, *Foundations of Political Analysis.*

91. For alternative views of the nature of economic justice, see for example Arthur and Shaw, *Justice and Economic Distribution,* 11–132.

92. See Waldo, *The Administrative State,* 199. Waldo writes, "We must stop assuming that there is but one uniform type of inefficiency—there are as many kinds as there are varieties of disease."

93. Samuel Bowles, David M. Gordon, and Thomas E. Weisskopf, *After the Waste-Land: A Democratic Economics for the Year 2000* (New York: M. E. Sharpe, 1990).

94. These examples are presented and discussed by Bowles, Gordon, and Weisskopf, *After the Waste-Land;* and by Mark Green and John F. Berry, *The Challenge of Hidden Profits: Reducing Corporate Bureaucracy and Waste* (New York: William Morrow, 1985).

95. Philip A. Hart, "Consumer Expenditures: 30 Percent Wasted," in *Current Economic Problems: A Book of Readings,* ed. Royall Brandis and Steven Cox (Homewood, Ill.: Richard D. Irwin, 1970).

96. Douglas F. Dowd, *The Waste of Nations: Dysfunction in the World Economy* (London: Westview Press, 1989).

97. For an account of externalities, for example, see Joseph E. Stiglitz, *Economics of the Public Sector* (New York: W. W. Norton, 1986), 178–98.

98. Nagatani, *Political Macroeconomics,* 64–65.

99. Ibid., 66.

100. James S. Coleman, "Properties of Rational Organizations," in *Interdisciplinary Perspectives on Organization Studies,* ed. Siegwart M. Lindenberg and Hein Schreuder (New York: Pergamon Press, 1993), 86.

101. Ibid., 86. Coleman adds the following footnote to the last sentence: "This fact, incidentally, invalidates the usual statement of the Coase theorem that the allocation of rights does not, in the absence of transaction cost, affect systemic outcome."

102. Ibid., 88. Coleman's second example concerns intellectual property rights, comparing efficiencies in the case where such rights are vested in the employee rather than in the employer (as in many universities) and the case where such rights are the company's (and the 3M Company is the instance he gives).

103. Yet other strategies for this deconstructive iteration, beyond appealing to the imperfect structure of the private market, are available in arguing that rational outcomes are suboptimal. For example, one line could explore the rationality of collusion between the self-interest of the entrepreneurs producing the privatized output and the self-interest of any public sector supervisors (or regulators) of the privatized programs. (One reason for supposing that supervision will be required is the rationality of monitoring whether the profit-conscious actions of the entrepreneurs are consistent with the public purposes of the privatized program.)

104. For example, see Madison, *The Hermeneutics of Postmodernity: Figures and Themes,* 106 and 114.

105. Ibid., 109.

106. Ibid., 114.

107. Ibid., 115.

108. Jacques Derrida, "Three Questions to Hans-Georg Gadamer," in *Dialogue and Deconstruction: The Gadamer-Derrida Encounter,* ed. Diane Michelfelder and Richard E. Palmer (Albany: SUNY, 1989), 53.

109. Fred R. Dallmayr, "Hermeneutics and Deconstruction: Gadamer and Derrida in Dialogue," in *Dialogue and Deconstruction,* 75–92; and Hans-Georg Gadamer, "Letter to Dallmayr," in *Dialogue and Deconstruction,* ed. Michelfelder and Palmer, 93–101.

110. The question is taken from a 1993 flyer advertising a meeting to hear Dr. Freeman; Joseph F. Freeman, *Government is Good: Citizenship, Participation and Power* (Columbia: University of Missouri Press, 1992).

111. Madison, *The Hermeneutics of Postmodernity,* 114.

112. Jean Baudrillard, "System of Objects."

113. Ibid., 10.

114. Ibid., 17, where Baudrillard quotes from Martineau, *Motivation in Advertising,* 50.

115. Ibid., 22.

116. Jean Baudrillard, *The Ecstasy of Communication,* trans. B. and C. Schutze (New York: Semitext(e), 1988), 59.

117. Baudrillard, "On Seduction," 149.

118. Ibid., 149.

119. Ibid.

120. For example, Jean Baudrillard, "Mirror of Production," in *Jean Baudrillard: Selected Writings,* 98–118.

121. Timothy Luke, "Touring Hyperreality: Critical Theory Confronts Informational Society," in *Critical Theory Now,* ed. Philip Wexler (London: Falmer Press, 1991), 6–8.

122. For example, see Serafina K. Bathrick, "How Mothers Quit Resisting and Managed to Love T.V.," *Critical Theory Now,* ed. Wexler, 145–64.

123. *Republic,* Book III, Section 10.

124. Baudrillard, "On Seduction," 154.

125. Baudrillard, "Simulacra and Simulations," 171.

Chapter 12. Postmodernity: Deterritorialization

1. Deleuze and Guattari, *Anti-Oedipus,* 222.

2. Mark Seem, Introduction, in Deleuze and Guattari, *Anti-Oedipus,* xxi. Seem's previous sentence reads, "The first task of the revolutionary, [Deleuze and Guattari] add, is to learn from the psychotic how to shake off the Oedipal yoke and the effects of power, in order to initiate a radical politics of desire free from all beliefs."

3. Deleuze and Guattari, *Anti-Oedipus,* 321.

4. Lyotard, *The Postmodern Condition.*

5. Ibid., 3.

6. Developments take different forms. For example, see Katherine B. Tyson, "A New Approach to Relevant Scientific Research for Practitioners: The Heuristic Paradigm," *Social Work* 37, no. 6 (1992). She argues (p. 552), "The positivist paradigm that defined social work research from 1949 to 1981 has failed to engender research that most practitioners find useful. . . . To remedy these inadequacies, social workers increasingly are turning to the heuristic paradigm, an up-to-date, scientific philosophy of research that draws from contemporary phi-

losophy of science and cultural, cognitive and linguistic studies and that endorses research as a tool for advocacy."

7. Yvonna Lincoln, ed., *Organizational Theory and Inquiry: The Paradigm Revolution* (Beverly Hills: Sage, 1985), 36.

8. John Van Maanan introduces his collection on qualitative methodology by writing, "The label qualitative methods . . . is at best an umbrella term covering an array of interpretive techniques which seek to describe, decode, translate, and otherwise come to terms with the meaning, not the frequency, of certain more or less naturally occurring phenomena in the social world." John Van Maanan, *Qualitative Methodology* (Beverly Hills: Sage, 1979), 9. There is a large literature on qualitative research; for example, see Catherine Marshall and Gretchen Rossman, *Designing Qualitative Research* (Newbury Park, Calif.: Sage, 1989); or, as cited in chapter 2, Tesch, *Qualitative Research.* Qualitative studies are not automatically postmodern and not automatically postpositivist. Many are modernist. See David A. Erlandson, Edward L. Harris, Barbara L. Skipper, and Steve D. Allen, *Doing Naturalistic Inquiry: A Guide to Methods* (Newbury Park, Calif.: Sage, 1993), x. As they write, "Naturalistic inquiry is not equivalent to qualitative inquiry."

9. See Yvonna S. Lincoln and Egon G. Guba, *Naturalistic Inquiry* (Beverly Hills: Sage, 1985), and Lincoln, ed., *Organizational Theory and Inquiry.*

10. Lincoln and Guba write, "Of the three 'paradigm eras,' the prepositivist is both the longest and the least interesting from a modern perspective; indeed, its lack of provocative acts and ideas is best illustrated by its very title—prepositivist. This era is simply a precursor to the more exciting period that followed" (Lincoln and Guba, *Naturalistic Inquiry,* 18). This characterization gives short shrift to the great accomplishments of this era, and it is a characterization that would be rejected by historians of science such as Pierre Duhem. The latter argues the position that no great break occurred between the scientific thinking of the Middle and Modern ages.

11. Lincoln and Guba, *Naturalistic Inquiry,* 19. They write, "Positivism may be defined as 'a family of philosophies characterized by an extremely positive evaluation of science and scientific method' (Reese, 1980, 450)."

12. Ibid., 29. Lincoln and Guba add, "[P]erhaps not so surprising, after all, when one contemplates that postpositivism is as much a reaction to the failings of positivism as it is a proactive set of new formulations."

13. Lincoln, ed., *Organizational Theory and Inquiry,* 33. Lincoln references Peter Schwartz and James Ogilvie, *The Emergent Paradigm: Changing Patterns of Thought and Belief,* Analytic Report 7, Values and Lifestyle Program (Menlo Park: Stanford Research Institute, 1979).

14. For an account of these shifts, see Lincoln, ed., *Organizational Theory and Inquiry,* 34–36.

15. David L. Clark, "Emerging Paradigms in Organizational Theory and Research," in *Organizational Theory and Inquiry,* ed. Lincoln.

16. Clark, "Emerging Paradigms in Organizational Theory and Research," 60, quoting J. Pfeffer, *Organization and Organization Theory* (Boston: Pittman, 1982), 7.

17. Clark, "Emerging Paradigms in Organizational Theory and Research," 76.

18. Ibid.

19. Ibid.

20. Karl E. Weick, *The Social Psychology of Organizing* (Reading, Mass.: Addison-Wesley, 1969), 108, quoting Piet Hein, *Grooks* (Cambridge: MIT Press, 1966), 17.

21. Clark, "Emerging Paradigms in Organizational Theory and Research," 69.

22. Ibid., 70.

23. Ibid., 71 and 73.

24. Lincoln, ed. *Organizational Theory and Inquiry,* 35.

25. Ibid.

26. Karl E. Weick, "Sources of Order in Unorganized Systems: Themes in Recent Organizational Theory," in *Organizational Theory and Inquiry,* ed. Lincoln, 109.

27. Ibid.

28. Ibid. Weick has also described the alternative view of organizations in terms of an unconventional soccer game. He repeats (p. 106) a 1976 version of his metaphor: "Imagine that you're either the referee, coach, player or spectator at an unconventional soccer match; the field for the game is round; there are several goals scattered haphazardly around the circular field, people can enter and leave the game whenever they want; they can say 'that's my goal' whenever they want to, as many times as they want to, and for as many goals as they want to; the entire game takes place on a sloped field, and the game is played as if it made sense."

29. Egon G. Guba and Yvonna S. Lincoln, *Fourth Generation Evaluation* (Newbury Park, Calif.: Sage, 1989), 158.

30. Lincoln and Guba, *Naturalistic Inquiry,* 36.

31. Ibid., 37.

32. Egon G. Guba, "The Context of Emergent Paradigm Research," in *Organizational Theory and Inquiry,* ed. Lincoln, 82.

33. See Marcia P. Harrigan and Rosemary L. Farmer, "The Myths and Facts of Aging," in *Gerontological Social Work,* ed. Robert L. Schneider and Nancy P. Kropf (Chicago: Nelson-Hall, 1992), 42–43.

34. Lincoln and Guba, *Naturalistic Inquiry,* 37.

35. Lex Donaldson, *In Defence of Organization Theory: A Reply to the Critics* (New York: Cambridge University Press, 1985), 103. Donaldson discusses Clegg and Dunkerley's views on organization theory as ideology (pp. 94–103). Clegg and Dunkerley's views appear in Stewart Clegg and David Dunkerley, *Organization, Class and Control* (London: Routledge and Kegan Paul, 1980).

36. Lincoln and Guba, *Naturalistic Inquiry,* 184.

37. Ibid., 184–85.

38. Ibid., 37.

39. Ibid.

40. Ibid.

41. Ibid.

42. Ibid., 39.

43. Ibid.

44. Ibid., 39–43. Descriptions of individual characteristics of operational naturalistic inquiry that follow are taken from these pages.

45. Ibid., 41.

46. Etzioni, *Modern Organizations,* 53. Etzioni gives the following quotation from Weber's *The Theory of Social and Economic Organization* in his account of Weber's rational structure of bureaucracy: "The organization of offices follows the principle of hierarchy; that is, each lower office is under the control and supervision of a higher one." He adds, "In this way no office is left uncontrolled. Compliance cannot be left to chance; it has to be systematically checked and reinforced."

47. Kathleen P. Iannello, *Decisions Without Hierarchy: Feminist Interventions in Organization Theory and Practice* (New York: Routledge, 1992), 12. She takes the quotation from W. Richard Scott, *Organizations* (Englewood Cliffs, N.J.: Prentice-Hall, 1981), 68. She adds,

"As Weber indicates, bureaucracy is a concept that encompasses many organizational characteristics, of which hierarchy is one. However, it can be argued that hierarchy is the key component of bureaucracy, around which channels of authority, systems of communication, and performance guidelines have developed."

48. Philip Cooke, *Back to the Future* (London: Unwin Hyman, 1990), 143.

49. Ibid., 143–53.

50. Albert Borgmann, *Crossing the Postmodern Divide* (Chicago: University of Chicago Press, 1992), 77.

51. Cooke, *Back to the Future*, 160–63. The following paragraph relies on this source.

52. Ibid. Cooke writes (p. 161) that there "has been a general growth in the proportion of part-time working in the advanced countries during the 1970s and 1980s. The highest rate of increase displayed has been in the Netherlands where the rate rose from 4 per cent to 50 per cent between 1973 and 1981 while in southern European countries such as Greece and Italy it remains at less than 10 per cent."

53. Hein Schreuder, "Coase, Hayek, and Hierarchy," in *Interdisciplinary Perspectives on Organization Studies*, ed. Lindenberg and Schreuder, 43.

54. Ibid., 43. The reference is to O. E. Williamson, *Markets and Hierarchies* (New York: Free Press, 1975), 7.

55. For example, see Gilles Deleuze and Félix Guattari, *A Thousand Plateaus* (Minneapolis: University of Minnesota Press, 1987).

56. Gilles Deleuze and Félix Guattari, *Kafka: Toward a Minor Literature*, trans. Dana Polan (Minneapolis: University of Minnesota Press, 1986), 3.

57. Julie Thompson Klein, *Interdisciplinarity: History, Theory, and Practice* (Detroit: Wayne State University Press, 1990), 21.

58. Hans Flexner, "The Curriculum, the Disciplines, and Interdisciplinarity in Higher Education," in *Interdisciplinarity and Higher Education*, ed. Joseph J. Kockelmans (University Press: Pennsylvania State University Press, 1979), 93.

59. For a listing of these and other distinctions, see Klein, *Interdisciplinarity: History, Theory, and Practice*, 104–105. For example, she notes another set of distinctions (Toulmin's) between compact disciplines (e.g., biology), would-be disciplines (e.g., behavioral sciences), and nondisciplinary activities (e.g., ethics). The distinction between highly codified (e.g., mathematics) and the less codified (e.g., social sciences) is taken from J. D. Thompson, R. W. Hawkes, and R. W. Avery. The distinction between high paradigm (e.g., chemistry) and low paradigm (e.g., political science) is taken from Lodahl and Gordon. The distinction between narrow and broad specialism is from A. Baum. The distinction between restricted sciences and configurational sciences (e.g., life sciences) is taken from R. D. Whiteley. The distinction between consensual and nonconsensual fields is from R. Rose. Citations may be found in Klein, *Interdisciplinarity: History, Theory, and Practice*, 215. An example given by Klein of a federated discipline is anthropology.

60. Centre for Educational Research and Innovation (CERI), *Interdisciplinarity: Problems of Teaching and Research in Universities* (Paris: Organisation for Economic Co-operation and Development, 1972), 35.

61. Klein, *Interdisciplinarity: History, Theory, and Practice*, 20–21.

62. CERI, *Interdisciplinarity: Problems of Teaching and Research in Universities*, 48–51.

63. Klein, *Interdisciplinarity: History, Theory, and Practice*, 38.

64. Ibid.

65. Michael A. Little and Jere D. Haas, *Human Population Biology: A Transdisciplinary Science* (New York: Oxford University Press, 1989), 3.

66. CERI, *Interdisciplinarity: Problems of Teaching and Research in Universities,* 25. See also Klein, *Interdisciplinarity: History, Theory, and Practice,* 17–73.

67. CERI, *Interdisciplinarity: Problems of Teaching and Research in Universities,* 25.

68. Little and Haas, *Human Population Biology,* 4.

69. Rustum Roy, "Interdisciplinary Science on Campus: The Elusive Dream," in *Interdisciplinarity and Higher Education,* ed. Kockelmans, 174.

70. Barry Smart, "Modernity, Postmodernity and the Present," in *Theories of Modernity and Postmodernity,* ed. Bryan S. Turner (Newbury Park, Calif.: Sage, 1990), 26. The Bauman citation is to Z. Bauman, "Is there a postmodern sociology?" *Theory, Culture and Society* 5, no. 2/3 (1988).

71. Smart, "Modernity, Postmodernity and the Present," 26.

72. For a caution about "the continuing rhetorical opposition of disciplinarity and interdisciplinarity," see Klein, *Interdisciplinarity: History, Theory, and Practice,* 105. She describes the opposition as "an oversimplified dichotomy that obscures the more subtle interactions that do take place."

73. Foster, ed., *The Anti-Aesthetic: Essays on Postmodern Culture* (Port Townsend, Wash.: Bay Press, 1983).

74. From "Qu'est-ce que la critique?" *Bulletin de la Société Française de Philosophie* 84, no. 2 (1990): 39, quoted in Miller, *The Passion of Michel Foucault,* 302. Miller writes, "As Foucault summed up this long historical development, 'I would say that critique is the movement by which the subject is given the right to discover the truth' by exercising 'an art of involuntary insubordination, of thoughtful disobedience.' "

75. Miller, *The Passion of Michel Foucault,* 303. Also, pp. 301 to 304, on which the account in this paragraph relies, offer a fuller summary of Foucault's views on "critique." A description of Foucault's understanding of "critique" can also be found in Christopher Norris, " 'What is enlightenment?' Kant according to Foucault," in *The Cambridge Companion to Foucault,* ed. Gutting, 174–75.

Chapter 13. Postmodernity: Alterity

1. Jacques Derrida, "Force of Law: The 'Mystical Foundation of Authority,' " in *Deconstruction and the Possibility of Justice,* ed. Drucilla Cornell, Michel Rosenfeld, and David Gray Carlson (New York: Routledge, 1992).

2. Ibid., 10.

3. Michel Foucault, "On the Genealogy of Ethics," in *Michel Foucault: Beyond Structuralism and Hermeneutics,* ed. Hubert L. Dreyfus and Paul Rabinow (Chicago: University of Chicago Press, 1983), 237.

4. Michel Foucault, Preface, in *Anti-Oedipus,* ed. Deleuze and Guattari, xiii.

5. Galen A. Johnson, Introduction, in *Ontology and Alterity in Merleau-Ponty,* ed. Johnson and Smith, xix.

6. Foucault, Preface, xiii.

7. Derrida, "Force of Law," 10.

8. Stephen K. White, *Political Theory and Postmodernism* (New York: Cambridge University Press, 1991), 76.

9. Foucault, Preface, xiii.

10. Félix Guattari, "The Postmodern Dead End," *Flash Art* 128 (May-June 1986): 40–41.

11. Foucault, Preface, xiii–xiv.

12. Ibid., xiii.

13. Ibid.

14. Amitai Etzioni, *The Spirit of Community: Rights, Responsibilities, and the Communitarian Agenda* (New York: Crown Publishers, 1993), 23.

15. Derrida, "Force of Law." For the argument that (p. xi) "Derridean deconstruction can, and indeed should, be understood as an ethical demand, provided that the ethics is understood in the particular sense given to it in the work of Emmanuel Levinas," see Simon Critchley, *The Ethics of Deconstruction: Derrida and Levinas* (Cambridge, Mass.: Blackwell, 1992).

16. Tzvetan Todorov, *The Conquest of America* (New York: Harper, 1987), 30, quoted in Ülker Gökberk, "Understanding Alterity: Ausländerliteratur between Relativism and Universalism," in *Theoretical Issues in Literary History,* ed. David Perkins (Cambridge: Harvard University Press, 1991), 155.

17. Jerold C. Frakes, *The Politics of Interpretation: Alterity and Ideology in Old Yiddish Studies* (Albany: SUNY, 1989), 17.

18. Ibid., 15.

19. Jean-François Lyotard and Jean-Loup Thébaud, *Just Gaming,* trans. Wlads Godzich (Minneapolis: University of Minnesota Press, 1985).

20. Albrecht Wellmer, *The Persistence of Modernity,* trans. David Midgley (Cambridge: MIT Press, 1991), 42, quoting Lyotard, *The Postmodern Condition,* 131.

21. The quote from Quine in chapter 7 (Quine, *Quiddities,* 3–4) on altruism may be recalled: "Altruism ranges from a passive respect for the interests of others to an active indulgence of their interests to the detriment of one's own. It ranges from the barely erogatory to the supererogatory on the other. What can be said for it?"

22. Department of Housing and Urban Development, "The Administrative Aspects of Model Cities Citizens' Organizations," *Model Cities Management Series,* Bulletin no. 6 (Washington, D.C.: Department of Housing and Urban Development, 1971), 2.

23. For a discussion of openness and the police, see Farmer, *Crime Control,* 164–69.

24. Foucault, "On the Genealogy of Ethics."

25. Ibid., 237.

26. Ibid.

27. After completing the writing of this text, I was glad to notice that another person had been struck with this etymological detail. An in-house publication contains this comment: "I've always been delighted by the etymological fact that aesthetic . . . is the opposite of anaesthetic. This means if doctors anaesthetize people, artists must 'aesthetize' them" (Elizabeth King, "Aesthetic and Anaesthetic," *V.C.U. Teaching* [1993]: 24).

28. Foucault, "On the Genealogy of Ethics," 230.

29. Ibid., 236.

30. Ibid., xiii.

31. Deleuze and Guattari, *Anti-Oedipus,* 362.

32. James Clifford, *The Predicament of Culture* (Cambridge: Harvard University Press, 1988), 95–96, quoted in Gökberk, "Understanding Alterity," 168.

33. Gökberk, "Understanding Alterity," 168.

34. Derrida, "Force of Law," 17.

35. Ibid., 18.

36. Gilles Deleuze and Félix Guattari, *Kafka: Toward a Minor Literature,* 19.

37. Ibid., 19.

38. Etzioni, *The Spirit of Community,* 247.

39. For some of Lyotard's views, see Lyotard, *The Postmodern Condition;* and Lyotard and Thébaud, *Just Gaming.*

40. Fraser cites Elizabeth V. Spelman, *Inessential Woman* (Boston: Beacon Press, 1988); and Denise Riley, *Am I That Name? Feminism and the Category of 'Woman' in History* (Minneapolis: University of Minnesota Press, 1988).

41. Nancy Fraser, "The Uses and Abuses of French Discourse Theories for Feminist Politics," in *Critical Theory Now,* ed. Philip Wexler (London: Falmer Press, 1991), 99.

42. For a defense of societal specialization, see Plato's *The Republic,* trans. Desmond Lee (New York: Penguin Books, 1955), passim.

43. Lyotard, *The Postmodern Condition,* xxiv.

44. Derrida, "Force of Law," 20.

45. Edith Wyschogrod, *Saints and Postmodernism: Revisioning Moral Philosophy* (Chicago: University of Chicago Press, 1990), xx.

46. Ibid., xxi.

47. Derrida, "Force of Law," 14.

48. Ibid., 27.

49. Ibid., 28.

50. Ibid., 27.

51. Ibid., 10.

52. Ibid. Also see Lyotard, *The Postmodern Condition;* and Lyotard and Thébaud, *Just Gaming.*

53. Thomas S. Szasz, *The Myth of Mental Illness: Foundations of a Theory of Personal Conduct* (New York: Dell Publishing, 1961), x.

54. Ibid., ix. Szasz adds, "Although mental illness might have been a useful concept in the nineteenth century, today it is scientifically worthless and socially harmful."

55. Ibid., front cover.

56. See the second paragraph of chapter 12.

57. Some, such as Aubert, explain that "each society organizes itself for the protection of the ruling classes against the socially inferior." This point is referenced in Ian Taylor, Paul Walton, and Jock Young, "The New Criminology," in *Crime and Justice,* vol. 1, ed. Leon Radzinowicz and Marvin Wolfgang (New York: Basic Books, n.d.), 652. Nevertheless, a postmodern move is to deny grand narratives.

58. For a characterization of Foucault's position, see John Caputo and Mark Yount, *Foucault and the Critique of Institutions* (University Park: Pennsylvania State University Press, 1993), 7. Caputo and Yount write, "Psychiatrists and psychologists, criminal justice professionals and social workers, confessors and spiritual directors: all produce the knowledge they apply. They create the knowledge they require in order to fashion functioning, well-formed individuals. They do not discover but invent; they do not 'liberate from' but 'produce for.' "

Selected Bibliography

Abrams, Robert. *Foundations of Political Analysis: An Introduction to The Theory of Collective Choice.* New York: Columbia University Press, 1980.

Agor, Weston H. *Intuition in Organizations: Leading and Managing Productively.* Newbury Park, Calif.: Sage, 1989.

Argyris, Chris. "Some Limits of Rational Man Organizational Theory." *Public Administration Review* 33, no. 3 (1973): 253–67.

———. "Organization Man: Rational and Self-Actualizing." *Public Administration Review* 33, no. 4 (1973): 346–53.

Argyris, Chris, and David A. Schon. *Organizational Learning: A Theory of Action Perspective.* Reading, Mass.: Addison-Wesley, 1978.

Arrow, Kenneth J. *Social Choice and Individual Values.* Rev. ed. New York: John Wiley, 1963.

Arthur, John, and William H. Shaw. *Justice and Economic Distribution.* 2nd ed. Englewood Cliffs, N.J.: Prentice Hall, 1991.

Avens, Roberts. *Imagination: A Way Toward Western Nirvana.* Lanham, Md.: University Press of America, 1979.

Barnard, Chester I. *Functions of the Executive.* Cambridge: Harvard University Press, 1938.

Baudrillard, Jean. *Jean Baudrillard: Selected Writings,* ed. Mark Poster. Stanford: Stanford University Press, 1988.

———. *America.* Trans. Chris Turner. London: Verso, 1989.

———. *Revenge of the Crystal: Selected Writings on the Modern Object and its Destiny.* Trans. Paul Foss and Julian Pefanis. London: Pluto Press, 1990.

———. *Seduction.* Trans. Brian Sugir. New York: St. Martin's Press, 1990.

Baum, Howell S. *The Invisible Bureaucracy: The Unconscious in Organizational Problem Solving.* New York: Oxford University Press, 1987.

Bauman, Zygmunt. *Hermeneutics and Social Science: Approaches to Understanding.* London: Hutchinson, 1978.

Benedict, Ruth. "Anthropology and the Abnormal." *The Journal of General Psychology* 10 (1934): 59–82.

Berger, Peter L., and Thomas Luckman. *The Social Construction of Reality: A Treatise in the Sociology of Knowledge.* Garden City, N.Y.: Doubleday, 1966.

Berman, Marshall. *All that is Solid Melts into Air: The Experience of Modernity.* New York: Simon and Schuster, 1982.

Best, Steven, and Douglas Kellner. *Postmodern Theory.* New York: Guilford Press, 1991.

Bleicher, Josef. *Contemporary Hermeneutics: Hermeneutics as Method, Philosophy and Critique.* London: Routledge and Kegan Paul, 1980.

Borgmann, Albert. *Crossing the Postmodern Divide.* Chicago: University of Chicago Press, 1992.

Boyd, Richard, Philip Gasper, and J. D. Trout. *The Philosophy of Science.* Boston: MIT Press, 1991.

Breton, Albert. *The Economic Theory of Representative Government.* Chicago: Aldine, 1974.

Brubaker, Rogers. *The Limits of Rationality: An Essay on the Social and Moral Thought of Max Weber.* London: George Allen and Unwin, 1984.

Buchanan, Allen. "Efficiency Arguments For and Against the Market." In *Justice and Economic Distribution,* 2nd ed., ed. John Arthur and William H. Shaw. Englewood Cliffs, N.J.: Prentice Hall, 1991.

Buchanan, James M. *The Supply and Demand of Public Goods.* Chicago: McNally, 1968.

Bunge, Mario. "Philosophy of Science and Technology." *Treatise on Basic Philosophy,* vol. 7. Dordrecht, The Netherlands: R. Reidel, 1985.

Burchell, Graham, Colin Gordon, and Peter Miller, eds. *The Foucault Effect: Studies in Governmentality.* Chicago: University of Chicago Press, 1991.

Cascardi, Anthony J. *The Subject of Modernity.* New York: Cambridge University Press, 1992.

Chambliss, Joseph J. *Imagination and Reason in Plato, Aristotle, Vico, Rousseau and Keats: An Essay on the Philosophy of Experience.* The Hague: Martinus Nijhoff, 1974.

Churchman, C. West. *The Systems Approach.* New York: Dell, 1983.

Committee on Standards of Official Conduct. *House Ethics Manual.* Washington, D.C.: US-GPO, 1992.

Cooke, Philip. *Back to the Future.* London: Unwin Hyman, 1990.

Cooper, Terry L. *The Responsible Administrator: An Approach to Ethics for the Administrative Role.* San Francisco: Jossey-Bass, 1990.

Cooper, Terry L., and N. Dale Wright, eds. *Exemplary Public Administrators: Character and Leadership in Government.* San Francisco: Jossey-Bass, 1992.

Cornell, Drucilla, Michel Rosenfeld, and David Gray Carlson, eds. *Deconstruction and the Possibility of Justice.* New York: Routledge, 1992.

Culler, Jonathan. *Ferdinand de Saussure.* Ithaca: Cornell University Press, 1976.

Cyert, Richard M., and James G. March. *A Behavioral Theory of the Firm.* Englewood Cliffs, N.J.: Prentice-Hall, 1963.

Deleuze, Gilles, and Félix Guattari. *Anti-Oedipus: Capitalism and Schizophrenia.* Trans. Robert Hurley, Mark Seem, and Helen Lane. New York: Viking Press, 1977.

———. *Kafka: Toward a Minor Literature.* Trans. Dana Polan. Minneapolis: University of Minnesota Press, 1986.

———. *A Thousand Plateaus.* Minneapolis: University of Minnesota Press, 1987.

Denhardt, Kathryn G. *The Ethics of Public Service: Resolving Moral Dilemmas in Public Organizations.* New York: Greenwood Press, 1991.

Denhardt, Robert B. *In the Shadow of Organization.* Lawrence: Regents Press of Kansas, 1981.

———. "Toward a Critical Theory of Public Organization." *Public Administration Review* 41, no. 6 (1981): 628–35.

———. *Theories of Public Organization.* Monterey, Calif.: Brooks/Cole, 1984.

Denhardt, Robert B., and Kathryn G. Denhardt. "Public Administration and the Critique of Domination." *Administration and Society* 11, no. 1 (May 1979): 107–20.

Derrida, Jacques. *Of Grammatology.* Trans. G. Spivak. Baltimore: Johns Hopkins University, 1976.

———. *Writing and Difference.* Trans. Alan Bass. Chicago: University of Chicago Press, 1978.

———. *Dissemination.* Trans. B. Johnson. Chicago: University of Chicago Press, 1981.

———. *Positions.* Trans. Alan Bass. Chicago: University of Chicago Press, 1981.

———. "Force of Law: The 'Mystical Foundation of Authority.' " In *Deconstruction and the*

Possibility of Justice, ed. Drucilla Cornell, Michel Rosenfeld, and David Gray Carlson. New York: Routledge, 1992.

Diamond, Michael A. "Organizational Identity: A Psychological Exploration of Organizational Meaning." *Administration and Society* 20, no. 2 (August 1988): 166–90.

Diwan, Romesh, and Chandana Chakraborty. *High Technology and International Competitiveness.* New York: Praeger, 1991.

Doswell, Andrew. *Office Automation: Context, Experience and Future.* Chichester, U.K.: John Wiley, 1990.

Downs, Anthony. *Inside Bureaucracy.* Boston: Little, Brown, 1967.

Dunleavy, Patrick. *Democracy, Bureaucracy and Public Choice.* Englewood Cliffs, N.J.: Simon and Schuster, 1992.

Dunn, William N., and Bahman Fozouni. *Toward a Critical Administrative Theory.* Beverly Hills: Sage, 1976.

Durbin, Paul T., ed. *Research in Philosophy and Technology,* vol. 1. Greenwich, Conn.: JAI Press, 1978.

Etzioni, Amitai. *Modern Organizations.* Englewood Cliffs, N.J.: Prentice-Hall, 1964.

———. *The Spirit of Community: Rights, Responsibilities, and the Communitarian Agenda.* New York: Crown Publishers, 1993.

Farmer, David J. *Civil Disorder Control: A Planning Program of Municipal Coordination and Cooperation.* Chicago: Public Administration Service, 1968.

———. *Crime Control: The Use and Misuse of Police Resources.* New York: Plenum Press, 1984.

———. *Being in Time: The Nature of Time in Light of McTaggart's Paradox.* Lanham, Md.: University Press of America, 1990.

Felts, Arthur. "Organizational Communication: A Critical Perspective." *Administration and Society* 23, no. 4 (February 1992): 495–513.

Feyerabend, Paul. *Against Method.* London: New Left Books, 1975.

Formaini, Robert. *The Myth of Scientific Public Policy.* New Brunswick, N.J.: Transaction Publishers, 1990.

Foster, Hal, ed. *The Anti-Aesthetic: Essays on Postmodern Culture.* Port Townsend, Wash.: Bay Press, 1983.

Foucault, Michel. *The Order of Things: An Archaeology of the Human Sciences.* Trans. Alan Sheridan-Smith. New York: Random House, 1966.

———. "On the Genealogy of Ethics." In *Michel Foucault: Beyond Structuralism and Hermeneutics,* ed. Hubert L. Dreyfus and Paul Rabinow. Chicago: University of Chicago Press, 1983.

Frankel, Boris. *The Post-Industrial Utopians.* Cambridge: Polity, 1987.

Freud, Sigmund. *Beyond the Pleasure Principle.* New York: W. W. Norton, 1961.

———. *Civilization and its Discontents.* Trans. James Strachey. New York: W. W. Norton, 1961.

———. *The Interpretation of Dreams.* New York: Modern Library, 1978.

Friedman, Milton, Homer Jones, George Stigler, and Allen Wallis, eds. *The Ethics of Competition and Other Essays.* Freeport, N.Y.: Books for Libraries Press, 1935.

Gadamer, Hans-Georg. *Truth and Method.* New York: Seabury Press, 1975.

———. "The Hermeneutics of Suspicion." In *Hermeneutics,* ed. Gary Shapiro and Alan Sica. Amherst: University of Massachusetts Press, 1984.

———. "Text and Interpretation." In *Dialogue and Deconstruction,* ed. Diane Michelfelder and Richard Palmer. Albany: SUNY Press, 1989.

Gawthrop, Louis. *Public Sector Management, Systems, and Ethics.* Bloomington: Indiana University Press, 1984.

Gergen, Kenneth J. *Toward Transformation in Social Knowledge.* New York: Springer-Verlag, 1982.

Gramsci, Antonio. *Selections from the Prison Notebooks of Antonio Gramsci.* Ed. Quinton Hoare and Geoffrey Smith. New York: International Publishers, 1972.

Griffin, David Ray. *Founders of Constructive Postmodern Philosophy.* Albany: SUNY, 1993.

Guba, Egon G., and Yvonna S. Lincoln. *Naturalistic Inquiry.* Beverly Hills: Sage, 1985.

Gulick, Luther, and Lyndall Urwick, eds. *Papers on the Science of Administration.* New York: Institute of Public Administration, 1937.

Habermas, Jürgen. *Knowledge and Human Interest.* London: Heinemen, 1971.

——. *The Structural Transformation of the Public Sphere: An Inquiry into a Category of Bourgeois Society.* Trans. Thomas Burger and Frederick Lawrence. Cambridge: MIT Press, 1989.

——. *The Theory of Communicative Action.* Vol. 1, *Reason and the Rationalization of Society,* and vol. 2, *Lifeworld and System: A Critique of Functionalist Reason.* Trans. Thomas McCarthy. Boston: Beacon Press, 1984 and 1987.

Hall, Calvin S., and Gardner Lindzey. *Theories of Personality.* New York: John Wiley, 1957.

Harmon, Michael M. *Action Theory for Public Administration.* New York: Longman, 1981.

Harmon, Michael M., and Richard T. Mayer. *Organization Theory for Public Administration.* Boston: Little, Brown, 1986.

Heidegger, Martin. "The Age of the World Picture." *The Question Concerning Technology and Other Essays.* Trans. William Lovitt. New York: Harper and Row, 1977.

Heilbroner, Robert L. *The Nature and Logic of Capitalism.* New York: W. W. Norton, 1985.

Henderson, Ernest F. *Symbol and Satire in the French Revolution.* New York: G. P. Putnam's Sons, 1912.

Hoesterey, Ingeborg, ed. *Zeitgeist in Babel: The Postmodernist Controversy.* Bloomington: Indiana University Press, 1991.

Honkapohja, Seppo, ed. *The State of Macroeconomics.* Oxford: Basil Blackwell, 1990.

Horkheimer, Max. *Eclipse of Reason.* New York: Seabury, 1974.

Horkheimer, Max, and Theodor Adorno. *Dialectic of Enlightenment.* Trans. John Cumming. New York: Seabury, 1972.

Horwitz, Robert H., ed. *The Moral Foundations of the American Republic.* Charlottesville: University Press of Virginia, 1977.

Hubbell, Larry. "Four Archetypal Shadows: A Look at the Dark Side of Public Organizations." *Administration and Society* 24, no. 2 (August 1992): 205–23.

Hummel, Ralph. *The Bureaucratic Experience,* 3rd ed. New York: St. Martin's Press, 1987.

——. "The Rise of Managerial Realism: Applied Phenomenology—A Symposium." *Public Administration Quarterly* 14, no. 1 (Spring 1990).

Iannello, Kathleen P. *Decisions Without Hierarchy: Feminist Interventions in Organization Theory and Practice.* New York: Routledge, 1992.

Jencks, Charles. *What Is Post-Modernism?* New York: St. Martin's Press, 1986.

——. *Post-Modernism: The New Classicism in Art and Architecture.* New York: Rizzoli, 1987.

Johnson, Lynn G. *The High-Technology Connection: Academic/Industrial Cooperation for Economic Growth.* Washington, D.C.: Association for the Study of Higher Education, 1984.

Katsiaficas, George. *The Imagination of the New Left: A Global Analysis of 1968.* Boston: South End Press, 1987.

Katz, Daniel, and Robert L. Kahn. *The Social Psychology of Organizations.* New York: John Wiley, 1966.

Klein, Julie Thompson. *Interdisciplinarity: History, Theory, and Practice.* Detroit: Wayne State University Press, 1990.

Knapp Commission to Investigate Allegations of Police Corruption and the City's Anti-Corruption Procedures. *Commission Report.* New York: George Braziller, 1973.

Knight, Frank H. "Ethics and the Economic Interpretation." *The Quarterly Journal of Economics* 36 (1922): 454–81. Reprinted in *The Ethics of Competition and Other Essays,* ed. Milton Friedman, Homer Jones, George Stigler, and Allen Wallis. New York: Books for Libraries Press, 1935.

Kolb, David. *The Critique of Pure Modernity: Hegel, Heidegger and After.* Chicago: University of Chicago Press, 1986.

Kuhn, Thomas. *The Structure of Scientific Revolutions,* 2nd ed. Chicago: University of Chicago Press, 1970.

Lan, Khiyong, and David H. Rosenbloom. "Public Administration in Transition?" *Public Administration Review* 52, no. 6 (November–December 1992).

Landau, Martin. "Redundancy, Rationality, and the Problem of Duplication and Overlap." *Public Administration Review* 29, no. 4 (1969): 346–58.

Laplanche, Jean. *Life and Death in Psychoanalysis.* Baltimore: Johns Hopkins University Press, 1976.

Laplanche, Jean, and Jean Baptiste Pontalis. *The Language of Psycho-Analysis.* New York: W. W. Norton, 1973.

Lash, Scott. "Modernity or Modernism? Weber and Contemporary Social Theory." In *Max Weber, Rationality and Modernity,* ed. Scott Lash and Sam Whimster. London: Allen and Unwin, 1987.

Laver, Michael. *The Politics of Private Desires.* New York: Penguin Books, 1981.

Lawson, Hilary. *Reflexivity: The Post-modern Predicament.* London: Hutchinson, 1985.

Leff, Gordon. *The Dissolution of the Medieval Outlook: An Essay on Intellectual and Spiritual Change in the Fourteenth Century.* New York: New York University Press, 1976.

Lerner, Allan W. "There Is More Than One Way To Be Redundant." *Administration and Society* 18, no. 3 (1986): 334–59.

Lewis, Carol W. *The Ethics Challenge in Public Service: A Problem-Solving Guide.* San Francisco: Jossey-Bass, 1991.

Lieberman, Philip. *The Biology and Evolution of Language.* Cambridge: Harvard University Press, 1984.

Lincoln, Yvonna, ed. *Organizational Theory and Inquiry: The Paradigm Revolution.* Beverly Hills: Sage, 1985.

Lindblom, Charles. "The Science of 'Muddling Through.' " *Public Administration Review* 19, no. 2 (1959): 79–88.

Lyotard, Jean-François. *The Postmodern Condition: A Report on Knowledge.* Trans. G. Bennington and B. Massumi. Minneapolis: University of Minnesota Press, 1984.

———. "Rewriting Modernity." *SubStance* 54 (1987): 8–9.

Lyotard, Jean-François, and Jean-Loup Thébaud. *Just Gaming.* Trans. Wlads Godzich. Minneapolis: University of Minnesota Press, 1985.

Madison, Gary B. *The Hermeneutics of Postmodernity: Figures and Themes.* Bloomington: Indiana University Press, 1988.

Mahler, Julianne. "The Quest for Organizational Meaning: Identifying and Interpreting the Symbolism in Organizational Stories." *Administration and Society* 20, no. 3 (November 1988): 344–68.

March, James G. *Decisions and Organizations.* Oxford: Basil Blackwell, 1988.

Martin, Daniel W. "Déjà Vu: French Antecedents of American Public Administration." *Public Administration Review* 47, no. 4 (1987): 298–301.

——. *The Guide to the Foundations of Public Administration*. New York: Marcel Dekker, 1989.

McCloskey, Donald N. *The Rhetoric of Economics*. Madison: University of Wisconsin Press, 1985.

McCurdy, Howard. *Public Administration: A Bibliography*. Washington, D.C.: American University, 1972.

McTaggart, John. *The Nature of Existence*. Vols. 1 and 2. Cambridge: Cambridge University Press, 1921 and 1927.

Michelfelder, Diane, and Richard E. Palmer, eds. *Dialogue and Deconstruction: The Gadamer-Derrida Encounter*. Albany: SUNY, 1989.

Miller, James. *The Passion of Michel Foucault*. New York: Simon and Schuster, 1993.

Mitcham, Carl, and Robert Mackey, eds. *Philosophy and Technology*. New York: Free Press, 1972.

Morgan, Gareth, ed. *Beyond Managerial Method: Strategies for Social Research*. Beverly Hills: Sage, 1983.

——. *Riding the Waves of Change: Developing Managerial Competencies for a Turbulent World*. San Francisco: Jossey-Bass, 1988.

——. *Imaginization: The Art of Creative Management*. Newbury Park, Calif.: Sage, 1993.

Morrow, William L. *Public Administration: Politics and the Political System*. New York: Random House, 1975.

Mosher, Frederick C. *American Public Administration: Past, Present and Future*. University: University of Alabama Press, 1975.

Mueller, Dennis C. *Public Choice II*. New York: Cambridge University Press, 1989.

Nagatani, Keizo. *Political Macroeconomics*. Oxford: Clarendon Press, 1989.

NASPAA Ad Hoc Committee. *Report of the Ad Hoc Committee on the Future of Public Service Education and Accreditation*. Chicago: NASPAA, 1992.

Niskanen, William A. *Bureaucracy and Representative Government*. Chicago: Aldine-Atherton, 1971.

Oldroyd, David. *The Arch of Knowledge*. New York: Methuen, 1986.

Ormiston, Gayle L., and Alan Schrift. *The Hermeneutic Tradition*. Albany: SUNY, 1990.

Osborne, David E., and Ted Gaebler. *Reinventing Government: How the Entrepreneurial Spirit Is Transforming the Public Sector*. Reading, Mass.: Addison-Wesley, 1992.

Ostrom, Vincent. *Intellectual Crisis in American Public Administration*. University: University of Alabama Press, 1973.

Ozouf, Mona. *Festivals and the French Revolution*. Cambridge: Harvard University Press, 1988.

Payad, Aurora. *Organization Behavior in American Public Administration: An Annotated Bibliography*. New York: Garland Publishing, 1986.

Popper, Karl. *The Logic of Scientific Discovery*. New York: Harper, 1959.

Quine, Willard V. *Quiddities: An Intermittently Philosophical Dictionary*. Cambridge: Harvard University Press, 1987.

Rabin, Jack, and James S. Bowman, eds. *Politics and Administration: Woodrow Wilson and the Study of Public Administration*. New York: Marcel Dekker, 1984.

Rabin, Jack, W. Bartley Hildreth, and Gerald J. Miller, eds. *Handbook of Public Administration*. New York: Marcel Dekker, 1989.

Rachels, James. *The Elements of Moral Philosophy*. New York: Random House, 1986.

Rhoads, Steven. *The Economist's View of the World: Governments, Markets and Public Policy.* Cambridge: Cambridge University Press, 1985.

Ricoeur, Paul. *Freud and Philosophy: An Essay on Interpretation.* New Haven: Yale University Press, 1970.

Rivlin, Alice. *Systematic Thinking for Social Action.* Washington, D.C.: The Brookings Institution, 1972.

Rizzo, Ann-Marie, and Dolores Brosnan. "Critical Theory and Communication Dysfunction: The Case of Sexually Ambiguous Behavior." *Administration and Society* 22, no. 1 (May 1990): 66–85.

Robbins, Lionel. *An Essay on the Nature and Significance of Economic Science.* London: Macmillan, 1962.

Rockmore, Tom, and Beth J. Singer. *Antifoundationalism Old and New.* Philadelphia: Temple University Press, 1992.

Rohr, John A. *Ethics for Bureaucrats: An Essay on Law and Values,* 2nd ed. New York: Marcel Dekker, 1989.

Rorty, Richard. *Philosophy and the Mirror of Nature.* Princeton: Princeton University Press, 1979.

———. *Consequences of Pragmatism.* Minneapolis: University of Minneapolis Press, 1982.

Rose, Margaret A. *The Post-Modern and the Post-Industrial: A Critical Analysis.* Cambridge: Cambridge University Press, 1991.

Rosenberg, Alexander. *Philosophy of Social Science.* Boulder: Westview Press, 1988.

Russell, Clifford S., ed. *Collective Decision Making: Applications from Public Choice Theory.* Baltimore: Johns Hopkins University Press, 1979.

Samuelson, Paul A., and William D. Nordhaus. *Economics,* 13th ed. New York: McGraw-Hill, 1989.

Sartre, Jean-Paul. *Imagination.* Ann Arbor: University of Michigan Press, 1962.

Schiesl, Martin J. *The Politics of Efficiency: Municipal Administration and Reform in America 1800–1920.* Berkeley: University of California Press, 1977.

Shapiro, Gary, and Alan Sica, eds. *Hermeneutics.* Amherst: University of Massachusetts Press, 1984.

Shils, Edward. *Tradition.* Chicago: University of Chicago Press, 1981.

Simon, Herbert A. *The Sciences of the Artificial.* Cambridge: MIT Press, 1969.

———. *Administrative Behavior: A Study of Decision-Making Processes in Administrative Organization.* 3rd ed. New York: Free Press, 1976.

Simon, Herbert, and James G. March. *Organizations.* New York: Wiley, 1958.

Tesch, Renata. *Qualitative Research.* New York: Falmer Press, 1990.

Thurow, Lester. *Head to Head: The Coming Economic Battle Among Japan, Europe and America.* New York: William Morrow, 1992.

Truzzi, Marcello. *Verstehen: Subjective Understanding in the Social Sciences.* Reading, Mass.: Addison-Wesley, 1974.

Turner, Bryan S. *Theories of Modernity and Postmodernity.* Newbury Park, Calif.: Sage, 1990.

Turner, Stephen P., and Regis Factor. *Max Weber and the Dispute over Reason and Value.* London: Routledge and Kegan Paul, 1984.

Vattimo, Gianni. *The Transparent Society.* Trans. David Webb. Baltimore: Johns Hopkins Press, 1992.

Waldo, Dwight. *Public Administration in a Time of Turbulence.* Scranton: Chandler Publishing, 1971.

———. *The Enterprise of Public Administration.* Novato, Calif.: Chandler and Sharp, 1980.

———. *The Administrative State: A Study of the Political Theory of American Public Administration,* 2nd ed. New York: Holmes and Meier, 1984.

Wamsley, Gary L., Robert N. Bacher, Charles T. Goodsell, Phil S. Kronenberg, John A. Rohr, Camilla M. Stivers, Orion White, and James F. Wolf. *Refounding Public Administration.* Newbury Park, Calif.: Sage, 1990.

Weber, Max. "Science as Vocation." In *From Max Weber,* ed. Hans H. Gerth and C. Wright Mills. New York: Oxford University Press, 1946.

———. *The Methodology of the Social Sciences.* Ed. Edward A Shils and Henry A. Finch. New York: Free Press, 1949.

———. *The Protestant Ethic and the Spirit of Capitalism.* Trans. Talcott Parsons. New York: Scribner, 1958.

———. *Economy and Society.* Ed. Guenther Roth and Claus Wittich. Berkeley: University of California Press, 1968.

Weick, Karl E. *The Social Psychology of Organizing.* Reading, Mass.: Addison-Wesley, 1969.

Wellmer, Albrecht. *The Persistence of Modernity.* Trans. David Midgley. Cambridge: MIT Press, 1991.

Wexler, Philip, ed. *Critical Theory Now.* London: Falmer Press, 1991.

White, Alan. *The Language of Imagination.* Oxford: Basil Blackwell, 1990.

White, Elliot, and Joseph Losco. *Biology and Bureaucracy: Public Administration and Public Policy from the Perspective of Evolutionary, Genetic and Neurobiological Theory.* Lanham, Md.: University Press of America, 1986.

White, Jay. D. "On the Growth of Knowledge in Public Administration." *Public Administration Review* 46, no. 1 (1986): 15–22.

———. "Action Theory and Literary Interpretation." *Administration and Society* 19, no. 3 (1987): 346–66.

White, Stephen K. *Political Theory and Postmodernism.* New York: Cambridge University Press, 1991.

Wildavsky, Aaron. *The Politics of the Budgetary Process.* Boston: Little, Brown, 1964.

Wisdom, John O. *Philosophy of the Social Sciences: A Metascientific Introduction.* Aldershot, U.K.: Avebury, 1986.

———. *Challengeability in Modern Science.* Aldershot, U.K.: Gower, 1987.

Wood, David, and Robert Bernasconi, eds. *Derrida and Différance.* Evanston: Northwestern University Press, 1988.

Wren, Daniel. *The Evolution of Management Thought,* 3rd ed. New York: John Wiley and Sons, 1987.

Wyschogrod, Edith. *Saints and Postmodernism: Revisioning Moral Philosophy.* Chicago: University of Chicago Press, 1990.

Index

Abrams, Robert, 122
Action: human, 84, 85. *See also* Behavior
Action learning research method, 167-68, 283 (n. 23), 284 (nn. 30, 32)
Administration: as business, 66; as science, 70-72, 85, 87, 101, 265 (n. 7), 270 (n. 44); as playacting, 100-101; as tentative, 241-42, 244; as ritual, 274 (n. 5). *See also* Management science
Administrative ethics, 71, 77-83, 85. *See also* Ethical enterprise
Administrative reports, 186
Administrative spirit, 171
Adorno, Theodor, 6, 37, 41, 45, 130, 140, 189
Agassi, Joseph, 87
Agor, Weston, 166
Airaksinen, Timo, 153
Alexander the Great, 45
All power to the imagination, 158, 159
Altruism, 107-108, 232-33, 295 (n. 21). *See also* Postmodern alterity
American dream, 52
American public administration: American element, 50-59, 69; public element, 59-63, 69; generic orientation, 60; programmatic orientation, 60; administration element, 63-68, 69; functional character, 63-65; programmatic character, 63-65; local character, 51-53; ambivalence about local character, 53-55; advantages of localism, 55; disadvantages of localism, 55-65
American Society for Public Administration, 77, 79, 92, 255 (n. 51)
Amish, 45, 163
Anaesthetic, 236, 295 (n. 27)
Anarchism, 115, 228, 238, 245. *See also* Quasianarchistic arrangements
Anaximander, 153
Anaximines, 153
Antiadministration, 160, 176, 227-29, 238, 240, 244, 245, 247

Antifascism, 229-31
Antifoundationalism, 274 (n. 4)
Antiinstitution and antiorganization, 217, 228, 243. *See also* Antiadministration
Apel, Karl, 26
Apollo and Apollonian, 46, 149, 258 (nn. 58, 60)
Appleby, Paul, 130
Applied phenomenology, 134, 135, 276 (n. 58). *See also* Phenomenology
Arborescent model of knowledge, 220, 222, 226. *See also* Rhizome
Archetypes, 142. *See also* Collective unconscious
Argyris, Chris, 132, 133, 191
Aristotle, 28, 30, 148, 164, 212, 233, 249 (n. 1)
Arrow, Kenneth, 98
Arrow's possibility theorem, 98, 124
"As if" exercise, 7
Assumptions of modernity discussion, 44-47
Athena, 78
Atlas, 78
Ausculation in depth, 172
Ausländerliteratur, 237
Austin, John, 152
Authorship of *Administrative Behavior,* 187-92. *See also* Deconstruction
Avens, Roberts, 164
Awash in a flux of images, 204

Bacon, Francis, 122, 221
Barnard, Chester, 30, 96, 97, 130, 189, 190, 191
Barthes, Roland, 149, 181
Baudrillard, Jean, 6, 41, 148, 149, 150, 153, 154, 155, 175, 177, 185, 204, 205, 207, 214, 229
Beccaria, Cesare, 56
Behavior, 84
Bélanger, Gérard, 108, 121, 202
Benchmarking, 56
Benedict, Ruth, 81
Bentham, Jeremy, 38

ABOUT THE AUTHOR

DAVID JOHN FARMER is Professor of Political Science and Public Administration, Virginia Commonwealth University. He received his bachelor of science degree from the London School of Economics, University of London, a master's degree from the University of Toronto and a master's from the University of Virginia, a doctorate from the University of London and one from the University of Virginia. He is author of *Crime Control: The Use and Misuse of Police Resources* (1984) and *Being in Time: The Nature of Time in Light of McTaggart's Paradox* (1990).